PEOPLE
GET READY

PEOPLE
GET READY

The Fight Against a Jobless Economy
and a Citizenless Democracy

Robert W. McChesney
and
John Nichols

NATION BOOKS
NEW YORK

Published by Nation Books, A Member of the Perseus Books Group
116 East 16th Street, 8th Floor, New York, NY 10003

Nation Books is a co-publishing venture of the Nation Institute and the
Perseus Books Group

Books published by Nation Books are available at special discounts for
bulk purchases in the United States by corporations, institutions, and
other organizations. For more information, please contact the Special
Markets Department at the Perseus Books Group, 2300 Chestnut Street,
Suite 200, Philadelphia, PA 19103, or call (800) 810-4145, ext. 5000, or
e-mail special.markets@perseusbooks.com.

DESIGNED BY LINDA MARK

Library of Congress Cataloging-in-Publication Data
Names: McChesney, Robert Waterman, 1952– author. Title: People get
   ready : the fight against a jobless economy and a citizenless democracy /
   Robert W. McChesney and John Nichols.
Description: New York : Nation Books, [2016] | Includes bibliographical
   references and index.
Identifiers: LCCN 2015040784 | ISBN 9781568585215 (hardcover)
Subjects: LCSH: United States--Economic conditions--2009- | United
   States—Social conditions. | United States—Politics and
government—2009–
   | Democracy--United States. | Labor—United States. | Technological
   innovations—Economic aspects—United States.
Classification: LCC HC106.84 .M3973 2016 | DDC 320.973—dc23 LC
record available at http://lccn.loc.gov/2015040784
ISBN: 978-1-56858-522-2 (e-book)

10 9 8 7 6 5 4 3 2 1

CONTENTS

Introduction: Welcome to the Future   1

ONE   Into the Maelstrom   13

TWO   A Jobless Economy?   43

THREE   Citizenless Democracy   115

FOUR   Democratic Infrastructure   151

FIVE   Overcoming the Democratic Disconnect   209

SIX   A Democratic Agenda for a Digital Age   245

        Statistical Appendix, R. Jamil Jonna   *277*
        Acknowledgments   *288*
        Notes   *291*
        Index   *343*

For Amy, Lucy, and Whitman

INTRODUCTION

Welcome to the Future

In the foolishness of their hearts they imagined that the maintenance and well-doing of the industrious poor were of greater consequence than the enrichment of a few individuals.

Lord Byron, 1812

THE FUTURE IS NOW. HERE'S HOW IT WORKS. A CHIP IMplanted in your finger (it's about the size of a grain of rice, you won't even remember that it's there) is going to open the door and start the ignition of the driverless car that will take you to the drive-thru window of a restaurant where you'll grab the breakfast you ordered, paid for, and scheduled for pick up with a phone app. Next stop: the community college job retraining center where you have been required to put in a few hours each week since automation wiped out your part-time job at the last plant still making anything in what's left of your hometown. The center is pretty much empty;

1

has been ever since the last big free-trade deal was approved and people started to realize that the good-paying jobs weren't coming back.
Besides, most training is done online now, with instructors working
from the distant call centers of offshored multinational corporations.
A pleasant if rather too-well-armed security guard informs you that
the center will be closing next week. You ask her what she will do next.
"I don't know," she answers. "I'm not in charge."

It is not "think different" or "be what's next" or "lean forward" that
is the defining statement of the future that is now. It is that last line:
"I'm not in charge." We are not in charge. In the midst of a technological revolution that is every bit as disruptive as the industrial revolution of two hundred years ago, the gadgets are all new, but the power
relations are all old. We're back to the Gilded Age, back to the age
before the Gilded Age, back to a future of plutocrats and peasants, of
masters and servants. We are told that this is a time of income inequality, and it is. But it is also a time of power inequality, where the ability
to determine what the future will look like and feel like and sound like
and taste like is concentrated in fewer and fewer hands. Every decision
that matters about our lives is being made by a corporate CEO or a
campaign donor or a programmer or a hacker or someone else we have
never met. We "choose" politicians by rote after elections so crude in
their messaging and so vapid in their content that most of us do not
bother to participate in them. The politicians themselves—with the
exception of an occasional Bernie Sanders or Elizabeth Warren—have
become rubberstamps for the trade deals, tax rates, and deregulations
demanded by an enriched and empowered one-tenth of one percent.
The rest of us are mere spectators. Many of us are not even aware that
the game we are watching isn't entertainment, isn't virtual reality. It is
our lives.[1]

Americans, like peoples across the world, must understand what
is at stake in this time of change. This book will speak about new
technologies, about virtual reality, about digital destinies, about the
automation of everything, and about the moment, not far from now,
when all the trends of the future that is now give way to what comes
next. Some things we know will occur. Tens of millions of Americans

who have the education, the training, and the ethic to do what we thought would be the work of a modern age will no longer be able to find that work. They will, as economist James Galbraith explains, be "not only unemployed but also obsolete."[2] Some of the disrupted and the discarded have felt obsolete for years, as they have slipped down the economic ladder from the assembly line to the warehouse to the convenience-store counter to the fast-food prep station. But their experience is being generalized. We will begin to recognize that what comes after the acceleration of automation that is only now beginning will not be some new way of working, some new industry, some new sector of the economy. The "genius" of the digital revolution—with all of its apps and smart technologies and advances in automation, with all of its blurring of lines between humans and machines, with all of its progress—is its exceptional efficiency. The changes that define the future that is now have nothing to do with job creation. Why would they? They are being developed and implemented by behemoth corporations that seek to maximize profits, not employment.

Despite what five justices on the United States Supreme Court might imagine, corporations are not people.[3] Corporations do not fret about the fact that millions of American workers have already been displaced, and that millions more will be displaced. They celebrate that fact. If a multinational corporation makes its product or delivers its service without having to pay as many human beings, all the better. That's why the value of the corporation's stock rises when it shutters factories and lays off workers. And if a big corporation can become huge by eliminating an industry, even wiping out a whole sector of the economy, then it is heralded as visionary and truly modern. And if that's a problem for the great mass of Americans who need work to sustain themselves and their families, it's a problem that will work itself out, eventually, thanks to the magic of the profit system. But the evidence is now in: technology writer and Silicon Valley entrepreneur Martin Ford is right when he notes that "there isn't another big sector of the economy to absorb all these workers."[4]

Yes, of course, that's a dystopian notion. But, remember, we live in the future that is now. Every day a virtual reality becomes just plain reality. There are miracles and there are marvels, but there are also reminders of what made those old science-fiction films so scary. What could be imagined, what can be imagined, is happening. Young men really are inserting grain-of-rice-sized microchips in their fingers in order to unlock doors and start cars—hoping that they will increase their employment prospects.[5] Fast-food restaurants really are taking orders with apps ("centralized ordering systems" that could "make cashiers redundant") and preparing them with robots ("automated kitchen equipment").[6] Multinational corporations really are investing in global knowledge-sharing schemes that openly propose to replace universities and community colleges—liberal arts and poetry, history and political science—with distance-learning "certificate" programs that train workers for a task, not a career.[7]

This is the story of now. And much of it is very fine, indeed. There is nothing wrong with disrupting drudgery, nothing wrong with making it easier to communicate, nothing wrong with trying new approaches that might work better than what came before.

But there is something wrong, something that is destructive rather than disruptive, something that is simply absurd about engaging in the wishful thinking that says a capitalistic system that by its nature prioritizes profit will somehow evolve for the better. It does not work like that. It never has and it never will.

So you have come to the wrong place if you are looking for another anti-technology rant. This is a book about the digital age and automation, about technology and technological change. But the real focus is on capitalism and politics, and on the fundamental question of how to bring the rest of us into the process of shaping a future that cannot be well or wisely shaped by the CEOs and bankers and bottom-line speculators who are now calling the shots. Seemingly endless stagnation, unemployment, underemployment, inequality, and growing poverty are the result of contemporary capitalism and the narrow range of policies countenanced by the political system, independent of the technological revolution we describe herein. The digital revolution is in the beginning stages of dramatically aggravating trends already firmly in place. We are concerned with the storm that results when these elements are put together.

We have participated in and written about the digital revolution from its early stages, and we remain highly engaged with it, but we do not come to this discussion as tech utopians. We have written about American and international political affairs for decades, but we do not come to this discussion as political utopians. We are realists, who have heard too many promises to imagine any technology—old or new—will change the political and economic realities that must be dealt with in order to assure that the changes now taking place will yield a just and equitable circumstance for the great mass of humanity. This explains our response to writer Paul Mason's powerful argument that "The End of Capitalism Has Begun," in a much-discussed 2015 article for the *Guardian*. Mason's rumination was introduced with a reassuring premise: "Without us noticing, we are entering the post-capitalist era. At the heart of further change to come is information technology, new ways of working and the sharing economy. The old ways will take a long while to disappear, but it's time to be utopian."[8] Mason explained that

> new forms of ownership, new forms of lending, new legal contracts: a whole business subculture has emerged over the past ten years, which the media has dubbed the "sharing economy." Buzzwords such as the "commons" and "peer-production" are thrown around, but few have bothered to ask what this development means for capitalism itself.
>
> I believe it offers an escape route—but only if these micro-level projects are nurtured, promoted and protected by a fundamental change in what governments do. And this must be driven by a change in our thinking—about technology, ownership and work. So that, when we create the elements of the new system, we can say to ourselves, and to others: "This is no longer simply my survival mechanism, my bolt hole from the neoliberal world; this is a new way of living in the process of formation."[9]

We are optimists and we appreciate Mason's optimism. Yet, our realism tells us that, as much as we can and do respect Mason's perspective, we also must acknowledge and embrace the observation of the writer Nigel Pollitt, who responded to Mason in a *Guardian* piece by explaining that

> much, not all, technological innovation depends on the desire to make profit. Is the proposition, seriously, that the myriad corporations and companies and individuals who build the robots that will make work vanish and abundance continuous, will give up their robots, and their robots' products—be these phones or fishmeal—for free?
>
> In the meantime, for every robot that comes online, that's several humans who lose their wages, unable to buy what the robot is making or vending. It doesn't add up, does it?[10]

Words like *sharing*, terms like *peer-production*, can be reassuring—until we are confronted with the stark reality of our progression. Ask a Kodak worker, if you can find one. Founded in 1888, Kodak was an iconic American company that put affordable cameras in our hands and gave us all kinds of ways to share the pictures we produced in the predigital age. Committed to innovation, Kodak employed the engineers who developed the digital camera and many of the photo-sharing innovations we now utilize. And this firm created and sustained lots of family-supporting jobs in the United States—especially in its headquarters city of Rochester, New York—and around the world.

In 1988, one hundred years after its founding, Kodak employed 145,000 people. But history, innovation, and a record of treating workers like human beings was no match for the new age of cell-phone communication and instantaneous photo-sharing using tools such as Instagram. In 2012, after the company filed for Chapter 11 bankruptcy protection, it was delisted from the New York Stock Exchange on a day when its value fell to $0.36 a share.[11] Employment tumbled as the company reorganized and by 2015 the total number of Kodak workers was less than 5 percent of what it was just a quarter century earlier.[12] At around the same time that Kodak was going bankrupt,

Instagram had thirteen million customers, who did almost all the work of snapping, editing, and sharing photos. How many actual human beings did Instagram employ when it was elbowing Kodak toward the dustbin of history? Thirteen. So it was that, while Kodak was crumbling, Facebook purchased Instagram for $1 billion, bringing what might have developed into a rival social network within its burgeoning monopoly. Kodak, the historically innovative company that employed those pioneering engineers and 145,000 other workers, was the past. Instagram, the company that let consumers do the work of sharing while employing just thirteen people, was the future. Yes, Instagram would grow as part of Facebook, but it would add employees at a microscopic rate: total Facebook employment as of March 2015 was 10,082, or only about 7 percent of the old Kodak figure. "This, in a nutshell, is why digital technology is changing our societies in such a profound way," explains Australian journalist Ian Leslie. "In a wired world, it costs virtually nothing to reproduce a photo or an e-book or a piece of software or to send it across the world. Small teams of designers or engineers can make products consumed and paid for by billions, creating vast wealth for their originators like Mark Zuckerberg. But the wealth doesn't 'trickle down' because digital goods require so few people to make them, and digitally organized workplaces require fewer people to run them."[13]

Or consider this: In 1964 AT&T was the nation's most valuable company, and was worth $267 billion in 2015 dollars. It employed 758,611 people. In late 2015 Google was the nation's second-most valuable company doing much of what AT&T did fifty years earlier, and a lot, lot more. It had a market value of $430 billion and employed around 55,000 people, which is 7 percent of AT&T's paid workforce in 1964. For every Google employee today, AT&T had fourteen workers five decades ago.[14]

This is reality. But it is not a reality that discredits utopian dreams or confirms dystopian cynicism. Rather, it is a reality that demands that Americans adjust their thinking about democracy such that the evolution of how we express our popular will keeps pace with the evolution of how we communicate, shop, and work. We cannot prevent that advance of digital technology and automation today any more than the Luddites could halt the advance of power looms and spinning frames. It is pointless to be against progress. The point is to shape progress, not as customers or consumers, not as clicks to be counted or employees struggling to synch ourselves into automated workplaces, but as citizens engaged in a democratic process of organizing a new economy that reflects our values and our needs.

This book seeks to foster that progress by identifying a place of reconciliation between the two poles outlined in the exchange between Paul Mason (whose optimism we relish) and Nigel Pollitt (whose realism we value) within a society that has already changed radically. We hope this reconciliation of optimism and realism will shape a multitude of incipient debates as that society begins to assess the scope and meaning of the changes we have already experienced, and the changes we are about to experience. The point of this reconciliation is not to calm the debate or to ease the tension. Quite the opposite. The point is to stir up the debate. We want to get the facts on the table, recognize where we are today, and then frame the arguments for how we might get to tomorrow.

That sounds easy. But what sounds easy is made difficult by the fact that the United States rarely if ever entertains serious discussions about economics. America is a country that is so big and so divergent that it rarely gets focused on a task until it is forced by a new reality (or perhaps an old reality presented in suddenly stark terms): a depression, a fascist threat, the violent suppression of a peaceful movement for racial justice, the destruction of our physical environment, the corruption of our governance. Remarkably, wonderfully, as the historian Harvey Kaye notes, America has throughout its history and especially across the past century met the most jarring of challenges with inspired and inspiring responses: a New Deal, a March on Washington followed by Civil Rights and Voting Rights Acts, Earth Day and the rapid enactment of Clean Air and Clean Water Acts, Watergate and the brief reforming of our politics.[15] But our experience of history and social movements tells us that the transformational moment in which we now find ourselves creates challenges that will not be well met by delaying action until after we are kicked in the head by an increasingly jobless economy. The condition in which some of us find ourselves already, and in which many of us will soon find ourselves, extends far beyond shuttered workplaces and boarded up Main Streets. It goes to the very marrow of our lives and our society, to questions of hope and hopelessness too profound to ignore. We have to get serious about addressing it before it metastasizes.

The great challenge of historical moments such as these, historical moments when we are experiencing economic and social change in something akin to real time, is that our attention is so easily drawn away from broad trends and focused on the evidence of those trends. It is the technological equivalent of noting the weird weather but missing the fact of climate change. Most of us recognize the changes that are taking place not as part of something bigger but as a "new normal" that may be vaguely frustrating at times (how many "devices" does it require to change the channel on a "Smart TV"?) but that keeps upgrading us so quickly that we barely bother to think about what it all means. This limits necessary questioning about whether we have the wherewithal and the authority to accept good change, reject bad change, and forge our own change. We get rid of our landlines and upgrade our iPhones, we kick the cassettes and CDs to the curb and download in a digital format the music we have always loved, we deposit our checks and pay our bills and schedule our travels without ever talking to human beings, we gather our information about politics from websites that reinforce our beliefs—or worse yet from negative ads and cable spin—and then we make decisions from a range of options dictated by the elites who manage the websites, pay for the ads, and produce the spin.[16]

The one thing Americans are in overwhelming agreement on, in poll after poll and election result after election result, is that neither major party has a plan for the future.[17] They're right. Neither party has a plan. Nor do most prominent politicians. The dissident campaigns that gained traction in the run-up to the 2016 presidential election, especially that of Bernie Sanders, connected with Americans who are deeply frustrated with an empty partisan discourse and a limited range of options. Yet, even as outsider campaigns gave voice to the frustration, they did little to foster necessary debates about the technological, economic, and social changes that feed that frustration. While Pope Francis may counsel that "contemporary man has not been trained to use power well," few political figures have thought deeply enough about the issues to recognize, as the pope did in his 2015 encyclical, that "our immense technological development has not been accompanied by a development in human responsibility, values and conscience."[18]

This lack of focus on the future creates a dangerous disconnect: sincere activism can be expended toward achievable goals but might then be upended by entirely predictable technological change. What do we mean by this? We are enthusiastic supporters of the movement to achieve a fifteen-dollar-an-hour minimum wage in the United States. Like a lot of Americans, we think the minimum wage should always be sufficient to ensure that a full-time worker and her family will live above the poverty line.[19] Yet, we know that, as wages rise for fast-food workers, multinational corporations will respond by replacing workers with robots. We know that even if the wages do not rise to a just and equitable level, the wave of automation that is coming will lead to mass dislocation in an industry that has become one of the few refuges for workers displaced by corporate downsizing and trade-related plant closings. We know this because the debate about where technological change is headed is already settled in the circles of those who intend to profit from that change.

A 2015 report from an influential strategic consulting and investment management firm, the Cornerstone Capital Group, warned that "it's not clear that cost inflation can be consistently offset by raising menu prices, so companies are considering new strategies to protect margins."[20] The report explains that "automation is currently complementing labor, particularly in the ordering process. Should wage pressure intensify, however, the focus will likely shift and companies will look to replace labor."[21]

That puts a whole new twist on discussions about wages and the future of work. The CEOs are well aware of the twist, but for the most part workers and activists are not. For the workers and their allies to negotiate effectively, they need to know what CEOs know, and they need to evolve their demands so that corporations cannot cynically raise wages for a handful of employees—with the ensuing favorable headlines that firms such as McDonald's and WalMart have already garnered for minute upticks in what they pay their workers—while eliminating jobs for the great mass of workers.[22] This evolution of demands must never go to the downward default position of accepting poverty wages as inevitable in a so-called new economy. Rather, demands must evolve upward to combine the requirement of a living wage with scheduling protections that renew the historic promise of "eight hours for work, eight hours for rest and eight hours for what you will" (such as those contained in the innovative "Retail Workers Bill of Rights" that we discuss in Chapter 5), with a broader societal recognition of the immediate need to provide support for workers who are displaced by automation, and with the longer-term recognition of the need for establishing economic structures that ensure that the benefits of the new economy are shared by all.

Instead of the narrowly defined elite discussion about "faster, cheaper, and more dynamic applications in foodservice," there needs to be a wide-open national discourse about what matters to Americans of every race, every ethnicity, every region, and every class. That is the discourse this book seeks to open because in this discussion can be found the seed of both political and economic democracy.

If we the people are going to make the future that is now our own, then we must begin a knowing, conscious fight for shared prosperity, genuine opportunity, and the full realization of the promise of new technologies. That full promise is being denied us at this point in our history. Through that denial, the promise of technology is being turned against us. The oppressive prospects of technology—to spy on us, to profit off our desperation and misery, to make us work harder for less, to control rather than to free us—are only beginning to be fully realized. Americans are unsettled by the realization. Polling shows that they see their circumstance as bad—and they fear that it is destined to get worse.[23]

We respect these sentiments. They are honest expressions of the fear and frustration fostered by economic uncertainty and empty politics.

But we do not accept them.

The future that is now is frightening and frustrating. It really is bad, and it really is getting worse. That's quantifiable. But from such moments have sprung great movements and what the author Grace Paley referred to as "enormous changes at the last minute."[24] The future that is next can be good, and it can get better. Dramatically better for Americans and for people around the world. Technology can help us to be happier, healthier, freer, and more connected to ourselves, to our families, and to communities. We can work less and enjoy our lives more. The tech utopian promise is real.

But there is no gadget that can get society from here to there. There is no app that will achieve the better and more humane life that is possible. There is no master plan from a CEO or Silicon Valley visionary. There is only us. We the people are the only force that can make a future worthy of our hopes and our humanity. And our only tool is the only tool that has ever taken the power to define the future away from the elites and given it to the whole of humanity: democracy.

chapter one

INTO THE MAELSTROM

IN JANUARY 2014 GOOGLE CHAIRMAN ERIC SCHMIDT APPEARED before the World Economic Forum in Davos, Switzerland, and acknowledged that due to rapid advances in technology, including some of the projects Google was working on, countless middle-class jobs that had seemed beyond the reach of computers and automation were going to be at risk in the near future. More and more middle-class workers were going to lose their jobs and there was little on the horizon to suggest there would be new jobs for them. This would be, according to Schmidt, the "defining" issue of the next two to three decades.[1]

Schmidt had no reason to raise this issue unless there was a basis for his concern. And he was not alone. At meetings of high-level technology executives and engineers, some public, some private, around the world over the past several years, few topics have garnered more attention than the radically changing nature of work and the prospect that it will change even more radically in the near future. But these issues are rarely raised with even the muted level of alarm expressed by Schmidt.

More often than not, the automation of whole sectors of the economy, and the ensuing displacement of workers, is discussed as "creative destruction," from which will emerge tremendous opportunities to cut costs and increase profits. These discussions of the jobs that are certain to be eliminated—and the whole industries that will be altered beyond recognition—are robust and enthusiastic.

Yet, they do not include the citizens, the workers, and the communities that are headed for creative destruction. That's jarring because Schmidt and his CEO compatriots are not futurists imagining some distant prospect. They are hard-edged business executives speaking about the here and now. And they speak about a reality that is well understood by the titans of the new tech monopolies and among the scholars who study labor and technology.[2] It is a reality that has profound significance for America, although there remains considerable disagreement about the precise nature of that significance. There are still tech utopians who say that the changes that are coming will invariably lead to the best of times—that people will work much less and enjoy greater access to healthcare, education, and economic security due to the vastly increased economic output. They tell us that society will generate the necessary tools to address environmental damage, overcome poverty, and turn the page to a glorious new chapter in history where economic scarcity no longer defines the human condition. But many of these utopians also acknowledge, as Schmidt does, that the transition to this new era will likely be marked by social upheaval the likes of which have only rarely been seen.

If there is consensus developing, it holds that an already troubling situation is about to get considerably worse. Harvard economist Edward L. Glaeser was blunt when he wrote in a 2014 paper that America's "most worrying social trend" was "the 40-year secular rise in the number and share of jobless adults."[3] And what comes next is an explosion of automation that will eliminate millions of additional jobs. That is an alarming notion that merits attention, debate, and intervention.

The sense of urgency ought to be heightened by the fact that the existing American political and social circumstance is ill prepared to respond to a massive wave of automation and dislocation. By now nearly everyone is familiar with the grotesque and historically unprecedented expansion of economic inequality in the United States over the past three or four decades. Likewise, poverty has increased sharply while upward mobility has almost disappeared.[4] Many Americans have experienced an "economic nightmare," as author and former *New York Times* columnist Bob Herbert put it, where "millions of hardworking men and women who had believed they were solidly anchored economically found themselves cast into a financial abyss, struggling with joblessness, home foreclosures, and personal bankruptcy." It wasn't just the result of the 2008 Great Recession. "From 1990 to 2008 the life-expectancy for the poorest, least well-educated white Americans fell by a stunning four years," notes Herbert. "For white women without a high school diploma, it fell by five years."[5]

Horrifying economic inequality extends from, and also extends, political inequality. The "rule of law," the foundation of democracy in America, is collapsing. The principle that all are equal before the law—with no one above it or below it—has become a sick joke in a society where unarmed African-American men and women are shot down by police officers while the billionaire bankers who crashed the global economy, and fund both political parties, have gone scot-free despite their legally dubious behavior. In some cases they have even received lucrative taxpayer bailouts.[6] Americans, *Rolling Stone* writer Matt Taibbi tells us, have "become numb to the idea that rights aren't absolute but are enjoyed on a kind of sliding scale [and] we've also learned to accept the implicit idea that some people have simply more rights than others. Some people go to jail, and others just don't."[7] In a state of extreme economic and social and political inequality, options for humane and workable responses to radical change disappear. This is the circumstance in which the United States finds itself as a digital revolution every bit as sweeping as the industrial revolution takes hold.

In recent years some of America's finest economists and writers have generated thoughtful and convincing proposals to create full employment at good wages, to rebuild the nation's infrastructure and urban areas, eliminate poverty, provide universal healthcare, greatly enhance political participation, reduce inequality, and transition to a sustainable green economy in one fell swoop.[8] The ideas emanate from other democracies and from America's own rich political economic traditions.[9] Many of these are proposals to maintain a largely capitalistic economy, albeit with a social democratic or Keynesian twist. Although these proposals corral some industries and all of them ask for billionaires and large corporations to pay more in taxes, they mostly allow corporations to continue on their merry way, arguably making even greater profits as a more prosperous middle class creates increased demand for their products.

Evidence suggests many of these proposals would be popular, even wildly popular, with most Americans. Yet none of these proposals has been taken seriously inside the corridors of power by those who run either of the political parties. Political science research by Stanford's David Broockman and the University of Michigan's Christopher Skovron concludes that on core policy issues legislators routinely think their own constituents are considerably *more* conservative than the polling data shows they actually are. This is true across the board but especially pronounced among conservative legislators. "The typical conservative legislator overestimates his or her district's conservatism by a whopping 20 percentage points. Indeed, he or she believes the district is even more conservative than the most right-leaning district in the entire country." Why? "Politicians feel much more accountable to the wealthy, party leaders, or interest groups than to rank and file voters' preferences," and "politically active citizens tend to be wealthier and more conservative than others."[10] Most reform proposals are dismissed as impractical and relegated to the netherworld of the loony-Left before they can even see the light of day.

The reason for this is clear: the United States is not a democracy, if by *democracy* we mean a government of the people, by the people, and for the people. That is the Big Lie of the official discourse. If anything, it is a "citizenless" democracy, an oxymoron if there ever was one. The only voice that matters in American politics, the voice that shouts down every other, is that of the wealthy few for whom creative destruction is a business practice rather than a threat.[11] Princeton's Martin Gilens and Northwestern's Benjamin I. Page have conducted exhaustive research on American politics. Their conclusion: "The central point that emerges from our research is that economic elites and organized groups representing business interests have substantial independent impacts on U.S. government policy, while mass-based interest groups and average citizens have little or no independent influence." If that is not clear enough, they add: "When a majority of citizens disagrees with economic elites or business interests, they generally lose. Moreover, because of the strong status quo bias built into the U.S. political system, even when fairly large majorities of Americans favor policy change, they generally do not get it."[12]

"Indeed, under most circumstance," Gilens writes in another recent study he conducted, "the preferences of the vast majority of Americans appear to have essentially no impact on which policies the government does or doesn't adopt."[13]

The problem here is not just that government policies are indifferent or hostile to those without great wealth. The two great and immediate existential threats to human existence—militarism and environmental catastrophe—proceed largely unchecked by public policy, regardless of popular concerns, and despite the fact that they affect rich and poor alike because they each have the capacity to radically degrade or terminate life as humans have experienced it for the past hundred thousand years on the planet. This is because very powerful interests see demilitarization and shifting away from fossil fuels as existential threats to *their* present lucrative positions, and no powerful interests have a direct stake in seeing the problems forcefully addressed. In the calculus of citizenless democracies, the rulers fiddle away and the "status quo" is not static but gets worse.

When understood as a "citizenless" democracy, the often lamented and lampooned ignorance of the American people takes on a different light. True, two-thirds of Americans cannot name a single member of the US Supreme Court, and a similar fraction cannot name the three branches of the federal government; only 15 percent can name the chief justice; and in 2010 over two in five Americans did not know who the sitting vice president was.[14] But this is not the cause of citizenless democracy; it is the effect. This is what one would rationally expect in what political scientist Sheldon Wolin character-ized as a "politically demobilized society, that is, a society in which the citizens, far from being whipped into a continuous frenzy by the regime's operatives, are encouraged at virtually every turn to be po-litically lethargic." It is a society in which people get precious little from the government, where austerity and rollbacks are the order of the day. Citizens are constantly reminded of the "political futility" of popular involvement in politics.[15] "There is a widespread sense," the scholar Tony Judt wrote in 2010, "that since 'they' will do what they want in any case—while feathering their own nests—why should 'we' waste time trying to influence the outcome of their actions?"[16] As the journalist Bob Herbert observed in his 2014 chronicle of contempo-rary America, "Something fundamental in the very character of the United States had shifted. There was a sense of powerlessness and resignation among ordinary people that I hadn't been used to seeing. The country seemed demoralized."[17]

In this context, it is rational that one abandon an interest in poli-tics, or social life broadly construed, and concentrate on looking out for number one. And in a context in which governments are increas-ingly felt to be divorced from responding to the expressed social and economic needs of its common citizens, that makes the focus on one's own bank account all the more important. But that is no way to live, for a person or a society. To paraphrase a point once made by the philosopher John Dewey: once an organism loses the sense that it can affect its environment, it starts to weaken and die.[18]

This is the context in which the next wave of automation is arriv-ing, and it could not be worse for the prospect of having the potential bounty shared with everyone and used for the benefit of building a healthy sustainable society. Unemployment, inequality, and poverty are best understood not, in the end, as economic problems, but instead as political problems. They require political solutions. And it would seem then that the United States, lacking those solutions, is poised for disaster.

But a country that is "poised for disaster" need not accept its fate. It can change. And there is reason to believe that it will, as Americans change.

Let's begin by looking at the bright side. It would be far worse if all the economic, environmental, and political problems of this nation were the triumphant result of an informed and enthusiastic citizenry, with voter turnouts the highest in the world, rather than the lowest. But such is not the case. The silver lining is that the demoralization and disconnect most Americans are experiencing within their citizen-less democracy is, in fact, the crack in the façade of an elitist political economy that activists can exploit to create a humane, sustainable, and citizen-run democracy. A credible roadmap to a much better future is being developed as extraordinary ideas, extraordinary movements, and extraordinary prospects are being developed by citizens who are almost never covered in what little remains of the news media. The common theme is that while challenges posed by an unprecedented wave of automation can be met, the solutions will not be cosmetic. They will require structural change in our political economy, and policies that are far outside the range countenanced by the nation's rulers. And there's the rub. If that is going to happen, it is going to take an army of aroused and informed citizens, rather than the marginal, though growing, coterie that presently exists.

One need not be a wild-eyed optimist or a naïve romantic to be certain that Americans can get this right. There is no need to deny that the coming years will be unusually turbulent, or that we will see a wrenching reconstruction of many institutions. The status quo is going to be turned upside down. Whether it is going to land in a good place will be determined by what the citizens of this nation do. If they fail to act, if all or most hands are not summoned to the deck, what awaits us may make the present day look like good times.

The state of present-day capitalism and what appears to be its likely future is one of stagnation—meaning ever-increasing inequality, poverty, austerity, and social insecurity. There is a crisis of unemployment and underemployment. Full employment, meaning, as economist Robert Pollin puts it, "an abundance of decent jobs," is "fundamental to

building a decent society."[19] A healthy economy that generates benefits for the bulk of the population, and not just society's owning class,
depends upon it.[20] And this is more than an economic issue. As technology writer Nicholas Carr puts it, people are "happiest when we're
absorbed in a difficult task, a task that has clear goals and that challenges us not only to exercise our talents, but stretch them." And that
is something most often found in work.[21] "When joblessness is high in
America," Herbert writes, "the nation's spirits inevitably are low."[22] Full
employment for more than a brief period has never been enthusiasti-
cally received by Wall Street, as it raises wages and shifts economic and
political power to employees. To some extent the decrepit state of the
contemporary labor market reflects the total control over government
economic policymaking by the wealthy.

The emerging automation wave that Eric Schmidt called attention
to at Davos is going to replace millions of jobs and alter the nature
of many of those jobs that remain. Some technology experts like Ben
Way expect a loss of 70 percent of existing jobs in the next three decades, with little hope that very many new jobs will emerge to replace
what is lost.[23] University of Pennsylvania sociologist Randall Collins
expects an unemployment rate in the neighborhood of 50 percent.[24]
One need not accept these predictions—they strike us as speculative
if not extreme—to see that at the very least what is about to transpire
is going to put *severe* downward pressure on wages and working conditions, which already are deplorable. "What does the 'end of work'
mean, exactly?" journalist Derek Thompson asked in a penetrating
examination of automation in a 2015 issue of the *Atlantic*. "It does not
mean the imminence of total unemployment, nor is the United States
remotely likely to face, say, 30 or 50 percent unemployment within
the next decade. Rather, technology could exert a slow but continual
downward pressure on the value and availability of work—that is, on
wages and on the share of prime-age workers with full-time jobs."[25]

Judt saw this coming in 2010: "Mass unemployment—once regarded as a pathology of badly managed economies—is beginning
to look like an endemic characteristic of advanced societies. At best,
we can hope for 'under-employment'—where men and women work

part-time; accept jobs far below their skill level; or else undertake skilled work of the sort traditionally assigned to immigrants and the young."[26]

Unemployment and underemployment of this magnitude have a way of capturing a person's attention like almost nothing else. With apologies to our friend Naomi Klein, this changes everything.

CAPITALISM ON STEROIDS

It is ironic that the digital revolution is central to the jobs crisis, because these same technologies have been roundly heralded heretofore as democratizing agents that shift power from the few to the many. Although we believe it is difficult to exaggerate the value that digital communication has brought to society as a whole, we also believe the evidence is clear that these technologies are not magical; how they are developed owes largely to the political economic context.[27] They can be forces for surveillance, propaganda, and immiseration as much as tools of liberation.[28]

What is striking is that the digital revolution exponentially increases one of the longstanding problems of capitalism—what the Irish engineer Mike Cooley terms "the gap between that which technology could provide society (its potential) and that which it actually does provide for society (its reality)."[29] The potential is wondrous. Artificial intelligence expert Neil Jacobstein notes that "exponential technologies may eventually permit people to not need jobs to have a high standard of living." He enthuses that "the emphasis will be less on making money and more on making contributions, or at least creating an interesting life."[30] Nor is this very far off in the future. One 2011 CNN report observed that "America is productive enough that it could probably shelter, feed, educate, and even provide health care for its entire population with just a fraction of us actually working."[31] The barrier to this brighter future, of course, is capitalism itself.

This gap between potential and reality is a long-term tension in capitalism that a number of our greatest economists—including some who in their times were among capitalism's mightiest champions—

have understood for the past 150 years. Today, the former chief economist of the International Monetary Fund, Harvard's Kenneth Rogoff,
bluntly states that with the technological revolution the "struggle for
subsistence will no longer be a primary imperative and capitalism's
numerous flaws may loom larger," leading to its possible demise.[32]
Capitalism's "structural crisis," as economist David M. Kotz puts it,
"has no easy path to a desirable solution. This historical moment may
be a turning point for humanity."[33] Economist and technology scholar
Jeremy Rifkin puts it baldly: "At the heart of capitalism there lies a
contradiction in the driving mechanism that has propelled it ever upward to commanding heights, but now is speeding it to its death."[34]

In a nation with a democratic governing system, one would reasonably expect that debates and study concerning the best uses of
these radical technologies to benefit all of society would dominate
political life. It certainly dramatically shifts the nature of progressive
and socialist analysis and strategic thinking. As prominent leftist theorist David Harvey notes: "An anti-capitalist movement has in the
current conjuncture to reorganize its thinking around the idea that
social labour is becoming less and less significant to how the economic engine of capitalism functions. Many of the service, administrative and professional jobs the left currently seeks to defend are on
the way out. Most of the world's population is becoming disposable
and irrelevant from the standpoint of capital."[35]

The role of markets and corporations and employment—indeed,
everything—would need to be reconsidered. Discussions would have
to occur concerning what the good life would be in a world where
work is largely unnecessary. Experiments would need to be conducted
on alternative types of enterprises and economic models. It would be,
in effect, the mother of all constitutional conventions. Where society
ended up would be impossible to predict, but wherever it did would
likely be the best possible place, because it would the product of democratic deliberation. And it is safe to say it would be a very different
place than where the current US political system is taking us.

Such an economic debate is unthinkable in the citizenless democracy of the United States, where the range of legitimate deliberation,

to quote media critic Jeff Cohen, extends all the way from GE to GM. There will be an "elite" debate on these issues—a debate premised on protecting elite interests—because the very system of capitalism is going to be in the crosshairs of history. "Today, the ability of free-market democracies to deliver widely shared increases in prosperity is in question as never before," a 2015 report by a commission co-chaired by former Treasury Secretary Lawrence H. Summers announced. "This is an economic problem that threatens to become a problem for the political systems of these nations."[36] The natives are going to get restless. As the *Economist* notes, "squeezing out" the middle class "could generate a more antagonistic, unstable and potentially dangerous politics."[37] Cato Institute researcher Brink Lindsey writes that "there is the threat that widening disparities between the elite and everybody else will prompt a political backlash against the whole system."[38]

The problem of a political system that is defined as a market, where issues can be made "important" or "unimportant" via the influence of campaign donations, lobbying, spin, and media manipulation, is that discussions of those disparities—and of their causes—are taken off the table. The level of corruption in contemporary politics would make Gilded Age icons like Jay Gould and Mark Hanna blush. American elections have become a disgrace, where a handful of unaccountable and often unknown billionaires finance the candidates, and the coin of the realm has become the entirely asinine negative political advertisement. America spends vastly more on its elections per capita than any other nation—and has made the ability to raise enormous amounts of money the sine qua non of political success for politicians of both major parties—yet it has extraordinarily low levels of voter turnout.[39] The American news media—including digital journalism—is in freefall collapse, as the number of paid reporters per capita has plummeted over the past twenty-five years.[40] What coverage remains of politics and elections tends to be superficial, and spoon-feeds the public what elites are saying. Most legitimate debates occur when elites disagree with each other. If elites are in agreement on an issue, or do not wish to talk about it, it almost never appears as a significant story in the news media. Nowhere is this more true than with economic issues, where corporate power and capitalism are off-limits to critical assessments.

Popular mythology—urged on by corporate public relations—has it that what is good about the economy is the result of entrepreneurs operating in free markets, and that the government's function is simply to screw things up with its endless barrage of counterproductive regulations. In fact, contemporary capitalism is very much a product of government policies and subsidies and the federal government is as necessary to the system as corporations and Wall Street. The US government, for example, every day works assiduously to advance the interests of the nation's largest corporations and wealthiest investors. Most of this work takes place within an elite consensus on goals and with the explicit desire that the public not interfere in the government's work. Nowhere is this more transparent than in the numerous major trade treaties that have been negotiated in the past three decades.

What is clear from our analysis is that there needs to be a rethinking of the relationship of capitalism to democracy, and a rethinking of what exactly is necessary for democracy to effectively exist, if people are going to make any progress in strengthening democracy. How can we turn citizenless democracies into bona fide democracies?

Prior to the emergence of modern capitalism, politics and economics were interchangeable; whoever controlled the government controlled the economy, and vice versa. The most politically powerful nobles were the wealthiest people. The idea of democracy prior to capitalism was the radical notion of politics controlled by propertyless citizens, which would give them command over property. "Democracy is when the indigent, and not the men of property, are the rulers," Aristotle noted at its birth.[41] It is why democracy was regarded as being synonymous with "communism" or some sort of one-class society; when poor people gained political power they would understandably reshuffle the property distribution and rules to eliminate wide disparities in property ownership and class privilege. It is why the very notion of democracy was widely, even universally, detested by the wealthy and the privileged throughout history. As recently as the founding of the

United States, for example, nearly all of those who wrote the Constitution or are considered founders, including Thomas Jefferson and James Madison, thought voting should be limited to property-holding white males. It wasn't even an issue for debate.[42]

One revolutionary change capitalism has brought to modern democratic governance was to split the elected control over the government from direct control over the economy, which is now in the hands of those with capital. The people who are elected to run the government generally are only coincidentally the same people who dominate in the marketplace and have the greatest fortunes. The power of government to curtail private property rights is strictly limited, compared to preindustrial societies. To capitalism's strongest advocates, like economist Milton Friedman, it was this core split in the disposition of power that created the space for "freedom" to flourish. It was one of the main reasons why markets and the sort of limited democracy found in places like the United States were made for each other.

But if capitalism changed the nature of the relationship of the economy to governance, it opened up a new defining debate concerning the relationship of democracy to the economy, one that has persisted since the dawn of the Republic. On one side is the classical position, one championed in much of liberal democratic theory, and embraced by much of the political left. This position holds that democracy is superior to capitalism and that the sovereign people of a nation have the fundamental right to determine through deliberation and debate what type of economy would best serve the nation, and with that, what sort of property ownership would be permitted. Many who advance this position view capitalism favorably, but they nonetheless understand that it must be the result of popular approval to be legitimate. And they are often open to the idea that the capitalist economy could be reformed and improved by political measures if that is the determination of the citizenry.

On the other side is the notion that property ownership, specifically the existing capitalist property ownership system, is the precondition for a free and decent society and that democracy is subservient to it.

Elected governments overstep their bounds to mess with the capitalist system in anything more than a mundane manner, and when they
do so they invariably invite tyranny, no matter how well intended the
policies may be. This is the conservative position in modern politics.
As Friedman put it in his classic 1962 work, *Capitalism and Freedom*,
the legitimate role of government is largely "to protect our freedom
both from enemies outside our gates and from our fellow citizens: to
preserve law and order, to enforce private contracts, to foster competitive markets." Any other function for government "is fraught
with danger."[43] "The only alternatives to free enterprise," eventual
Supreme Court Justice Lewis Powell wrote in his 1971 memo for the
Chamber of Commerce, "are varying degrees of bureaucratic regulation of individual freedom—ranging from that under moderate
socialism to the iron heel of the leftist or rightist dictatorship."[44] And
the first freedom, the single inviolable human right that no government no matter how democratic has the right to interfere with, is the
right for individuals or private businesses to maximize profits from
their investments.

If the former position envisions a strong democracy, where all
power resides with the citizenry, the latter position envisions a caged
democracy with a limited mandate; the real action in the laissez faire
world is in the private sector, and that is where the best and most talented people logically and invariably gravitate. "The best minds are
not in government," Ronald Reagan is reputed to have said. "If any
were, business would steal them away."[45] The main job of governance
is to make sure the profit system works smoothly, contracts and private property are respected and enforced, the dispossessed are kept in
line, and, if there is an economic crisis, the government intervenes as
necessary to make it lucrative for businesses and wealthy individuals
to invest again. Big government is A-OK when it advances the interests of capital—though this point best not be emphasized to a general
audience; for everyone else, "small" government is the order of the
day. Governance is best when it is left to those who fully appreciate
that the needs of investors come first and foremost. And that is most
likely to happen if most everyone else tunes out politics and focuses

on other matters. The problem, of course, is that we are entering into a period where change will come so rapidly that, when citizens tune back in, tens of millions of them could be left with nothing.

When a capitalist economy is literally shaking apart, when it is in severe crisis, the demand that the political system address enormous social and economic problems rises. This is where we see political results that involve potentially fundamental realignment and restructuring, as when a democratic nation elects a government that is explicitly committed to shifting the economy away from capitalism, to something generally called socialism.[46] But the tension between these approaches plays out in all capitalist democracies in the form of ongoing debates about the proper role of the government in directing and participating in the economy: what should it be permitted to do and whose interests should it represent. In the strong democracy view, for example, economic planning by the state is imperative to determine how best to approach a number of fundamental issues, including environmental policy, urban development, economic infrastructure, and many forms of social security and well-being. In the limited democracy view, outside of the military or police functions, these are decisions best determined by the profit calculations of business and investors. The market is infallible, and it is imperative that flawed humans not interfere with its genius. The role of government is to facilitate and protect the profit system.

This split corresponds to a series of crucial battles that determines just how effective and sweeping popular governance can be. To advocates of a strong democracy, institutions, rules, and policies should be put into place to encourage active and informed participation by as much of the population as possible. As political scientist Robert A. Dahl puts it, citizens in a democracy must "possess the political resources they would require in order to participate in political life pretty much as equals."[47] The playing field should be leveled so those without means can effectively govern as equals of those with substantial means. To conservatives, such an approach is foolhardy if not downright corrosive of freedom, for effective popular participation in politics, just as much as an "activist" government, is to be discouraged.

DEMOCRATIC INFRASTRUCTURE

A debate persists over what we term *democratic infrastructure*. As Dahl writes, "Political equality requires democratic political institutions."[48] The term *infrastructure* comes from economics. An advanced economy does not exist because entrepreneurs or businesses have the right to invest and can do whatever they please. It exists because elaborate communication, transportation, sanitation, energy, and legal infrastructures provide a foundation that makes commerce possible. Establishing this infrastructure is largely the province of the government, even if the state's job is to coordinate private interests to get it done effectively. The beauty of infrastructure projects is that they are accessible to everyone and have tremendous "spillovers," or "positive externalities," meaning they generate considerable value for others and for society as a whole.[49] Without such an infrastructure, an advanced economy cannot exist.

So it is with democracy. The right to vote means little without

- the infrastructure of effective elections, such that one-person, one-vote is the order of the day, and races allow genuine competition
- the rule of law
- stringent limits on money in politics
- limits on the power of the judiciary to act in an arbitrary and unaccountable manner
- the effective ability to launch effective new parties or associations
- free trade unions with effective collective bargaining
- open, transparent governance
- a credible, independent, and uncensored free press/news media
- universal free schools with civic education
- a basic level of economic and social security, which is only limited by the overall productive capacity of the society
- an environment that can sustain and nurture life.

In short, a credible democratic infrastructure requires ground rules and institutions that empower the weakest in society so they can effectively be the political equals of the wealthiest members of society, and that prevent the wealthy few from having excessive influence. It also includes "breakers" to prevent the establishment of such proven enemies of democracy as

- corruption
- private monopolistic control over the economy
- significant economic inequality
- government secrecy and surveillance
- government propaganda
- militarism

These six tend to go hand-in-hand.[50] The civil liberties that most Americans cherish—the freedoms of speech, press, and religion; the right to assemble; the right to privacy—thrive when there is a strong democratic infrastructure. Without one, these freedoms tend to be on insecure ground, at least to the extent their exercise threatens those in power. We agree with the writer and lawyer Elliot Sperber, who argues that "this infrastructure of democracy" must be as "inalienable" as the political rights we cherish.[51] Hungarian scholar Zoltan Tibor Pallinger, who has direct experience in building democracies in formerly communist nations, defines "democratic infrastructure" as the "institutions, instruments and procedures provided by the state that render the use of democratic rights possible."[52]

A vibrant democratic infrastructure does not necessarily presuppose a particular economic structure; it could be accompanied by an economy where private property, markets, and profit-making proliferate. Theoretically, a strong democratic infrastructure could be accompanied by a class-based economy in which wealth and economic power belong disproportionately to those at the very top, but for such an economy to exist would require that its proponents convince the preponderance of the population of its merits in a fair fight. Such a democratic infrastructure is simultaneously nonpartisan and also at the heart of contentious politics. This would be a paradox, except it simply confirms the truth that democracy is not a neutral or value-free undertaking. Democracy has many winners, but it also has losers: those who benefit by its absence or at least its diminution.

A commitment to strong democracy demands an array of infrastructural policies that can be, at times, highly controversial. Along these lines, consider the right to free labor unions and effective collective bargaining. Wendell Willkie, corporate president and free enterprise champion turned 1940 Republican presidential candidate, explained the need for unions and collective bargaining by noting that "for labor the essential content of freedom is different in today's society from what it was in the agricultural society of an earlier age. Men no longer able to own, or aspire to own, small businesses and farms have sought new solutions for a need which all Americans must respect—the need to control for themselves the circumstances which dictate their working lives."[53]

According to Willkie, labor unions deserved to be accorded permanence because they were a necessary foundation of modern democracy. He was right: the evidence is clear that unions, in addition to the value they generate for their own members, reduce overall economic inequality and also provide people without property a means for more effectively participating in the political process.[54] So strong unions produce a double win in terms of democratic infrastructure. This is well understood and accepted in most advanced democracies, including the United States from the 1930s until recently, but it is obviously a controversial proposition today, as unions raise labor costs and generate understandable enmity from employers, who have considerable self-interest in seeing unions weakened or eliminated.

The state of this democratic infrastructure at any time generally corresponds to a broader political culture, which informally send cues to the citizenry about what their role is and who is legitimately entitled to make political decisions. It promotes what can be a dominant *weltanschauung*, or general broad-based political culture. When a democratic infrastructure is dynamic and growing, notions of fairness, justice, egalitarianism, and public service are respected and widespread.

Trust between people increases. Provocative new ideas are put in play and subject to debate. When the democratic infrastructure is weak or in decline, the political culture shrivels, self-interest reigns, and demoralization and pessimism ascend. Then the only rational reason to enter public life is to use it as a way station to an eventual job in the private sector where you can cash in your public-sector chips, or just for purposes of flat-out corruption.

The battle over a democratic infrastructure has ebbed and flowed over the course of American history, as it has in other democratic nations. After four decades of relentless attack on the democratic infrastructure, it has severely shrunk in the United States today, and much of what remains is in jeopardy. This is the main reason why the great existential economic crisis we are experiencing has been aggravated by a pathetic and corrupt political response. For many Americans its constituent parts now seem foreign or radical—or are even entirely unknown—when they are in fact at the heart of the American struggle for democracy.

The advocates of unrestrained capitalism and limited government can and often do trump democracy. But the United States has seen many circumstances in which democracy has won out and the democratic infrastructure has been built out. We are in another moment when this is going to happen. But to understand the task at hand, we must begin by understanding the possibility itself. In our view, the moral of the story is clear: if you win the battle for democratic infrastructure, you almost certainly will win the war for controlling the nation, and the economy. It is here, on this battlefield, more than anywhere else, that the outcome will determine whose future it will be, or if there will be much of a future at all. It is where those concerned about how America responds to the jobs crisis we are facing must turn their attention. In a time of crisis, it means everything.

The historical review of democratic infrastructure and weltanschauung also contributes to a more productive understanding of how social change is actually made. It reveals how each of the disparate interests that work on one part of building a democratic infrastructure have a decided interest in seeing the other parts succeed as well.

Competition between them is best regarded as the proverbial "circular firing squad," and unless there is overall success, and a changed weltanschauung, no single campaign can earn more than marginal victories, and those victories will prove difficult, if not impossible, to maintain. That may seem too abstract for a rallying cry, but the underlying principle needs to guide the work.

With regard to unifying rallying cries, it is hard to take issue with Klein when she argues that "the overriding principle must be to address the twin crises of climate change and inequality at the same time."[55] Herbert offers up another, related, candidate, for "overriding" status: "The crucial impact of employment on virtually every facet of American society is the reason activists with widely different agendas might be induced to rally around a sustained campaign to wipe out joblessness and unemployment. If America cannot get its act together on the jobs front, its many other serious wounds will not heal."[56]

We believe Herbert is right, too, and in the context of automation, it leads almost certainly to a broader discussion of how economic and political power is exercised in the United States.

The United States has been here before. During the Progressive Era of a century ago, a tremendous popular surge launched seven decades of democratic advancement. In many respects, the core problems we face today were anticipated then. What is clear from what happened a century ago is how central social movements were to the process of building out a democratic infrastructure and changing the weltanschauung. This provides a context for reviewing and assessing the unusually rapid growth of grassroots activism in recent years on an array of issues mostly related to elements of the democratic infrastructure. It grows on fertile ground: polling shows that the vast majority of Americans believe big business has too much control over their lives and way too much influence over government.[57] "The inability of traditional politics and policies to address fundamental challenges has fueled an extraordinary amount of experimentation in communities across the United States," a 2015 report by the Next System Project noted. "Unbeknownst to many, literally thousands of on-the-ground efforts have been developing."[58] Because media coverage has been virtually nonexistent, many Americans who might be sympathetic or curious are left entirely in the dark.

An understanding of democratic infrastructure and weltanschauung can also help us pierce through the pessimism that overpowers countless Americans and renders them inactive because they believe social change for the better is impossible. It is perhaps human nature to see change as very slow and incremental. The belief that tomorrow will look pretty much like today is awfully difficult to argue with most days of most lives. So what we see around us today is what we will very likely see when we wake up tomorrow. The problem with this approach is that it cannot account for social change except in retrospect. No one saw the civil rights movement or the feminist movement or the gay rights movement or the environmental movement erupting in the years before they happened. If people did, the movements would have happened earlier. The Knights of Labor and the Congress of Industrial Organizations seemingly came out of nowhere when they burst on the scene. No one anticipated the Occupy explosion of 2011. After movements emerge, many people act like they saw them coming all along and they were fully anticipated; the sense of surprise is quickly forgotten.

There is something even more important about this. When fundamental social change comes, as Klein writes, "it's generally not in legislative dribs and drabs spread out evenly over decades. Rather it comes in spasms of rapid-fire lawmaking, with one breakthrough after another." These are periods in which the democratic infrastructure is built up and the weltanschauung has shifted dramatically. Klein captures this well:

> When major shifts in the economic balance of power take place, they are invariably the result of extraordinary levels of social mobilization. . . . During extraordinary historical moments—both world wars, the aftermath of the Great Depression, or the peak of the civil rights era—the usual categories dividing "activists" and "regular people" became

meaningless because the project of changing society was so deeply woven into the project of life. Activists were, quite simply, everyone.[59]

This is the sort of moment we are entering. We have no idea when exactly or under what terms. But what we can do is prepare and get ready. In short, we agree with Chris Hedges that in historical terms, the United States is entering a period where the status quo cannot remain as it is, and radical, even revolutionary, change is almost certain to come.[60] What we do know, and what will be the best indicator of a new moment, is the weltanschauung will shift. Crises that had appeared insurmountable will now appear like opportunities to make a much better world than had ever existed before. There will doubtlessly be many important differences between the coming period of activism and those of the past century; the singular importance of the environment comes to mind. There is one other crucial difference that emerges from our research: the very nature of the economy will be a front-burner issue as never before. The great issue of the coming generation will be expanding democratic values and principles— building out the democratic infrastructure if you will—into economic institutions and practices.[61]

THE REAL F-BOMB

But movements to expand the democratic infrastructure, and create a just and sustainable society, will not be the only response to stagnation, inequality, economic crisis, and, most important of all, mass unemployment. It is not all roses and lilies. In times of crisis, as mainstream political parties, institutions, and thinkers increasingly are mired in varying degrees of corruption, failure, incompetence, and stupefaction, there will be movements born of immense anger and frustration on the political right. We know from looking at other nations in our times that face these economic crises—like Greece today—and from the decade of the 1930s, when most of the world met these standards—that a particular deadly scourge is likely to appear: fascism.[62] The term *fascism* carries more baggage than a fleet of luxury ocean liners, and it is absurd and counterproductive to think of it as being embodied *in toto* by the Nazi or Italian experience in the 1930s.* Nevertheless, allowing for that proviso, there is much to learn from its history.

The connection between mass unemployment and fascism is almost universally accepted by scholars of the subject. "Because capitalism goes into crisis," historian Dave Renton writes, "because it forces millions into unemployment, so there are conditions in which bitterness grows." Indeed, it was only with the skyrocketing unemployment of the early 1930s that the Nazi Party in Germany moved from the margins to power.[63] President Franklin D. Roosevelt emphasized this point at every turn. "Democracy is not safe if its business system does not provide employment and produce and distribute goods in such a way as to sustain an acceptable standard of living."[64] "Democracy has disappeared in several great nations," FDR said on another occasion, "not because the people of those nations disliked democracy, but because they had grown tired of unemployment and insecurity, of seeing their children hungry while they sat helpless in the face of government confusion and government weakness."[65]

What mass unemployment means in the coming years, Judt writes, is a "return to dependency upon the state."[66] This is not only because millions are out of work, but because in such a depressed environment capitalism does not generate profits anywhere near satisfactory for investors and businesses. The state needs to intervene much more

---

* *Fascism* has become a widely used term in many different ways over the years. And there is a valuable literature on the topic. In some cases it is applied to any non-democratic authoritarian capitalist society—almost always military dictatorships—the kind the United States has routinely supported for the past seventy years. See Noam Chomsky and Edward S. Herman, *The Washington Connection and Third World Fascism: The Political Economy of Human Rights,* Volume I (Boston: South End Press, 1979). For our purposes, we prefer Robert O. Paxton's approach. Calling fascism "the major political innovation of the twentieth century," he regards it as "dictatorship against the left amidst popular enthusiasm." Mass support is a defining feature, which is why the run-of-the mill police state does not qualify. "Fascism," he writes, "was a new invention created afresh for the era of mass politics. It sought to appeal mainly to the emotions by the use of ritual, carefully stage-managed ceremonies, and intensely charged rhetoric." See Robert O. Paxton, *The Anatomy of Fascism* (New York: Alfred A. Knopf, 2004), pp. 3, 16.

aggressively not only to create jobs but also to create the conditions, including the markets, for profitable investment. The government needs to make the system work with bold action because obviously the traditional mechanisms to stimulate the economy have failed, or else the economy would not be in a depression. The private economy is dead in the water. As Thompson put it in his sober assessment of automation, for Americans to effectively address the coming waves of unemployment and underemployment, "it is almost certain that the country would have to embrace a radical new role for government."[67] The only issue is what the nature of the radical new role will be.

In the 1930s and 1940s the solution of the worldwide democratic Left to the problem of mass unemployment was the New Deal, or Keynesianism, or what was termed *social democracy*. The government would tax the rich or borrow their idle capital at very low interest rates and then put that money to work on public-works programs, and to fund numerous social programs that would benefit the poor and working class. The government would support free trade unions and progressive taxation and other measures to reduce inequality. Then workers would use their incomes to purchase goods and services and capitalists would make profits and have incentive to make additional private investments. And, because many of these measures built out the democratic infrastructure, the process of rejuvenating the economy also greatly strengthened effective popular participation in governance. "We have begun to bring private autocratic powers into their proper subordination to the public's government. The legend that they were invincible—above and beyond the processes of a democracy—has been shattered," FDR said in his second inaugural address in 1937. "We have always known that heedless self-interest was bad morals; we know now that it is bad economics."[68]

No one studied these policies at the time more perceptively than Michal Kalecki, the brilliant Polish economist who synthesized the work of Karl Marx and John Maynard Keynes.[69] In a 1943 essay, Kalecki noted that Keynesian policies worked: "Clearly higher output and employment benefits not only workers, but businessmen as well, because their profits rise." Yet, there was a paradox: in all democratic nations, "big business opposed consistently experiments for increasing employment by Government spending." Kalecki noted that "the businessmen in the slump are longing for a boom," so, he wondered, "why do they not accept gladly the 'synthetic' boom which the Government is able to offer them?"[70] Kalecki then provided the answer: if people in a nation realize that their elected governments can use public spending to create full employment, and maintain it permanently, it would undermine the fundamental idea of capitalism that business and private investment are the natural and best and only possible director for the economy, and make labor far more powerful. This would be disastrous. "It is true," Kalecki wrote,

> that profits would be higher under a regime of full employment than they are on average under *laissez-faire*; and even the rise in wage rates resulting from the stronger bargaining power of the workers is less likely to reduce profits than to increase prices. . . . But "discipline in the factories" and "political stability" are more appreciated by the business leaders than profits. Their class instinct tells them that lasting full employment is unsound from their point of view and that unemployment is an integral part of the normal capitalist system.[71]

Seven decades later, as the US government failed to take aggressive steps to end the recession and create full employment, economist Paul Krugman conceded that Kalecki's analysis—which he had once dismissed as extreme—was the best explanation for the pathetic state of affairs.[72]

But in the 1930s, unlike the first half of the 2010s, governments had no choice but to aggressively address economic depression and mass unemployment. Kalecki writes that "one of the important functions of fascism, as typified by the Nazi system, was to remove capitalist objections to full employment." Nazi Germany was the one country where big business did not oppose government spending to generate full employment. The appeal of the Nazi system was that "the State machinery is under the direct control of a partnership of big business with fascist upstarts." The dislike of government spending on social programs to create full employment is overcome by "concentrating Government expenditure on armaments." Finally, Kalecki writes, "'discipline in the factories' and 'political stability' under full employment are maintained by the 'new order', which ranges from the suppression of trade unions to the concentration camp." In times of severe crisis, fascism was the preferred option for big business over democracy.[73]

In the interwar years, fascism had widespread, though by no means universal, support from the wealthy and powerful, particularly if it was seen as the best bet, so to speak, in the battle against socialism. Winston Churchill was far from an outlier in the 1920s when he voiced loud approval of Italian fascism, viewing it the proven way to "rally the masses of the people" and provide "the necessary antidote to the Russian poison."[74]

This is obviously a sensitive point, as it calls into question how deep the capitalist commitment to civil liberties and democracy is, and some right-wingers have twisted themselves into intellectual pretzels in their efforts to portray fascism as a left-wing movement that is hostile to capitalism, markets, and profits.[75] This is entirely unconvincing. What is true is that historical research reveals that "real capitalists, even when they rejected democracy, mostly preferred authoritarians to fascists," as the renowned historian of fascism Robert O. Paxton notes. But, he adds, "whenever fascists reached power, to be sure, capitalists mostly accommodated with them as the best available nonsocialist solution." Paxton also acknowledges that fascist parties sometimes used stridently anti-capitalist rhetoric to gin up support when out of power: "Whenever fascist parties acquired power, however, they did nothing to carry out these anticapitalist threats. By contrast, they enforced with the utmost violence and thoroughness their threats against socialism. . . . Once in power, fascist regimes banned strikes, dissolved independent trade unions, lowered wage earners' purchasing power, and showered money on armaments industries, to the immense satisfaction of employers."[76]

"We stand for the maintenance of private property," Adolf Hitler proclaimed on more than one occasion. "We shall protect free enterprise as the most expedient, or rather the sole possible economic order."[77] Analysis of economic data from the 1930s reveals that in Nazi

Germany "the class which benefited most from fascist rule was the layer of big industrialists and landowners."[78] The same was true in fascist Italy, which has been described as a "crony capitalist, oligarchical system."[79] For this reason the economist Harold J. Laski wrote in 1937 that "fascism is nothing but monopoly capitalism imposing its will on those masses whom it has deliberately transformed into its slaves."[80]

This was certainly how it was understood by anti-fascists in the United States from the late 1930s until 1945, when the worldwide struggle between fascism and democracy dominated everything. Fascism was a global menace that threatened all capitalist democracies, and not a foreign phenomenon explained by some opaque and macabre national characteristics of Germans or Italians. Germany was not some backwater land filled with superstition and zealotry before 1933; it had Europe's wealthiest and most advanced economy, and it was roundly considered the beacon of European culture in the early twentieth century. The idea that the Nazis could assume power was considered utterly preposterous almost until the moment they did. Many Americans, including President Franklin Roosevelt and Vice President Henry A. Wallace, understood that in times of severe economic crisis, all bets are off. Then a nation's demons can be exploited, and America had its share, starting with extreme white racism. "The first truth is that the liberty of a democracy is not safe if the people tolerate the growth of private power to a point where it becomes stronger than the democratic state itself," Roosevelt said in 1938. "That, in its essence, is Fascism—ownership of Government by an individual, by a group, or by any other controlling private power."[81]

To FDR and Wallace, the domestic fascist threat in the United States was a grave concern and it came primarily from "monopolists" and "cartelists," who to protect their privileges "would sacrifice democracy itself." "If we define an American fascist as one who in case of conflict puts money and power ahead of human beings, then there are undoubtedly several million fascists in the United States," Wallace wrote. He explained that "the American fascist would prefer not to use violence. His method is to poison the channels of public information."[82] In the view of FDR and Wallace, a fascist power grab would not require a violent rupture so much as a quiet takeover orchestrated by elements of the capitalist class. The United States would experience its own home-grown All-American fascism. "They claim to be super-patriots, but they would destroy every liberty guaranteed by the constitution," Wallace wrote. "Their final objective toward which all their deceit is directed is to capture political power so that, using the power of the state and the power of the market simultaneously, they may keep the common man in eternal subjection."[83]

The journalist George Seldes wrote widely during these years on the domestic fascist threat, especially the significant support major American industrialists showed for fascism, even during World War II, and what a weak job the US news media did of exposing it.[84] "American fascism will not be really dangerous," Wallace wrote in 1944, "until there is a purposeful coalition among the cartelists, the deliberate poisoners of public information, and those who stand for the K.K.K. type of demagoguery."[85]

Fortunately, fascism was defeated, both externally and internally, but there are important lessons to be drawn from this period. First, although fascism is officially detested by nearly every American since World War II, it is striking that so many of the developments associated with fascism have become commonplace in the United States since 1945: massive government spending on armaments and militarism; seemingly endless wars barely understood by most Americans; growing inequality; massive monopolistic firms that dominate the economy far more than in FDR's era; weak and feeble news media that largely propagate elite opinion; a governing system that is mostly if not entirely in the pocket of the wealthy; the disappearing rule of law; and what seems like near ubiquitous and unaccountable surveillance of private citizens.[86] That's a sobering list.[87]

Second, and more daunting, one of the core aspects of fascism everywhere was to destroy democratic infrastructure. Contemporary Republicans should pause and consider the agenda they have embraced in their fight to eliminate labor unions and collective bargaining; undermine public education; scrap progressive taxation; mangle Social Security and Medicare; make voting more difficult for poor people;

increase government secrecy; allow unlimited corporate and billionaire spending on politics; privatize government activities so that public monies flow increasingly to private business; disregard all concerns for the environment; and reject Dwight Eisenhower's wise counsel about the threat posed by a military-industrial complex. Perhaps as daunting is the ineffectual resistance and periodic support shown by the Democratic Party on many of these issues. We are not suggesting that the people pushing these policies are fascists; we are simply noting that these policies are body blows to what remains democratic in American politics, and their removal could have a disastrous effect on the ability to have a peaceful, humane, and democratic resolution of the crises before us. And we can only wonder what Franklin Roosevelt or Henry Wallace would have made of this situation.

In 1942 the sociologist Robert S. Lynd wrote an introduction to Robert A. Brady's book on the power of big business, and its relationship with the government in Europe and the United States. Brady presented a dark picture of corporate-government collusion to the detriment of the rest of society. "One stout weapon remains in the hands of the little people at the grass roots of democracy," Lynd noted: "no one dares to challenge in frontal attack the basic democratic thesis."[88] With the shrinking of the democratic infrastructure, we are uncertain if Lynd's observation will remain true, especially in a time of deep economic problems. So many people, especially young people, are alienated from the political process and to them the word *democracy* is more a hollow cliché than a meaningful concept. Polling data shows that the commitment of Americans (as well as people worldwide) to the idea of living in a democracy has weakened considerably in recent years, especially among younger people.[89]

In recent years, for the first time in our lives, we have heard people talk about how democracy is failing and overrated, because, they say, the governments we constitute "cannot solve our problems." These are words that send chills down our spines. They open a door to a place we cannot afford to go. In turbulent times, bad things can happen. The anti-democratic raw material for a fascist surge certainly exists: America is infected with what Taibbi diagnoses as "a profound hatred of the weak and the poor, and a corresponding groveling terror before the rich and successful."[90]

That is not what America should be. And that is not, we believe, what America will be. We believe the majority of Americans are progressive and deeply desirous of living in a just, humane, and democratic society.[91] But that does not guarantee that they do, or that they will. For that reason, the battles to protect and extend elements of the democratic infrastructure move front and center as battles for survival in an age of daunting economic and social change. Only with a full embrace of democracy can we put ourselves in position to turn the economic revolution we are in the midst of experiencing into humanity's greatest victory, rather than its worst nightmare.

We take as a point of beginning the message with which Naomi Klein ended her most recent book. "There is little doubt that another crisis will see us in the streets and squares once again, taking us all by surprise," she wrote.

> The real question is what progressive forces will make of that moment, the power and confidence with which it will be seized. Because these moments when the impossible seems suddenly possible are excruciatingly rare and precious. That means more must be made of them. The next time one arises, it must be harnessed not only to denounce the world as it is, and build fleeting pockets of liberated space. It must be the catalyst to actually build the world that will keep us all safe. The stakes are simply too high, and time too short, to settle for anything less.[92]

Eric Schmidt is right, and so is Naomi Klein. The unemployment, poverty, and calamity resulting from the merger of the profit system with the coming wave of automation will be the defining issue of the coming decades. Capitalism as we know it and governance as we know it are ill prepared to define the future in favor of humanity. We cannot settle for that. We cannot settle for anything less than political and economic democracy because nothing less will create and sustain the America—and the world—that we have a right and a responsibility to demand.

chapter two

A JOBLESS ECONOMY?

I T IS IMPOSSIBLE FOR MOST OF US TO CONCEIVE OF A SOCIETY without jobs. But it is not frivolous to ask whether there will be anywhere near enough jobs to provide employment for all the people who require incomes, and whether the wages and conditions of the jobs that exist will be remotely close to satisfactory for a credible economy or a democratic society. This requires examining the role of technology and automation in the American capitalist economy and the relationship of technology to the pursuit of profit.

UNEMPLOYMENT AND CONTEMPORARY CAPITALISM

To understand the jobs picture in any capitalist economy, the point of beginning is the rate of economic growth. As a rule, when economies are growing rapidly, they tend to reach maximum employment levels, and often approach what has traditionally been defined as "full employment." With labor becoming scarce, wages increase and good times abound. When economies are sluggish and have declines in investment

CHART 1. Percentage of Quarters with 6 Percent or Greater Real GDP Growth, 1930–2015

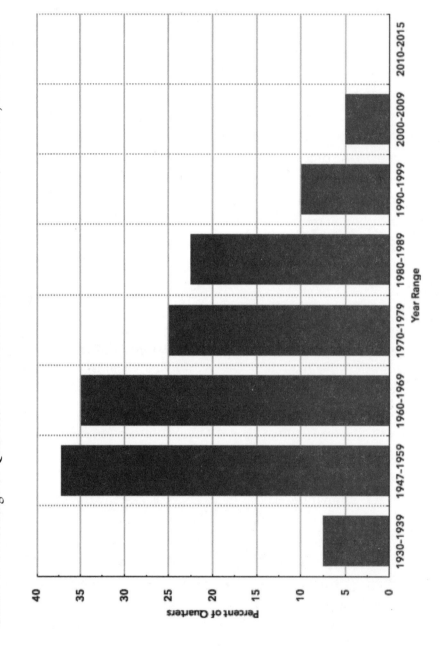

and output, people are put out of work and jobs become scarce. The plethora of unemployed workers puts downward pressure on wages.

The foundation of our analysis of the jobs picture is provided in Chart 1, which was developed by economist Fred Magdoff; it demonstrates that the rate of growth in American capitalism has been on a downward trajectory for a good five decades, and that the process has accelerated in the new century.[1] Our measure is the percentage of quarters in a time period in which the real growth rate exceeded 6 percent.[2] These quarters of 6 percent annual growth point to periods that are boom times by any calculation. The Great Recession since 2008 has aggravated and highlighted the problem of slow growth, such that economists across the political spectrum now speak openly of the United States economy as being in a period of long-term secular stagnation.

Another way to express the downward growth trajectory of US capitalism is to look at private investment, which is the heart and soul of a capitalist economy. As Chart 2 reveals, private investment has been declining as a percentage of Gross Domestic Product. It uses a ten-year moving average to smooth out the fluctuations and provide a clearer trend line. Unless there is a large increase in government spending to compensate for the decline—which is a controversial policy option in a capitalist economy—everything else being equal, slower growth rates and higher levels of unemployment result. Indeed, even more striking is the massive and increasing amount of cash that corporations are holding, as shown in Chart 3. This "unemployed" capital is a sign of a stagnating economy, with profitable investment opportunities growing so scarce that firms would rather sit on their cash than risk it in real investments.

Why exactly US capitalism—and world capitalism, for that matter—has been and is stagnant with no end in sight is a crucial issue that can be traced in part to the way in which monopoly-finance capital produces stagnation. That's another discussion, however.[3] Our concern at this point is with the jobs picture, and Chart 4 demonstrates that unemployment has been increasing in general while capitalism has

CHART 2. Net Private Non-Residential Fixed Investment as a Percentage of GDP, 1949–2013

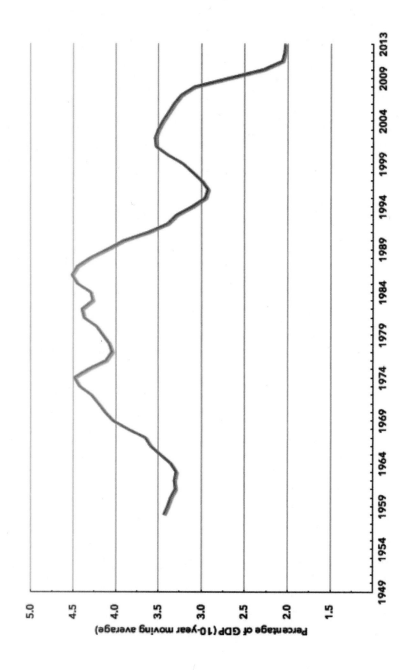

CHART 3 Cash and Short-Term Investments of the Top 1,200 Non-Financial US Firms, 1970–2013

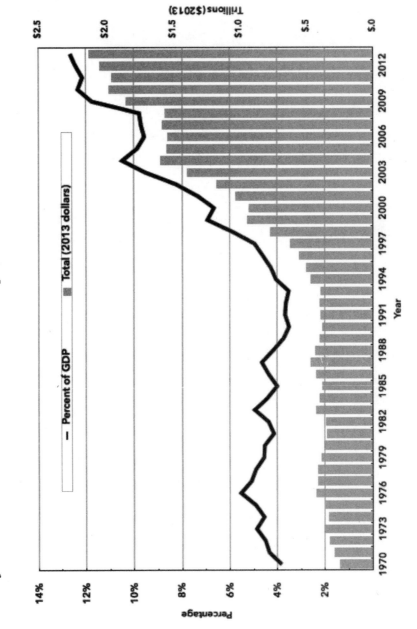

CHART 4 Official and Hidden Unemployment, 1962–2014

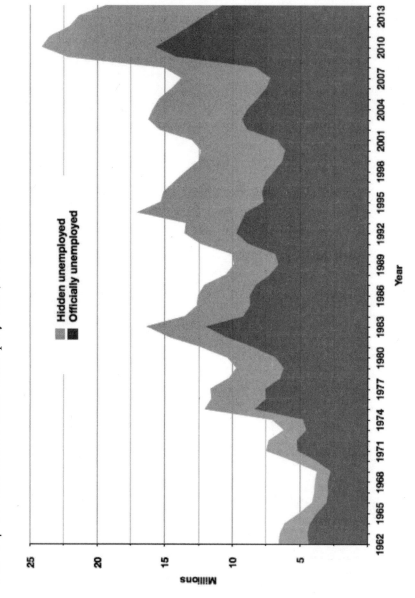

CHART 5 Duration of Job Losses in Selected Recessions

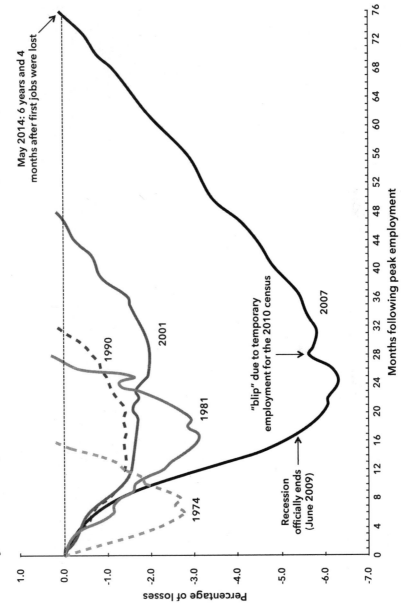

May 2014: 6 years and 4 months after first jobs were lost

1990

2001

1981

1974

"blip" due to temporary employment for the 2010 census

2007

Recession officially ends (June 2009)

Percentage of losses

1.0
0.0
-1.0
-2.0
-3.0
-4.0
-5.0
-6.0
-7.0

Months following peak employment

0 4 8 12 16 20 24 28 32 36 40 44 48 52 56 60 64 68 72 76

been tending toward stagnation. We provide here not only the total amount of "official" unemployment, but a broader assessment that includes people who have dropped out of the labor market and are no longer actively seeking employment—that is, people who constitute the "hidden unemployed."

What is important about these first four charts is that they reveal that the employment situation in the United States is not simply a function of a short-term boom-and-bust business cycle. It is, instead, a longer-term problem of stagnation, such that even as the economy recovers after a downturn, it takes longer to return to the levels of employment seen in previous expansions, and the recessions can grow more severe and last longer.

Chart 5 continues in this vein. It shows how many months it has taken in each recovery since the early 1970s for the economy to regain the jobs lost to the downturn. Every single recovery has taken longer than the previous one, with the most recent Great Recession especially sluggish. On a weaker foundation, the system overall is more susceptible to panics and crashes of the 1929 and 2008 variety. In this scenario, there are other developments that reveal deterioration in the employment situation facing workers, beyond the traditional official rate of unemployment.

Consider the situation facing young workers. Chart 6 demonstrates that the economy is generating fewer middle-class jobs, and an increasing proportion of the jobs provide incomes at poverty levels. This is what economists call "labor market polarization"—great jobs for those at the top, a mountain of crappy jobs at the bottom, and fewer and fewer jobs in between.[4] Studies reveal that this is a phenomenon across all sixteen European Union nations as well.[5] This growth in dismal jobs is not because workers are less productive. Chart 7 shows the growing split between the growth in Gross Domestic Product and household income since the 1970s. Put another way, from 1945 to the early 1970s, as workers' productivity increased, so did their wages by a comparable percentage. Since the 1970s, worker output has grown, in some cases sharply, but wages have stagnated.[6]

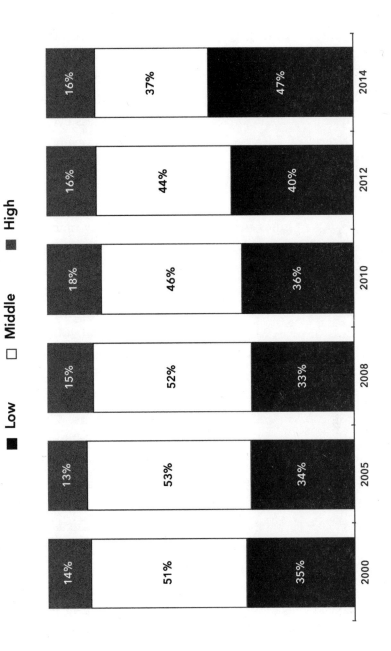

CHART 6 Changes in Job Growth by Median Wage for Selected Periods, 2000–2014

CHART 7 Index of Real Median Household Income and Real GDP, 1967–2013 (1967 = 100)

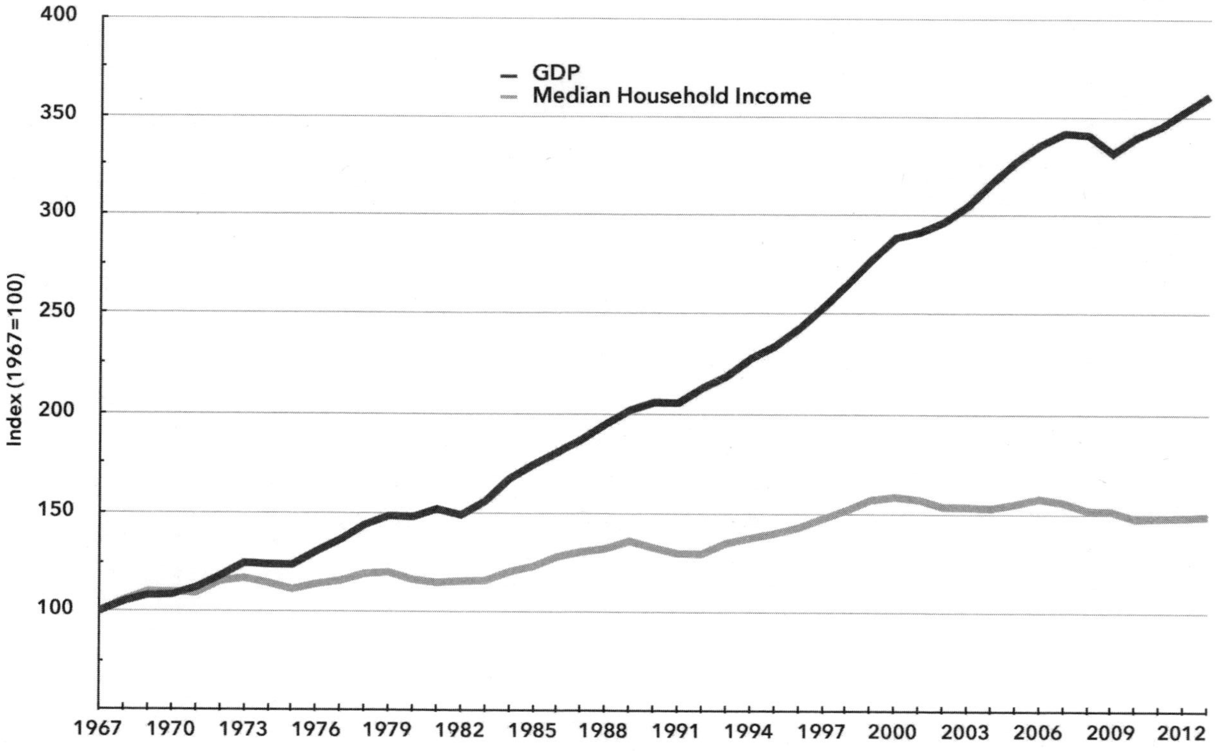

53

CHART 8 Median Wage and Salary Income of Persons 18–24 Years Old, Without College Experience, 1964–2014

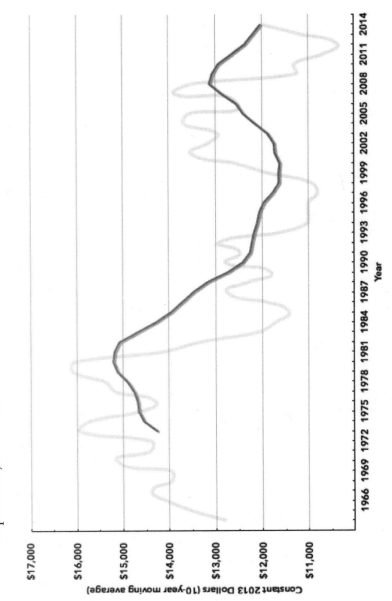

Downward pressure on wages and working conditions is a consequence of the deteriorating jobs picture. When the Associated Press examined this issue in 2013, its report highlighted illustrative comments from a working-class woman in Appalachia, who said, "If you apply for a job, they're not hiring people, and they're not paying that much to even go to work." Children, she said, have "nothing better to do than to get on drugs."[7] Chart 8 shows the decline in wages for young workers without a college education. Since 2000 the real wages for young people, both high school and college graduates, have plummeted.[8] But it goes back decades. One of us left school to work at a lumberyard in the mid-1970s and earned an income that would translate into around $75,000 annually in 2015 dollars. Back then this sort of unionized blue-collar job seemed good but unremarkable, and was taken predominantly by people who had a high school education, if that. Today, the young people completing college whom we encounter would consider a job with that salary and its relatively lavish benefits the equivalent of winning the Irish Sweepstakes.

In this environment, it is not surprising that significant numbers of people have dropped out of the labor market and are no longer actively looking for work. As economist Tyler Cowen notes, "Most of the measured declines in employment participation have been coming from younger men, not early retirees." He explains that "adult males are seceding from the workforce—or being kicked out—in frightening numbers. Few of these individuals are wealthy playboys."[9] In 2014 16 percent of men between the ages of 25 and 54 were not working; in the late 1960s, the figure was 5 percent.[10] The percentage of women in the workforce peaked in the late 1990s and is now back to levels not seen since the 1980s. Charts 9 and 10 document these trends.

In fact, the drop-off in labor participation rates has been especially striking since 2000, when the historic increases stimulated by women joining the labor force began to reverse. How significant a factor is this? Economic observers note that the official labor force participation rate has been declining continually, from an annual average of 67.1 percent in 2000 to 62.5 percent in 2015. This translates to the dis-

CHART 9 Labor Force Participation Rate, Males, 1948–2014

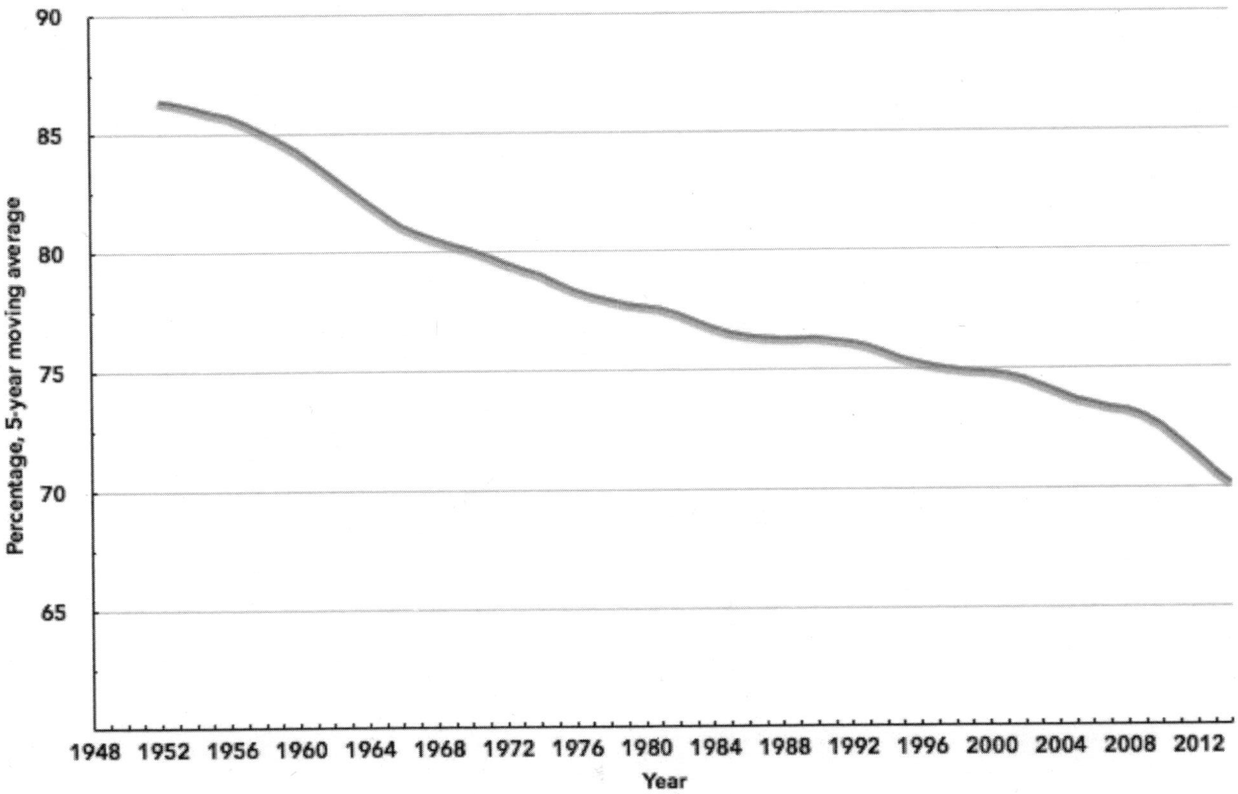

CHART 10 Labor Force Participation Rate, Females, 1990–2014

appearance of close to 7.2 million workers from the official labor force in 2015 (see Chart 11 sources in the Statistical Appendix). However, in this case (as in so many others), the official labor statistics are inadequate. Indeed, if we estimate how many more jobs would be needed to maintain the level of civilian employment that existed in 2000, the picture changes dramatically.[11] Chart 11 does just this, revealing that the economy would need to generate nearly 14 million more jobs in 2015 if all those workers who have left the labor market since 2000 had remained in it and had jobs. The number, not to mention the trend, of these "missing jobs" is staggering and puts the employment crisis in a very different light from the official pronouncements of the officials who boast about "continual job growth."[12]

This data creates a certain cognitive dissonance for those Americans who spent much time in 2014 and 2015 listening to politicians and pundits crow about how the unemployment rate was under 6 percent and the economy was partying like it was 1999. "Right now," Gallup CEO Jim Clifton said in February 2015, "we're hearing much celebrating from the media, the White House and Wall Street about how unemployment is 'down' to 5.6%. The cheerleading for this number is deafening. The media loves a comeback story, the White House wants to score political points and Wall Street would like you to stay in the market." Clifton, head of one of the top public opinion survey organizations in the world, adds:

> None of them will tell you this: If you, a family member or anyone is unemployed and has subsequently given up on finding a job—if you are so hopelessly out of work that you've stopped looking over the past four weeks—the Department of Labor doesn't count you as unemployed. That's right. While you are as unemployed as one can possibly be, and tragically may never find work again, you are *not* counted in the figure we see relentlessly in the news—currently 5.6%. Right now, as many as 30 million Americans are either out of work or severely underemployed. Trust me, the vast majority of them aren't throwing parties to toast "falling" unemployment.

CHART 11 Estimated Number of Missing Jobs Since 2000 Peak in Labor Force Participation

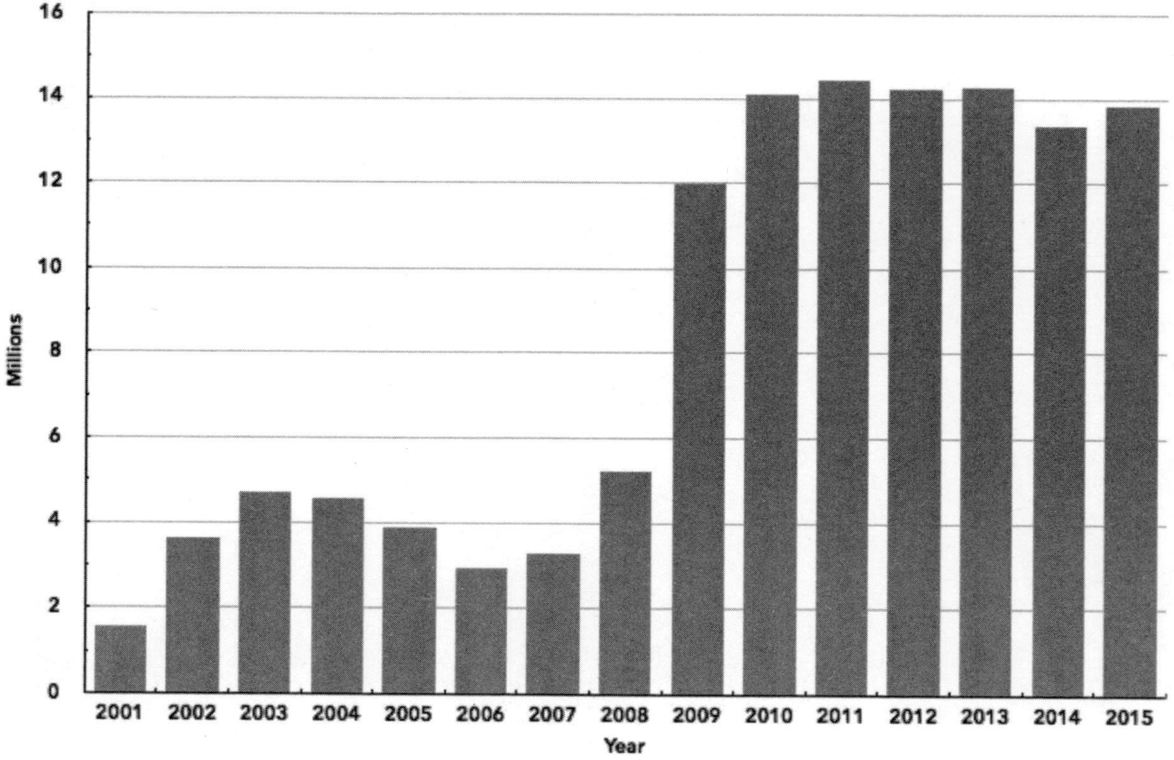

CHART 12 Working Poor, Hidden Unemployed, and Officially Unemployed, 1968–2014

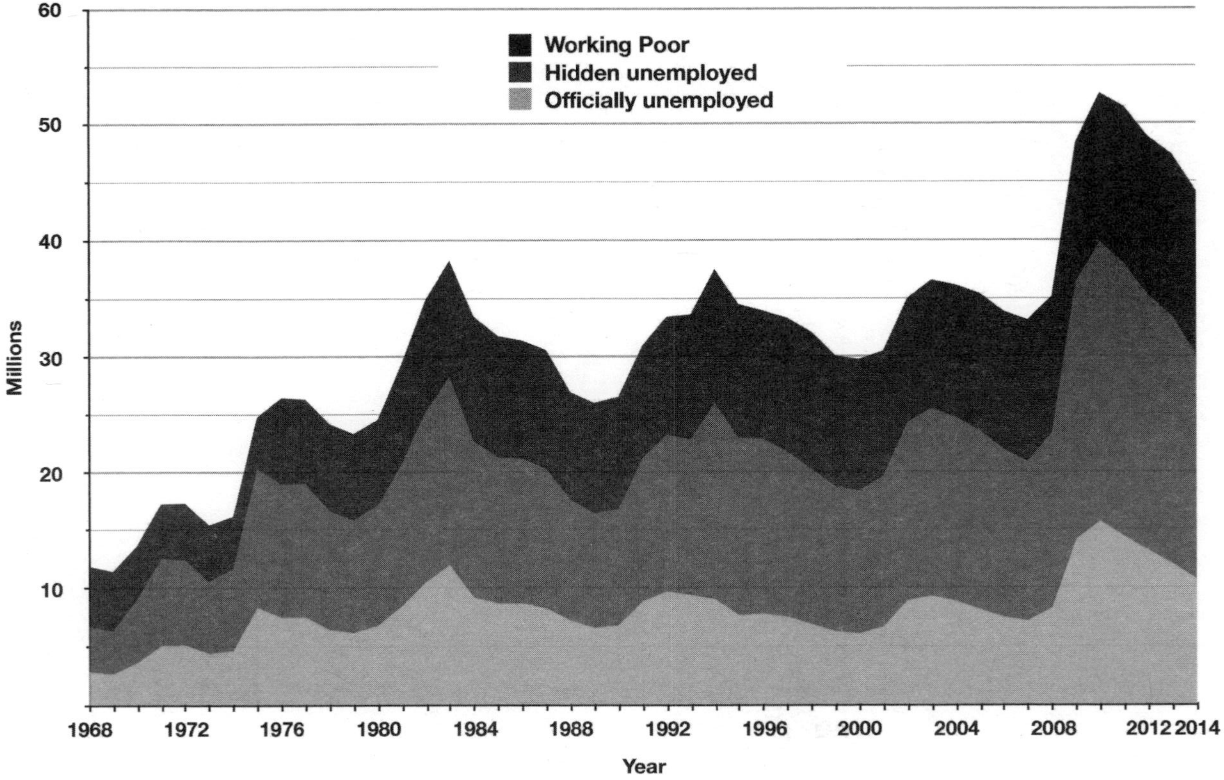

There's another reason why the official rate is misleading. Say you're an out-of-work engineer or healthcare worker or construction worker or retail manager: If you perform a minimum of one hour of work in a week and are paid at least twenty dollars—maybe someone pays you to mow their lawn—you're not officially counted as unemployed in the much-reported 5.6%. Few Americans know this.

Yet another figure of importance that doesn't get much press: those working part time but wanting full-time work. If you have a degree in chemistry or math and are working ten hours part time because it is all you can find—in other words, you are severely underemployed—the government doesn't count you in the 5.6%. Few Americans know this.[13]

Chart 12 describes the world as it is experienced by Americans and illuminated by Jim Clifton's data. It provides a comprehensive picture of those officially unemployed, as well as those who are underemployed, those who have given up looking for work, and also those working at poverty wages. This is the real unemployment and underemployment picture, and it is not pretty.

In this real world, the one not inhabited by politicians and pundits, by the first decade of this century the labor market had changed so much in the United States and other industrial nations that some economists wrote of the emergence of a "precariat," a new category beneath the traditional working class.[14] This precariat referred to a hodgepodge of part-time and freelance jobs where the workers had no rights, security, or benefits, and generally not much income—hence their precarious material and psychological state of existence. Members of the precariat are often educated and qualified for far better employment but are unable to find any positions.[15] The *Economist* calculates that roughly a third of the "employed" young people in the advanced economies have these "informal and intermittent jobs." Further, it notes somberly that research suggests that young people who enter such a dubious labor market often get "scarred"; they face a "wage penalty" of up to 20 percent for a good two decades, and the scarring is passed down to subsequent generations.[16] As the economist John Schmitt put it in 2009, the power imbalance between this workforce and their employers "is a central cause of the problems facing the low-wage workers."[17]

A contributing factor in the decline of wages and working conditions for workers has been the disintegration of the trade union movement in the United States.[18] Union membership has collapsed from roughly a third of American workers in the 1950s and a quarter of American workers in the 1970s to around 11 percent today, and a mere 6.6 percent in the private sector.[19] The real numbers for union membership had dropped from 17.7 million in 1983, when the United States was just coming out of a severe recession, to 14.5 million in 2013, when the United States was more than four years into a much-discussed "recovery."[20] Chart 13 illustrates this decline.

Prior to the 1960s, union membership was overwhelmingly in the private sector; so we begin to separate public from private in the graph in 1984, when the data becomes reliable. Public-sector unionization remained more robust for a number of years in the 1990s and 2000s because state and local governments were prohibited from engaging in the sort of aggressive union-busting campaigns that became increasingly common in the private sector, and it is generally implausible to threaten to move public-sector labor overseas to low-wage locales. However, since 2011 anti-labor state governors and legislatures in states such as Wisconsin, Michigan, and Indiana began to eliminate protections for public-sector workers, leading to the relatively new phenomenon of declining public-sector unionization rates.[21] The quantitative decrease in overall unionization rates has become a qualitative change: organized labor now simply struggles to stop the continued erosion; even in many states where they were once strong, unions are no longer in a position to embark on major organizing drives and win outright victories in fights for higher wages and benefits. Chart 14 documents the number of strikes and work stoppages over the past six decades. Without the credible threat of a strike, management has little to

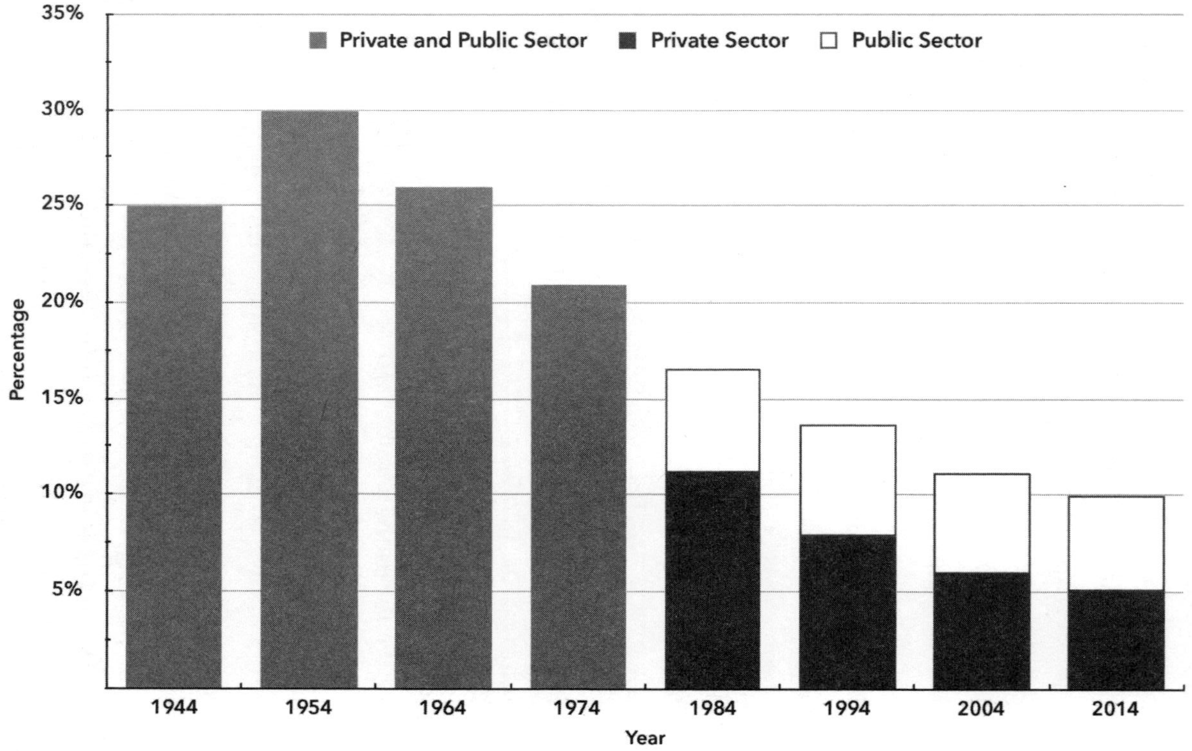

CHART 13 Union Membership as a Percentage of Total Employed Workers, 1944–2014

fear. As Schmitt puts it, "The huge decline in unionization in the private sector has decimated the U.S. working class, which depends on the union wages and benefit premium to secure a middle-class standard of living."[22] Schmitt is talking about the broad working class, as even workers who do not belong to unions benefit when wages are higher across the economy.

These developments in the labor market both reflect and play a huge role in generating the massive increase in economic inequality that has been such a subject of conversation over the past few years.[23] Most studies suggest that between one-fifth and one-third of the increase in economic inequality among men is due to the decline in unions, what one expert terms "the devastation in the labor movement."[24] Back in 1979 over half of American workers—often union workers—had pensions connected to their jobs; today it is around one-third.[25] In a nutshell, income that once went to workers is now going to owners and bosses.[26] Whereas the CEO of a large company made around twenty times more than the average worker in 1965, by 2013 the ratio had grown to nearly three hundred to one.[27] To put it another way, if the United States had the same income distribution in 2015 that it had in 1979, $1 trillion in income going to the top 1 percent would instead go to the bottom 80 percent.[28] A study by economists Michael Greenstone and Adam Looney concludes that "most men were earning substantially less in 2009 than men of similar ages and education did in 1969, adjusted for inflation."[29]

Chart 15 shows, decade by decade, how the income shares have changed over the past eighty years. What this chart cannot convey is that this portends not only inequality but, in a stagnant economy, increasing poverty. By 2013 an Associated Press study concluded that four out of five American adults "struggle with joblessness, near-poverty or reliance on welfare for at least parts of their lives, a sign of deteriorating economic security and an elusive American dream."[30] The popular notion that poverty is something experienced largely by people of color—and that white people were "middle class"—has

64

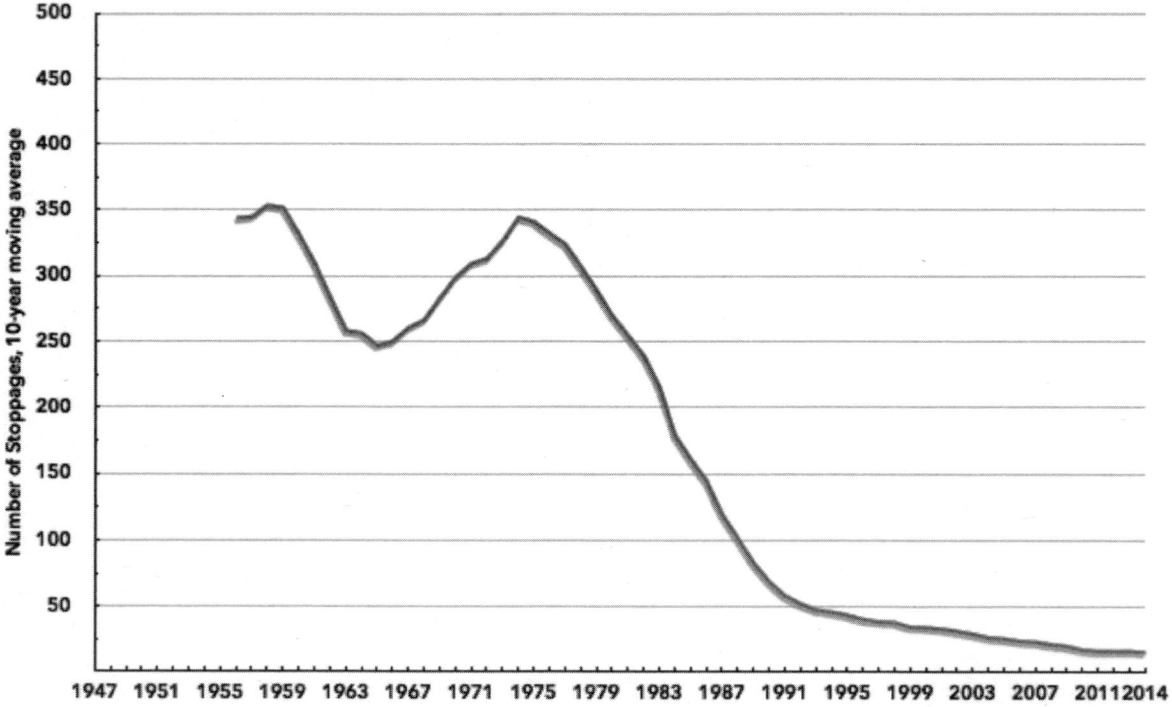

CHART 14 Number of Work Stoppages Idling 1,000 Workers, 1947–2014

blown up like a trick cigar on April Fool's Day.* Although people of color remain disproportionately among the ranks of the poor, they are being joined by a wave of working-class and middle-class whites moving down the economic ladder.[31] The flip side of this coin is that upward economic mobility—people's ability to improve their lot compared to that of their parents—has all but disappeared.[32] The United States that was once broadly viewed as "the land of opportunity" today ranks near the bottom of advanced economies for social mobility.[33]

The Great Recession that began in 2008 aggravated problems in the labor market and shifted the matter to another level altogether.[34] Chart 16 shows the increase in long-term unemployment, people who have been out of work for at least fifteen weeks. That is not necessarily the worst of it. The vast majority of the jobs lost in the recession were considered "mid-wage," while the majority of the new jobs created in the recovery were "low-wage."[35] The stock market skyrocketed and fortunes were made on Wall Street, but as *New York Times* financial reporter Felix Salmon put it, "These days a healthy stock market doesn't mean a healthy economy, as a glance at the high unemployment rate or low labor-market participation rate will show."[36] In fact, when corporations announce plant closings and layoffs in the United States, media outlets report that the news does "wonders" for stock prices.[37]

---

* This growing inequality and poverty makes liberal and progressive economists apoplectic. Lower incomes mean there is less and less consumer demand for products and services, so businesses have less incentive to make new investments, and to hire more workers who then have more income, which reinforces stagnation and makes significant long-term growth all but impossible. It makes the overall economy weaker and more susceptible to panics and crises. Despite the existence of proven policies to counter stagnation, elite policymakers refuse to countenance policies that would forcefully address inequality or strengthen the power of workers to gain better wages and working conditions, not to mention secure, long-term employment. The business-as-usual approach means that nothing in this chapter is likely to change for the better going forward. For that to happen, the narrow business-as-usual range of debate has to be obliterated.

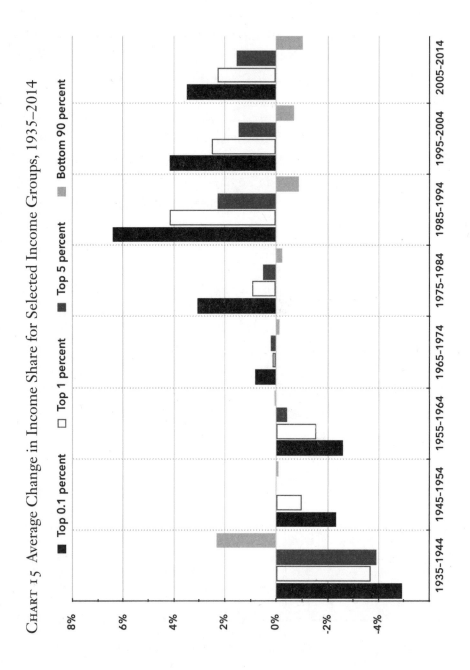

CHART 15 Average Change in Income Share for Selected Income Groups, 1935–2014

CHART 16 Unemployed for at Least 15 Weeks as a Percentage of the Labor Force, 1962–2014

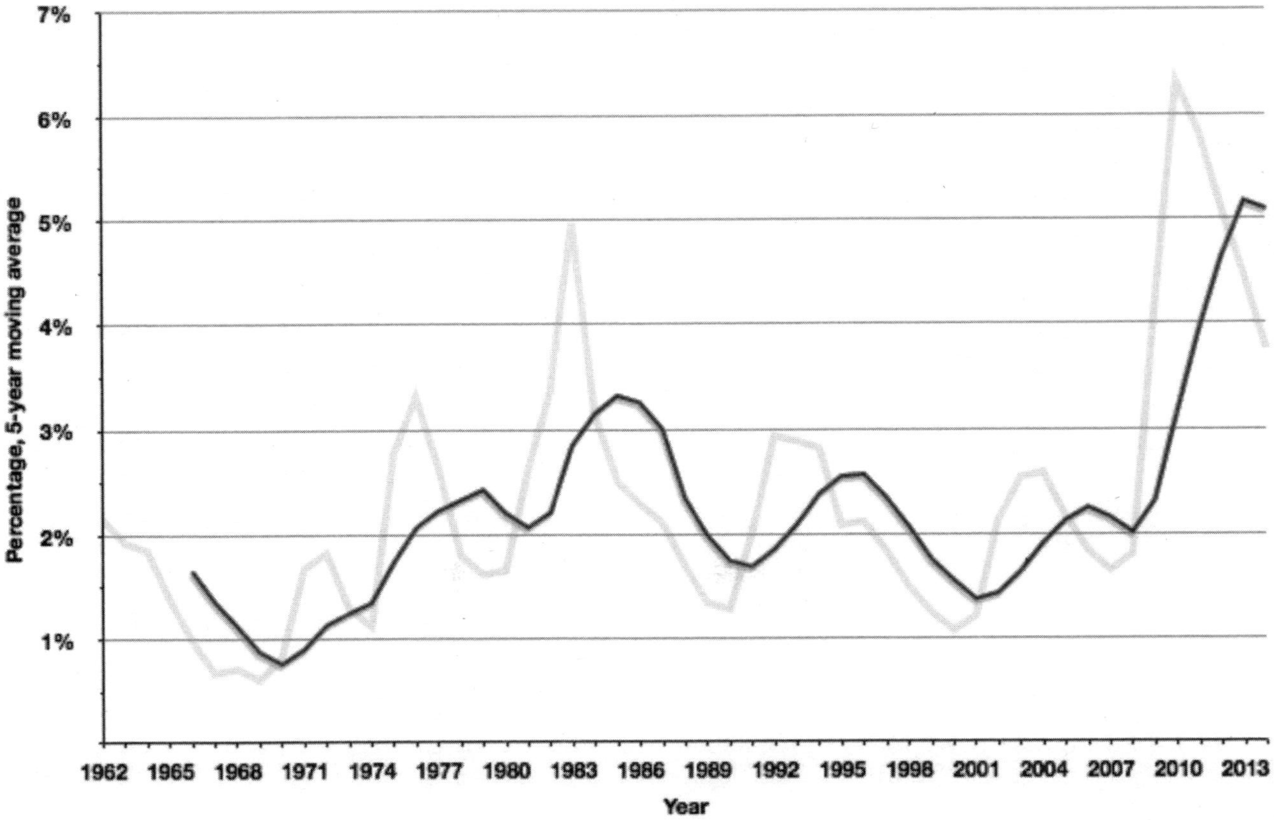

ENTER TECHNOLOGY AND CREATIVE DESTRUCTION

Analysis of this phenomenon does not merely point to the traditional meme that fat cats have rigged the game to get even fatter while others starve. Job-killing technology, in many instances, provided an explanation for the lack of job growth during the recovery of 2009–2013. This contradicts some longstanding and deeply held conventional wisdom, especially among economists. The general notion has been an optimistic one; as the *Economist* put it, "Although innovation kills some jobs, it creates new and better ones, as a more productive society becomes richer and its wealthier inhabitants demand more goods and services."[38] But the link between increasing private investment and rising employment appears to be weakening. American capitalism seems to have turned a corner: increases in private investment and worker productivity no longer necessarily lead to commensurate increases in employment or real incomes.[39]

As business reporters Bernard Condon and Paul Wiseman explain, "Technology is used by companies to run leaner and smarter in good times and bad, but never more than in bad. In a recession, sales fall and companies cut jobs to save money. They turn to technology to do tasks people used to do. Then it hits them: They realize they don't have to re-hire the humans when business improves, or at least not as many."[40] The Nobel-prize winning economist Michael Spence put it this way in 2013:

> Growth and employment are thus diverging in advanced countries. The key force driving this trend—technology—is playing multiple roles. The replacement of routine manual jobs by machines and robots is a powerful, continuing, and perhaps accelerating trend in manufacturing and logistics, while networks of computers are replacing routine white-collar jobs in information processing. Part of this is pure automation. Another important part is disintermediation—the elimination of intermediaries in banking, online retail, and a host of government services, to name just a few affected areas.[41]

Most Americans are aware that monopolized online sales and distribution operations (such as Amazon, for example) have decimated local bookstores and record shops, as well as chain operations such as Borders Books and Virgin Megastores. But disintermediation is also wiping out jobs at small, medium-sized, and large businesses that used to sell everything from computer hardware and software to airline tickets, toys, and contact lenses.[42]

As Chart 17 indicates, the one hundred largest US companies (in terms of total annual revenue) are able to generate more US revenues and earn more US profits with fewer American workers, and the process appears to be accelerating.* These one hundred firms accounted for 43 percent of US GDP in 2013, up from 26 percent in 1950, so this trend is hardly on the periphery of the economy.[43] There is the palpable sense that technology is destroying more jobs than it is creating, an issue we will take up in short order.

For young people it is arguable that the employment picture is as dismal as it has been at any time since the Great Depression of the 1930s, and for college graduates it may be worse. The Federal Reserve Bank of New York in 2014 determined that 46 percent of recent college graduates were working at jobs that did not require a BA.[44] That is bad news not only for college graduates but for high school graduates, "who find themselves competing with college graduates for basic jobs in service businesses."[45] Even before the Great Recession of 2008, the Bureau of Labor Statistics forecast that two-thirds of the jobs available between 2008 and 2018 would not require *any* post-secondary education.[46] As the journalist Derek Thompson concludes, "The job market appears to be requiring more and more preparation for a lower and lower starting wage."[47] The *Economist* announces that young people

---

* As the statistical appendix demonstrates (see notes to Chart 17), if the data is expanded to the top one hundred global firms—that is all workers (foreign and domestic) and all revenues (foreign and domestic)—it does not alter the pattern of steadily increasing returns per worker. If anything it appears that the ratio of revenues (or sales) to workers actually *increases* for these firms when foreign sales and employees are included. We stick to the United States because the data is more comprehensive for illustrating historical trends.

CHART 17 US Revenue and US Gross Profit per Employee of the Top 100 US Firms, 1953–2013

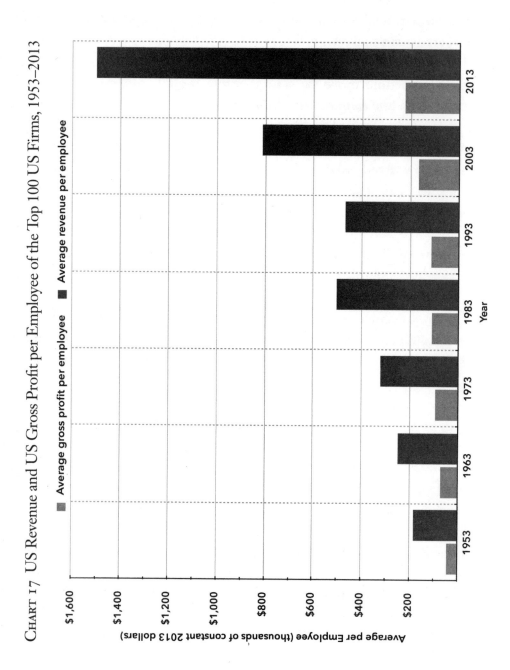

are experiencing an "epidemic of joblessness."[48] *Newsweek* character-izes young Americans as constituting "Generation Screwed."[49] There are nowhere near enough jobs, and the jobs that do exist, to employ the vernacular, suck.[50]

By 2015 the precariat is evolving into a cybertariat, as digital tech-nologies become more central to organizing and even constituting labor.[51] The *Economist* credits the ubiquity of the smartphone for mov-ing freelancing from the margins to the center of capitalism.[52] By 2025 experts anticipate that one of every three global labor "transactions" will be conducted online as part of the "on-demand" or "crowd labor" economy, with a few gigantic digital hiring hall corporations using their networks and apps to get temp labor for employers.[53] Informal work, or freelancing, already accounts for around one-third of the US workforce, fully 53 million workers, according to an Edelman Berland report prepared for the Freelancers Union.[54] A *Christian Science Mon-itor* report stated that up to 50 percent of the new jobs in the recov-ery were freelance positions.[55] Economic Modeling Specialists Intl., a labor market analytics firm, calculated that by 2014 some 18 percent of all US jobs were performed by part-time freelancers or part-time independent contractors. There was a 60 percent increase in the num-ber of these part-time gig jobs from 2001.[56]

Proponents of the informal or 1099 sector—taken from the "in-dependent contractor" 1099 form used by the Internal Revenue Ser-vice—play up the freedom, power, romance, and adventure that come with being one's own boss, and for some of those 53 million workers that is no doubt the case as they swashbuckle their way to fame and fortune, or at least personal satisfaction. But as one *New York Times* examination concludes, many of these workers are "less microentre-preneurs than microearners. They often work seven-day weeks, trying to assemble a living wage from a series of one-off gigs."[57] According to the Government Accounting Office, these freelance workers are twice as likely as traditional full-time employees to have an annual income under $15,000.[58]

The venture capital firm SherpaVentures argues that this new freelance sector is the wave of the future and a win-win for everyone.

"Perpetual hourly employment is often deeply inefficient for all parties involved," one of their reports states.[59] While many freelancers may disagree and wish for something more stable and remunerative, American corporations are A-OK with the new world order. "Major corporations," Lawrence Summers and British parliamentarian Ed Balls noted in 2015, "have opted to use subcontracting to perform basic functions, and many workers are now classified as independent contractors, eroding basic labor-law protection." Accordingly, data reveals that the percentage of male workers who have worked with the same firm for at least ten years has dropped sharply over the past two decades, especially for younger workers.[60] "What once was a relationship" between firms and their employees, one reporter explains, "is now a transaction."[61] Businesses "have found that having a large nontraditional workforce makes them more competitive."[62] While the *Economist* has no illusion that this new freelance-based "on-demand" economy is a good thing for workers, it nonetheless regards the process as unstoppable.[63] Arguably the leading expert on the emergence of the cybertariat is Ursula Huws. "We are now living in a period," she wrote in 2015, when there has been "a sea change in the character of work."[64]

It is left to the acclaimed pro-market economist Tyler Cowen to capture the logic of where all of this is going: "We will move from a society based on the pretense that everyone is given an okay standard of living to a society in which people are expected to fend for themselves much more than they do now. I imagine a world where, say, 10 to 15 percent of the citizenry is extremely wealthy and has fantastically comfortable and stimulating lives, the equivalent of current-day millionaires, albeit with better health care."[65]

The other 85 to 90 percent of us? Not so much.

Whatever the society Cowen imagines, with the economic foundation that he describes, it will not be a democracy. Nor will it enjoy the rule of law or even be much of a civilization. And this is before we add to the mix the digital technological revolution, which is redefining the economy and employment across the board. This is a process that in crucial respects is only just beginning, and it is coming at us at what seems like historical warp speed. How will that change things?

A VERY SHORT HISTORY OF AUTOMATION

It is anything but a coincidence that the modern explosion in technologies correlates closely with the rise of modern industrial capitalism. Technology "was a tool in the arsenal of capitalist competition, the purpose of which was to increase the efficiency of labor," economist James Galbraith writes, noting that in core respects that remains every bit as true today. "The big function of the new technologies is to save labor costs."[66] Businesses also develop technologies to allow them greater control over the work process and to minimize the power of labor. "The logic of capitalism, when combined with the history of scientific and technological progress, would seem to be a recipe for the eventual removal of labor from the processes of production," Nicholas Carr writes. "Machines, unlike workers, don't demand a share of the returns on capitalists' investments. They don't get sick or expect paid vacations or demand yearly wages. For the capitalist, labor is a problem that progress solves."[67]

For this reason, workers have always had skepticism toward labor-saving technology, and it has sometimes been the subject of, for lack of a better term, intense class struggle. Most literature understandably focuses on the Luddites in 1810s England, but they were hardly anomalous. The great historian of capitalism Sven Beckert notes that, at the very beginning of the industrial system in 1770s England, entrepreneurs' very first "innovations sometimes even brought down the wrath of their neighbors, who dreaded the job losses the innovators caused." "Fear of mob violence," he adds, drove some fledgling capitalists to move their residences "away from the places they had made their inventions."[68]

Despite technology's role in eliminating and altering jobs, it has also been seen as a uniquely progressive force for raising living standards. In 1930 the visionary economist John Maynard Keynes introduced the specter of "technological unemployment"; he defined this as "unemployment due to the discovery of means of economizing the use of labor outrunning the pace at which we can find new uses for labor." He considered it "only a temporary phase of maladjustment."[69]

Once the Great Depression had passed and was mostly forgotten, Keynes's concerns about technological unemployment did not find much currency in the economics profession.[70] The conventional wisdom concerning technology, especially technology that affects jobs, is that it is a net positive. It is true that some people lose in the short run because they are displaced, but as the economy grows, new industries arise and new employment opportunities appear. The lousiest and most mind-numbing jobs are the ones that tend to get replaced by machines, and the new jobs tend to require more education and skill and be more rewarding, we are told. The huge percentage of the population who would have worked in agriculture in the nineteenth century or manufacturing in the twentieth century invariably move on to bigger and better things when the nation needs far fewer workers to grow the food or make the products. It is a sign of progress.

Our concern is not with routine technological innovation or even with major product invention. What concerns us is what economists call a "general purpose technology" (GPT). As business scholars Erik Brynjolfsson and Andrew McAfee write, this refers to "a small group of technological innovations so powerful they interrupt and accelerate the normal march of economic progress."[71] In the past, economists Joseph Schumpeter, Paul Baran, and Paul Sweezy characterized these as "epoch-making" innovations because they so radically altered the course of capitalist development.[72] These GPTs tend to be energy, transportation, and communication technologies, because radical changes in those areas redefine all markets, not just a specific industry or sector. They tend to have enormous geographical effects, extending markets and increasing effective demands for products. The classic examples of GPTs are steam power, electricity, railroads, and the internal combustion engine. In some cases, like railroads and automobiles, GPTs can drive massive waves of investment that lead to enormous spin-off industries. In these cases, the new technologies can drive a capitalist economy to much higher rates of investment, growth, and employment than would exist otherwise.

Computers and digital communication, connected by networks, are the newest GPTs, and by most accounts they are equal if not superior to any that have preceded them. They not only expand the size and scope of markets, they also radically lower the costs of production. As the leading scholar on automation, David F. Noble, has emphasized, the emergence of computers and automation was driven to no small extent by the military coming out of World War II and into the Cold War. From that base, "it took hold within industry, especially within those industries tied closely with the military and the military-sponsored technical community."[73] In November 1946 *Fortune* magazine published a large color spread on the "Automatic Factory." "The threat and promise of laborless machines is closer than ever . . . all the parts are here," it reported.[74]

Even at first blush, it was clear that something rather different from previous mechanization and ultimately revolutionary was at hand, and this was more than a little disconcerting. It is striking how sober the first response to automation was, even, or dare we say especially, by the one person closest to the science. On the heels of the very first computers being built, MIT professor and cybernetics pioneer Norbert Wiener speculated in 1950 that it would probably take two decades for automation to overhaul and dominate the economy. He wrote that the process

> will lead to an immediate transition period of disastrous confusion. We have a good deal of experience as to how the industrialists regard a new industrial potential. Their whole propaganda is to the effect that it must not be considered as the business of the government but must be left open to whatever entrepreneurs wish to invest money in it. We also know that they have very few inhibitions when it comes to taking all the profit out of an industry that is there to be taken, and then letting the public pick up the pieces.

"The automatic machine," he concluded, "is the precise economic equivalent of slave labor. Any labor which competes with slave labor must accept the economic conditions of slave labor. It is perfectly clear that this will produce an unemployment situation, in comparison with which the present recession or even the depression of the thirties will seem a pleasant joke."[75]

Some of the period's sharpest minds took notice. Kurt Vonnegut's first novel, 1952's *Player Piano*, was a dystopian tale about a near-future society where most work has been replaced by automation. It drew from Vonnegut's experience seeing the introduction of computer-operated machinery in the General Electric plant where he worked after the war.[76] Bertrand Russell wrote an essay in 1951 that asked "Are Human Beings Necessary?" as a response to computing. He concluded that "we shall have to change some of the fundamental assumptions upon which the world has been run ever since the beginning of civilization."[77] Critical theorist Erich Fromm addressed automation in his 1955 book, *The Sane Society*, and he was not immediately enthusiastic: "Is not the mode of work in itself an essential element in forming a person's character? Does completely automatized work not lead to a completely automatized life?[78] That same year, University of Cambridge engineer R. H. MacMillan asked whether humans might be "in danger of being destroyed by our own creations." Mac-Millan argued that "the rapidly increasing part that automatic devices are playing in the peace-time industrial life of all civilized countries" might in time pose the same peril for humanity as nuclear weapons.[79] This point was not lost on Wiener, who mused, "Those of us who have contributed to the new science of cybernetics thus stand in a moral position which is, to say the least, not very comfortable."[80]

By the mid-1950s governments and policymakers turned their attention to automation. In 1955 a subcommittee of the Joint Committee on the Economic Report of the United States Congress held two weeks of hearings on "Automation and Technological Change." It generated numerous examples of what automation had accomplished in only a few years. For example, two workers now assembled one thousand radios a day, whereas that had required two hundred workers previously. One man in a Ford plant ran a single machine that did the work once done by between thirty-five and seventy workers, and forty-eight workers could now do what had taken four hundred workers twice as long to accomplish.[81] In 1958 UNESCO devoted a full volume of its *International Social Science Bulletin* to a series of papers on the "Social Consequences of Automation." "Although it may be wise to remain skeptical toward the illusory hope of a golden age within our reach and toward the fear of unemployment, which the same people usually experience simultaneously," the *Bulletin*'s editors wrote in their foreword, it is possible "to detect a vital turning point in the history of our societies."[82]

The one group with its head most directly on the chopping block was labor. Carr's review of automation concludes that industrial planners saw it as a way to lessen the role and importance of labor unions. "The lesson would prove important: in an automated system, power concentrates with those who control the programming."[83] In 1949, in a letter to United Auto Workers (UAW) president Walter Reuther, Wiener informed Reuther that he had, without success, "made repeated attempts to get in touch with the Labor Union movement, and try to acquaint them with what may be expected of automatic machinery in the near future." Reuther telegrammed his enthusiasm for such a meeting, though it appears they simply maintained a correspondence for the next three years.[84]

It is no surprise that the trade union movement demonstrated a concern with what was happening. The International Labour Office held a conference on automation and employment in 1957; it was optimistic that "the long-run outlook is good," while acknowledging severe "short-run problems" with displaced labor.[85] Reuther's public statements reflected both sentiments. "We know that you cannot hide from technological progress," he told a Congress of Industrial Organizations–sponsored "National Conference on Automation" in 1955. "We know, too, that the labor movement, which is itself a progressive movement, must not stand in the way of scientific improvements."[86] "We cannot afford to hypnotize ourselves into passivity," Reuther told the UAW convention that same year, with "the comforting thought, that in the long run, the economy will adjust to labor displacement and disruption which could result from the Second Industrial Revolution as it did from the First."[87]

Perhaps the most sophisticated and prescient assessment of automation and its relationship to US capitalism came in a 1957 private report by the renowned Marxist economist Paul M. Sweezy.[88] Sweezy

examined the engineering research on leading technological developments, including automation and computerization and came away
impressed. "These new technological developments are comparable in
importance to the steam engine in its day, and in due course will have
effects of a no less revolutionary character."[89] Because automation was
capable of creating "closed-loop" processes, it could and would eliminate the worker.

> The purpose of automation is to cut costs. In all cases it does this by
> saving labor. In some cases, it saves capital too. . . . Whether displaced
> workers will find other employment depends upon whether new jobs
> are being created as rapidly as the rate of displacement plus the rate
> at which new workers are coming on the labor market. And this in
> turn depends on a variety of forces most of which are only related
> indirectly, if at all, to the processes of automation.

A "probable long-run effect of automation," Sweezy wrote, "is what
some economists have called a 'shift to profits,' that is to say, an improvement in the share of national income accruing to the owners of
capital, or at least a slowing down of any tendency that may exist for
the share of capital in the national income to decline." Unless there
were significant public-policy interventions, especially in education,
"we could conceivably be faced with the problem of what to do with
millions of 'misfits,' people who would not be employable in the more
advanced industries and would therefore have no way of sharing in the
benefits of increased productivity. Some of these people might become
and remain totally unemployed, but it seems more likely," Sweezy observed, that "the bulk of them would provide a low-wage labor force
for a sector of marginal, substandard, exploitative industries."
  Sweezy outlined crucial problems in what later came to be known
as software and hardware that needed to be resolved before automation could truly explode, but he had no doubt that those problems
would eventually be solved. "The present period of preparation and
gestation will be followed by periods of very rapid introduction of
the new automatic techniques. . . . What this may mean had better

be left for the present to the writers of science fiction." To those who dismissed computerization and automation as no big deal, Sweezy responded, "Come back in another thirty years. The transformation of society implicit in the new technologies will then be in full swing and you will be able to see signs of it on every hand." What Sweezy grasped well before all others was that automation, unlike most other innovations, ultimately *saved on capital in a manner almost as striking as how it saved on labor.* This meant that it propelled the productive capacity of society to incredible heights, and therefore exacerbated a central problem under modern capitalism of firms being able to sell at a profitable price all that they are capable of producing.[90]

By the early 1960s automation had burst into the popular consciousness, and caution was thrown to the wind.[91] One writer caustically labeled it the period of "automation hysteria."[92] RAND economist Richard Bellman predicted that in short order a mere 2 percent of the population would be able to produce all of society's material goods. One writer in 1964 noted that "*Fortune, Newsweek,* the *Advanced Management Journal,* and many other periodical and professional organs, indicate the potential of cybernation for wiping out not only most blue-collar jobs but also most office and 'middle management' positions." Construction work, too, was projected as soon to be extinct, or at least greatly reduced.[93] "It is often claimed that automation is nothing more than the latest stage in the evolution of technological means for removing the toil from work," *Newsweek* editor Robert E. Cubbedge wrote in his popular 1963 book *Who Needs People? Automation and Your Future.* "The assertion is misleading. There is a very good possibility that automation is so different in degree as to be profoundly different in kind; that it poses unique problems for society, by challenging patterns of work, education, manufacturing, and distribution."[94]

It also became the stuff of politics. The 1962 *Port Huron Statement*—the visionary manifesto of the newly created Students for a Democratic Society (SDS) and the 1960s New Left, written primary by the young activist Tom Hayden—gave considerable attention to automation, which, he wrote, "is transforming society in ways that are scarcely comprehensible." Automation "is destroying whole categories of work" while "it paradoxically is imparting the opportunity for men the world around to rise in dignity from their knees." But such promise—an "economic utopia"—was impossible in a system with "elitist control," where "automation is initiated according to its profitability."[95]

On March 22, 1964, the "Ad Hoc Committee on the Triple Revolution" submitted a fourteen-page memorandum to President Lyndon Johnson, where the "cybernation revolution" was positioned alongside human rights and militarism as the main challenges to modern societies. The memo, which was signed by current and future Nobel Prize winners Linus Pauling and Gunnar Myrdal as well as the publisher of *Scientific American*, warned the president that

> as machines take over production from men, they absorb an increasing proportion of resources while the men who are displaced become dependent on minimal and unrelated government measures—unemployment insurance, social security, welfare payments. These measures are less and less able to disguise a historic paradox: that a growing proportion of the population is subsisting on minimal incomes, often below the poverty line, at a time when sufficient productive potential is available to supply the needs of everyone in the United States.[96]

The memo called for a guaranteed basic income—not based upon one's labor—for all Americans to solve the problem.

Although this memorandum has largely been forgotten, it had considerable influence at the time. Indeed, in his final sermon, delivered on March 31, 1968, before an audience in the thousands at Washington DC's National Cathedral, Dr. Martin Luther King Jr. invoked the "triple revolution" and the importance of automation and cybernation at the beginning of his presentation. "Through our scientific and technological genius, we have made of this world a neighborhood and yet we have not had the ethical commitment to make of it a brotherhood," King observed in words few others could muster. "But somehow, and in some way, we have got to do this. We must all learn to live together as brothers or we will all perish together as fools."[97]

Automation generated a provocative set of arguments on the political left. Marxist theorist Herbert Marcuse captured the dilemma in his influential *One-Dimensional Man*, published in 1964, using Marx's nomenclature of "dead labor" to refer to capital goods. "Now automation seems to alter qualitatively the relationship between dead and living labor; it tends to the point where productivity is determined 'by the machines and not by the individual output.' Moreover, the very measurement of individual output becomes impossible."[98] Two leftist activists argued that same year in *Monthly Review* that "the cybernation revolution poses an impasse for socialists also: it presents us with nothing less than the liquidation of the working class as a significant component of society. When human industrial labor is obsolescent, to project a worker's state becomes an anachronism." They stated that the memo on "The Triple Revolution" was correct, and a basic income should be guaranteed to all Americans independent of their labor.[99] Sweezy and his *Monthly Review* co-editor Leo Huberman disagreed: "Our conclusion can only be that the idea of unconditionally guaranteed incomes is not the great revolutionary principle which the authors of 'The Triple Revolution' evidently believe it to be. If applied under our present system, it would be, like religion, an opiate of the people tending to strengthen the status quo [and] far from inaugurating an era of regeneration, it would merely tend to dull the sense of anger and outrage which is the natural human reaction to a society as corrupt and shameful as ours." Instead, they called for socializing the economy so that the surplus generated by automation was controlled by society as a whole, not by the owners of a handful of large corporations.[100]

Organized labor, having suffered through relatively high levels of unemployment in the late 1950s and early 1960s, no longer saw, nor welcomed, the promise of automation. The Department of Labor estimated that two hundred thousand jobs were being lost to automation each year in the early 1960s; and in industry after industry output was up while employment levels were down.[101] AFL-CIO president George Meany said that automation was "rapidly becoming a curse to this society . . . in a mad race to produce more and more with less and less labor and without any feeling [as to] what it may mean to the whole economy." The business trade publication *Printers' Ink* concluded in 1964 that the American workforce was "frightened and uncertain of its future."[102]

It was not only student activists, labor, and people on the left who were concerned about automation, though they were at the forefront. The eventual 1978 Nobel Prize winner in economics, Herbert Simon, published his book *The Shape of Automation for Men and Management* in 1965. A computer scientist and a pioneer in artificial intelligence as well as an economist, Simon wrote that "in our time, computers will be able to do anything a man can do."[103] President John F. Kennedy referred to unemployment caused by automation as "the major domestic challenge of the 1960s."[104] "If men have the talent to invent new machines that put men out of work," he stated in 1962, "they have the talent to put those men back to work."[105]

Yet there was considerable anxiety over the prospect that new jobs might not appear to replace those being lost. In August 1964 President Johnson formally created the National Commission on Technology, Automation, and Economic Progress to examine the issues and file a report, first and foremost "on whether technological change is a major source of unemployment." The ultimate report, published in 1966, extended its mandate to consider "the fear" that eventually technology "would eliminate all but a few jobs, with the major portion of what we now call work being performed automatically by machine." It was a prestigious fifteen-member commission, including UAW head Reuther, IBM chair Thomas Watson, five other corporate leaders, and the intellectuals Daniel Bell and Robert Solow. The 1966 report concluded optimistically that government policies could successfully address unemployment arising from automation. It asserted that automation was a progressive development, and that "the vast majority of people quite rightly have accepted technological change as beneficial."[106]

What is perhaps most striking for our purposes is what the commission did end up recommending in its report. It said that the technological threat to employment only underscored the crucial need for the government to "fulfill the promise of the Employment Act of 1946: 'a job for all those able, willing, and seeking to work.'" The report called for the federal government to "be an employer of last resort, providing work for the 'hard-core unemployed' in useful community enterprises." It specifically mentioned the sort of "unmet human and community needs" where this labor, and the new technologies, could be deployed as improving healthcare, transportation, and housing, and battling air pollution and water pollution—in short, a massive expansion of spending on vital infrastructure and cleaning up the environment. Moreover, to ensure that everyone benefited by "the abundance" generated by technological advances, the report called for a guaranteed annual income for all Americans, which would effectively end poverty. The report also specified that it was imperative that traditionally disadvantaged communities receive "compensatory" resources such that their public education gave them the capacity to participate alongside those from more privileged sectors. And it called for a commitment to "improvements in public education" overall, with free schooling for all Americans through grade fourteen.[107]

These recommendations are breathtaking from the present vantage point because they are so radical, and they were agreed to by some of the leading CEOs in the nation. Indeed, the report even went so far as to urge firms to use automation to "humanize" the workplace and develop the new technologies in such a manner as to make the work experience more rewarding for the worker.[108] By the late 1970s or 1980s, with the changing political currents, one can only imagine how a subsequent commission on automation might have considered these issues. Indeed, one can "only imagine," because no such independent body ever came into existence. This was the one and only time in American history that automation and employment were formally studied and considered by an official government commission.

The early to middle 1960s proved to be the high-water mark for popular recognition of automation as an important social and economic issue, and a problem demanding political attention. What is striking is that these writers posed almost the exact same concerns, questions, framing, and even solutions that are being raised today; they were simply fifty years ahead of their time. Why did the issue of automation drift into the background? The easy answer is that the alarmist concerns of the early 1960s did not materialize, as the capacity for firms to deploy automation to replace most human jobs was greatly exaggerated. When we now see how laughably primitive computers and digital technology were fifty years ago, the predictions made at the time seem preposterous. This experience has probably been a factor in making economists and observers of all stripes gun-shy about predicting automation's elimination of most jobs, lest they be confused with the tinfoil-hat UFO crowd from the same time period. Whatever the precise reason for the shift, automation and displacement were no longer "news" after the mid-1960s. Chart 18 documents the decline in stories mentioning automation in the *New York Times* from 1955 through February 2015.

But the disappearance of automation as a political issue owes to more than the exaggerated claims of the early 1960s. To a large extent it reflected the fact that organized labor, aside from a handful of progressive unions like the United Electrical Workers (UEW), the International Association of Machinists, and more recently National Nurses United, threw in the towel. This shift in focus was encouraged in the late 1960s by the virtual disappearance of unemployment with the booming economy that accompanied the Vietnam War. It was also encouraged by the persistent management stratagem to label any critic of automation a "Luddite," as if asking questions about whether all automation was always good was tantamount to saying that society should abandon cooked food, electricity, and indoor plumbing.[109]

In the decades that followed, when unemployment became a political issue, the major public concern regarding job losses was with the many millions shifted to overseas low-wage locales. This aspect of globalization was not unrelated to computerization. Martin Wolf of the *Financial Times* writes that "information technology has turbo-charged globalization by making it vastly easier to organize global supply chains, run 24-hour global financial markets, and spread technological know-how."[110] As leading economists have

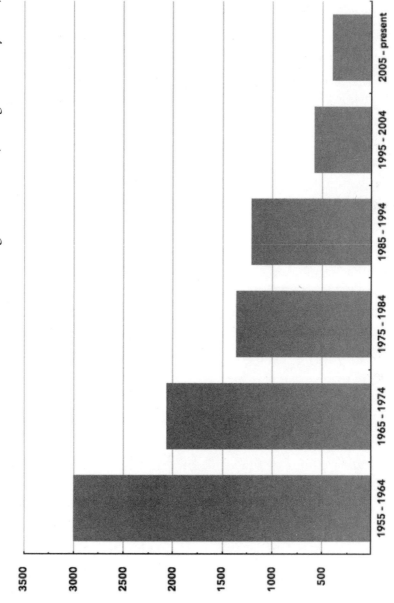

CHART 18 Number of *New York Times* Stories Mentioning Automation (through February 2015)

noted, computer technology and the Internet have made it "easier for businesses to outsource or relocate all or part of their operations to countries where wages, labor, and environmental standards are low."[111] Moreover, globalization made automation appear necessary. "If America hopes to match foreign competition," *Time* magazine wrote in 1983, "it may have to rely more heavily on automation."[112] That same year, *Fortune* wrote of "the race to the automatic factory," with none of the alarmism of a generation earlier. It was now a very good thing, a competitive requirement to keep up with the Japanese.[113] This argument won the day, at least to some extent because, until the latest recession, it seemed that the system could generate enough new jobs—albeit not especially good jobs in many cases—to prevent a full-throttle jobs crisis.[114]

By the 1990s only a few iconoclastic and heterodox economists and writers continued to study the issue and sound alarm bells about radical changes in the labor market. In 1995 economist Jeremy Rifkin argued that impending improvements in "software technologies are going to bring civilization ever closer to a near-workerless world." The great historian of economic thought Robert Heilbroner said the effect of automation on the economy was "a problem that we will be living with for the rest of our own and our children's lives," and that it "ought to become the center of a long-lasting and deep-probing conversation for the nation."[115]

It didn't. Instead, beginning in the 1990s, the Internet moved from the margins of our social and economic lives to become a nearly ubiquitous medium in the space of a decade. It quickly came to be regarded as the great new communication medium. When business pages and cable news shows considered computers and digital communication, they focused on the bounty it provided for web surfers and consumers, the challenge for existing businesses, and the magnificent new opportunity for investors and entrepreneurs. By the second decade of this century, the digital revolution had redefined the era in its image, and had entered the bone marrow not only of media and communication but of every aspect of the economy. Indeed, the three most valuable corporations in the US economy in the autumn of 2015 were Internet/computer firms—as well as five of the top ten and twelve of the top thirty-one, and that does not include related firms like General Electric and Disney—and only a few of them even existed in the 1960s.[116] The critics of the 1960s were not wrong that an explosion was coming. They were just a little off on the sequence, scope, and timing.

Nor does this mean that automation, or the powerful application of computers and networks to the economy, slowed down or became passé. To the contrary, it continued its persistent increase, but it simply became part of the woodwork, a necessary option for businesses to be competitive.[117] In this context, Nobel Prize–winning economist Wassily Leontief provided a more optimistic vision of automation's effects in 1983 at a Paris conference. "How will working people adjust themselves to being on the job only a few hours a day?" he asked.[118] Three years later, Leontief and economist Faye Duchin released their detailed examination of automation, which projected that it was likely to replace many millions more jobs by 2000. At the same time, they argued that "the computer revolution" by the year 2000 "will be no more advanced than the mechanization of European economies had advanced by, let us say, the year 1820."[119] In recent times, near-work-erless factories run by computer programs have become common. Thanks to computerized programs and robotics, for example, US steel industry production rose from 75 million tons to 120 million tons between 1982 and 2002, while the number of steelworkers fell from 289,000 to 74,000.[120] In the 1960s, for another example, a single textile worker operated five machines, each able to run a thread through the loom at one hundred times per minute. By 2014 machines ran at six times that speed and a single operator supervised one hundred looms.[121] Office work increasingly became the target of automation and computerization.[122]

To some extent, this process was so comprehensive and overwhelming—and part of a broader digitalization of all aspects of social life—that it eluded sustained analysis, as water escapes the comprehension of the proverbial fish. It certainly paved the way for what was and is about to come. American jobs were being radically changed by technology, and more than a few were being lost to technology, but until the Great Recession it did not seem to be much of a loss. And even then, as Galbraith put it, "you can't distinguish a job lost to technology from a job lost to a business slump. The two are, actually, the same thing."[123]

To some economists, who believe they can see what is in front of them as long as they keep their eyes glued to the rear-view mirror, this settles the matter. The future will look like the past. Technology will have no fundamental effect upon employment levels and need not concern policymakers when they address unemployment. But to an increasing number of engineers, computer scientists, investors, business leaders, business and economic reporters, and scholars—and more than a few eminent economists—the economy stands at a precipice, and society is facing the type of revolutionary GPT that occurs maybe once a century, if that. "There is a wave of what certainly appears to be labor substitutive innovation. . . . It appears technology is permitting very large-scale substitutions," Summers observed in 2015. "Probably, we are only in the early innings of such a wave."[124]

THE SECOND HALF OF THE CHESSBOARD

The question that jumps out is, why now? Why isn't this a warmed-over version of the early 1960s automation hysteria that proved to be bogus? The answer begins, appropriately enough, in the 1960s with Gordon Moore, a computer engineer and a founder of Intel. Moore wrote an article in 1965 in which he projected, in effect, that due to continuous technological improvements, the computing power one could buy for a dollar would double every year for a good ten years. This became Moore's Law. He later suggested that it would double every two years, and most observers have come to use the notion that it would double every eighteen months. People once anticipated that Moore's Law would peter out or at least slow down over time, but it has proven resilient and astonishingly accurate. "Over and over again," Brynjolfsson and McAfee write, "brilliant tinkering has found ways to skirt the limitations imposed by physics."[125]

What does this mean? By the early 1980s, for example, the cost of computer power relative to manual computing power was eight thousand times less than what it had been thirty years earlier.[126] It took scientists a decade of intensive work to sequence the three billion base pairs in the human genome by 2003. By 2013, a single computer facility could sequence that much DNA in a day.[127] More recently, the *Economist* reports, "the new iPhones sold over the weekend of their release in September 2014 contained 25 times more computing power than the whole world had at its disposal in 1995."[128]

What becomes clear is that if Moore's Law is extended for an appreciable period of time, the growth becomes mind-boggling. The futurist Ray Kurzweil is famous for explaining this with the parable of the person who invented the game of chess in sixth-century CE India. The inventor presented the new game to the local emperor, who was so impressed that he invited the inventor to name his reward. The inventor asked for a single grain of rice on the first day—then two grains on the second day, four grains on the third day, eight grains on the fourth day, and so on, with the number of grains to continue doubling every day for sixty-four days, to account for every square on the chessboard. The emperor instantly agreed, surprised by such a modest request. After ten days, the gift was around a thousand grains. After twenty days it was a million grains. After thirty days it was a billion grains, and then after thirty-two days, or halfway through the chessboard, the total was four billion grains, about one large field's quantity. But thereafter the doubling became astronomical. By the time one got to the sixty-fourth square, the number of grains would be eighteen quintillion, vastly more rice than has ever been produced in history. The emperor obviously could not comply. (In some versions of the story, the inventor is beheaded by the angry emperor.) "Kurzweil's point," Brynjolfsson and McAfee write, "is that constant doubling, reflecting exponential growth, is deceptive because it is initially unremarkable."[129]

If we return to Moore's Law, and begin in the 1960s, we are now entering the second half of the chessboard. The "exponential growth eventually leads to staggeringly big numbers, ones that leave our intuition and experience behind." Chart 19 provides a graph of what doubling looks like, beginning in 1960 at a rate of fifty computer "instructions per second" and doubling every eighteen months. To fit this chart on the page, all the spectacular growth in the "first half" of the chessboard barely registers before 2008. We are now at the part of the curve that is shooting straight up like an oil-well gusher. Even if the rate of growth eventually does slow down, we are deep into uncharted terrain, as though we have traveled through a wormhole to some distant galaxy.[130] As Brynjolfsson and McAfee note, "Things get weird in the second half of the chessboard."[131] In their view, the world is at an inflection point, where all sorts of operations that only recently were thought impossible for computers and uniquely the province of humans—driverless cars, anyone? robot "nurses"?—will be easily done by computers, and soon other tasks that presently are considered unthinkable for computers will become standard fare. The most striking feature may well be how very quickly this will take place in historical terms.

To put the moment we are entering in perspective, consider the analysis of Gill A. Pratt. Until 2015 Pratt served as Program Director at the Pentagon's Defense Advanced Research Projects Agency (DARPA), where he oversaw work on robotics. This is important because DARPA has been at the center of technological innovation throughout the digital era. Pratt argues that humanity may be on the verge of experiencing something comparable in impact to the "Cambrian Explosion," referring to the relatively brief period 540 million years ago when life underwent an astonishingly rapid diversification, including arguably the evolution of vision. It was crucial for the subsequent development of complex and intelligent life. Pratt outlined a series of related and complementary breakthroughs in robotics and computing that will make it possible for machines "to replicate the performance of many of the perceptual parts of the brain," including, ironically enough, vision itself. At the very least, Pratt observes, "the effects on economic output and human workers are certain to be profound." He refuses to predict when exactly this will occur, "as the timing of tipping points is hard to predict," but it is on its way.[132]

CHART 19 Theoretical Growth in Computing Power

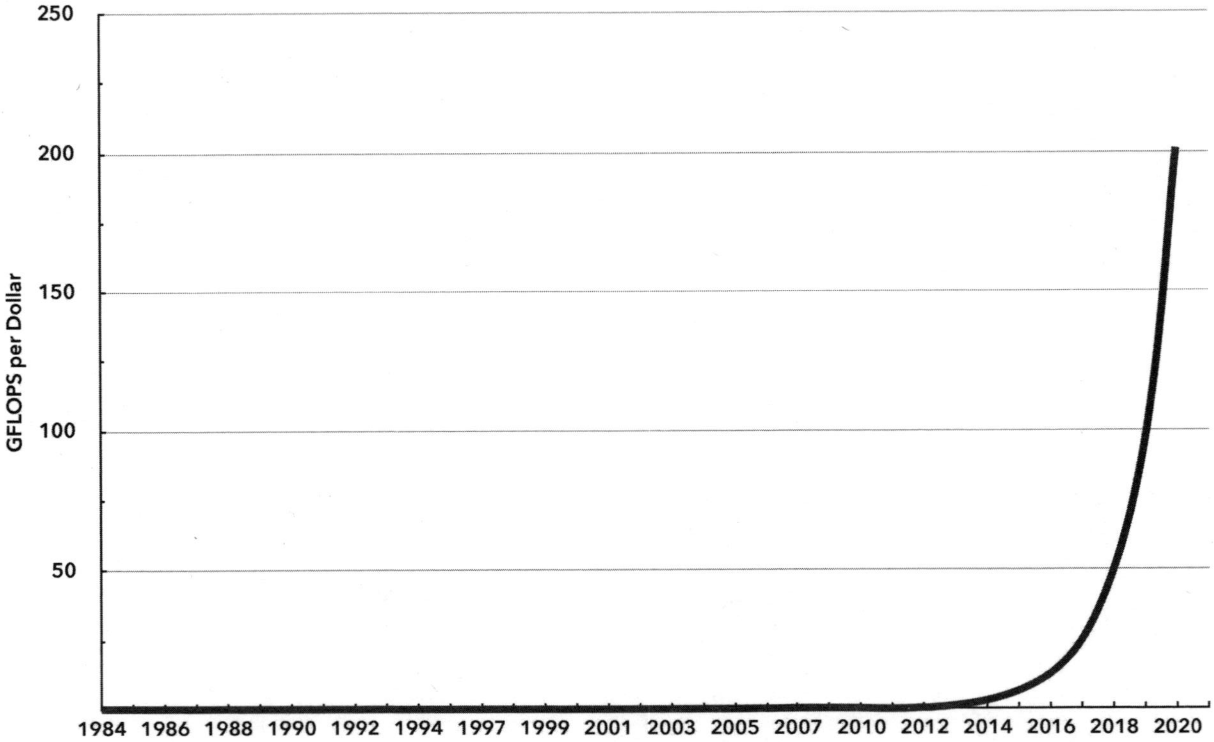

In this context it is almost banal to discuss Deep Blue, the IBM computer that defeated Garry Kasparov, the world champion, in a game of chess in what seems like the computer dark ages of 1997. Or even IBM's Watson computer from 2011 that was able to defeat all human competition in television's game of *Jeopardy*. This was done in real time and required the computer to interpret oral questions filled with wordplay and irony.[133] It was not just a gimmick. As Martin Ford notes, "IBM is already positioning Watson to play a significant role in fields like medicine and customer service."[134] "Artificial intelligence has become vastly more sophisticated in a short time," the *New York Times* reports, "with machines now able to learn, not just follow programmed instructions, and to respond to human language and movement."[135]

Computers can now access an unimaginably large body of stored information that is growing by leaps and bounds and process that information almost instantaneously with ever more sophisticated algorithms. This is what is referred to as "big data."[136] Computers, as Nicholas Carr explains, may never be able to replicate "tacit" or "procedural" knowledge, which refers to the stuff we do without thinking about it, like riding a bike or driving a car. Instead, computers are very good at "explicit" or "declarative" knowledge, which is the stuff we do that we can write down instructions for, like how to change a flat tire or solve a quadratic equation. "The superhuman speed with which computers can follow instructions, calculate probabilities, and receive and send data," Carr notes, "means that they can use explicit knowledge to perform many of the complicated tasks we do with tacit knowledge." Driverless cars are just the tip of that iceberg. The implications for automation are striking, if not revolutionary. "Even highly trained analysts and other so-called knowledge workers are seeing their work circumscribed by decision-support systems that turn the making of judgments into a data-processing routine."[137]

Much of this "big data" is accumulated in the "cloud," a group of enormous "server farms" controlled by a handful of massive corporations like Google, Apple, Amazon, and Microsoft. The cloud becomes the rational and most cost-effective way for businesses to store and analyze their data. One of the great benefits and therefore consequences of cloud computing, according to Vincent Mosco, the leading scholar on the subject, is that it "essentially deepens and extends opportunities to eliminate jobs and restructure the workforce." This is, in fact, a primary selling point that cloud computing firms use to drum up business.[138] (That seems fitting, as these vast corporate server farms "virtually run themselves," Carr writes.[139]) Ford observes that with "the migration of much of the intelligence that animates mobile robots" into the cloud, it makes it possible "to build less expensive robots, since less onboard computational power and memory are required, and allows for instant software upgrade across multiple machines."[140] In the meantime, for the same reason, as the *Economist* notes, cloud computing is also ideal for harnessing freelance workers to replace higher-paid labor.[141]

Another possibility opened up by being in the second half of the chessboard is the "Internet of Things," a term for the billions of human-made devices that are connected to each other on a universal computing infrastructure. Each of these devices has its own Internet address, and will communicate with other devices more than with people. "That's the whole point of the thing," technology writer Michael Miller enthuses, "to connect just about everything in the aptly named Internet of Things." It promises "more automatic, and more intelligent services provided by interconnected smart devices—with a minimal amount of human interaction."[142] "Make no mistake," author Samuel Greengard writes, "we are entering a brave new world of immersive and embedded technology. . . . It's entirely clear that a more technology-centric world is in the cards."[143]

Depending upon the source, by 2020 or very soon thereafter, it is expected that there will be as many as fifty billion such devices, and only a small fraction of them will be personal computers, tablets, or smartphones controlled by individual humans. "Engineers expect so many of these connected devices," Philip Howard writes in his book *Pax Technica*, "that they have reconfigured the addressing system to allow for 2 to the 128th power addresses—enough for each atom on the face of the earth to have 100 addresses."[144] Much of the economy will run through the Internet of Things. As Carr notes, "Manufacturers are spending billions of dollars to outfit factories with network-connected sensors, and technology giants like GE, IBM, and Cisco, hoping to spearhead the creation of an 'Internet of Things,' are rushing to develop standards for sharing the resulting data."[145] Soon one-half of German manufacturing investment is going to building out the Internet of Things, and PricewaterhouseCoopers expects global investment in the industrial Internet to top $500 billion by 2020.[146] That does not seem like so much when one considers that Cisco Systems forecasts that by 2022 the Internet of Things will generate $14.4 trillion in cost savings and revenue.[147] A large share of these savings will come by eliminating jobs. "Business processes that once took place among human beings are now being executed electronically," economist and technology theorist W. Brian Arthur puts it. Commerce is increasingly managed through "a huge conversation conducted entirely among machines."[148]

In conjunction with all this, an open source Robot Operating System (ROS) "is rapidly becoming the standard software platform for robotics development," according to Ford. "The history of computing shows pretty clearly that once a standard operating system, together with inexpensive and easy-to-use programming tools, becomes available, an explosion of application software is likely to follow." What does this mean? "It's a good bet," Ford says, that "we are, in all likelihood at the leading edge of an explosive wave of innovation that will ultimately produce robots geared to nearly every conceivable commercial, industrial, and consumer task."[149]

Robotics expert Ben Way anticipates the next decade will see a qualitative leap in what robots can do, which will radically increase their range and efficiency.[150] These "robots" are far more sophisticated in their abilities and their applications than the clunky machines of old movies. They will be not only in factories, they will be everywhere.

Then there is 3D printing, which Jeremy Rifkin describes as the "manufacturing" model that accompanies an Internet of Things economy.[151] This is the until-very-recently-unimaginable process of having a "printer" stamp out a three-dimensional product that one designs on one's computer. The possibilities are endless—it has used plastic and metals to create the products—and they look to revolutionize manufacturing, such that whole categories of workers can cease to be a factor. *Forbes* magazine compares it to the emergence of the industrial revolution and the assembly line. "3D Printing will be a game changer."[152] And this is not on some dude's drawing board in Palo Alto. It is already in existence and widely used, as Brynjolfsson and McAfee note: "It's used by countless companies every day to make prototypes and model parts." Then, to put an exclamation point on their analysis, they say that 3D printing, robotics, driverless cars, and computers like Watson "are not the crowning achievements of the computer era. They're the warm-up act."[153]

WHAT DOES THIS MEAN FOR JOBS?

In short, as we get to the second half of the chessboard, the ability of employers to cost-effectively deploy their new tools and tactics of organization increases, dare we say it, exponentially. Any way you slice it, the outlook is bad, very bad, for workers. The *Economist* has been at the forefront of studying and writing about the issue.[154] "Until now," it wrote in 2014, "the jobs most vulnerable to machines were those that involved routine, repetitive tasks. But thanks to the exponential rise in processing power and the ubiquity of digitized information ('big data'), computers are increasingly able to perform complicated tasks more cheaply and effectively than people."[155] As computer science reporter Federico Pistono puts it, "Millions of algorithms created by computer scientists are frantically running on servers all over the world, with one sole purpose: do whatever humans can do, but better."[156] What does this mean? "The combination of big data and smart machines will take over some occupations wholesale; in others it will allow firms to do more with fewer workers."[157]

In earlier stages of automation, Brynjolfsson explains, firms automated the physical work but required humans to be the control system. Now the control system can be automated, and when it is, "then it is less clear what the role for humans is."[158]

The *Economist* notes that new technologies also make it possible for firms to "reshape" those jobs that remain, so that they can "be done by less skilled contract workers."[159] "In case after case," Carr writes, "we've seen as machines become more sophisticated, the work left to people becomes less so."[160] This was anticipated first by Harvard Business School professor James R. Bright in his 1958 book *Automation and Management*. "It seems that the more automatic the machine, the less the operator has to do," Bright wrote. "The progressive effect of automation is first to relieve the operator of manual effort and then to relieve him of the need to apply continuous mental effort."[161]

In 1966 Bright filed a report for President Johnson's National Commission on Technology, Automation, and Economic Progress: "The lesson should be increasingly clear; it is not necessarily true that highly complex equipment requires skilled operators. The 'skill' can be built into the machine." With his orientation toward management, Bright was the first dissenting voice regarding the notion that automation required workers to have better education and training: "I suggest that excessive educational and skill specification is a serious mistake and potential hazard to our educational and social system. We will hurt individuals, raise labor costs improperly, create disillusion and resentment, and destroy valid job standards by setting standards that are not truly needed for a given task."[162] He was decades ahead of his time.[163] As Tyler Cowen puts it, most of these new jobs that interact with sophisticated machines "won't be much harder than, in today's world, operating a tollbooth on the New Jersey Garden State Parkway, a job performed by both man and machines."[164] Thompson's examination of labor in the *Atlantic* concludes that "most jobs are still boring, repetitive, and easily learned."[165]

Indeed, as the *Economist* notes, the *de-skilling* of the remaining jobs can be seen as providing a way station to their eventual elimination.* "Gobbetising jobs with the aim of parceling them out to people who don't see or need to see the big picture is not that different from gobbetising them in a way that allows automation. Often the first activity

---

* This insight is hardly new; it was made in 1776 at the beginning of the industrial revolution by Adam Smith in *The Wealth of Nations*, when he wrote how simplifying labor processes made it easier to replace workers with machines. See Adam Smith, *The Wealth of Nations* (New York: Modern Library, 2000), p. 4.

may prove a prelude to the second."[166] The magazine offers up Uber as an example of a business that may well be "a forerunner to an eventual system that has no drivers at all."[167]

Martin Ford points to a New York–based start-up, Work Fusion, which sells software to firms to automate big projects formerly done by office workers. Where people are still needed, the software recruits freelance workers online to do the temp work, and then the software monitors what the workers do to learn from them so that their jobs, too, can be automated. "As the freelance workers do their jobs they are, in effect, training the system to replace them. That's a pretty good preview of what the future looks like."[168] "The combination of advanced sensors, voice recognition, artificial intelligence, big data, text-mining, and pattern-recognition algorithms, is generating smart robots capable of quickly learning human actions, and even learning from one another," writes former US Labor Secretary Robert Reich. "If you think being a 'professional' makes your job safe, think again."[169]

So exactly which jobs are on the chopping block? "Accountants may follow travel agents and bank tellers into the unemployment line as tax software improves. Machines are already turning basic sports results and financial data into "good-enough" news stories," the *Economist* writes. "A taxi driver will be a rarity in many places by the 2030s or 2040s. That sounds like bad news for journalists who rely on that most reliable source of local knowledge and prejudice—but will there be any journalists left to care? Will there be airline pilots? Or traffic cops? Or soldiers?"[170] A report in the *New York Times* adds "counselors, salespeople, chefs, paralegals and researchers" to the list.[171] Or consider utility meter readers. In 2001, 56,000 American workers held that job. By 2010 the number was down to 36,000. By 2023 the number is expected to be zero.[172]

Consider that the four most common occupations in the United States are retail salesperson, cashier, food and beverage server, and office clerk. Nearly 10 percent of the labor force, over fifteen million workers—more workers than there are in Texas and Massachusetts combined—are so employed. Thompson notes that these jobs are highly susceptible to automation.[173] Ford sees 50 percent of fast-food jobs disappearing, and argues it is likely there will be "explosive growth of the fully automated self-service retail sector—or, in other words, intelligent vending machines and kiosks."[174] Or consider driverless cars. Robotics scientists like MIT's Daniela Rus make a powerful and convincing case that the impending shift to a driverless world—the technology is in its final stages—will be much more efficient, vastly improve the transportation system, and do wonders for the environment and the quality of life.[175] One problem: the most common occupation for American men is driving some sort of vehicle, be it automobile, bus, or truck. What happens to them?[176]

Then there are the two sectors of the economy harboring the most professionals—health care and education. They "are under increasing pressure to cut costs," Reich notes. "And expert machines are poised to take over."[177] A 2014 article asked: "Robot Replacing Nurses: Is It Really That Far-Fetched?" The answer:

> Dr. Rosalind Picard, professor at the Massachusetts Institute of Technology (MIT), recently told the British Broadcasting Corporation (BBC) that robots should be made available to healthcare providers (nurses and physicians) in order to enhance healthcare delivery. However, when pressed by the interviewer to guarantee that robots will not fully replace nurses as a way for hospitals to save money, she answered: "You know, when people are in charge all kinds of things can happen . . . right?"[178]

For education "entrepreneur" John Katzman, the great question is, "How do we use technology so that we require fewer highly qualified teachers?"[179]

The better question may be: What jobs *aren't* susceptible to elimination or radical de-skilling and downsizing by automation? Computer entrepreneur Peter H. Diamondis and technology reporter Steven Kotler concur. Within a decade, they write, robots "will make up the majority of the blue-collar workforce." They will be doing everything from "shelf-stocking" inventory at Costco to "burger-slinging" at McDonald's.[180] That's not all. Ford argues that the last remaining labor-intensive areas in agriculture—primarily picking—are soon to be susceptible to automation.[181]

In manufacturing, the original target of automation, the list is endless. "Being newly able to do brain work will not stop computers from doing ever more formerly manual labour," the *Economist* reports. "It will make them better at it."[182] This is probably where the invasion of the revolutionary new robots will be noticed first. "Robots deployed in manufacturing today," the *Wall Street Journal* reported in 2015,

> tend to be large, dangerous to anyone who strays too close to their whirling arms, and limited to one task, like welding, painting or hoisting heavy parts. The latest models entering factories and being developed in labs are a different breed. They can work alongside humans without endangering them and help assemble all sorts of objects, as large as aircraft engines and as small and delicate as smartphones. Soon, some should be easy enough to program and deploy that they no longer will need expert overseers.

Robots are getting much lighter, they can be repurposed easily and can do delicate work humans find very difficult and once regarded as impossible for machines. "One company promises its robots eventually will be sewing garments in the U.S., taking over one of the ultimate sweatshop tasks."[183]

The one proviso historically offered by economists was that low wages slow down the incentive for businesses to turn to automation. The "good news" for manufacturing workers was that, as long as they did not press management for higher wages or better working conditions, they might keep some of their jobs. How has this worked in practice? A firm like Nissan relies upon robots for its factories in Japan, but its factories in India rely on cheap local labor.[184] Indeed, a good deal of economic analysis of the speed and intensity of technological innovation and diffusion is based upon the cost of labor. When wages are relatively low, innovation slows down, and when wages are high, firms have a greater incentive to turn to automation. The logic is that as American labor costs continue to decline, firms will be more likely to hire real workers and less inclined to turn to automation, or to move manufacturing jobs abroad to low-wage locales.

As we enter the second half of the chessboard, that economic thinking can be filed next to the discredited notion that market economies always gravitate toward full employment, or that market economies tend to reduce inequality.[185] "China, India, Mexico, and other emerging nations are learning quickly," Rifkin writes, "that the cheapest workers in the world are not as cheap, efficient, and productive as the information technology, robotics, and artificial intelligence that replaces them."[186] A recent study by University of Chicago economists Loukas Karabarbounis and Brent Nieman found that labor's share of GDP has been declining in those three nations as well as most of the other nations they examined. Their explanation? Advances in information technology caused the price of plant, machinery, and equipment to drop, so companies have shifted investment away from labor and toward capital. They determine that in the United States almost one-half of the decline in the share of labor in the national income can be attributed to businesses' replacing workers with computers and software.[187]

By 2012 the global sales of industrial robots was a $28 billion annual market, and the fastest-growing market is China, where robot installations have been increasing at a 25 percent annual rate since 2005.[188] China still has a long way to go, as it has just thirty robots per 10,000 manufacturing employees compared to South Korea (437), Japan (323), Germany (282), and the United States (152), according to the International Federation of Robotics, a trade group. The research firm IHS Technology projects that robot sales in China will increase from 55,000 units in 2014, to 211,000 units in 2019.[189]

Consider Foxconn, the largest maker of electronic components in the world and the largest exporter in Greater China. Foxconn is single-handedly responsible for manufacturing nearly half of the consumer technology in the world, and much, if not most, of what Americans own in terms of smartphones and tablet computers. It has annual revenues of $135 billion and is the third-largest employer in the world, with 1.2 million workers. Foxconn grabbed its market share by providing a low-paid and heavily exploited workforce for Western firms, working in conditions right out of a Charles Dickens novel. In 2010, world attention shifted to Foxconn's factories that produced Apple products following a string of suicides by its workers. Soon thereafter, Foxconn began an aggressive program to eventually replace many, or most, of its workers with one million robots.[190] Foxconn CEO Terry Gou said in 2015 that the firm has been adding thirty thousand industrial robots annually since then, and the process is being accelerated to the point where he expects robots and automation to complete 70 percent of its assembly-line work by 2018. Gou eventually foresees a "robot army"—Foxconn has invested heavily in robotics research—as a way to offset labor costs. "I think in the future young people won't do this kind of work, and won't enter the factories," Gou says.[191] Foxconn is not an outlier or some kind of "futurist" firm.[192] It is part of a trend. The headline of a 2015 *New York Times* report from China said it all: "Cheaper Robots, Fewer Workers." It explained that

> a few low-tech industries, like garment manufacturing, are moving from China to places that still have very low wages, like Bangladesh. But many industries, particularly electronics, are still moving factories to China. That is because so many of the parts suppliers are now in China that it is often more costly to do assembly elsewhere. So although building robots to replace workers is seldom cheap, a growing number of companies are finding it less costly than either paying ever-higher wages in China or moving to another country.[193]

We doubt that automation will replace most labor in China, India, or the global south in the near term; there is still more than enough cheap labor.[194] We also doubt that firms such as Foxconn anticipate a workerless world in the visible future—although Gou says the firm already has a fully automated plant in Chendu that works 24/7 with the lights off. But there is not much doubt that Foxconn managers intend to use the company's vast resources and immense market power to create a permanent low-cost position worldwide,

combining low wages with the most advanced technology.[195] For the
Foxconn business model to survive, it must ensure that the dominant
and unrivaled manufacturing infrastructure and networks built in
China remain attractive as automation increases in prominence and
lessens the importance of a cheap, non-unionized labor force. But
the historical clock is ticking. One industry analyst says that there
will be a few million manufacturing jobs left in 2040. In 2003 there
were 163 million manufacturing jobs worldwide.[196]

All of this is bad news for a capitalist economy, which needs workers with decent incomes so they can become consumers who purchase
products. That is when capitalists make profits and have incentives
to invest and expand the economy. The loss of jobs and therefore the
shrinking of a consumer base with disposable income is a recurring
problem in capitalist economies, and it provides a good shorthand description of the Great Depression. It looks to be our fate again in
one form or another. As Galbraith puts it, the United States is experiencing "a permanent move toward lower rates of employment in the
private, for-profit sector."[197]

But can the same computer technology that seems to be aggravating the problems of capitalism also provide a solution? One of the
attributes of earlier GPTs, like railroads and automobiles, is that they
stimulated a massive body of investment (and employment) in related
industries that became powerhouses in their own right. Consider
automobiles. We both grew up in the industrial Midwest—in Cleveland and southeastern Wisconsin, respectively—during the heyday
of the Rust Belt, back before there was much rust. From Buffalo and
Pittsburgh in the east to Cleveland, Akron, Toledo, and Detroit in
the middle, and on to Gary, Chicago, and Milwaukee in the west, gigantic factories producing steel, glass, rubber, machine tools, and the
like were ever-present, in addition to the iconic auto plants. Millions
of people earned good wages and the economies were strong, and at
the center of it all was the automobile. That doesn't even begin to
factor in all the construction and real estate development—that is,
suburbanization—and other ancillary industries that resulted as well.
One can make the case that automobilization was a central factor

in the health of US capitalism for much of the twentieth century. It more than offset the losses to employment that the automobile had created by ending the "ecology of horse and plow and the semi-modern technology of the railroad and the streetcar."[198]

Is anything like this occurring or on the horizon due to computerization and the Internet? To our knowledge, Galbraith has studied that question as much as anyone, and his answer is an emphatic "no." "With computers and the Internet, this scope for secondary employment is far less." Indeed, the evidence is that the opposite is the case. "The ratio of jobs killed to jobs created in this process is high," Galbraith writes. "Moreover, many of those displaced are not only unemployed but also obsolete." One of the virtues of computerization and the Internet proves to be a great problem for a capitalist economy: it not only saves on labor, but it also saves on capital, as it becomes so much more efficient.[199] Ironically, perhaps the only tangible new sector of jobs for humans has been provided by Rifkin, who states that "there is one last surge of work: in the next 35 years we will have to put the infrastructure of the automated economy in place—robots are not going to do that." Exactly how many jobs that will require is unclear, but Rifkin notes that "this transformation will keep two more generations busy but the downside is of course that the smarter technology gets, the less workers it needs to run it properly." And, this "surge of work" is paving the way for the end of work by mid-century.[200]

People who study the list of the most common occupations find it to be largely the province of the types of jobs that predated the computer and are now in its crosshairs. "Nine out of 10 workers today are in occupations that existed 100 years ago," Thompson writes, "and just 5 percent of the jobs generated between 1993 and 2013 came from 'high tech' sectors like computing, software, and telecommunications. Our newest industries tend to be the most labor-efficient: they just don't require many people."[201] Apple directly employs less than 10 percent of the one million workers around the globe involved in producing and selling its products; many of those nine hundred thousand gig and contracted jobs seem like good candidates for the digital chopping block in the future.[202] Amazon, for another example, already uses some fifteen thousand robots in its warehouses.[203] Moreover, those humans who remain on the payroll tend to experience exactly what one would expect in any other sector of the economy: in a labor market marked by a massive surplus of desperate workers, working conditions can revert to levels once regarded as barbaric.[204]

It is difficult to see where new jobs—certainly the tens of millions of new jobs that will be needed—are supposed to come from. As economic historian Robert Sidelsky puts it, the stock response from optimists is that society needs to "simply train people for better jobs." The problem here is that "technological progress is now eating up the better jobs, too."[205] There are not enough "specialized new digital jobs, like people who create apps," a business reporter writes, "no matter how we're educating people. Our new industries simply aren't labor-intensive."[206] When Sidelsky pressed the optimists to describe some of the "many new types of jobs" that will be created, they came up with "lead drivers of multi-car road trains" in the coming era of driverless cars, "big data analysts, or robot mechanics. That does not sound like too many new jobs to me."[207]

In 2014 Pew conducted a "Future of the Internet" survey of nearly two thousand technology experts on how advances in robotics and artificial intelligence might affect the economy and employment in the coming decade. Half of these experts expected no loss in employment, even though "this group anticipates that many jobs currently performed by humans will be substantially taken over by robots or digital agents by 2025." What evidence provided the basis for this optimism about job creation? They offered "faith that human ingenuity will create new jobs, industries, and ways to make a living, just as it has been doing since the dawn of the Industrial Revolution."[208] So that's it? No need for evidence, just have faith? From scientists?

Pistono had an experience like ours when he attempted to locate tangible examples or a credible explanation of what the new industries might be and where new jobs might come from to replace the ones being lost. "I have read several books, watched hundreds of debates and interviews on the subject, and I have not so far heard a single argument to support the idea that we can make this work, or how."[209] By the end of 2014, former Treasury Secretary Lawrence Summers stated that he no longer believed that the automation process would create new jobs to replace the ones it was eliminating. "This isn't some hypothetical future possibility," he said. "This is something that's emerging before us right now."[210] Due to automation, "there is no reason to believe there will be jobs for all people at socially acceptable wages," the commission on the state of the US economy headed by Summers and Balls concluded in 2015. "The rapid pace in computer innovation of routine tasks has rightfully worried policymakers, as this scale of automation has little precedent in industrialized economies."[211]

In 2013 two Oxford University scholars published a detailed research paper that concluded that 47 percent of existing US jobs—including many "middle-class" service jobs—were at "high risk" of being eliminated due to automation.[212] This has led some respected observers to predict unemployment rates in the coming decades in the 50 percent range. We are dubious about the value of making predictions of that nature, because there are so many factors no one can anticipate. It is possible that unemployment will be buffered by scads of presently unforeseeable new jobs, though even then it is hard to see how they will be particularly good jobs. We need to be mindful of Amara's Law, named after systems engineer Roy Amara: "We tend to overestimate the effect of a technology in the short run and underestimate the effect in the long run."[213]

What we are comfortable saying—and what we believe must be said loudly and emphatically—is that the present course is taking *all* the trends toward increased inequality and poverty already in existence and making them worse. Technological displacement of workers, Summers correctly concludes, "is likely to be a substantial factor pushing toward more inequality in the future."[214] No evidence provided by *anyone* suggests otherwise. And that alone, not a prospective frightening rate of unemployment decades down the road, should be more than enough to get everyone's attention.

This conclusion comes as no surprise to labor unions and progressive economists. Paul Krugman writes that "we could be looking at a society that grows ever richer, but in which all the gains in wealth accrue to whoever owns the robots."[215] But the exact same conclusion is being reached by many of those who are enthralled with capitalism and enamored with the new technologies, and who benefit materially by what is taking place. Brynjolfsson and McAfee stand as arguably the world's greatest cheerleaders for automation and what they refer to as "the second machine age." But they acknowledge that "the gains, however large, have been concentrated among a relatively small group of winners, leaving the majority of people worse off than before."[216] The *Economist* writes that "the prosperity unleashed by the digital revolution has gone overwhelmingly to the owners of capital and the highest-skilled workers."[217] It will continue into the future and "will contribute to pressure to reduce labour rights in all sorts of situations."[218] The *Economist* also notes there is a "squeezing out" of the middle class, whose emergence in the twentieth century "was a hugely important political and social development across the world."[219]

There are crucial existential questions that the new era of artificial intelligence, robotics, and computerization brings to the forefront. "It's apparent," Greengard notes, "that society is hitting a tipping point where humans are engineering our own obsolescence."[220] What is the relationship of humans to their machines?[221] At what point are they no longer "our" machines? What does *human being* mean? What makes us happy? Or, the question that technology historian George Dyson posed: "What if the cost of machines that think is people who don't?"[222] Organizations like the Future of Life Institute, funded in part by Tesla founder Elon Musk, the Lifeboat Foundation, and the recently created Center for the Study of Existential Risk at Cambridge University all address the "existential risks" for humanity posed by genetic engineering, nanotechnology, and artificial intelligence, particularly as we approach the so-called singularity, the hypothetical moment when artificial intelligence surpasses the human intellect. As renowned Cambridge astrophysicist Sir Martin Rees puts it, the risk is exponentially greater because of "the ease with which a single person or company can cause catastrophic harm."[223] In July 2015 the Future of Life Institute released a letter signed by some three thousand artificial intelligence researchers and sixteen thousand other noted scholars calling for a global ban on offensive autonomous military weapons. "Artificial Intelligence (AI) technology has reached a point where the deployment of such systems is—practically if not legally—feasible within years, not decades, and the stakes are high: autonomous weapons have been described as the third revolution in warfare, after gunpowder and nuclear arms."[224]

We share these concerns. For our purposes, this technological revolution is of singular importance because it is contributing to an unsustainable future, and the crises of unemployment, inequality, and poverty are the direct and visible manifestations. Martin Ford is spot-on when he writes that "the problem is not with technology; it is with our economic system, and it lies specifically in that system's inability to continue thriving in the new reality that is being created."[225] We would only add this: it is not even an economic problem as much as it is a political one, because the only plausible way to solve the great structural problems facing the economy will be through politics.

THE GREAT PARADOX(ES)

Whatever the virtues of capitalism, computerization and automation substantially elevate two related core paradoxes that are intrinsic to the profit system.

The first core paradox is that capitalism rewards businesses and investors for engaging in certain types of behavior and punishes them for not engaging in such behavior. When all businesses respond the same way, however, it creates major problems no one wanted, or it makes existing small problems much larger. The classic example is how businesses respond to an economic slowdown. The prudent course for an individual firm is to cut back on prospective investment and lay off workers and marshal resources—minimize losses—until a turnaround appears on the horizon. But when all firms follow the same course, and stop investing while laying off millions of workers, the recession grows much worse and proves far more intractable. All businesses suffer as a result, not to mention workers and everyone else.

What is rational for the individual capitalist produces utterly irrational results when it is done by capitalists as a whole.

Likewise, for individuals it is regarded as commendable financial management when people save money instead of spending their entire income. The individual who is willing to forgo immediate consumption will become wealthier in the long run and have far more money to use for consumption. It is also good for the economy, since increased savings means there is more money for investment, and the overall economy can grow at a faster rate, with the result being higher incomes for everyone. But if everyone follows that course and increases their savings, overall consumption plummets and the economy can enter a recession. If the economy is already in a recession, a high rate of savings can slow down any recovery and contribute to a depression. Then incomes stagnate or fall, and the benefits of saving are lost. Economists have a term for this phenomenon: it is called "the paradox of thrift." What is rational behavior for the individual produces disastrous consequences when everyone does it.

So it is with automation. The profit system pushes firms to automate as much as possible, and to de-skill remaining jobs as well. Firms that do not compete on these terms will be defeated in the marketplace, their profits will be lower, and management heads will roll. If a firm does not get its act together, the business will go under. For the individual firm this makes perfect sense, and there really isn't any choice. But when all firms in the economy automate and de-skill as much as possible, it means that there is substantially less demand for the products many of them produce, and the economy stagnates. When what seems utterly progressive, dynamic, and rational for an individual firm is done by all of them, it produces an economy that is marked by low growth and mounting inequality and poverty. In an extreme case, the fruits of automation may then be denied to all.

The second core paradox of the profit system is that computerization and automation greatly enhance a criticism of capitalism that goes back to the time of Karl Marx, who with Friedrich Engels wrote in *The Communist Manifesto* that capitalism "cannot exist without constantly revolutionising the instruments of production."[226] This was the basis for arguably Marx's strongest and most persistent critique—what David Harvey terms the "central contradiction" of capitalism in the Marxist tradition—and the one that never goes away: the system inexorably generates an increasing gap between what the economy is capable of producing—both quantitatively and qualitatively—and what it actually produces.[227] In the present time, this inability for capitalism to successfully sell at a profit all that it can produce leads to stagnation, underinvestment, unemployment, and never-ending demands for austerity. But there is a larger, existential conflict between the increasingly advanced capacity to produce and what the economy actually produces as it awaits the green light from capitalists confident in their ability to maximize profits.

This insight was not reserved to those who were hostile to the capitalist system. The great nineteenth-century liberal economist John Stuart Mill, a contemporary of Marx, regarded capitalism as ideally suited for developing technology and expanding the productive capacity of a society, but he was dubious about its long-term suitability for a decent society.

> Hitherto it is questionable if all the mechanical inventions yet made have lightened the day's toil of any human being. They have enabled a greater population to live the same life of drudgery and imprisonment, and an increased number of manufacturers and others to make fortunes. They have increased the comforts of the middle classes. But they have not yet begun to effect those great changes in human destiny, which it is in their nature and in their futurity to accomplish.

In Mill's mind, it was "only in the backward countries of the world that increased production is still an important object: in those most advanced, what is economically needed is a better distribution, of which one indispensable means is a stricter restraint on population." He chastised his fellow economists for their overriding belief that "the test of prosperity is high profits," and that the existing economic system was the optimal human condition for the rest of time. "The increase of wealth is not boundless," he wrote. "I know not why it should be [a] matter of congratulation that persons who are already richer than any one needs to be, should have doubled their means of consuming things which give little or no pleasure except as representative of wealth."

In Mill's view, capitalist development would rightly lead to what he termed a "stationary state," where the endless pursuit of ever more profit would no longer exist. Such a

> society would exhibit these leading features: a well-paid and affluent body of labourers; no enormous fortunes, except what were earned and accumulated during a single lifetime; but a much larger body of persons than at present, not only exempt from the coarser toils, but with sufficient leisure, both physical and mental, from mechanical details, to cultivate freely the graces of life, and afford examples of them to the classes less favourably circumstanced for their growth. . . . The best state for human nature is that in which, while no one is poor, no one desires to be richer, nor has any reason to fear being thrust back by the efforts of others to push themselves forward.[228]

By the end of the second decade of the twentieth century, capitalism had undergone extraordinary growth in productive capacity—the modern US industrial economy exploded in size in the five decades following the Civil War—and the greatest and most original-thinking economists of the time returned to the paradox of spectacular productivity alongside spectacular deprivation. The visionary economist Thorstein Veblen regarded that as the exact description of the American economy. "The mechanical industry of the new order is inordinately productive," he wrote in 1919.

> So the rate and volume of output have to be regulated with a view to what the traffic will bear—that is to say, what will yield the largest net return in terms of price to the business men who manage the country's industrial system. Otherwise, there will be "overproduction," business depression, and consequent hard times all around. . . . That is to say, in no such community can the industrial system be allowed to work at full

capacity for any appreciable interval of time, on pain of business stagnation and consequent privation for all classes and conditions of men.
The requirements of profitable business will not tolerate it. So the rate
and volume of output must be adjusted to the needs of the market, not
to the working capacity of the available resources, equipment and man
power, nor to the community's need of consumable goods.

To Veblen this was a tragic state of affairs, as the technology that
produces this state of affairs "is in an eminent sense a joint stock of
knowledge and experience held in common by the civilized peoples."
Were it not "being manhandled by ignorant business men with an
eye single to maximum profits, the resulting output of goods and services would doubtless exceed the current output by several hundred
percent."[229]

In 1930, as capitalism entered the worst depression of the twentieth century, and as the world was in the midst of "a bad attack of economic pessimism," Keynes wrote a short piece to remind people that
the problems of the economy were due not to its weakness, but rather
to its extraordinary productivity. He noted that US factory output per
worker was 40 percent greater in 1925 than in 1919. He projected that
within readers' lifetimes, the number of workers needed to "perform
all the operations of agriculture, mining, and manufacture" would be
reduced by 75 percent. Keynes hypothesized that in a century's time,
the "economic problem" would be solved, and very little human labor
would be required to provide all people with living standards at least
eight times greater than those of 1930.[230] He thought it would possibly
lead to more than a little angst as people struggled, for the first time in
human existence, with the prospect that the "economic problem" was
no longer all-consuming. Keynes wrote of reaching "our destination
of economic bliss," and with that a shift in human nature.[231]

Keynes's insight regarding human nature is of particular importance. "Industriousness has served as America's unofficial religion
since its founding," Thompson writes in the *Atlantic*. "The sanctity
and preeminence of work lie at the heart of the country's politics,
economics, and social interactions. What might happen if work goes

away?" Keynes's pessimism at least for the short term is well founded. "The paradox of work is that many people hate their jobs," Thompson notes, "but they are considerably more miserable doing nothing." This leads Thompson to a provocative conclusion: "Most people do need to achieve things through, yes, *work* to feel a lasting sense of purpose. To envision a future that offers more than minute-to-minute satisfaction, we have to imagine how millions of people might find meaningful work without formal wages."[232]

Keynes wrote *before* anyone anticipated how computerization and digital communication networks would turn everything upside down. "The development of automation and cybernation in the last two decades signals the end of the long, long era in which the inevitability of scarcity constituted the central fact of human existence," Baran and Sweezy wrote in their seminal 1966 work *Monopoly Capital*.[233] Herbert Marcuse, a close confidant and frequent correspondent of Baran, grasped the implications, much like Keynes: "Complete automation in the realm of necessity would open the dimension of free time as the one in which man's private *and* societal existence would constitute itself. This would be the historical transcendence toward a new civilization."[234] But the outcome was not inexorable. "The central question is whether the prevailing relations of production promote or block, encourage or discourage the translation of these potentialities into practice," Baran and Sweezy added. "The appearance and the widening of the gap between what is and what could be, demonstrate thus that the existing property relations and the economic, social and political institutions resting upon them have turned into an effective obstacle to the achievement of what has become possible."[235]

The growth in the economy's capacity to produce since the 1930s, or even the 1960s, has been extraordinary, much as these economists anticipated. If the experts we used as counsel for this chapter are anywhere near accurate, the next four or five decades could make the twentieth century look like the twelfth century.

In popular economic theory, such revolutionary increases in productive capacity are supposed to translate into higher living standards, much shorter workweeks, richer public infrastructure, and a greater overall social security. Society should have the resources to tackle vexing environmental problems with the least amount of pain possible. In fact, however, nothing on the horizon suggests that this is in the offing. As automation and computerization take productive capacity to undreamed-of heights, jobs grow more scarce and are de-skilled, many people are poorer, and all the talk is of austerity and seemingly endless cutbacks in social services. There is growing wealth for the few combined with greater insecurity for the many. Washington, we've got a problem.

The false assumptions, of course, are that the benefits of the technology accrue to more than the owners of the firms deploying the technologies. And also that capitalists have incentive to produce far more than they do to satisfy the needs of people worldwide. In fact, Veblen had it right: capitalists produce as much as they do only as long as it remains profitable to do so. Producing more than that lowers prices and lessens profits. In short, to follow Keynes's logic to a place he did not go, capitalism would seem to have little or no reason to exist if the "economic problem" is solved, so it is imperative that the economic problem remain. For business and wealthy investors to continue to win, everyone else has to lose.

In our view, the evidence points in one direction: the economy needs to be fundamentally reformed, if not replaced. Capitalism as we know it is the wrong economic system for the material world that is emerging. This is a radical conclusion, but it is not made merely by radicals. The number of true believers who think leaving firms and wealthy investors alone to do as they wish will ultimately solve the employment problem and give us a great economy that can be the foundation for a vibrant democracy is shrinking, primarily because it is a faith-based position. There are also some who have a similar faith that technology is innately progressive and all-powerful, so it can and will solve capitalism's problems for us. They tell us that all we have to do is get out of the way, make some fresh popcorn, and grab a front-row seat as the future unfolds.

But researching this book, what has been striking to us is that many, perhaps most, of the people who have studied these matters—

from across the political spectrum—recognize that if the system is left alone, it will not right itself. Instead, structural changes are needed, and government will have to play the central role in determining and instituting these changes. Even those who believe that the existing capitalist system provides benefits that make it worth saving realize that significant reforms and government policy interventions are necessary to prevent intolerable outcomes. "It's time to start discussing what kind of society we should construct around a labor-light economy," Brynjolfsson and McAfee conclude. "How should the abundance of such an economy be shared? How can the tendency of modern capitalism to produce high levels of inequality be muted while preserving its ability to allocate resources efficiently and reward initiative and effort? What do fulfilling lives look like when they no longer center on industrial-era conceptions of work? How should education, the social safety net, taxation, and other important elements of civic society be rethought?"[236]

Where markets and business and private investment figure into the new economy is a matter to be studied, debated, and resolved; we only know that it cannot be the same as what we have had for generations. The solutions to the employment and economic crises in the United States are political. The great debate is over what types of reforms there should be, and what type of system we should end up with. A core responsibility of the democratic state is to provide the ground rules and basis for an economy that will best serve the democratically determined needs of the people. An unavoidable part of this debate is to take up the issues last taken seriously in the 1960s: How should technology best be deployed to serve human needs? Never has the need for such a democratic debate and policymaking been greater than it is today.

chapter three

CITIZENLESS DEMOCRACY

HERE CAN BE NO DEMOCRACY IN AMERICA WITHOUT IN-
formed, engaged, and active citizenry. Everyone knows this.
It's an eternal construct that runs through the historical and
emotional understanding of the United States.[1] But what if the *citizens*
are expunged from democracy? What if citizens are told that, on the
issues of greatest consequence, their services are no longer required?
What if politicians get completely comfortable with the fact that—
except perhaps for a few pre-election weeks when it is necessary to suggest differently—they will always defer to concentrated wealth rather
than the popular will? What if, when citizens seek to engage, they are
overwhelmed by propaganda and victimized by voter suppression? Can
what remains be called a democracy? Of course not. Yet, this is the
current state of "democracy" in America. This is how it is experienced
now by the vast majority of Americans. And this is the essential challenge Americans face as they grapple with the pressing issues posed
by technological change, stagnation, and the threat of an increasingly
jobless economy.

The United States retains the façade of democracy. It remains a democracy on paper and in our hearts. But ours is, increasingly, a citizenless democracy. In the interregnum between the Progressive Era and the New Deal, Supreme Court Justice Louis Brandeis would write without irony that "the most important political office is that of the private citizen." Ninety years on, no one who is serious about the American scheme of things today would suggest, except for purposes of comedy, that the private citizen holds any position of importance. Oligarchs and their servants call the shots for the feudal serfs of corporate capital. This would be an unacceptable circumstance at any time in history, but it is an absolutely devastating development in a moment of great economic and social change.

The United States, like many other nations, is at an impasse. A spectacular digital revolution has the capacity to solve the "economic problem," as defined by Keynes, and to make a revolutionary turn *for the better* in the human condition. Under the best of circumstances and sufficient democratic participation and leadership, the curse of widespread unemployment and poverty could, like a caterpillar, become the butterfly of a post-scarcity democracy, where no one suffers from economic insecurity and all are able to develop their faculties in a manner historically available only to the privileged. But this very same technological revolution can also generate an opposite outcome. It all comes down to a series of political decisions that people and governments will make regarding how these technologies will be deployed, how the wealth generated by change will be distributed, and what sort of political and economic institutions will prevail in the twenty-first century.

With the exception of questions of war and peace, nowhere are debates about the role of government more vital than when they involve great economic issues. The way in which economic debates are resolved, the way in which economic policy is set, determines the future of the United States and its people. How could it be otherwise? The issues are definitional. The decisions set acceptable levels of employment and unemployment; they influence how and where jobs will be created, and whether those jobs will pay a living wage and provide humane working conditions; they determine how corporations and individuals will be taxed, and at what rate and for what purpose; they establish regulations (or a lack of regulations) for banks and brokers, and for the interactions of those banks and brokers with families and communities; and they make choices about global trade policy that assume virtual constitutional authority, inasmuch as trade agreements can literally trump a nation's laws. When new issues arise, when new challenges develop, the response of the government locks in approaches and policies—including regulatory frameworks—that decide how the economy will work for decades to come. It is in these debates that the United States decides whether the future belongs to the billionaires or the rest of us. Yet, the rest of us are shunted aside rather than invited to participate.

This aggressive disregard for the people is made possible by a decay of democratic infrastructure that is now so severe that citizens are, for the most part, an afterthought when it comes to decision-making about the economy. This feeds an alienation that is confirmed by appallingly low voter-turnout rates, especially among the young and the poor. People are "voting with their feet," but they have nowhere to go. In the absence of an engaged citizenry, economic crimes are committed and the criminals are rewarded. Don't believe us? Let's return to the scene of the crime of this century: the bailout of the bankers who crashed the global economy in 2008.

TOO IMPORTANT FOR DEMOCRACY

Members of Congress rarely acknowledge that, when it comes to the most important economic choices, power does not rest with them, let alone with the people of the United States. Yet, when Congresswoman Marcy Kaptur appeared in Michael Moore's 2009 film *Capitalism: A Love Story*, he asked her, "Do you think it's too harsh to call what has happened here a coup d'état? A financial coup d'état?"

"I could agree with that," said Kaptur, one of the longest-serving members of the current Congress, a key player on the powerful House Appropriations Committee, and a former domestic policy adviser to

President Jimmy Carter. "I could agree with that. Because the people here really aren't in charge. Wall Street is in charge."[2]

Kaptur is right about the influence of economic elites on issues of concern to their bottom lines—an influence that is now so immense that, even when the wealthy cause a crisis, they are rewarded. But what Kaptur says about relatively well-recognized catastrophes such as the Wall Street crash and the economic meltdown that extended from it goes double for catastrophes that are in the making. How can a country that cannot have a reasonable, realistic, and ultimately useful debate when an issue of enormous consequence is staring it in the face—say, for instance, the collapse of the global economy—possibly embark upon the necessary discussion about a digital revolution that may be every bit as disruptive as the industrial revolution? How can a political process that does not dare question the authority of economic elites whose greed and lack of foresight so obviously created a crisis for the great mass of Americans begin to ask the right questions about a jobs crisis that is still in the making? How can citizens challenge a new generation of cyber elites, often working in conjunction with the same old investment bankers and Wall Street charlatans? How do people who are struggling just to get by cut through the spin that claims that the cruelest of cuts must be accepted as the "creative destruction" of a new age? How can America possibly debate the future when so many issues of consequence are taken off the table in the present?

After Wall Street speculators crashed the global economy in 2008, it was obvious that the people were not in charge. Instead of cracking down on the speculators, Congress started writing checks to bail them out. "Think about what these banks have done. They have taken very imprudent behavior, irresponsible. They have really gambled, all right? And in many cases, been involved in fraudulent activity," Kaptur explained. "And then when they lost, they shifted their losses to the taxpayer." The big banks are coddled. "Their bed is feathered," complained Kaptur, who explained that, when it comes to representing the interests of the great mass of citizens who need a strong government to counter the influence of corporate power, "Congress has really shut down."[3]

Kaptur's assessment was correct. She got credit for her frankness. But no real change. What was briefly repaired was broken again by the same powerful interests that did the initial damage. The pulled-punches "reforms" contained in the 2010 Dodd-Frank legislation that attempted to impose a mild measure of regulation on big banks were being undone just a few years later; so much so that Republican lawmakers joked openly and unapologetically about the success of their efforts to "undermine aspects of Dodd-Frank."[4] A 2014 Center for Public Integrity study concluded that "less than six years after a massive financial crisis drove the U.S. banking system to the edge of collapse, leading to a $700 billion government bailout and a recession that destroyed as much as $34 trillion in wealth, bankers and lawmakers are working in concert to undermine Dodd-Frank, an 849-page law designed to prevent another failure."[5]

Even when the people win, they lose. And, eventually, a lot of the people give up. This explains how, in the parlance of politics, issues can be taken *off the table*. For the elites to prevail, it is no longer necessary that the people accept all the spin, all the propaganda, all the lies. It is sufficient if citizens are simply overwhelmed by an empty and dispiriting politics that never seems to go right. If nothing that is fixed remains fixed, why bother trying? Why bother voting?

The bank bailout in 2008 provides the most glaring example of how this works, and of how a crisis of economic policy becomes a crisis for democracy. Michael Moore made a movie about it and, to this day, political figures on the left and right grumble about it—including, notably, cynics like former House Budget Committee chairman Paul Ryan, who engineered Republican support for the bailout in 2008 and then decried the deal as his party's vice-presidential nominee in 2012. The cynicism is bipartisan. Former President Bill Clinton, who signed legislation that eliminated the Glass-Steagall barrier against risky banking practices (and who journalist Robert Scheer aptly observed "bears as much responsibility as any politician for the worst economic crisis since the Great Depression"[6]) had the nerve to deliver a 2012 Democratic National Convention address in which he complained about politicians who "want to get rid of those pesky financial regulations designed to prevent another crash and prohibit future bailouts."[7]

There's a reason why Ron Suskind titled his book on the Wall Street bailout and its aftermath *Confidence Men*. The classic definition of a "confidence man" points to a scam artist who wins the trust of people by feigning care and concern. Then, when the victims let their guard down, placing their faith in the confidence man to do right by them, the defrauding begins. Suskind revealed the hidden history of Wall Street and the White House in the months and years following the 2008 meltdown, and how political and economic elites "manufactured" confidence when they should have been taking necessary steps to eliminate the threat posed by "too-big-to-fail" banks and the pathologies that extend from them.[8] But the "confidence man" analogy goes for economic debates in general. We are told to relax because the smartest men in the room have this covered. In fact, what they are covering are their own backsides and their own greed. The more complex an issue becomes—and the more money that is at stake—the more the confidence men seek to take that issue off the table. "If 'Too Big to Fail' and 'Too Connected to Fail' have become the slogans justifying the repeated government bailouts of some major banks and insurers such as A.I.G., these firms' continued resistance to tighter government restrictions might be summed up as 'Too Complex to Regulate,'" observed Andrea Orr of the Economic Policy Institute.[9]

"THE SYSTEM IS RIGGED"

The same argument is peddled when tax policy is debated. Americans are told that tax cuts for the wealthy and for multinational corporations must simply be accepted on faith as the necessary cost of doing business in modern times. The argument has gone so well that, since Dwight Eisenhower was president, the top federal income tax rate has collapsed from 91 percent to 70 percent to 50 percent to 39.6 percent under a Democratic president who is decried by his right-wing critics as a socialist.[10] The rate decline does not begin to tell the story of the extent to which corporations and billionaires have restructured the tax code to avoid paying their fair share—and to literally redistribute wealth upward. "[Every] few months there's a new report on big corporations working the system," says Senator Elizabeth Warren. "One recent report showed that, of the big corporations in the S&P 500, 115 paid less than 20% in taxes. Another report claimed that, of 280 of the biggest corporations in the country, 78 paid nothing in taxes during one of the last three years."[11] Billionaire Warren Buffett reminds us that, thanks to loopholes that let investors like him avoid taxes, his rate is lower than that of his secretary. Indeed, says Buffett, he's often "the lowest-paying taxpayer in the office."[12]

For much of the twentieth century, this state of affairs would have been unthinkable. Progressive income taxation—in which the richest Americans pay at a higher marginal rate than those with lower incomes—was accepted as good for the economy and good for democracy. Everyone knew that progressive taxation enhanced equality, and that it communicated to rich and poor alike that Americans were "all in this together." Progressive tax policy was part of the democratic infrastructure.

But no longer. Americans have been told for decades now that they must accept supply-side strategies that are so convoluted in their construction, and so obviously flawed in their execution, that former President George Herbert Walker Bush—no liberal he—famously referred to them as "voodoo economics." Anyone who pays attention to the data knows that, as Rick Unger of *Forbes* has explained, while tax-cut proposals "can save the wealthy a healthy chunk of money" they "are highly unlikely to do much of anything for our economy." Writing for one of the most pro-business publications in America, Unger argues that, "we have an obligation to consider the benefits of a tax cut versus the long-term damage to the country."[13]

Yet, when it comes to tax debates, virtually all Republicans and most Democrats refuse to adopt even this simple standard of fiscal and social responsibility. In so doing, they shut down serious discussion about how tax policy shapes our economic reality, and about how tax policy could be used not merely to fund government but to address issues that Democrats and Republicans, liberals and conservatives, agree are challenging the stability of society. Income inequality is now broadly accepted as a serious issue in the United States. No surprise there, as the gap not just between the rich and poor but between the exceptionally rich and everyone else is widening at an exponential rate.

University of California-Berkeley economics professor Emmanuel Saez determined that the top 1 percent of Americans captured 91 percent of all income gains from 2009 to 2012, the initial years of recovery from the Great Recession. Saez based his research on pretax, pre-government-benefit income, explaining, "That's the key stat to think about how the market allocates incomes in the first place. Anybody should be worried that the recovery from the Great Recession has been so skewed in terms of market incomes."[14] Justin Wolfers, a senior fellow at the Peterson Institute for International Economics, did additional research on the later years of the recovery and determined that "so far all of the gains of the recovery have gone to the top 1 percent."[15] *All* of the gains.*

Economic Policy Institute research on tax cuts and loopholes for the wealthy indicates that they have played an outsized role in expanding income inequality, such that "roughly 30 percent of the rise in post-tax, post-transfer inequality is attributable to erosions in the redistributive nature of tax and budget policy." Yet, while "tax policy [provides] one of the more concrete policy levers affecting inequality," the lever is not used. In fact, it is frequently pushed in the wrong direction.

Consider this: the billionaire-funded front groups that for years have tried to generate support for balancing budgets with "entitlement reform" invariably propose to "Fix the Debt" with an egalitarian sounding abstraction they call "shared sacrifice." There's always plenty of sacrifice on the part of poor and the elderly. But the share that the billionaires and corporate CEOs get to keep invariably ends up as . . .

---

* Confirming what he refers to as "the narrative that the economic recovery so far has only boosted the incomes of the rich, and it has yielded no improvement for the bottom 99 percent of the distribution," Wolfers noted that "after adjusting for inflation, the average income for the richest 1 percent (excluding capital gains) has risen from $871,100 in 2009 to $968,000 over 2012 and 2013. By contrast, for the remaining 99 percent, average incomes fell by a few dollars from $44,000 to $43,900."

more. A 2013 study of the inner workings of Wall Street mogul Pete Peterson's "long campaign to get Congress and the White House to cut Social Security, Medicare and Medicaid while providing tax breaks for corporations and the wealthy" found that many of the CEOs who had signed on to letters calling for austerity "head firms that pay a negative tax rate, like Honeywell, GE, Boeing and Verizon. And as the Public Accountability Initiative notes, many lobby to preserve costly tax breaks for the wealthy (including the 'carried interest' tax loophole that made Peterson a rich man) and to prevent a tax on Wall Street speculation."[16]

"Fix the Debt" firms are even pushing for a "territorial tax system" that will increase the debt by $1 trillion over ten years and encourage the offshoring of American jobs. Why would supposed debt slayers favor this boondoggle? Because, the Institute for Policy Studies calculates, at least sixty-three "Fix-the-Debt firms would divvy up a $134 billion windfall."[17] No way that proposal would get traction, right? Wrong. Speaker of the House Paul Ryan, the Wisconsin Republican who formerly chaired that powerful House Ways and Means Committee, has long been a staunch supporter of the "territorial tax" scheme, which would let US-based multinational corporations avoid paying taxes on dividends they receive from foreign affiliates—a huge tax break for corporations and an invitation to offshore operations. No surprise there. Ryan is always pitching proposals to balance budgets on the backs of working people (Medicaid vouchers, raising the retirement age, gambling Social Security money on Wall Street) while opposing tax hikes for wealthy campaign donors and corporations.[18]

What was surprising was the 2013 Reuters report headlined: "Obama might back territorial tax system: business chief."[19] The president had just been reelected after he ripped Republican presidential nominee Mitt Romney and Ryan—the party's vice-presidential standard bearer—for proposing tax breaks for billionaires and corporations that would not "invest in our children's education or rebuild our roads or put more folks back to work."[20] Now a White House official was telling Reuters that, while the president was not up for "a pure territorial system" he was "eager to 'pursue corporate tax reform that lowers the rate.'"[21] Obama's impure compromise of 2015 was to tax the off-shore profits of corporations at a rate of 14 percent—as opposed to the statutory federal income tax rate of 35 percent. Citizens for Tax Justice, the watchdog and advocacy group responsible for ground-breaking reports of corporate tax evasion, examined the Obama plan and concluded that "it's hard to see why his approach makes sense. The companies currently holding profits in foreign tax havens accumulated these profits over a period when the statutory federal income tax rate stood at its current 35 percent. These companies shifted some of their profits offshore to avoid paying the statutory rate on their U.S. profits, and they should not receive a reward for dodging their tax bills in the form of a substantially lower tax rate."[22]

Yes, it is hard to see how this approach makes much sense, unless of course tax proposals that ask wealthy individuals and corporations to pay their fair share are *off the table*. And, for the most part, they are. Not officially off the table, mind you. President Obama and others still float tax-the-rich proposals, and they can even get a bit of traction. But the option of seriously taxing the rich, as happened in the days of radicals like Richard Nixon and Gerald Ford, is so far off the table that it is ridiculed. The Washington groupthink is as ubiquitous as it is favorable to the elites. In 2015, when Vermont Senator Bernie Sanders and Illinois Congresswoman Jan Schakowsky introduced a modest proposal to close corporate loopholes, with an eye toward raising needed revenues and removing incentives to move jobs overseas, *Forbes* explained that the proposal was "swimming against the tide of conventional thinking" because so many "policymakers today take it for granted that foreign investment must be subsidized through the tax code."[23]

Not popular wisdom, mind you. Polls routinely show that there is overwhelming support for taxing billionaires and banks at substantially higher rates. A February 2015 AP survey found that "68 percent of those questioned said wealthy households pay too little in federal taxes; only 11 percent said the wealthy pay too much." Fifty-six percent of those surveyed favored substantial new taxes on the immense capital gains of the rich (including 46 percent of Republicans) while just 16 percent were opposed. New taxes on banks were winning by a margin of almost four to one. The people weren't signaling a desire for minor tinkering with the tax code, observed the AP analysis. "The findings echo the populist messages of two liberal senators—Warren of Massachusetts and Sanders of Vermont."[24] In other words, when it comes to tax policy, the popular will is with one senator who says "the system is rigged"[25] and another who complains that the United States is becoming "a plutocracy . . . of the rich, for the rich and by the rich."[26]

But popular will does not steer the debate, or the policymaking, in Washington or most state capitals these days. If it did, the government would not merely be taxing corporations and the rich. It would be creating millions of jobs right now, urgently studying the changes and challenges posed by automation and anticipating the threat of an increasingly jobless economy. Unfortunately, for all the talk among politicians and pundits about their reverence for "job creators"—the current term of art for tax-dodging corporations and billionaires—job creation is also off the table. Way off.

FORGETTING FULL EMPLOYMENT

When the Great Recession was at its worst, in the fall of 2009, unemployment "peaked" at 10 percent. The United Nations reported that the United States and other developed countries were experiencing "a jobs crisis" with "sustained and devastating impacts on individuals, families, households and their communities." Job losses, the UN explained, had "pushed countless families into financial and economic hardship, resulting in the loss of homes to foreclosure and increases in poverty, debt and bankruptcy, especially in the United States and other advanced economies."[27] A *US News and World Report* headline asked "Is Unemployment the Worst since the Great Depression?"[28] (Answer: Not quite, but "it won't take much to get it to the worst since the Great Depression.") *CNN*'s Lou Dobbs spoke of an "unemployment nightmare." The *New York Times*'s Bob Herbert declared, "We're hurtin' and there ain't much healin' on the horizon."[29]

Unfortunately, the misery has not ended, even if the news media coverage of it has. The official unemployment rate did begin to decrease after hitting its peak in the fall of 2009. Five years later, it finally fell below 6 percent, and it continued to creep down to 5.5 percent in mid-2015.[30] As we note in Chapter 2, the "official" unemployment rate is only one of the many strands of data about unemployment produced by the Bureau of Labor Statistics. While there is an "official" unemployment rate identified as the "U-3" figure that is reported each month as the measure of what percentage of folks have jobs and what percentage do not, there is also an "unofficial" rate, the "U-6" figure, that more precisely measures the number of Americans who are not just unemployed but also those who have given up actively looking for work and those so "underemployed" that are unlikely to be able to support themselves or their families.[31] *Forbes* says, and we agree, that the "unofficial" U-6 number is "a better (though still flawed) indicator of labor market conditions." While the U-3 number is unreasonably optimistic, the U-6 number is realistic.

The two numbers are very different. For instance, while the "official" unemployment rate was 5.5 percent in March 2015, when there was much celebration about the recovery from the Great Recession, the "unofficial" rate was 10.9 percent. That's right, almost six years after the official unemployment rate "peaked" in 2009, the realistic unemployment rate in 2015 was still at a level that 2009 reports characterized as a "nightmare." For many Americans this is indeed a living nightmare of epic proportions. The pioneering analysts of modern American inequality Chuck Collins and Felice Yeskel long ago argued that there is "economic apartheid in America," producing powerful evidence of connections between racial disparity and economic inequality. Nowhere is this more evident than in the jobless data of not just the recent past but right now.[32] The *Atlantic* reminds us that "the unemployment rate for blacks has always been at least 60 percent higher than for whites."[33] Among young African American men today, joblessness is five times higher than for white Americans.[34] In deindustrialized urban communities, the number of people who are out of work is generally high, but for the young people of color, unemployment rates as high as 30 percent, 40 percent, 50 percent are startlingly common.[35]

Put another way: for millions of Americans, it is always a "worst since the Great Depression" moment. And in many regions their number is growing, as college graduates who thought their professional degrees would be tickets to the middle class find themselves competing for disappearing jobs with their parents.[36] What makes things even worse is that there is no Great Depression, nor even Great Recession, urgency on the part of the political class regarding joblessness in America. Instead of recognizing the need for action and intervention, there is celebration that things are "headed in the right direction"—along with a constant redefinition of the right direction. Unemployment rates that just a few decades ago were broadly seen as unreasonable are now accepted as "the new normal."

In the summer of 2012, as Democrats were renominating Barack Obama at a convention where speakers heralded the president's "new American Dream economy," the official unemployment rate was 8 percent and the actual rate was 14.7 percent.[37] Those numbers were higher than in 1984, when that year's Democratic nominee, Walter Mondale, decried high unemployment and the hopelessness of a nation where "the help-wanted ads are full of listings for executives, and for dishwashers—but not much in between."[38] Of course, politicians adjust their rhetoric based on their status as incumbents or challengers. But should we really accept that numbers that thirty years ago meant "working Americans are worse off, and the middle class is standing on a trap door" are now economically and politically acceptable?[39] If we do, then we should also accept that the goalposts aren't being moved, they are being taken down. After the Bureau of Labor Statistics reported in early 2015 that 295,000 Americans had filed for unemployment benefits, former White House counselor Bill Curry noted, "Economists called it good news, as the number was less than 300,000; that's the line they say separates good news from bad. But it isn't much less. . . . Job growth is anemic. Still, economists say things are going so well we can raise interest rates. They call that good news—though they don't say for whom."[40]

This is a relatively new development that speaks volumes about the disconnect between politics and people, and that provides a jarring reminder of how much effort it will take to get official Washington focused on debates about automation and the displacement of workers in a "new economy." Coming out of the Great Depression in the 1930s it was understood for a good two generations that pursuing policies to achieve full employment was a crucial issue for the government, perhaps second in importance only to national defense. After witnessing the rise of fascism in nations with catastrophic levels of joblessness, full employment was understood as necessary for both economic and political stability. It was a core component of the democratic infrastructure.

In the 1970s, when a spike in unemployment and inflation numbers stirred concerns about a possible recession—yes, there was a time in America when officials anticipated rather than merely responded to economic challenges—Minnesota Senator Hubert Humphrey and California Congressman Augustus Hawkins pushed for what came to be known as the "Humphrey-Hawkins Full-Employment Act." The measure proposed that the government establish standards for acceptable unemployment rates: not more than 3 percent for persons aged 20 or over and not more than 4 percent for persons aged 16 or over.[41] More important, Humphrey and Hawkins proposed that, if the private sector appeared to be falling short of those goals, the government would create a "reservoir of public employment." This was a Keynesian response, and it had a lot of popular appeal. The Humphrey-Hawkins proposal was embraced by Democratic presidential contenders, endorsed by newspaper editorial pages, and signed into law by President Jimmy Carter as the Full Employment and Balanced Growth Act of 1978. To this day, Duke University public policy professor William Darity Jr. reminds us, "The law charges the public sector with the responsibility of direct job creation."[42] Unfortunately, the charge has not been kept. What were originally proposed as standards were reimagined as "goals." Triggers for New Deal–style interventions were replaced with requirements for annual reports by the chairman of the Federal Reserve. The dream that serious economic planning and stability might replace chance and misery was dashed by a Democratic president and Congress in 1978 and abandoned altogether in the realigned America of Ronald Reagan. The year 1983, when full employment was supposed to be achieved under the law, began with a national unemployment rate of 10.4 percent; states such as Michigan and West Virginia had jobless rates over 15 percent; and 21.2 percent of African Americans were out of work.

Reagan refused to take meaningful action to address unemployment, and he refused even to consider creating a "reservoir of public employment." Reagan peddled an anti-Keynesian fantasy that said the worst possible approach to unemployment was for the government to start creating jobs. And this fantasy has held ever since. Democratic presidents may support some stimulus spending in hard times—especially if it is linked to tax breaks, as was Barack Obama's 2009 plan—while Republicans just want the tax breaks.

There are still a few outliers like Michigan Congressman John Conyers Jr., who in 2013 rejected the happy talk of recovery from the Great Recession and instead proposed what he called the "Humphrey-Hawkins Full Employment and Training Act." Though the bill title was nostalgic, the senior member of the House was recognizing contemporary challenges and anticipating jobless economics: "Since 2000 more than 50,000 manufacturing facilities in the U.S. have closed and roughly 50,000 industrial jobs have been lost each month," he explained, adding that

> now service sector jobs, where the remaining two-thirds of all workers are currently employed, are disappearing. Because of, but not limited to technology advances, these middle-income jobs are not likely to come back, effectively hollowing out . . . America's middle class and leaving millions of unemployed and underemployed workers with limited future prospects. The effect of these trends on American jobs were significantly aggravated by the "Great Recession."[43]

"During the Great Depression, President Roosevelt's New Deal put millions of Americans back to work building roads, dams, bridges, parks and electrification systems," Conyers concluded. "There is no reason why America cannot have a 21st century 'New Deal,' where unemployed Americans can be gainfully employed rebuilding our crumbling infrastructure and strengthening our communities."[44] Actually, there is a reason. Unlike in the period from the 1930s through the 1970s, when presidents and Congresses and the media were prepared to engage in serious debates about joblessness and government intervention to achieve full employment, the initiative by Conyers has gone absolutely nowhere. Even on the cusp of a Great Recession, even under a Democratic president with a Democratic Senate and for a time with a Democratic House, full employment was off the table. Just where Ronald Reagan wanted it. And it is a non-story in the news media.

Reagan's great contribution—if it can be called that—to debates about jobs and economic policy in the United States was to convince most of the political class, virtually all of the media, and a substantial portion of the American people that Keynes and FDR were wrong about the role government could play in addressing the loss of jobs, income, and opportunity. As we've noted, Reagan began his presidency by declaring, on the cusp of a scorching recession, that "in this present crisis, government is not the solution to our problem; government is the problem." Reagan turned the United States hard against industrial policy and investment in job creation, and harder still toward a policy of deferring to corporations with regard to essential issues such as domestic investment and global trade. It was a disastrous turn, as an irony of history illustrates. In early 1983, when unemployment in America was near its peak, Reagan told the country that everything was going to be fine because he has just visited a Chrysler plant in Fenton, Missouri, "where 1,700 workers are being called back to a newly modernized plant."[45]

There were two Chrysler plants in Fenton. But no more. When the Great Recession hit, Chrysler slid into bankruptcy. It got a huge government bailout, which supposedly "saved the auto industry." But, under the North American Free Trade Agreement, production was moved from one plant to Canada and from the other to Mexico. As the second plant was shuttered in Fenton in 2009, thousands of United Auto Workers union members rallied outside it. The local UAW president told the crowd, "This is no longer a business issue, but a social issue. The corporations failed and they had to borrow from the U.S. taxpayers. Now they want to carry U.S. taxpayers' money across the borders."[46]

Which brings us to trade policy—the economic issue that presidents since Reagan have worked hardest to keep off the table.

TRADE DEALS: "WHERE THE REAL KNIFE WAS PUT IN THE FLESH"

For Americans who seek the debate that must be had about the intersection of technology and society—and about the damage that is done when political and economic and media elites take issues off the table—Kaptur has some counsel: consider how this country handles trade policy. This, she says, is "where the real knife was put in the flesh."[47]

As with debates about technological change and the dislocation that extends from it, debates about trade policy are portrayed as complicated—too complicated for citizens and even for members of Congress to understand. As with debates about technological change, debates about trade policy are portrayed as delicate—too delicate to be trusted to popular opinion or popular intervention. As with debates about technological change, debates about trade policy are portrayed as essential—too essential to question the deals that are done or the deals that will be done. Those who raise concerns about the economic and social disruption that results from flawed trade policies are constantly portrayed as ill-informed or simply emotional about change that is inevitable. Critics of specific free-trade agreements and the broader model of international arrangement on which they are constructed find themselves dismissed by the likes of Anne O. Krueger, a top International Monetary Fund official, as having just two motivations: "One was fear; the other a desire to protect vested interests."[48]

Media outlets amplify this jingoism, rarely asking if there might be reason to fear, never considering that the "vested interests" are working families and the planet.

The *Wall Street Journal* editorial page preaches the free-trade gospel with abandon, griping about how "on the right and the left you get critics who are protectionist," while the *New York Times* features cheerleading headlines about "Globalization that Works for Workers at Home."[49] And political leaders of both parties declare that, even if past trade deals have never turned out as well as promised, opposition is pointless—and dangerous. Yes, President Obama acknowledged in a 2014 speech, there may be "pushback" against new trade deals, opposition based on "a public perception generally that trade has resulted in an erosion of our manufacturing base as companies moved overseas in search of lower-wage labor." Yes, Obama acknowledged that the perception might even have basis in fact—but he explained: "That horse is out of the barn [since] much of that shift in search of low-wage labor has already occurred."[50]

The message, delivered from every direction, is "shut up and give up."

One of the mistakes that is made in analyzing the failed politics of our times is to look for a "vast right-wing conspiracy" or the machination of a "hidden hand." In fact, economic and political elites are often quite open about their goals. Noam Chomsky suggested a quarter century ago that the great question is the obvious one: "whether democracy and freedom are values to be preserved or threats to be avoided."[51] Without saying so in precise terms, CEOs and newspaper editors and presidents tell us that, when an issue is really important, democracy and freedom are, indeed, threats to be avoided. It is, Americans are constantly reminded, better to let the technocrats, the self-interested and permanently engaged lobbyists, handle the complicated issues. Don't trust your own experience of shuttered factories and broken unions, let the experts who got us this far lead us deeper into the abyss. This goes double when debates involve future arrangements, on issues such as trade policy and automation. One of the reasons why the political discourse in the United States seems to whipsaw from crisis to crisis is that technocrats and the CEOs they work for are not inclined to put issues on the table when citizens could still have a role in developing policies. Best to tell the people *after the fact* that everything has been settled and that their prospects for repairing the damage done are slim because *that horse is out of the barn.*

As America approaches what must be a great debate about the changes that a digital age will usher in; as we consider the implications of technological changes that will eliminate millions of jobs, de-skill many of the jobs that remain, and create only a handful of new positions for digital managers and robot repairwomen; and as we look for ways in which to share rather than concentrate the wealth yielded by reducing workforces, it is vital to understand that the United States has been here before—frequently. And that the United States has messed up—badly. The problem was not that the people were too "protectionist," too fearful, too confused to make the right demands. The problem was that the people were aggressively discouraged from making demands that were every bit as appropriate, and far more necessary for society, than the demands of the CEOs and the bankers.

For more than thirty years, under Democratic and Republican presidents, with the approval of Congresses controlled by both parties, the United States has embraced trade and investment policies that the American Federation of Labor–Congress of Industrial Organizations argues "have reflected the influence of powerful corporate interests. They protect what's important to corporate America but do little or nothing to safeguard the rights of workers and the environment here and around the world. They fuel a race to the bottom in living standards."[52]

That race to the bottom has been measured, charted, detailed, and revealed. The data is devastating. Since Congress approved the North American Free Trade Agreement (NAFTA) between the United States, Canada, and Mexico in 1993, after a push by Democratic President Bill Clinton and Republican House Minority Whip Newt Gingrich, presidents and "opposition" leaders have in remarkably bipartisan fashion adopted a long list of Free Trade Agreements (FTAs) and related deals. Each of these FTAs has made it easier for multinational corporations to move jobs to countries with lower wages, fewer union protections, weaker environmental regulations, and lousier records of defending human rights. The result has been a hollowing out of American manufacturing that is well recognized in the communities that are on the frontlines of the deindustrialization of the United States. In 2001, shortly after a Republican-controlled Congress worked with President Clinton to provide China with most-favored-nation trading status, there were 398,887 private manufacturing facilities in the United States. A decade later, according to the Bureau of Labor Statistics Quarterly Census of Employment and Wages, the number had fallen to 342,647—a loss of 56,190 factories.[53]

It gets worse. According to a 2015 study by Public Citizen's Global Trade Watch, "the aggregate U.S. goods trade deficit with Free Trade Agreement (FTA) partners is more than five times as high as before the deals went into effect, while the aggregate trade deficit with non-FTA countries has actually fallen."[54] Trade deals as they are now done do not benefit the US economy, they benefit multinational corporations. Indeed, says US Senator Sherrod Brown, D-Ohio, "our trade deals amount to corporate handouts and worker sellouts."[55]

The biggest sellout is of democracy itself. Trade agreements in recent decades have established so-called Investor-State Dispute Settlement (ISDS) mechanisms. When a trade agreement that includes such a mechanism—as, for instance, did NAFTA—is approved by the Congress and signed by the president, multinational corporations are afforded a new avenue for challenging government laws and regulations in the United States. And the avenue is a friendly one for the corporations: an international tribunal, or "court," that has the authority to impose penalties on nations that pass laws that the tribunal determines to have erected a barrier to a foreign corporation maximizing profits. The penalties put actual economic pressure on nations to back away from taking steps to protect workers, farmers, consumers, and the environment. "Investor-state challenges were rare before the new millennium, but have become increasingly popular tools for corporations to use when challenging regulations they object to," explains Zach Carter, a former member of the steering committee of Americans for Financial Reform who writes about the impact of trade policy on domestic regulations. "Under the North American Free Trade Agreement, for instance, companies including Exxon Mobil, Dow Chemical and Eli Lilly have attempted to overrule Canadian regulations on offshore oil drilling, fracking, pesticides, drug patents and other issues."[56]

This is an extreme example of how issues are taken off the table—and of how popular movements that beat corporations in domestic-policy debates can still be thwarted. But it is increasingly popular in an age of globalization and ever-expanding corporate reach. That reach concerns progressive populists and honest conservatives. "[Under] ISDS, U.S. investors abroad and foreign investors in the United States can collect damages from the treasuries of their host governments by virtue of the judgments of arbitration panels that are entirely outside of the legal structure of the respective countries," observes Daniel Ikenson, the director of the Cato Institute's Herbert A. Stiefel Center for Trade Policy Studies. "This all raises serious questions about democratic accountability, sovereignty, checks and balances, and the separation of power."[57]

When progressive reformers from Americans for Financial Reform and Cato Institute libertarians are in agreement, that ought to put issues on the table. In a functional democracy, where political parties compete on the basis of ideas and issues, revelations about "secret tribunals" with the power to impose fines on Americans for passing laws would be a call to the barricades. Yet, after the 2014 elections shifted control of the US Senate to Republicans who had spent the previous six years seeking to derail Barack Obama's presidency, Republican Senate Majority Leader Mitch McConnell embraced Obama's request for "Fast Track" Trade Promotion Authority to allow the president to negotiate a sweeping new Trans-Pacific Partnership trade deal without consulting Congress. Even as he admitted that "it's an enormous grant of power, obviously, from a Republican Congress to a Democratic president," McConnell said he was comfortable letting Obama do the deal without the procedural hurdles. Why? The Republican leader explained that "what the American people are saying is they want us to look for areas of agreement, and this certainly is one of them."[58]

No, they're not.

In 2014 Hart Research Associates and Chesapeake Beach Consulting polled Americans on the question of whether Congress should grant "Fast Track" authority to the president. Sixty-two percent of those surveyed said they were opposed, while only 28 percent expressed support—and only 12 percent were firmly in favor of the idea. "Demographically, opposition is very broad, with no more than one-third of voters in any region of the country or in any age cohort favoring fast track," reported the pollsters. Then they did something fascinating. Recognizing that Americans get limited information about trade debates, the pollsters set out "to simulate a public debate over the merits of fast track and the proposed TPP trade deal, by presenting each respondent with an equal number of arguments made by organizations supporting and opposing fast track." With more information, overall opposition rose to 65 percent.[59]

McConnell was entirely wrong about the will of the people, a fact that could not have escaped the wily career politician. But the senator had a clear sense of his political responsibility in a country where men like McConnell understand the "democratic infrastructure" as a network of campaign donors and lobbyists. The top donors to McConnell's 2014 reelection bid were individuals and political action committees associated with the "Securities and Investment" industries—ardent supporters of free trade.[60] McConnell was also clear that he would not be called out for rejecting the popular will. In an age of steadily stenographic media coverage of economic debates, there is little or no accountability on complex issues for politicians such as Mitch McConnell—or Barack Obama.

When Obama was bidding for the Democratic presidency nomination in 2008, he defined himself as a candidate of "hope and change" in a number of ways. He thrilled labor audiences in primary states such as Wisconsin by denouncing policies that had saddled the United States with NAFTA, the permanent normalization of trade with China, and yawning trade deficits. Obama promised to scrap the secretive, "backroom-deal" negotiating style of "Fast Track" agreements that elbowed the Congress and the American people out of the process. He talked about renegotiating NAFTA to add safeguards for the environment and labor rights. If Canada and other trading partners rejected changes, Obama said he was open to exiting the agreements altogether. It seemed as if a new day was dawning when it came to the trade policy—or, at the very least, in the approach of a too-frequently-compromised Democratic Party.[61]

Then came reports that Obama's senior economic adviser, Austin Goolsbee, had quietly assured the Canadians that the candidate's statements were not to be believed—that his populist appeals in working-class towns battered by trade-related layoffs and factory closings "should be viewed as more about political positioning than a clear articulation of policy plans."[62] When the news broke, before the critical Ohio primary, Obama aides pointed political journalists toward reports that his rival for the Democratic nomination, Hillary Clinton, had apparently had aides provide similar "not to worry" assurances to the Canadians. Reporters who had never bothered to connect the dots between trade policies, shuttered factories, and the righteous indignation of Ohio workers were lapping up the "he-said, she-said" scrap.[63] The controversy grew so intense that Obama had to address it. He told a Cleveland TV station: "I think it's important for viewers to understand that [the claim that he was saying one thing to workers and another thing to Wall Street elites and foreign governments] was not true."[64]

Obama lost Ohio, but he won enough other states to secure the nomination. Then, within days of assembling the delegates he needed, *Fortune* magazine featured an interview with the candidate headlined "Obama: NAFTA Not So Bad after All."[65] Reminded that during the primary season he had referred to NAFTA as "devastating" and suggested he might use an opt-out clause in the trade agreement between the United States, Canada, and Mexico, Obama replied, "Sometimes during campaigns the rhetoric gets overheated and amplified."

"Politicians are always guilty of that, and I don't exempt myself," Obama continued. Abandoning the tough talk of just a few months earlier, Obama sounded an awful lot like the free-trader the Canadians had been assured he would be. All that primary-season rhetoric about fighting to protect workers, was just, Obama said, another way of "opening up a dialogue." *Fortune* was satisfied. "The general campaign is on, independent voters up for grabs, and Barack Obama is toning down his populist rhetoric—at least when it comes to free trade." Yes, of course, the business magazine observed, NAFTA would remain "the bugaboo of union leaders, grassroots activists and Midwesterners who blame free trade for the factory closings they see in their hometowns." But the CEOs and the bankers could rest assured, *Fortune* chirped, for "the presumptive Democratic nominee suggests he doesn't want to unilaterally blow up NAFTA after all."[66]

Journalist and commentator David Sirota summed the whole charade up when he explained, "Here you have a policy—NAFTA—that is among the most unpopular policies of the last generation, according to polls. Here you have a candidate who campaigned against it in the primary. And within weeks of getting the general election, here you have that same candidate running to Corporate America's magazine of record to reassure Wall Street about that same policy."[67] President Obama did more than that. Despite opposition from the workers and environmentalists and human rights activists he promised to represent, he signed sweeping free-trade agreements with South Korea, Colombia, and Panama.[68] And in his 2015 State of the Union Address the president announced that he wanted to work with McConnell and the Republicans to enact the biggest trade agreements since NAFTA: the Trans-Pacific Partnership (TPP) with Asian countries and a Transatlantic Trade and Investment Partnership (TTIP) with Europe.

Members of Obama's own party, led by Senators Elizabeth Warren and Bernie Sanders, raised objections. But the president was having none of it. He ripped on his fellow Democrats and labor unions that raised entirely legitimate democracy concerns about specific threats to financial regulations—saying they "don't know what they're talking about." The president actually compared his own party's progressives to the conspiracy theorists on the right. Recalling that Tea Party activists had tried to derail healthcare reform with claims that

"ObamaCare" would create "death panels," the president said, "Some-one coming up with a slogan like 'death panels' doesn't mean it's true. The same thing is true on this."[69]

Why is President Obama using all of his political capital, and then some, to advance an issue embraced by his ostensible political opponents and detested by most of the Americans who voted him into office twice? The answer has everything to do with the reshaping of American politics so that, when citizens try to cut through the spin, when they get engaged and decide to put an issue on the table, they find themselves pushing against stenographic media, big-money politics, and the structural barriers to democracy itself. Welcome to citizenless democracy.

OUR SHRIVELED POLITICAL CULTURE

Nothing says "shut up and give up" quite so effectively as a candidate who tells the people that he will champion their interests on a complex issue that matters greatly to them and then, upon his nomination and election, signals that he cannot possibly deliver on the promise. It bakes in cynicism about politics and about what is possible in a democracy—signaling that the fundamental issues really are off the table. This is the means by which unelected bankers and billionaires most effectively and steadily define the popular discourse, placing issues of concern to their bottom lines out of reach for the great mass of citizens. Then, the elites need only convince a handful of policy-makers who are, for reasons of campaign finance, eternally beholden to them. The bigger the issue, invariably, the more "off-limits" it is. In this calculus, politics becomes boring, as it does not discuss that which matters most. Voters check out from the electoral process, and citizens question the value of organizing around issues. This is fine by the elites, and by the political mandarins who implement their agenda. It is devastating for democracy.

The news media plays a crucial role in keeping democracy citizen-less, as the examples we have focused on illustrate. Mainstream journalism, even at its best, generally takes its cues for what the range of legitimate debate is on an issue by what political and economic elites say about the issue. That is considered "professional" and "nonpartisan." If elites are all in concert on an issue—as with ending progressive taxation, abandoning full employment as a serious policy objective, or fast-tracking secretive trade deals—the news media rarely provides much if any critical analysis. That would be "unprofessional" and "ideological." In the current crisis that is decimating the commercial model for journalism, the amount of resources for actual hard-digging into the actual planning and ambitions of the powerful is generally non-existent, and not something corporate owners have shown much inclination to encourage.

As for political journalism, with a few fine exceptions, it is mostly pointless gossip and nutritionless assessments of spin and polls. With regard to political campaigns the journalism hits rock bottom. Rather than note that the emperor is wearing no clothes, or that the complete corruption of the electoral process by what former US Senator Russ Feingold describes as "legalized bribery"[70] makes a mockery of self-government, the news media plays along with the fiction that the elections accurately represent the will of the people, and that elected "representatives" will represent the interests of the voters. That hardly anyone votes by global democratic standards is almost never mentioned, as this would call into question the general hype about democracy-in-action proffered otherwise, and it would force TV pundits in particular to confront directly the asininity of political advertising, the campaign lingua franca of these times. It would also require a persistent and unyielding exposure of the influence of billionaires over the election process.[71]

Each new election cycle consolidates the power of those who would manipulate not just the politics of the country but a crony capitalist enterprise so rewarding that tiny "investments" of campaign contributions yield "returns" now measured in billions. Las Vegas casino mogul Sheldon Adelson gave roughly $200 million to various and sundry conservative causes and candidates in 2012.[72] By 2014 his wealth had risen to $40 billion—helped along, the smart betting suggests, by the relaxed approach of federal, state, and local regulators and investigators to complaints about unsavory business practices.[73] It is true that $200 million sounds like a lot of money, but Adelson is so rich that he could spend $200 million *every week for three straight years* and still be a billionaire. He can find that cash in his spare-change jar. But that misses the point: buying politicians is not a high-end consumer good for Adelson, or the other billionaires and corporations that bankroll American politics today. It is an investment. What does Adelson get for his $200 million? A smooth ride to the top. According to *Forbes*, "Adelson added more to his fortune than any other person (in the world)" in 2013 and his ranking on the magazine's 2014 list of the billionaires moved to No. 8.[74] That placed him a rung or so below brothers Charles and David Koch, whose "donor network" steered at least $400 million into the 2012 campaign cycle and then came back with plans for a "$300 Million Spending Spree" in the non-presidential campaign season of 2014.[75] But Adelson was a rung or so above members of the Walton family, who have for years used their Walmart largesse to slather candidates who are ready to attack public education with campaign cash and structural support.[76]

So much money flows into campaigns, and the lobbying that polices the governments that extend from those campaigns, that each new election cycle sets new records for campaign fund-raising and expenditures—with total spending for the federal, state, local, judicial, and referendum races of 2012 surpassing $10 billion.[77] The records are barely noted as they are surpassed so quickly and so steadily. What is noted, albeit briefly, are the announcements that point to the next plateau. When it was revealed that the network of billionaires established by the Koch brothers to advance their business agenda planned to spend almost $900 million to influence the politics of 2016, it was news—for a day. But instead of raging against the acquisition of government by non-state players with little or no interest in the common good—as the crusader editors of old did—the news of the latest Koch initiative on behalf of favored Republicans inspired today's major media outlets to fevered speculation about whether and how Democratic donors might match the spending.[78]

The deplorable state of American governance is not an accident. Those economic elites and their mandarins are, in fact, endeavoring on a regular basis to make American democracy less functional and less real. Their most overt machinations are evident to engaged citizens and members of Congress, who raise an appropriate outcry when the activist majority on the US Supreme Court hands down a particularly egregious decision to flood more money into politics, as was the case with the 2010 *Citizens United v. Federal Election Commission* and 2014 *McCutcheon v. Federal Election Commission* rulings, or when a similar majority invalidates key sections of the Voting Rights Act, as was the case with their 2013 *Shelby County v. Holder* ruling. The 2014 headline on an analysis for the Reuters news service by Constitutional Accountability Center chief counsel Elizabeth B. Wydra got it right: the mantra of the court majority led by Chief Justice John Roberts has become "Easier to Donate, Harder to Vote."[79]

America's two major political parties differ rhetorically on plenty of issues, and they are each quick to accuse the other of every manner of atrociousness. Yet the Republicans and Democrats are remarkably collaborative when it comes to gaming the system. "Our giving is very equal between parties across the country," Walmart's Brooke Buchanan says of corporate political action committee donations that in 2012 split 51 percent Republican and 49 percent Democratic—and who prove the maxim "the rich get richer" no matter which party is in power.[80] There really are populist Democrats such as Sanders and Warren who want to tax the rich and bust the banks, just as there really are Republicans such as Congressmen Justin Amash and Walter Jones Jr. who want to do something about crony capitalism—especially as it sustains a military-industrial complex that benefits (and benefits from) both parties.[81] But in an age that supposedly prizes "disruption," the real disrupters are often treated as political pariahs.

The Democratic Party's impulse toward progressive populism appears to be stronger and more broadly based than the Republican opposition to crony capitalism. Yet, despite what Rush Limbaugh says, the Democratic Party is not exactly threatening Wall Street. Democratic presidents are managerial as opposed to radical, as are most Democrats in Congress. After the party suffered a severe set-back in the 2014 midterm elections, author William Greider noted that "instead of addressing [the reality of economic misery and uncertainty in an agonizingly slow recovery] and proposing remedies, the Democrats ran on a cowardly, uninspiring platform: the Republicans are worse than we are. Undoubtedly, that's true—but so what?" President Obama and his party, said Greider, "have no credible solutions to offer. To get serious about inequality and the deteriorating middle class, Democrats would have to undo a lot of the damage their own party has done to the economy over the past thirty years."[82]

Like the Republicans, the Democrats want to chalk up political wins and to enjoy the power associated with those wins. As such, the party is more than willing to compromise not just policies but principles if there are funds to be raised or strategies to be implemented. So Democrats think, and act, a lot like Republicans when it comes to maintaining the infrastructure of democracy, which is to say they are not all that interested in the work. When Republican National Committee chairman Reince Priebus and the RNC restructured their 2016 nominating process in a way that made it less friendly to voters and more friendly to campaign donors—by cutting the number of debates and collapsing the schedule in a way that favored well-funded and establishment-friendly candidates—there was no great outcry from Democrats. In fact, New Hampshire Democratic Party chairman Ray Buckley, a vice chairman of the Democratic National Committee, explained that the Democrats would probably follow the Republican lead on a number of scheduling issues because, after all, "it is a choreographed dance that includes the RNC, the DNC, and of course, the states."[83]

By the fall of 2015, in fact, there was a good case to be made that when it came to scheduling debates, the Democratic National Committee was doing more damage to democracy—and to its own prospects—than the Republican National Committee. Two months after the Republican presidential candidates had started debating, the Democratic contenders were still waiting to take the stage. The Democratic schedule was so constrained, so restrictive, and so obviously intended to protect frontrunner Hillary Clinton from scrutiny that candidate Martin O'Malley, a former governor of Maryland who eight years earlier had backed Clinton, told a DNC meeting:

> Think about it. The Republicans stand before the nation, malign our president's record of achievements, denigrate women and immigrant families, double-down on trickle-down, and tell their false story. We respond with crickets, tumbleweeds, and a cynical move to delay and limit our own party debates. Four debates and only four debates—we are told, not asked—before voters in our earliest states make their decision. This is totally unprecedented in our party. This sort of rigged process has never been attempted before.

Calling for more debates, O'Malley bluntly declared, "We are the Democratic Party, not the Undemocratic Party. If we are to debate debates, the topic should be how many, not how few."[84]

As the stilted and dysfunctional 2016 campaign developed, it became increasingly evident that both of the nation's dominant political organizations had become Undemocratic Parties.

WHAT IF THEY GAVE AN ELECTION AND NOBODY CAME?

The great mass of Americans are not invited to the dance, so it should come as no surprise that they do not attend.

Voter participation in the United States, the first and most basic measure of democratic engagement, is declining to record-low levels. The decline has been sharp; so dramatic, in fact, that it raises profound questions about the viability of the American electoral process as a structure for engaging the great mass of citizens—and for constructing local, state, and federal governments that represent and advance the interests of the great mass of citizens.

Consider this: the 2014 midterm elections in the United States were the most costly in the history of the republic—with an overall price tag far in excess of the more than $4 billion formally reported for congressional elections.[85] They were aggressively fought and for good reason: a great deal was at stake. Control of the US Senate was up for grabs, and with it the ability of President Obama and his Democratic allies to guide the legislative agenda of the nation, to secure approval of nominees to the US Supreme Court and the federal bench, to open up or shut down investigations, to force compromises on questions of taxation and spending. At the state level, where the brutal battles over labor rights, public education, and social services had played out over the previous four years, the overwhelming majority of governorships and legislative seats were up for election.[86] Former Republican National Committee chairman Haley Barbour announced that "the most important election for Republicans is 2014, not 2016." Vice President Joe Biden echoed the theme. "Folks," he shouted at a rally in Iowa, "this election is even more important than the two elections [where] you elected Barack and me."[87]

Even allowing for election-season hyperbole, it was clear that this election was a big deal. The wealthiest and most self-interested billionaires in America wore their hands out signing checks to finance the most intense campaigning the country had ever seen in a midterm election. The president jetted from battleground state to battleground state on a frenzied final schedule that literally had him crossing paths with top Republican campaigners on airport tarmacs. Thousands of candidates ran themselves ragged, tens of thousands of volunteers woke early and went to bed late in a final push toward an Election Day that produced results so dramatic that they drew not just domestic but international attention. The top-line results were good news for Republicans who took control of the US Senate, held the US House, and expanded their position of strength in the states. Yet, as the *New York Times* noted in an editorial published a week after the election, while the numbers were "bad for Democrats, [they were] even worse for democracy."[88]

If you met three Americans who were of voting age on the morning after Election Day 2014, two of them did not cast a ballot. The two nonvoters would, on balance, be younger and poorer than the one voter—meaning that a small, older, and relatively affluent minority picked the winners and defined the governance of the most powerful country in the world for the next two years. According to an analysis by *U.S. News and World Report*, "in exit polls from [the] midterms, for example, only 13 percent of voters were under 30. Nonvoters are also more racially diverse than the voting. . . . More than 40 percent of likely nonvoters in the 2014 elections identified as Hispanic, black or other racial/ethnic minorities, compared with 22 percent of likely voters."[89] Vermont Senator Sanders reflected on those figures and said, "We should not be satisfied with a 'democracy' in which more than 60 percent of our people don't vote and some 80 percent of young people and low-income Americans fail to vote."[90]

According to United States Elections Project estimates, just 33 percent of the voting-age population cast a ballot for the highest office on the ballot. That's less than the 36 percent turnout figure generally reported after the 2014 elections because the United States disenfranchises millions of American adults who are imprisoned, on probation, on parole, or who face other roadblocks to being able to vote.[91] But even using the restrictive standards that get us to the 36 percent figure, the collapse in participation was dramatic. The nation's most populous states, all of which had contests for governor, lower-level statewide posts, congressional seats, and in some cases US Senate seats, saw dismal turnout: 28 percent in Texas, 29 percent in New York, 31 percent in California. Forty-three states reported turnouts of less than 50 percent, which meant that their elections were decided by a minority of eligible voters.[92]

Turnout in 2014 was the worst since 1942, when the United States had just entered World War II. And a number of states, as *U.S. News and World Report* noted, "saw nosedives of crazy proportions"—drops of 10 percent or more from the rates seen in the relatively low-turnout 2010 election.[93]

Let's make this more concrete. Following both the 2010 and 2014 midterm elections, the pundits and news media were pontificating about how Americans had rejected Obama's policies and wanted a more conservative approach to governing. The implication was that millions of Americans got a taste of the Democrats and then switched over to the Republicans. One could logically conclude that Americans were clinically insane as they flip-flopped every two years from Democratic landslides to Republican landslides. In fact, very little of that happened. Instead, the younger and poorer Democrats simply stopped voting in midterm elections at much greater rates than did older and wealthier Republicans. This point is well understood in Republican circles, where repressing the voter turnout—especially among younger, poorer, and non-white citizens—has become job one for state governments over the past six years. But the approach is not new. In 1980 conservative political strategist Paul Weyrich laid out the strategy when he told a gathering of right-wing organizers, "I don't want everybody to vote. Elections are not won by a majority of people. They never have been from the beginning of our country, and they are not now. As a matter of fact our leverage in the elections quite candidly goes up as the voting populace goes down."[94]

Mission Accomplished! In the 2014 election the Republicans won a whopping 59-seat advantage over the Democrats in the 435-member House of Representatives. Thanks to gerrymandered district lines—drawn largely by Republicans who won control of statehouses in the low-voter-turnout off-year elections of 2010—the Republicans were able to win 57 percent of the House seats with only 51 percent of the total votes for the 435 House races. But this is where it gets interesting: 2014 Republican House candidates nationwide—winners and losers—received the votes of only 16 percent of the voting-age citizens of the United States, less than 1 in 6 Americans. Things are around the same in the Senate, where all the Republican candidates for the hundred Senate seats received votes from just under 21 percent of the voting-age population, or one in five Americans.[95] And, again, this is the "majority" party, with commanding control of Congress and a determination to use its power. But what sort of "mandate" did they really have with such flimsy popular support?* Matters were only marginally better for the Democrats the last time they controlled both the House and the Senate, following the 2008 election. The party's

---

*Note to pundits: Can we please stop using the phrase "the people have spoken" after each of these low-turnout elections? How about: "If you meet six people, maybe one of them wanted this result."

candidates received the votes of 26 and 28 percent of the voting-age population, respectively, or just more than one in four.

Groups that monitor voter turnout, such as the International Institute for Democracy and Electoral Assistance, regularly rank the United States near rock bottom on global turnout measures.[96] Voter turnout in the United States is less than half that of countries with established electoral systems that actually promote high levels of participation. "Regardless of which metric of eligibility you use," statistician Howard Steven Friedman noted in a 2012 *Huffington Post Politics* piece, "the United States has one of the lowest voter turnouts of any of the comparator countries."[97]

Compare the United States with Germany, a large stable democracy with which the United States is in frequent competition and collaboration. When we interviewed Germans about elections practices, the first thing they told us was that their country did not have a perfect democracy. Yet, the 2013 elections that Germans generally identified as dull and that produced a predictable finish, drew a turnout of just under 72 percent. That was almost 20 percent more than the turnout in 2012 among the overall voting-age population of the United States.[98] But Germans were not electing a president. Germans were choosing a new Bundestag, which in turn would identify a chancellor. So, though the electoral structures are different, the 2013 German election closely paralleled the 2014 election for the US House of Representatives. If we make this comparison, then Germany, after a "boring" election that drew a turnout on the low side of historic patterns, is doubling midterm election participation in the United States. And Germany's turnout rates are far from the highest among established democracies around the world. In France, turnout in the 2012 presidential election topped 80 percent. In Sweden, turnout for the 2014 parliamentary elections was 86 percent. Uruguay's 2014 presidential election drew more than 90 percent.[99] Those countries are not outliers. The United States is.

The United States is barely on the democratic grid when it comes to representative democracy. The International Institute for Democracy and Electoral Assistance ranks the United States 120th among countries of the world for turnout by eligible voters, and 138th for turnout among voting-age adults.[100] Turnout in the United States among eligible voters used to be higher—often above 70 percent in presidential and midterm elections during the nineteenth century and still coming close to 65 percent among eligible voters and the overall voting-age population as recently as 1960. But the research of the United States Election Project reveals a marked decline since the 1970s.[101]

Americans tend to vote more during periods of crisis and when they believe their vote might actually make life better. The 1924 presidential election was held in relatively prosperous and tranquil times. In a three-way race where the Progressive candidate Robert M. La Follette drew 16 percent of the vote, President Calvin Coolidge coasted to victory with 15.7 million votes, or 54 percent of the total cast. Twelve years later, in the Great Depression election of 1936, the Republican presidential candidate, Alf Landon, was demolished by FDR, getting only 36.5 percent of the vote in what is regarded as perhaps the greatest landside in American presidential history. But loser Landon got almost one million *more* votes than winner Coolidge did in 1924. What happened? The turnout rate of voting-age Americans increased from 44 percent in 1924 to 57 percent in 1936. Roosevelt did not cruise to victory by convincing Republicans to switch teams. Instead, many millions of Americans came to the polls for the first time and voted for the Democrat. Indeed, in 1936 FDR got over 14 million *more* votes than the combined 1924 vote of La Follette and the Democratic candidate, John W. Davis. FDR came very close to getting more votes on his own in 1936 than *all* three presidential candidates—Coolidge, Davis, and La Follette—together received in 1924.

If the promise of American democracy is ever going to realized, it will not be because the dwindling number of mostly older, whiter, and richer voters start to cast ballots for different candidates and parties. It will be because of a surge of new voters. Turnout will need to get much closer to 80 percent to be legitimate. And that means guaranteeing the right to vote for all voting-age Americans, making it the aggressive policy of the government to do all it can to encourage people to vote, and to ensure that elections decide essential issues that are now held off the table. This is what Bernie Sanders and his supporters are talking about when they speak of "a political revolution." No change of consequence, certainly no change for the better, will come within the narrow confines of the low-information, low-engagement, low-turnout politics that now defines our "democracy."

How did America's politics become so decayed and dysfunctional? Why is this country barreling toward citizenless democracy? The way to answer that question is to examine the democratic infrastructure, and to recognize the necessary role it plays in sustaining a strong democracy. America has a rich and notable history in this regard, one that has played a prominent role in the nation's development and that has inspired the world. Today's rulers prefer that this history be ignored. If, on the other hand, the history is restored to the people, it provides a remarkable set of tools for renewing and extending democracy in America. It is time to exhume the tools. With this history of the development of democratic infrastructure we can better understand the current predicament, and generate a vision and a roadmap for truly empowering citizens to make the essential *economic* issues that are now *off the table* the essential *political* issues they must be. This is the key to making the United States into a self-governing society, and to making the United States of the twenty-first century a place of prosperity and hope for all Americans.

chapter four

DEMOCRATIC INFRASTRUCTURE

T HE IMMENSE ECONOMIC PROBLEMS THAT ARE BEING AGGRA-
vated and accelerated by the technological revolution
raise fundamental issues that require popular involvement
to be resolved in a humane and sustainable manner. Ours is a citizenless democracy, where core political and economic decisions are
made by the wealthy few for the wealthy few. Consequential economic issues are off the table. Voting is hard. Money rules the day.
Instead of guiding the ship of state, the vast majority of Americans
are on individual rafts in the middle of the ocean watching that ship
sail off into the distance. Citizens need democratic infrastructure to
be effective participants in governance, but the democratic infrastructure of the United States seems to be disappearing faster than
the polar ice caps.

The good news is that there is a rich and underappreciated tradition in American history that respects the importance of a credible
democratic infrastructure, and that has fought for its development—

sometimes with considerable success. Those wealthy few who are on top now, along with their pawns in the political and pundit classes, tell us that serious efforts to expand the democratic infrastructure of the United States would violate the terms laid out in the Constitution, to which they swear unrivaled fealty. The most emphatic defenders of the status quo wrap themselves in the flag and claim that what the United States has today is the freest and best society possible—that contemporary America is exactly what the wisest of the founders intended. All other versions of democracy pale by comparison, and any reform effort to alter the US system would lessen our freedoms. They are wrong about the history, and wrong about democracy.

CONSTITUTIONS AGAINST DEMOCRACY?

Constitutions in democratic societies are important. It is in the writing of these documents that nation-states set the specific terms for how citizens shall direct governance. Constitutions mandate much, though rarely all, of what citizens understand as democratic infrastructure. Constitutions also provide guidance for elected bodies and organized citizens to fill in the rest of the democratic infrastructure, and define how easy it is for the people of a new age to amend old rules. "A constitution," political scientist Robert Dahl has written, should "maintain political institutions that foster political equality among citizens and all the necessary rights, liberties, and opportunities that are essential to the existence of political equality and democratic governance."[1] Constitutions are not the only place these matters are determined, but they are central to the process.[2] So what do we learn by assessing how the democratic infrastructure has been understood in the American constitutional traditions? That is a loaded question, as a close reading reveals, as we use the plural to talk about constitutional *traditions*. Not only are there multiple ways to understand the US Constitution, there are fifty state constitutions and *hundreds* of state constitutional conventions, many of which have dealt with the democratic infrastructure. It is only by considering the range of American constitutional traditions that we can begin to answer the question about democratic infrastructure.*

The first point is that the framers of the Constitution flunked miserably Dahl's test for a democratic constitution. The immediately obvious problem is that African Americans and Native Americans were written out of the picture as potential citizens of the new country. They were only to be used by whites for the advantages of whites. Writer and activist Staughton Lynd is spot-on when he states that the United States "was founded on crimes against humanity directed at Native Americans and African-American slaves." This was not a regrettable footnote to the nation's founding and history, but it was at the center, a fact which still remains underappreciated to this day.[3]

Most of the founders of the nation were well aware that slavery was morally wrong and intellectually indefensible. Thomas Jefferson's original version of the Declaration of Independence included a paragraph on slavery in its bill of offenses committed by King George:

> He has waged cruel war against human nature itself, violating its most sacred rights of life and liberty in the persons of a distant people who never offended him, captivating and carrying them into slavery in another hemisphere, or to incur miserable death in their transportation hither. . . . And he is now exciting those very people to rise in arms among us, and to purchase that liberty of which he had deprived them, by murdering the people upon whom he also obtruded them: thus paying off former crimes committed against the liberties of one people, with crimes which he urges them to commit against the lives of another.

---

* In the early days of the American experiment, each state was required to establish its own constitution. Since then, it has been a standard that states have constitutions. As we will explain later in this chapter, they are much more dynamic documents than the US Constitution. Many states have held, and continue to hold, constitutional conventions not just to write the documents but to update them. Others have established relatively easy processes for amending constitutions by petitioning to schedule referendum votes on particular issues.

This contradictory paragraph says it all: simultaneous outrage at the British for enslaving Africans and forcing them to the New World along with outrage that the British were now encouraging the same slaves to revolt. Perhaps that is why the paragraph was deleted from the final draft, and no mention of slavery appears in the document.[4] (Indeed, Gerald Horne and other historians make a convincing argument that it was the fear of the burgeoning British anti-slavery movement—with its sympathy for slave uprisings, and the English Court of King's Bench 1772 *Somerset v. Stewart* ruling that chattel slavery was unsupported by English common law—that motivated slaveholders and merchants dependent upon slavery to throw in with the American revolution.[5]) Historians debate the precise role of slavery in the constitutional debates that followed a decade later; the federal Constitution makes no explicit mention of slavery, but deems each slave three-fifths of a person for the purpose of counting state populations and thereby apportioning political representation in the US House of Representatives.[6]

With but a handful of glorious exceptions, like Thomas Paine—whose 1775 essay "African Slavery in America" was a scathing indictment of the institution and a call for its termination—and the Pennsylvania radicals, the white supremacy that was embedded into the culture was either accepted or actively promoted.[7] But the Constitution is also a dubious product for democracy even when looking strictly at the white male population as the relevant group of prospective citizens, which is what the framers did.

While they were deeply concerned with preventing tyranny, the intent of the federal Constitution was *not* to promote democracy, even among those of European descent. This analysis was best put by the scholar and future president Woodrow Wilson in 1893:

> The federal government was not by intention a democratic government. In plan and structure it was meant to check the sweep and power of popular majorities. The Senate, it was believed, would be a stronghold of conservatism, if not of aristocracy and wealth. The President,

it was expected, would be the choice of representative men acting in the electoral college, and not of the people. The federal Judiciary was looked to, with its virtually permanent membership, to hold the entire structure of national politics in nice balance against all disturbing influences, whether of popular impulse or of official overbearance. Only in the House of Representatives were the people to be accorded an immediate audience and a direct means of making their will effective in affairs. The government had, in fact, been originated and organized upon the initiative and primarily in the interest of the mercantile and wealthy classes. Originally conceived in an effort to resolve commercial disputes between the States, it had been urged to adoption by a minority, under the concerted and aggressive leadership of able men representing a ruling class.

Wilson also observed that "there can be a moneyed aristocracy, but there cannot be a moneyed democracy." In subsequent generations the forces of democracy would rise up in the United States with frequent success, Wilson noted, but in the first decades of the Republic, "the conservative, cultivated, propertied classes of New England and the South practically held the government as their own."[8] In 1800 in New York City, for example, a mere 25 percent of white men were eligible to vote. The property requirement for white male voters did not end in the nation until North Carolina eliminated it in 1856.[9] And the poll tax was not formally eliminated until 1964.[10]

Wilson, like many other observers to this day, charitably conceded that the framers were mostly distrustful of those without substantial property because they believed the poor were incapable of having a will of their own and could therefore be misled by some artful charlatan to the ruin of the republic; that is, the tyranny of the majority. As people became more educated and responsible owners of property themselves, they would be trusted with full participation in the governing process. As numerous historians have demonstrated, however, the framers were more than genteel patricians on the lookout for their dim-witted and gullible brethren in the lower orders. Their more pressing concern, as historian Alexander Keyssar puts it, was "that men who were financially strapped would band together to defend their own interests."[11]

The revolution against Britain had been fought by the poor and those of limited means, and they did so inspired by the radical democratic words of Thomas Paine in *Common Sense*. It is for that reason that Benjamin Franklin told Paine that he, Paine, "was more responsible than any other living person on this continent for the creation of what are called the United States of America."[12] The vision of the farmers and artisans who attended to battle was not a war to simply switch flags and end up with a native ruling class over them. It was to create a far more egalitarian and fair society that they participated in governing. Shays' Rebellion of 1786–1787 is the best known of a number of popular uprisings throughout this period that alarmed the elites that gathered in Philadelphia to draft the Constitution in the summer of 1787.[13]

Indeed, the federal Constitution was in significant part a reaction to a series of more democratic state constitutions that had already been drafted and approved in the new Republic. The most radical was written in the summer and fall of 1776 in Pennsylvania by a group that included Franklin and Paine. Much of the momentum came from rural farmers, the poor, artisans, and the mid-level merchants of Philadelphia, who by 1775 had become, as William Hogeland puts it, "a powerful street constituency in favor of American independence as a way to promote economic equality."[14] The Pennsylvania constitution allowed for universal male suffrage and the election of a powerful unicameral legislature for one-year terms. The judiciary and executive branches were weak, and no bill could become law after being passed until it had been in print for a year so citizens could respond to it. It also called for the state to promote public education and the establishment of universities. The first assemblies elected under this constitution "began passing laws to regulate wealth and foster economic development for ordinary people." Laws specifically were passed, according to Hogeland, to "restrict monopolies, equalize taxes, abolish slavery, and otherwise pursue, now through legitimate government, the old goals of popular agitation."[15]

So when the lawyer Edmund Randolph of Virginia opened the proceedings for the first meeting of the United States Constitutional Convention, he was blunt. "Our chief danger," he told a group that included George Washington, "arises from the democratic parts of our constitutions." As Hogelund observes, like Randolph, the founders' use of the term *democracy* was pejorative, "sometimes to mean mob rule, sometimes to mean unchecked representation, and sometimes to mingle the two." The states with their more popular constitutions and suffrage laws were the problem. "None of the constitutions," Randolph said, "have provided sufficient checks against the democracy."[16]

When today's "conservatives" demand a return to the original vision of the US Constitution, they often celebrate these anti-democratic elements—its minimizing the power of one-person, one vote; its lack of any "positive rights" outlining what citizens might expect from their government; for a few, even its appointment rather than direct election of US senators as signs of genius and the basis for individual freedom. From there it is a short leap to regarding the Constitution as a full-throttle endorsement of "free market" capitalism with a Gilded Age disregard for the poor and working class, who are "free" to pull themselves up by their bootstraps, as the saying goes. This interpretation is self-serving; it takes the US Constitution out of context. It eliminates the actual, and rich, traditions that do exist. It turns the Constitution into a cardboard rationale for what the contemporary dominant interests favor today and going forward.

Two critical points of context are these: first, the US Constitution dealt with the political economy it knew and anticipated would continue. There was no speculation about what the economy might or might not look like—as well as should or should not look like—one hundred or two hundred or three hundred years down the road, any more than sane people would do today. It was written in the context of a mercantile economy based overwhelmingly on agriculture and significantly on slave labor. It was an economy with private property, but it was decidedly preindustrial capitalist in economic terms.

Capitalism, as we now know it, is based on the competition of individual capitalists to get ever-richer through the pursuit of profit, in a never-ending manner; it generally requires a propertyless urban working class to provide the labor to generate the profits. Such a growth of private capital leads to routine overall economic growth, and that increased economic output continually increases the material wealth of the society. That is what is revolutionary about capitalism and distinguishes it from all its economic predecessors. But capitalism in that sense was not even close to existence in 1787. Ninety percent of adults worked in agriculture, and there was only one bank—Alexander Hamilton's Bank of New York, founded in 1784—in the entire country. There were few cities and none had a population of more than 100,000. It took weeks to travel overland from Maine to Georgia, or to cross the Atlantic.[17] Routine annual economic growth was largely unknown anywhere in the world before the nineteenth century.[18] That explains why in the US Constitution or the debates about the Constitution, terms like *corporations*, *profits*, *competition*, *enterprise*, *growth*, and *markets* are nowhere to be found. Many of those terms would not become widely used for several generations.* Indeed, the use of the term *capitalism* to describe this revolutionary new economic system begins in Germany in the 1880s, and only gains common usage in English and French at the beginning of the twentieth century.[19]

Moreover, the US Constitution was drafted during an era in which the notions that the endless increase of one's wealth and property is good both for society and, as important, a person's inherent right—

---

* The capitalism roundly celebrated today as commanded from on high through the vessel of the US Constitution proved to be an acquired taste deep into America's history. In his 1861 State of the Union Address—in the era when capitalism's contours were indeed becoming visible—President Abraham Lincoln closed his speech, which had focused on the raging Civil War, by stating, "In my present position I could scarcely be justified were I to omit raising a warning voice against this approach of returning despotism." The despotism that so concerned Lincoln was "the effort to place capital on an equal footing with, if not above, labor in the structure of government." Lincoln elaborated on the notion: "Labor is prior to and independent of capital. Capital is only the fruit of labor, and could never have existed if labor had not first existed. Labor is the superior of capital, and deserves much the higher consideration." This only scratches the surface of Lincoln's remarkable statement about the relationship of capital and labor to democracy. Abraham Lincoln, State of the Union Address, December 3, 1861, http://www .presidentialrhetoric.com/historicspeeches/lincoln/stateoftheunion1861.html.

central, even necessary, postulates of a modern capitalist society—
were considered dubious, if not folly. As Franklin put it in 1783:

> All the Property that is necessary to a Man, for the Conservation of
> the Individual and the Propagation of the Species, is his natural Right,
> which none can justly deprive him of: But all Property superfluous
> to such purposes is the Property of the Publick, who, by their Laws,
> have created it, and who may therefore by other Laws dispose of it,
> whenever the Welfare of the Publick shall demand such Disposition.
> He that does not like civil Society on these Terms, let him retire and
> live among Savages. He can have no right to the benefits of Society,
> who will not pay his Club towards the Support of it.[20]

To the extent Americans got a sense of the industrial capitalism
then in its very earliest stages in England, there was no groundswell,
let alone a consensus, that this was at all desirable for the United States.
In his 1785 *Notes on the State of Virginia*, Thomas Jefferson wrote "Let
our workshops remain in Europe."[21]

Then, as corporations began to proliferate in the first few decades
of the nineteenth century, the framers, not to mention many others,
while recognizing corporations' economic advantages, were immediately and deeply concerned about the ability and commercial incentive
of corporations to corrupt and destroy the political system.[22] Jefferson
wrote on this topic with some regularity in the last two decades of
his life.[23] In 1816, for example, in a letter to Pennsylvanian George
Logan, he wrote: "I hope we shall . . . crush in its birth the aristocracy
of our monied corporations which dare already to challenge our government to a trial of strength, and to bid defiance to the laws of their
country."[24]

The second critical point of context is that in 1787 many of the
states had constitutions that included or enabled their legislatures to
enact positive rights and social welfare provisions. These were striking
by the standards of those times, and inspiring even for these times.
Shouldn't this tradition be every bit as important to understanding
American history? These state constitutions were generally much

more democratic undertakings than the US Constitutional Convention, the products of sometimes significant popular participation. These were the values of the (white male) American people, to the extent they were consulted. The federal Constitution understandably regarded positive rights and social welfare provisions as being handled at the more democratic state level—where most of the work of government was to take place—and not a federal affair. For that reason, as scholar Cass Sunstein puts it, "the Constitution's framers gave no thought to including social and economic guarantees in the bill of rights."[25] Constitutional historian Emily Zackin writes that because of the centrality of state constitutions at the time, "while the Bill of Rights may reflect a suspicion of the federal government, we cannot infer from this document that even its drafters were suspicious of all government."[26] Indeed, the preamble to the Constitution states the very purpose of the federal government is "to form a more perfect Union, establish Justice, insure domestic Tranquility, provide for the common defense, promote the general Welfare, and secure the Blessings of Liberty to ourselves and our Posterity." When one looks at the writings of the framers on what the functions of government be, they were anything but modern-day free-market libertarians.[27]

Consider the matter of public education. It is not mandated in the federal Constitution. Does that mean the framers did not regard it as essential for the nation, or that it should not be paid for and conducted by the government? Of course not. The Northwest Ordinance of 1787, later reaffirmed by the first Congress in 1789, set the statehood conditions for the territories west of the Appalachian mountains to enter the union on equal footing with the original thirteen states. Chief among the requirements was the establishment of "schools and means of education" which were "necessary to good government and the happiness of mankind."[28] No less than John Adams, among the least sympathetic of the founders to popular suffrage and democratic governance, put the matter of education this way in 1785: "The whole people must take upon themselves the education of the whole people and be willing to bear the expenses of it. There should not be a district of one mile square, without a school in it, not founded by a charitable individual, but maintained at the public expense of the people themselves."[29]

The same is true on the matter of economic inequality. Jefferson is on record in 1785 as writing about the use of aggressive government action to reduce economic inequality, an intervention he regarded as highly desirable and necessary for effective governance.[30] "I am conscious that an equal division of property is impracticable. But the consequences of this enormous inequality producing so much misery to the bulk of mankind, legislatures cannot invest too many devices for subdividing property, only taking care to let their subdivisions go hand in hand with the natural affections of the human mind."[31] Noted educator and Federalist Noah Webster stated in 1787 that political equality required "a general and tolerably equal distribution of landed property."[32] Only a few years following the passage of the Constitution, James Madison argued in an essay titled "On Parties" that it was imperative to establish genuine "political equality among all," and a main way to accomplish that was by "the silent operation of the laws, which, without violating the rights of property, *reduce extreme wealth towards a state of mediocrity, and raise extreme indigence toward a state of comfort*" (our emphasis). Because this program was not spelled out in the federal Constitution does not mean the founders found it unimportant or improper.

Late in his life, as Madison prepared his notes on the constitutional debates for publication, he wrote that his views on suffrage had matured and changed in the intervening years. "The right of suffrage," he now wrote, "is a fundamental Article in Republican Constitutions." He reasserted his belief that, for the republican system to succeed, the government needed to reduce the great wealth of the few to benefit those without property. He no longer thought of the Constitution as primarily necessary to protect the few from the tyranny of the majority. Instead, Madison changed course and now defended majority rule as the single "vital principle of republican government."[33] After reviewing this and other evidence, Dahl writes, "I have little doubt that if the American Constitutional Convention had been held in 1820, a very different constitution would have emerged from the deliberations."[34] That same year, noting the Constitution's complicity with slavery, future president John Quincy Adams wrote, "The constitution is a compact with Hell, and a life devoted to its destruction would be a life well spent."[35]

CONSTITUTIONS ON MILITARISM

It is ironic and colossally tragic that the two areas where the US Constitution and Bill of Rights anticipated and spoke most directly to raging perennial threats to democracy—threats that preceded capitalism and that will survive it as well—are today those provisions that are almost entirely ignored. These are the limitations on militarism and the recognition of the crucial role of the government in guaranteeing the existence of a viable independent press, or news media. Both relate strongly to the deep concern of the framers to prevent corruption, which they regarded as a deadly threat to any governing system. "My wish," Madison said, "is that the national legislature be as uncorrupt as possible." The Articles of Confederation, which preceded the Constitution, strictly prohibited any person working for the United States or any state government from accepting "any present, emolument, office or title of any kind." As law professor Zephyr Teachout writes, "Charges of corruption and its variants were an essential force in the creation of the Constitution, and part of almost every debate about government structure."[36]

The first great imperative for promoting (or protecting) a democratic infrastructure are the sections in the federal Constitution limiting the capacity of the government to engage in war. At least six of the state constitutions drafted prior to 1787 had phrases similar to this one from the Pennsylvania and North Carolina constitutions: "As standing armies in time of peace are dangerous to liberty, they ought not to be kept up."[37] The US Constitution strictly limits the war-making power of the president and puts the power to declare war and the obligation to raise funds to pay for war in the hands of Congress. The Constitution's purpose was "clogging rather than facilitating war," as delegate George Mason stated to broad approval during the Constitutional Convention.[38] The point of the Second and Third Amendments—the "military amendments," as constitutional scholar Akhil Reed Amar terms them—"centrally focuses on the structural issue of protecting civilian values against the threat of an overbearing military. No standing army in peacetime can be allowed to dominate civilian society, either openly or by subtle insinuation."[39]

The framers, men like Madison and Jefferson, were classically educated. They saw that warfare, militarism, and endless imperialism had sounded the death knell for Greek democracy, the Roman Republic, and the democratic prospects for the great nations of contemporary Europe. Both Jefferson and Madison were obsessive on this point. "Even under the best forms of government," Jefferson observed, "those entrusted with power have, in time, and by slow operations, perverted it to tyranny."[40] "Perhaps it is a universal truth," Madison wrote to Jefferson in 1798, "that the loss of liberty at home is to be charged to the provisions against danger, real or pretended, from abroad."[41] Madison put it best in his timeless declaration that

of all the enemies of true liberty, war is, perhaps, the most to be dreaded, because it comprises and develops the germ of every other. War is the parent of armies; from these proceed debts and taxes; and armies, and debts, and taxes are the known instruments for bringing the many under the domination of the few. In war, too, the discretionary power of the Executive is extended; its influence in dealing out offices, honors and emoluments is multiplied; and all the means of seducing the minds, are added to those of subduing the force, of the people. The same malignant aspect in republicanism may be traced in the inequality of fortunes, and the opportunities of fraud, growing out of a state of war, and in the degeneracy of manner and of morals, engendered in both. No nation can preserve its freedom in the midst of continual warfare.[42]

In his 1796 "farewell address" to the nation—a letter written with the assistance of Alexander Hamilton and read before at least one branch of Congress annually for the past 150 years, and a great inspiration to the anti-imperialist movements of the late nineteenth and early twenti-eth centuries—President Washington cautioned his peers and future generations to "avoid the necessity of those overgrown military estab-lishments, which, under any form of government, are inauspicious to liberty, and which are to be regarded as particularly hostile to Repub-lican Liberty."[43]

Aside from the numerous continental campaigns to seize lands from the indigenous populations as well as Mexico, the United States heeded the spirit of the Constitution and its framers for much of its history, generally demobilizing immediately after a declared war. "As late as the 1930s," political scientist Walter Dean Burnham observes, "the U.S. Army contained scarcely more men under arms than the hundred thousand to which the Treaty of Versailles limited Ger-many."[44] Much of military and naval war production was under state control and when wars generated vast fortunes, as happened during the Civil War and World War I, scandals ensued. In the 1930s US Sen-ator Gerald Nye of North Dakota denounced the munitions industry as "an unadulterated, unblushing racket."[45] When America entered the Second World War, President Franklin D. Roosevelt stated, "I don't want to see a single war millionaire created in the United States as a result of this world disaster."[46] FDR was obsessive on this point. In his 1944 State of the Union Address, he observed that "for two long years I have pleaded with the Congress to take undue profits out of war."[47]

That seems like the ancient history of some very different nation. Following World War II the United States abandoned its commitment to being a peacetime nation unless in a formally declared war and be-came what Madison feared: a continual warfare society.[48] A massive and self-perpetuating military-industrial complex was created in a few short years, largely outside civilian review or control, which is now hard-wired to some of the largest private corporations. It is a huge profit center for investors. This military-industrial complex has ex-tended the power of the executive branch relative to Congress in ways that are beyond all previous understanding.[49] Any effort to strengthen the democratic infrastructure must address the problem of continual warfare head-on, and the wisdom and counsel of the framers provides the necessary starting point.

THE CONSTITUTION AND A FREE PRESS

Everyone is familiar with the First Amendment's prohibition on government interference with the press. This is something that has inspired advocates of liberty worldwide, and of which Americans are justifiably proud. But understanding the Constitution's commitment to a free press as a negative right—as something the government cannot do to citizens who wish to engage in journalism—is only half-right. In the haze of the past century of commercially driven news media, nearly all Americans have lost sight of the fact that the American free press constitutional tradition has a second component, every bit as important as the prohibition against prior restraint and censorship: it is the highest duty of the government to see that a free press actually exists so there is something of value that cannot be censored. It is difficult to exaggerate the importance of this issue at the beginning of our country.

In 1787, as the Constitution was being drafted in Philadelphia, Thomas Jefferson was ensconced in Paris as minister to France. From afar he corresponded on the singular importance of the free press. Jefferson wrote:

> The way to prevent these irregular interpositions of the people is to give them full information of their affairs thro' the channel of the public papers, and to contrive that those papers should penetrate the whole mass of the people. The basis of our governments being the opinion of the people, the very first object should be to keep that right; and were it left to me to decide whether we should have a government without newspapers, or newspapers without a government, I should not hesitate a moment to prefer the latter. But I should mean that every man should receive those papers and be capable of reading them.

For Jefferson, just having the right to speak without government censorship is a necessary but insufficient condition for a free press, and therefore democracy. It also demands that there be a literate public, a viable press system, and that people have easy access to this press.

But why, exactly, was this such an obsession to Jefferson? In the same letter, Jefferson praises Native American societies for being largely classless and happy, and criticizes European societies—like the France he was witnessing firsthand on the eve of its revolution—in no uncertain terms for being their opposite. Jefferson also stakes out the central role of the press in stark class terms when he describes the role of the press in preventing exploitation and domination by the rich over the poor:

> Among [European societies], under pretence of governing they have divided their nations into two classes, wolves and sheep. I do not exaggerate. This is a true picture of Europe. Cherish therefore the spirit of our people, and keep alive their attention. Do not be too severe upon their errors, but reclaim them by enlightening them. If once they become inattentive to the public affairs, you and I, and Congress, and Assemblies, judges and governors shall all become wolves. It seems to be the law of our general nature, in spite of individual exceptions; and experience declares that man is the only animal which devours his own kind, for I can apply no milder term to the governments of Europe, and to the general prey of the rich on the poor.[50]

In short, a free press has an obligation to call out, to challenge, to undermine the natural tendency of propertied classes to dominate politics, open the doors to corruption, reduce the masses to effective powerlessness, and eventually terminate self-government.

James Madison was every bit Jefferson's equal in his passion for a free press. Together they argued for it as a check on militarism, secrecy, corruption, inequality, and empire. Near the end of his life, Madison famously observed, "A popular government without popular information or the means of acquiring it, is but a Prologue to a Farce or a Tragedy or perhaps both. Knowledge will forever govern ignorance, and a people who mean to be their own Governors, must arm themselves with the power knowledge gives."[51]

An institution this important to the very existence of democracy is not something you roll the dice on and hope you get lucky. There was no sense in this period (and for a long time thereafter) that as long as the government did not censor newspapers, private citizens or businesses would have sufficient incentive to produce a satisfactory press. Indeed, the Constitution's creation of the Post Office was above all else a commitment to seeing that newspapers were distributed effectively and inexpensively. That is why Jefferson and Madison met with President Washington and urged him to name as the first postmaster general the most prominent and radical of the country's pamphleteers, Thomas Paine.[52] For the first century of American history most newspapers were distributed by the mails, and the Post Office barely charged newspapers anything to be delivered. (In around 10 percent of the cases, newspaper delivery through the mails was free.) It was quite consciously a subsidy by the federal government to make it economically viable for many more newspapers to exist than would otherwise be the case. Newspapers constituted more than 90 percent of the Post Office's weighted traffic, yet provided only about 10 percent of its revenues. If the United States government subsidized journalism in the second decade of the twenty-first century as a percentage of GDP to the same extent it did in the first half of the nineteenth century, it would spend in the area of $35 billion annually.[53]

This was the case through much of the nineteenth century. The Post Office was by far the largest and most important branch of the federal government, with 80 percent of federal employees as of 1860. Delivery in major cities was often two or three times daily, six or seven days per week. Newspaper subsidies constituted a policy that worked magnificently; the United States had vastly more newspapers than any other nation on a per capita basis during this period. When Alexis de Tocqueville made his journey across America in the 1830s, he was astounded by the prevalence of newspapers far beyond that to be found anywhere else in the world. "The number of newspapers," he wrote, "exceeds all belief." He wrote of the close

relationship between newspapers, equality, and democratic governance. "The power of newspapers must therefore increase as men
become equal." It was no accident or the consequence of free markets; it was due to explicit government policies and subsidies.[54]

Although this second component of the American free press tradition has been largely forgotten since the advent of the commercial era of journalism, the US Supreme Court, in *all* relevant cases,
has asserted its existence and preeminence. In the Supreme Court's
1927 *Whitney v. California* case, Justice Louis Brandeis concluded,
"Those who won our independence believed that the final end of the
State was to make men free to develop their faculties; . . . that the
greatest menace to freedom is an inert people; that public discussion
is a political duty; and that this should be a fundamental principle
of American government."[55] In perhaps the greatest free press case
in Supreme Court history, *Associated Press v. United States* (1945), in
his majority opinion, Hugo Black wrote that the First Amendment
"rests on the assumption that the widest possible dissemination of
information from diverse and antagonistic sources is essential to the
welfare of the public, that a free press is a condition of a free society."[56] Justice Potter Stewart noted that "the Free Press guarantee is,
in essence, a *structural* provision of the Constitution" (Stewart's emphasis). It required government policies to guarantee its existence.
"The primary purpose of the constitutional guarantee of a free press
was," he added, "to create a fourth institution outside the Government as an additional check on the three official branches." Stewart
concluded: "Perhaps our liberties might survive without an independent established press. But the Founders doubted it, and, in the
year 1974, I think we can all be thankful for their doubts."[57] In his
opinion in the 1994 case *Turner Broadcasting System v. FCC*, Reagan
appointee Justice Anthony Kennedy concluded, "assuring the public
has access to a multiplicity of information sources is a governmental
purpose of the highest order."[58]

It is understandable why this rich recognition of the constitutional commitment to a free press declined by the end of the nineteenth century: newspaper publishing became extremely lucrative

and the subsidies disappeared or came to play a smaller role. But today, with the emergence of the Internet, the commercial journalism model based upon advertising providing the lion's share of the revenues is disintegrating. There are far fewer paid reporters and editors on a per capita basis, accounting for both old and new media, than there were twenty-five years ago. Most of governance and the relationship of governance to commercial interests go unreported, and few people have any idea what is happening. It is Jefferson's and Madison's worst nightmare, and there is nothing on the horizon to suggest a commercial solution to the problem. It is high time for Americans to embrace their full constitutional rights and demand policies and subsidies to create a viable, competitive, independent, and uncensored news media. Much as the framers understood, it is difficult to imagine how anything remotely close to a democratic society can exist unless this happens.[59]

CHANGING CONSTITUTIONS

There is one aspect of the Constitution that has not been ignored, to the resounding approval of those who like the status quo: it is notoriously difficult to revise or update. The US Constitution has been amended only sixteen times in the past 220 years; two of those were the prohibition amendments that cancelled each other out, and six other amendments were largely noncontroversial bookkeeping measures.

Consequently, the 1791 document including the Bill of Rights remains largely intact, with a mere eight significant amendments since George Washington left office, and three of those were the great Reconstruction amendments that passed on the heels of the nation's bloodiest war—when defeated Southern states could not participate.[60] Not only is the Constitution out of date, constitutional scholar Daniel Lazare writes, but "by imposing an unchangeable political structure on a generation that has never had an opportunity to vote on the system as a whole, it amounts to a terrible dictatorship of the past over the present." Because it is "virtually impossible to alter the political structure in any fundamental way," Lazare adds, Americans have "one of the most unresponsive political systems this side of the former Soviet Union."[61]

Before anyone reports Lazare to Homeland Security or the National Security Agency, recall that this was precisely Jefferson's position as well. "Each generation is as independent as the one preceding, as that was of all that had gone before. It has then, like them, a right to choose for itself the form of government it believes most promotive of its own happiness," Jefferson wrote in 1816. He called on the Constitution to be amended so that there would be a new constitutional convention every "nineteen or twenty years," such that every generation would have the opportunity to create its own politics and governance.[62]

This is, again, where states provide a rich alternative approach in American history; unlike the federal Constitution, popular involvement in *state* constitutions is encouraged. "The realm of state constitutional law is a beehive of activity," one scholar writes.[63] This began back in the 1770s and 1780s, when states were routinely meeting to draft and redraft constitutions, and has continued to this day.[64] By 2005 the fifty states had held a combined 233 constitutional conventions, adopted 146 different constitutions, and ratified over six thousand amendments to their existing constitutions.[65] Around ten thousand amendments have been submitted to voters for consideration. As Zackin put it in her cleverly titled book, Americans have been "looking for rights in all the wrong places."[66]

If you want to see what democracy looks like, put Washington DC in your rearview mirror and head to the states. It is here that the battles for a democratic infrastructure have been waged. In general, what one finds when examining state constitutions is that "Americans have used their constitutions to demand protective and interventionist government," beginning in the mid-nineteenth century.[67] In the constitutions of the various states one finds provisions to address the concern that Jefferson and Madison highlighted, the need to improve the lives of those without property. It is here, for example, that numerous states, as a result of popular organizing, have put in place constitutional protections for the right to collective bargaining, and, more recently, the right to a clean and sustainable environment.[68]

The most important area of state constitutional involvement in positive rights and building a democratic infrastructure has unquestionably been education. "Every state constitution," legal scholar Katherine Twomey writes, "includes a clause requiring the state legislature to establish a free system of public schools for children residing within its borders."[69] Universal public education dates back to Horace Mann and the common school movement of the 1830s, and it was a rejection of the European system of a liberal education for the children of the privileged and vocational training for the children of the masses.[70] As Townsend Harris of the New York City Board of Education advocated in 1847, "Open the door to all—let the children of the rich and poor take their seats together and know no distinction save that of industry, good conduct, and intellect."[71] In this sense the vision for American public education was fiercely egalitarian. The notion was best expressed in 1907 by John Dewey: "What the best and wisest parent wants for his own child, that must the community want for all its children. Any other ideal for our schools is narrow and unlovely; acted upon, it destroys our democracy."[72]

Every bit as important as promoting equality and fairness, as education historian Diane Ravitch has emphasized, is that "the essential purpose of the public schools, the reason they receive public funding, is to teach young people the rights and responsibilities of citizens . . . to sustain our democracy." This was the idea from the very beginning; education for a role in the economy was secondary.[73] When Texas declared its independence from Mexico in 1836, it stated, "It is an axiom of political science that unless a people are educated and enlightened it is idle to expect the continuance of civil liberty or the capacity for self-government."[74] Public education has been a cornerstone of the democratic infrastructure. So much of what is democratic—indeed, so much of what is truly exceptional—about America can be attributed to it. Its rejuvenation and development are imperative to any vision of a healthy democratic infrastructure.

A US CONSTITUTION FOR MODERN TIMES?

Following the Gilded Age of the final decades of the nineteenth century, the United States became a substantially more democratic nation in the seven decades from 1900 to 1970. For starters, with the 1971 passage of the Twenty-Sixth Amendment to the Constitution allowing eighteen- to twenty-year-olds to vote, the United States finally—195 years after the Declaration of Independence, 182 years after the passage of the Constitution, and 108 years after Lincoln's Gettysburg Address—theoretically granted suffrage to the entire population of adult citizens. It took decades of ferocious and heroic organizing and political struggle to win the franchise for poor people, women, young people, Native Americans, African Americans, and other people of color. Six or seven decades earlier, suffrage was restricted mostly to white males; and a century before that, to mostly rich white males. Theodore Roosevelt won a massive landslide victory in the 1904 presidential election . . . with the votes of 15 percent of the adult population. That looks like democratic nirvana compared to Thomas Jefferson's overwhelming landslide reelection to the presidency a century earlier. Jefferson got a whopping 73 percent of the total vote that was cast in 1804—impressive enough until one realizes it accounted for less than 3 percent of the nation's population. (Part of the reason for this astonishing statistic is that only 11 of the nation's 17 states even held popular votes for president in 1804.)[75]

There were ebbs and flows to be certain over these seven decades from 1900 to 1970, but the expanded democracy generated a variety of crucial policies that probably would have not been enacted, left to the whims of traditional elites. These include progressive income taxation, inheritance taxation on the wealthy, the right to form trade unions, abolishing child labor, social security, expanded universal public education and higher education, Medicare, unemployment insurance, and a variety of regulations to protect the environment, workplace safety, and consumers. Much of this dealt directly and indirectly with building out the democratic infrastructure, making it possible for all citizens to participate more effectively in the political system. Throughout this period elected bodies worked to limit the role of money in elections. Citizens won the right to elect judges in most states, while initiatives, referenda, and recalls were put into place. In 1913 the Seventeenth Amendment to the US Constitution was passed, requiring the direct election of senators. The first great wave of this democratic surge took place during the Progressive Era, the first fifteen years of the twentieth century.

We turn now to the 1930s and 1940s, a period of great relevance for Americans today, perhaps more than any other. Then, even more so than today, unemployment was extremely high by historical standards. In such an environment traditional policies fail and are discredited, and the center collapses. Unemployment has a way of getting a person's attention more than almost any other issue and has inspired new social forces demanding reform or revolution. Some nations responded with sharp lurches toward fascism, like Germany; others enhanced their democracies and moved moderately to the left, like the United States. Fascism was an extraordinary and un-precedented development for democracies. Prior to 1900 no one considered the idea that an advanced industrial society could have popular movements to explicitly *end* democracy; it went against ev-erything people knew.[76]

In the late 1930s and early 1940s, as tens of millions of people worldwide would lose their lives in the battle against fascism, the United States wrestled with a fundamental question: what can the na-tion do, the world do, to see that the specter of fascism never raises its head again to threaten humanity's survival? What institutions and practices, what democratic infrastructure, are required to lessen the chances of falling into the bottomless pit of fascist tyranny?

In 1938 FDR singled out the economic problems in the United States that he associated with the rise of fascism. It arises in nations where people have "to go without work, or to accept some standard of living which obviously and woefully falls short of their capacity to pro-duce." It is then that people feel "the oppressive sense of helplessness under the domination of a few, which are overshadowing our whole economic life." It was the greed, corruption, and power of monopolistic

big businesses that Roosevelt saw as the motor force for fascism. And
for that reason he authorized a comprehensive study of economic concentration with an eye to breaking up monopolistic power. "The power
of a few to manage the economic life of the nation must be diffused
among the many or be transferred to the public and its democratically
responsible government. If prices are to be managed and administered,
if the nation's business is to be allotted by plan and not by competition,
that power should not be vested in any private group or cartel, however
benevolent its professions profess to be."[77]

This anti-monopoly thrust was curtailed as the nation entered full
war preparations with the start of the European war in 1939. The
United States entered the war in 1941, and it was at this moment,
with clarity and conviction, that President Roosevelt and others laid
out a vision of how to ensure the survival and growth of democracy.
Of course FDR had incentive to define the war effort in noble terms
to galvanize enthusiasm among the mass of the population for the
immense sacrifices required during wartime. But historians who have
studied the matter are convinced that it was far more than that; this
was an issue dear to FDR and to many people in the United States at
the time.[78] The signal statements were the "Four Freedoms" and the
"Second Bill of Rights." It was a part of the weltanschauung, or dominant world view, that crystallized in the later 1930s—a period with
a thriving labor union movement and immense popularity for government programs like Social Security—that saw the United States
become a much more progressive and democratic nation. "For the
past several years," Republican presidential candidate Wendell Willkie
wrote in 1940, "practically everybody claims to be a liberal."[79]

FDR unveiled the Four Freedoms in his January 1941 State of the
Union Address to Congress. He offered up four universal principles
for a free and democratic world, which he hoped would define the war
against the Axis powers:

> In the future days, which we seek to make secure, we look forward to
> a world founded upon four essential human freedoms.

The first is freedom of speech and expression—everywhere in the world.

The second is freedom of every person to worship God in his own way—everywhere in the world.

The third is freedom from want—which, translated into world terms, means economic understandings which will secure to every nation a healthy peacetime life for its inhabitants—everywhere in the world.

The fourth is freedom from fear—which, translated into world terms, means a world-wide reduction of armaments to such a point and in such a thorough fashion that no nation will be in a position to commit an act of physical aggression against any neighbor—anywhere in the world.

That is no vision of a distant millennium. It is a definite basis for a kind of world attainable in our own time and generation.[80]

In short, the war was not being fought merely to defeat an enemy. It was a pivot point after which nothing would be the quite the same. Countries would change, and for the better, recognizing that the best defense against totalitarianism was the shaping of a good society where poverty and militarism were to be eliminated. These were core freedoms that all people deserved. And Roosevelt was certain that, after struggling through the Great Depression and World War II, that Americans were ready for the change.

The Four Freedoms became a big deal. "The people of the United States through their President have given the world a new Magna Carta of democracy," wrote newspaper editor William Allen White.[81] By early 1942, after America entered the war, it was these criteria that would be used by a majority of Americans to explain why the nation was at war. A May 1942 Intelligence Survey showed that the Four Freedoms "have a powerful and genuine appeal to seven persons in ten." It became a battle for public opinion, albeit a bit one-sided. Even the conservative *Saturday Evening Post*—whose president Walter D. Fuller was chairman of the board of the vehemently anti–New Deal National Association of Manufacturers—threw in the towel. It ran FDR-inspired paintings by Norman Rockwell on covers of four consecutive issues, each devoted to one of the Four Freedoms.[82]

Three years after the Four Freedoms speech, in his 1944 State of the Union Address, as victory in the war was all but certain, FDR introduced the idea of his economic bill of rights, or what has been called the Second Bill of Rights. It is worth reading Roosevelt's precise words:

> It is our duty now to begin to lay the plans and determine the strategy for the winning of a lasting peace and the establishment of an American standard of living higher than ever before known. We cannot be content, no matter how high that general standard of living may be, if some fraction of our people—whether it be one-third or one-fifth or one-tenth—is ill-fed, ill-clothed, ill-housed, and insecure.
>
> This Republic had its beginning, and grew to its present strength, under the protection of certain inalienable political rights—among them the right of free speech, free press, free worship, trial by jury, freedom from unreasonable searches and seizures. They were our rights to life and liberty.
>
> As our Nation has grown in size and stature, however—as our industrial economy expanded—these political rights proved inadequate to assure us equality in the pursuit of happiness.
>
> We have come to a clear realization of the fact that true individual freedom cannot exist without economic security and independence. "Necessitous men are not free men." People who are hungry and out of a job are the stuff of which dictatorships are made.
>
> In our day these economic truths have become accepted as self-evident. We have accepted, so to speak, a second Bill of Rights under which a new basis of security and prosperity can be established for all regardless of station, race, or creed.
>
> Among these are:
>
> - The right to a useful and remunerative job in the industries or shops or farms or mines of the Nation;
> - The right to earn enough to provide adequate food and clothing and recreation;

- The right of every farmer to raise and sell his products at a return which will give him and his family a decent living;
- The right of every businessman, large and small, to trade in an atmosphere of freedom from unfair competition and domination by monopolies at home or abroad;
- The right of every family to a decent home;
- The right to adequate medical care and the opportunity to achieve and enjoy good health;
- The right to adequate protection from the economic fears of old age, sickness, accident, and unemployment;
- The right to a good education.

All of these rights spell security. And after this war is won we must be prepared to move forward, in the implementation of these rights, to new goals of human happiness and well-being.

America's own rightful place in the world depends in large part upon how fully these and similar rights have been carried into practice for our citizens. For unless there is security here at home there cannot be lasting peace in the world.[83]

Few would question that FDR is one of the three or four most important presidents in American history, and by many accounts he and Lincoln are the greatest. Here he is calling for radical, even revolutionary, additions to the rights guaranteed to all Americans, with the spectacular policy implications that necessarily follow. In effect he is saying that unemployment and poverty should be unconstitutional, a massive amount of democratic infrastructure must be created, and monopolistic big business is now officially a dubious force.

FDR did not seek constitutional amendments. Instead he asked Congress to "explore the means for implementing this economic bill of rights—for it is definitely the responsibility of the Congress so to do." FDR recognized that there were dangers of a "rightist reaction" that would not only oppose the Second Bill of Rights but would seek "to return to the so-called 'normalcy' of the 1920's." FDR was unsparing in his assessment of his opponents. He famously had said in

1936 that his was the first administration in a generation to directly challenge "business and financial monopoly," and as a result, "they are unanimous in their hate for me—and I welcome their hatred."[84] Now, he was even more pointed. If the rightist reactionaries triumphed as the nation entered the postwar years, he said, "then it is certain that even though we shall have conquered our enemies on the battlefields abroad, we shall have yielded to the spirit of Fascism here at home." The enemies of freedom were the businesses and their "selfish pressure groups who seek to feather their nests while young Americans are dying."[85]

What makes this moment even more extraordinary was that the Second Bill of Rights was not a partisan undertaking. In 1940 FDR defeated the Republican Willkie, a businessman and self-described champion of free enterprise, for the presidency.[86] As the party's titular head, Willkie remained in the public eye, and he prepared to run for president again in 1944. But Willkie made a point of embracing proposals by FDR that he said made sense for America and the world. By 1942 the Republican was a strong proponent of the Four Freedoms, and he was commissioned by President Roosevelt to travel the world meeting with World War II allies. Not only did Willkie find himself in agreement with FDR, he criticized him from the left, on the grounds that not enough was being done to battle racism against African Americans.[87] After Willkie dropped out of the 1944 race for the Republican nomination, he published a book, *An American Program*, with seven essays on what should be done in America regardless of which party won the White House that November.

An American Program is an astonishing statement, and says quite a bit about the weltanschauung. Willkie fully supports expanding Social Security, making taxation more progressive, and ensuring that the government do what must be done to guarantee a "reasonably high level of employment." It is necessary that "every child in America grows up with the basic necessities of education, good food, adequate clothing, medical care and a decent home."[88] Most striking, Willkie emphatically supports organized labor and collective bargaining. "Labor's inherent right to strike," he wrote, "is the basis of all its rights. . . . Every thoughtful American knows today that a strong labor movement is one of the greatest bulwarks against the growth of fascistic tendencies and consequently is necessary for our democratic way of life."[89] Willkie, the former corporate president, shares FDR's distaste for large powerful corporations: "Monopolies and monopolistic prices threaten the very existence of the free enterprise system."[90] So close was Willkie to FDR, including on the component parts of the Economic Bill of Rights, that the two of them broached the idea of forming a new political party to unite all the liberals in the nation, and leave the Southern segregationists and big business "reactionaries" to have their own party.[91] Alas, Willkie died suddenly in October 1944 at age fifty-two and FDR died six months later, so nothing came of it.

With FDR in poor health and then gone, the Second Bill of Rights never got anywhere in Congress. For Americans, there was one notable program that grew from the Second Bill of Rights: the GI Bill, which was signed into law in June 1944. The bill gave veterans access to vocational training and higher education, as well as housing and medical benefits while in school, and low-interest loans for buying homes and starting businesses. It was no small contribution to postwar society—indeed, it is regarded as a definitional legislative accomplishment—but it was just a fraction of what FDR thought necessary for the entire population.[92] Vice President Henry Wallace never wavered; he argued in 1944 that to defeat fascism in the postwar era, the great benefits of the "immense and growing volume of scientific research, mechanical invention and management technique" needed not only to be promoted, but the benefits were to be shared across society. Wallace argued this required political "inventions" comparable in scope to the economic inventions. His grave warning was that "fascism in the postwar inevitably will push steadily for Anglo-Saxon imperialism and eventually for war with Russia. Already American fascists are talking and writing about this conflict and using it as an excuse for their internal hatreds and intolerances toward certain races, creeds and classes."[93]

Coming out of the war, many Americans assumed the battle to permanently defeat fascism would continue, as would the democratic advances of the people. In 1946, for example, Congressman Wright Patman, a Democrat from Texas, wrote that "there are many strong symptoms of fascism in our own democratic society. True, this movement in the United States masquerades under other names than the discredited one of fascism, but whatever it may be called, its peculiar characteristics are alarmingly evident." Patman, a nationally prominent populist and New Dealer who served nearly five decades in Congress, listed several requirements to minimize the threat of fascism: high-quality public education for all Americans regardless of their economic background; guaranteed full employment and a strong labor movement; and to "make certain that the existing government operates honestly and efficiently." As Patman concluded: "no really strong democracy has fallen before fascism."[94] Patman requested the Legislative Reference Service of the Library of Congress to make a detailed analysis of the historical record of fascism, so the American people and government could take steps to minimize any prospective success in the United States. The 206-page report concluded by characterizing fascism as a system that "favors big business, strengthens the position of heavy industries, retains enough of the profit system to permit the elite to build up personal fortunes . . . facilitates cartelization, and spends huge sums for military purposes." Moreover "free collective bargaining and self-government by labor organizations is abolished."[95] The conclusions dovetailed with the general thrust of the Four Freedoms and the Second Bill of Rights.

Over at the Federal Communications Commission, New Dealer Clifford Durr led the campaign to make radio broadcasting more diverse and less a pawn to commercial and big business interests. The "Blue Book" campaign of the immediate postwar years was the most radical effort to rein in the commercial broadcasting system since its inception, and was done with the clear recognition that a powerful democratic media was mandatory to prevent the weakening of democracy and the rise of fascism.[96] But very quickly any momentum to directly attack fascism disappeared, and all attention went to addressing the "communist" threat. It was as if World War II had never happened. Anti-fascism was suspect, unless the critic made it abundantly clear that communism was every bit as evil, as Patman did in his foreword to the 1947 fascism report.[97] And eventually anti-fascism just became suspect, period. The liberal New Dealer Durr, who had a distinguished career at the FCC, was redbaited out of office and had trouble finding suitable employment for years.[98]

That last hurrah for the issues in the Second Bill of Rights came in 1948. Wallace bid for the presidency on the ticket of a new Progressive Party, opposing President Harry Truman and more cautious Democrats on a third-party platform that not only embraced the component parts of economic bill of rights but also included a strong call for demilitarization that was right out of the Four Freedoms. Wallace also called for an end to Jim Crow, recognizing and embracing much of what Willkie and civil rights campaigners such as A. Philip Randolph were saying how racial division had to be ended for the nation as whole to progress. Though polls showed him to be competitive early on, Wallace's numbers declined as the former vice president faced relentless redbaiting attacks. Historians suggest that Wallace's candidacy forced Truman to support integration of the military and wage hikes.[99] But Wallace, and the drive for a Second Bill of Rights, were finished.

By the end of the 1940s the country experienced a massive red scare—"fear itself" returned with a vengeance—which ended labor's surge and put it on the defensive, and established a continual warfare economy. By 1949, if not earlier, to advocate loudly what the president had proposed in January 1944 might be enough to cost a person her job, and it certainly would have stigmatized someone as insufficiently patriotic, if not a red. The weltanschauung had seemingly turned on a dime. But, crucially, the Red Scare was not a return to the normalcy of the 1920s, as FDR feared; most of the existing New Deal reforms and much of the democratic infrastructure were too popular to be rolled back. They provided the foundation for the next democratic surge in the 1960s.

The Four Freedoms and the Second Bill of Rights were most influential abroad. The United States occupied Japan and oversaw the Allied occupation of Germany. In both cases the occupiers were concerned with putting in place a democratic infrastructure that would minimize if not eliminate the prospect of a return of fascism.* Notorious anti–New Deal General Douglas MacArthur, who directed the postwar US occupation of Japan, boldly advocated for the creation and protection of labor unions as a bulwark against the return of authoritarian rule.[100] The Japanese constitution, which the US effectively wrote, included most of the original Bill of Rights as well as the Second Bill of Rights. It even included the strongest anti-militarism provisions ever written into any nation's constitution, basically banning the existence of armed forces.[101] Moreover, the American occupiers spared no expense bankrolling a large and diverse news media, which they insisted had to be critical of the occupiers to be legitimate. Much the same took place in Germany, with regard to labor rights, press support, and the new constitution that Germans wrote, though in Europe anti-communism curtailed the extent of anti-fascist work.[102] Neither nation is perfect in 2015, but the constitutions and infrastructure put in place in the late 1940s have certainly contributed to Germany and Japan being at the very top of the lists of the most democratic nations in the world.[103]

The influence of the Second Bill of Rights, Sunstein notes, also "played a major role in the Universal Declaration of Human Rights, finalized in 1948 under the leadership of Eleanor Roosevelt and publicly endorsed by American officials at the time."[104] The terminology of the Universal Declaration is, at times, almost interchangeable with the Second Bill of Rights. As Sunstein writes, "All over the globe, modern constitutions follow the Universal Declaration in creating social and economic rights, sometimes using its precise words. They guarantee citizens a wide range of social entitlements."[105] "These principles are chiefly rooted in the 1948 *Universal Declaration of Human Rights*," constitutional scholar Judith Blau observes, "and became the basis of constitutions written in the last half of the 20th century as colonies gained their independence or were incorporated

---

* There were obviously other motives as well, of a geopolitical nature. In particular, the obsession with communism and the Left altered the nature of the occupations, especially in Germany. There de-Nazification slowed down so all hands could be on deck to battle the threat ostensibly posed by the Soviet Union and its supporters.

into older constitutions." Blau's review of the 194 existing national constitutions found that some two-thirds of them include most of the planks of the Second Bill of Rights.[106]

The great political scientist Robert Dahl once asked this rhetorical question: "If our constitution is as good as most Americans seem to think it is, why haven't other democratic countries copied it?"[107] Well, we now know they *have* copied it and been inspired by it—only it was the one generated in the 1940s that was never quite made part of the federal Constitution here.[108]

THE DEMOCRATIC SURGE OF THE 1960S AND EARLY 1970S

Perhaps it was a coincidence, but this period of democratization culminated in a long period of unusually strong economic growth from the late 1940s to the early 1970s. Moreover, as one historian put it, this postwar period "had been the most economically egalitarian period in U.S. history, the point on the graph where the bounty was shared most equitably, and unemployment was at historic lows." The year 1972 proved to be the apex of real earnings for male workers in American history.[109] "America was on a roll during those Eisenhower-Kennedy-Johnson years," Bob Herbert writes. "Economic, social, and cultural doors were being flung open one after another. There was a buoyancy to the American experience that was extraordinary."[110]

The 1960s and early 1970s are a relevant period for us not only because it is so recent and immediately precedes the citizenless democracy we now inhabit, but because that was the first generation that actually grappled in some way with the notion of a post-scarcity society. In 1965, in his commencement address at the University of Michigan, President Lyndon Baines Johnson launched with great fanfare his plans for a "Great Society," to be built on the spectacular growth in the nation's productive capacity wrought by "unbounded invention."

> The Great Society rests on abundance and liberty for all. It demands an end to poverty and racial injustice, to which we are totally committed in our time. But that is just the beginning.

The Great Society is a place where every child can find knowledge to enrich his mind and to enlarge his talents. It is a place where leisure is a welcome chance to build and reflect, not a feared cause of boredom and restlessness. It is a place where the city of man serves not only the needs of the body and the demands of commerce but the desire for beauty and the hunger for community.

It is a place where man can renew contact with nature. It is a place which honors creation for its own sake and for what it adds to the understanding of the race. It is a place where men are more concerned with the quality of their goals than the quantity of their goods.

LBJ proposed a dramatic build-out of the democratic infrastructure to end poverty, build magnificent cities, and repair nature.[111] Though he failed—and "continual warfare" was a factor in his downfall—this was arguably the first credible post-scarcity vision from someone in power, and it is the prospect facing Americans and humanity today, as least in terms of what we are technologically capable of accomplishing. Compared to the present historical moment, however, what is striking about the 1960s is, even in turbulent times, the overall optimism that difficult social problems could be solved.

There is a measure of irony that most of the great social movements of the 1960s and early 1970s—civil rights, black power, environmental, student, consumer, antiwar, feminist, Chicano, Native American, and gay—were fueled by the conviction that American society was deeply flawed and required radical transformation. A record percentage of young people were getting college educations and upward mobility was the order of the day. By contemporary standards political corruption barely existed. But, by historical standards, an aroused citizenry was dissatisfied and thought America had to do better, and had to go places no democracy had ever gone before. Militarism, racism, environmental calamity, sexual discrimination, inequality, poverty, mindless materialism, and endless commercialism—all had to end. And an astonishing number of young people—including the sort of upper- and middle-class youth that were the bulwark of conservatism in most societies—thought capitalism was a dying economic system and that corporations were dangerous parasites.

During this period the center of gravity for American politics moved to the left on a number of fundamental issues. In 1954 Republican President Dwight Eisenhower wrote to his brother that "should any political party attempt to abolish social security, unemployment insurance, and eliminate labor laws and farm programs, you would not hear of that party again in our political history. Among them are H.L. Hunt (you possibly know his background), a few other Texas oil millionaires, and an occasional politician or business man from other areas. Their number is negligible and they are stupid."[112] Fifteen years later that sentiment was ever more entrenched and extended. The baseline for participation in public discourse—with but a few exceptions, primarily generated by wealthy businessmen and their shock troops of increasingly discredited white supremacists and segregationists—was a commitment to a relatively strong democracy and an enhanced democratic infrastructure. And this happened when capitalism was hitting on all cylinders. The weltanschauung, or dominant worldview, had changed.

Some sense of the shifting tides can be found in the 1972 platform of the Democratic Party, which had nominated George McGovern as its presidential candidate after a successful grassroots insurgency campaign. McGovern, who had supported Henry Wallace's campaign for president in 1948, was probably the most left-wing major party presidential candidate in US history. "Our traditions, our history, our Constitution, our lives, all say that America belongs to its people. But the people no longer believe it," the platform began. "They feel that the government is run for the privileged few rather than for the many—and they are right." It went on to call for (and we paraphrase):

- A guaranteed job for all Americans, with government providing employment if necessary at a living wage
- Huge expansion of public spending projects to rebuild cities, create mass transportation networks, address pollution, and build housing for the poor

- Tax reform to promote a much greater commitment to "progressive taxation" to generate equitable distribution of income and wealth
- Stepped-up antitrust action to break-up "shared monopolies" like those found with the massive corporations that dominated the automobile, steel, and tire industries—that is, *restructure the oligopolistic basis of American capitalism* (our emphasis)
- Establishing a national economic commission to examine the role of large multinational corporations in the economy to see if federal chartering of corporations is necessary to reduce their influence
- Policies to directly attack the concentration of economic power in fewer and fewer hands
- Extension of trade union rights to workers in the nonprofit and public sector
- Support of a grape boycott to assist the farmworkers in their campaign to establish a union
- Establishing universal comprehensive health insurance controlled, financed, and administered by the federal government so all Americans are covered at all times; that is, Medicare for everyone
- Supporting equalization of spending among school districts to end the disparity between the caliber of public education based upon family income
- Actively supporting community policing
- Recognizing human rights of prisoners and fundamentally restructuring prisons to make them effective rehabilitation facilities
- Reestablishing the congressional role in military affairs, reducing military spending, and ending secrecy, except where absolutely necessary
- A total overhaul of the campaign-finance system with clear limits on donations to prevent candidates from being "dependent on large contributors who seek preferential treatment." Also, an increase in public funding of elections.

- Universal voter registration by postcard, abolition of the Electoral College, and a run-off election for president if no candidate gets at least 40 percent of the vote

That is just a taste of what was included.[113] In short, the 1972 Democratic Party platform effectively called for the fulfillment of FDR's and Henry Wallace's anti-fascist democratic vision, along with a broader commitment to the great issues that had emerged subsequently. Put another way, it embraced all the economic social policies raised by A. Philip Randolph and Martin Luther King Jr. in their 1966 Freedom Budget, and the Freedom Budget was taken directly from FDR's Second Bill of Rights.[114]

What is almost as striking is the Republican Party response. Its platform certainly positioned itself to the right of the Democrats, but it was nothing like what would become *de rigueur* for the GOP by the 1980s and thereafter. The basic contours of the welfare state were supported, and when Nixon won his landslide victory over McGovern it was no referendum on the core New Deal policies like Social Security or the right to form trade unions, or on the more recent turns to environmental and consumer regulation. After the 1964 debacle in the presidential election, the Goldwater wing of the party was marginalized and licking its wounds. In the early 1970s the Republican Party had a significant liberal wing in Congress, made up of people like Senators Lowell Weicker, Edward Brooke, and Charles Percy and Representatives Pete McCloskey and John Anderson.

In fact, the Nixon administration (1969–1974) is noted for its passage of trailblazing environmental and consumer legislation, far more sweeping than anything that would follow. "Clean air, clean water, open spaces—these should once again be the birthright of every American," Nixon said in a lengthy discussion of the environment in his 1970 State of the Union Address. "This requires comprehensive new regulations." He bragged that his program "will be the most comprehensive and costly program in this field in America's history."[115] More than a few commentators have observed that on balance the Nixon administration was well to left of the Democratic administrations of Bill Clinton and Barack Obama. It was not that Richard Nixon was some sort of closet lefty by any stretch of the imagination; it was the nature of the times.[116] Civilian (non-military) spending by the government hit a peak never seen before or since.[117]

To get a better sense of these times it is imperative to get away from the elites. What drove both parties leftward were the social movements of the period, particularly the civil rights, student, antiwar, and black power movements, joined later by the women's and environmental movements.[118] There were numerous other related currents that held considerable importance. Perhaps the most significant of these was the movement inspired by consumer advocate Ralph Nader, who by most polls was among the most respected Americans in that period, for people across the political spectrum and across the generations. Nader, a proponent of small "d" strong democracy as well as competitive markets, worked tirelessly to advance open governance and effective regulation of big business on behalf of consumers and workers. His work, according to many, had saved more lives than that of any other living American save Dr. Jonas Salk, the creator of the polio vaccine. Nader made the case to young Americans that government could be a positive force in improving both the economy and people's lives, and that a career in public service was not only honorable, but a superior way to give one's life value and meaning.

Simultaneously, there was an enormous counterculture that developed among young people—largely, though not exclusively, from the white middle class, outwardly typified by "hippies"—with a vast culture of music, magazines, FM radio, and underground newspapers. To no small extent this tradition has been erased from history, or it has been replaced with caricatures and stereotypes that do it no justice. Sometimes these hippies and those many they influenced were associated with the activist New Left, but often they were apolitical or only marginally active.[119] This counterculture was decidedly radical in values and lifestyles, with an emphasis on creativity, community, egalitarianism, nonviolence, and a rejection of the acquisitive materialism of consumer culture, which was regarded as ethically and morally bankrupt. While most attention has focused on recreational drug use, rock music, loosening sexual mores, or flamboyant fashion, what is most striking for our purposes is their thoroughgoing rejection of dominant social attitudes and the belief that society needed to radically change.[120] Nothing expressed this worldview better, and to a larger audience, than Yale law professor Charles Reich's 1970 bestseller, *The Greening of America*. Reich projected that the counterculture would lead ultimately to a political revolution by the sheer power of its eventual effective replacement of the Corporate State.[121]

Reich's vision is worth considering:

> There is a revolution coming. It will not be like revolutions of the past. It will originate with the individual and with culture, and it will change the political structure only as its final act. It will not require violence to succeed, and it cannot be successfully resisted by violence. It is now spreading with amazing rapidity, and already our laws, institutions and social structure are changing in consequence. It promises a higher reason, a more human community, and a new and liberated individual. . . .
>
> This is the revolution of the new generation. Their protest and rebellion, their culture, clothes, music, drugs, ways of thought, and liberated life-style are not a passing fad or a form of dissent and refusal, nor are they in any sense irrational. The whole emerging pattern, from ideals to campus demonstrations to beads and bell bottoms to the Woodstock Festival, makes sense and is part of a consistent philosophy. It is both necessary and inevitable, and in time it will include not only youth, but all people in America.[122]

It is easy to laugh at what seems like the absurdity of the counterculture today, as it appeared to get so easily co-opted by Madison Avenue and corporate America in subsequent years.[123] But it certainly scared the bejesus out of older people—especially people in power—who wondered why so many young people were rejecting that which they worked so hard to acquire. In some respects, this was the first "post-scarcity" generation—the heirs to Mill and Keynes—grappling with what the point of life is in an era when accumulating material goods was no longer necessary for survival.

It was the anarchist writer Murray Bookchin who first understood this. He linked the computer revolution to post-scarcity societies, and imagined the ability for humanity to create truly egalitarian, self-governing, libertarian, and environmentally sound societies. In a series of essays in the late 1960s, Bookchin wrote that the conditions were ripe, for the first time in history, for what he termed "post-scarcity anarchism." Rebellious American youth, Bookchin wrote, have

> produced invaluable forms of libertarian and utopian affirmation— the right to make love without restriction, the goal of community, the disavowal of money and commodities, the belief in mutual aid, and a new respect for spontaneity. Easy as it is for revolutionaries to criticize certain pitfalls within this orientation of personal and social values, the fact remains that it has played a preparatory role of decisive importance in forming the present atmosphere of indiscipline, spontaneity, radicalism and freedom.

He added: "In the era when technological advances and cybernation have brought into question the exploitation of man by man, toil and material want in any form whatever, the cry 'Black is beautiful' or 'Make love, not war' marks the transformation of the traditional demand for survival into a historically new demand for life."

Bookchin concluded that the United States was "at a point in history when the boldest concepts of utopia are realizable." It was based on the "steady destruction in the United States of the myth that material abundance, based on commodity relations between men, can conceal the inherent poverty of bourgeois life." Two years after Bookchin penned these words the great uprising in Paris of May-June 1968 took place, with slogans like "All Power to the Imagination" and "Be Realistic: Demand the Impossible" conveying these exact sentiments.[124]

In a weltanschauung where this was a relatively widespread presence and where the Black Panther Party had captured the eyes of the world, the democratic socialist Martin Luther King Jr. and eventual Green Party presidential candidate Ralph Nader were the moderates.* Astonishingly, organized labor, the longstanding nemesis of capital and organized wealth, where socialists frolicked, often was cast in the uncharacteristic role of conservative bastion, or at least as a defender of the status quo. To some extent this owed to the immediate postwar purging of the radical and communist organizers who built up many of the great American trade unions in mid-century; this stripped the movement of many of its most principled and visionary activists. Organized labor still aggressively supported liberal candidates for office, and some elements of it were strong proponents of civil rights, but it tended to be uncomfortable with criticism of the military-industrial complex and the war in Vietnam, and had little apparent sympathy for the student left, black militants, or the counterculture. It did not appear to enjoy being outflanked on the political left, and was very cool toward the 1972 McGovern campaign, despite that campaign's having what was possibly the most pro-labor platform for a major party in US presidential election history.

---

* Here is a sample of the voice of moderation, from King's 1967 speech announcing his opposition to the war in Vietnam: "The war in Vietnam is but a symptom of a far deeper malady within the American spirit, and if we ignore this sobering reality, we will find ourselves organizing 'clergy and laymen concerned' committees for the next generation. They will be concerned about Guatemala and Peru. They will be concerned about Thailand and Cambodia. They will be concerned about Mozambique and South Africa. We will be marching for these and a dozen other names and attending rallies without end unless there is a significant and profound change in American life and policy. . . . This is the role our nation has taken, the role of those who make peaceful revolution impossible by refusing to give up the privileges and the pleasures that come from the immense profits of overseas investments. I am convinced that if we are to get on to the right side of the world revolution, we as a nation must undergo a radical revolution of values. We must rapidly begin the shift from a thing-oriented society to a person-oriented society. When machines and computers, profit motives and property rights, are considered more important than people, the giant triplets of racism, extreme materialism, and militarism are incapable of being conquered. A true revolution of values will soon cause us to question the fairness and justice of many of our past and present policies." Martin Luther King Jr., "Beyond Vietnam," New York, New York, April 4, 1967, http://mlk-kpp01.stanford.edu/index.php/encyclopedia/documentsentry/doc_beyond_vietnam/.

During the late 1960s and early 1970s several reforms were enacted to expand and deepen the democratic infrastructure. As noted,
voting rights were extended to all Americans over eighteeen. The
primary process was opened up so voters could have more influence
over their party's nomination process. Congress passed the toughest
federal campaign-finance laws ever, all with the intent of getting the
influence of wealth out of the electoral process.[125] Public broadcasting
was finally authorized in 1967, with the implicit charter to provide
a voice to the underserved parts of the population.[126] Colleges and
universities were serving an enormous number of first-generation students, with what seems today like virtually free tuition at great public
universities. The federal government began funding public education
in 1965 to bring poor school districts closer to those standards found
in schools in more affluent communities.[127] Poverty was in decline
and both parties were committed to the war on it. Economic inequality was at an all-time low, assisted by high rates of unionization and
progressive income taxation. Only the war, and the stain of militarism,
stood as an intractable barrier, and the antiwar movement and New
Left had that scourge in their sights.

And that's not all. Scholars like Cass Sunstein persuasively argue
that had Hubert Humphrey won the 1968 presidential election—he
came very close—the Supreme Court would have ruled soon thereafter to, in effect, make FDR's Second Bill of Rights part of the Constitution: that is, given that the Constitution required the establishment
of a number of democratic infrastructure initiatives, and given that
all people are entitled to a basic standard of living so they can effectively participate in society, poverty and excessive inequality were, in
effect, unconstitutional.[128] Likewise, it probably would have mandated
equal public-education spending for all children, thus ending the
class-biased system that had been aggravated by suburbanization.[129]
Outside the court, activists came close to having television commer-
cials aimed at children prohibited, and even launched a debate about
whether prisons were necessary any longer.[130]

Everywhere one turned it seemed that wealth and privilege were
on the defensive and the democratic infrastructure was being built out

in an unprecedented manner. "From 1969 to 1972," political scientist David Vogel writes, "virtually the entire American business community experienced a series of political setbacks without parallel during the postwar period."[131] In his introduction to the 1971 bestseller, *America, Inc.*, Nader said the great issue of the coming decade would be the fight to democratize the control of corporations, so shareholders would not have exclusive power, and big business would no longer be a "mindless, parochial juggernaut."[132] To those atop the economy, the nation's traditional rulers, it must have seemed like the inmates were running the asylum.

THE 1970S AND THE CRISIS OF DEMOCRACY

The conservative magazine *National Review* commissioned a poll in 1971 to gauge the opinions of college students on twelve representative campuses. Among the findings was that almost half the students favored "socialization of basic U.S. industries," and that 75 percent would see no problem with Marxists teaching citizenship courses in public schools.[133] Business was on the run, and in its public pronouncements often sounded defensive and conciliatory toward its critics, and eager to establish its commitment to being socially responsible.*

Between 1969 and 1971 a spate of articles appeared in the business press and trade publications addressing the diminished prestige of business and the apparent embrace of socialist ideas by what seemed like a large segment of the population, and especially young people.

---

* It was left to the entirely unrepentant Milton Friedman to grab big business by the collar, much like when Don Corleone shook Johnny Fontane and told him to stop crying and to "act like a man" in *The Godfather*. In a 1970 article in the *New York Times*, Friedman wrote that businessmen who think they are protecting free enterprise by accepting that their businesses have a social responsibility to solve social problems like discrimination and pollution "and whatever else may be the catchwords of the contemporary crop of reformers" are only making matters worse. "Businessmen who talk this way are unwitting puppets of the intellectual forces that have been undermining the basis of a free society these past decades." He introduced, instead, the Friedman doctrine: "The Social Responsibility of Business is to Increase its Profits." Period. See Milton Friedman, "The Social Responsibility of Business Is to Increase Its Profits," *New York Times*, September 13, 1970, p. 33.

These were business people talking to each other and strategizing about what best to do. The most influential communication of this period, by a wide margin, was the Lewis Powell Memorandum of August 1971. It was a confidential memo, prepared for the US Chamber of Commerce and only distributed to a few score corporate executives and wealthy investors, but it created ripples that helped define recent history. When Powell was nominated and confirmed for a position on the US Supreme Court later that year, the memo's existence was unknown and did not arise in his confirmation hearings. Indeed, the Senate hearings were more a coronation than a review, and the collegial tone of the amiable and respected moderate Southern corporate lawyer was contrary to the alarmism and distress of his memo.[134]

What we are dealing with "is quite new in the history of America," Powell wrote. "The assault on the enterprise system is broadly based and consistently pursued. It is gaining momentum and converts. . . . Business and the enterprise system are in deep trouble, and the hour is late." He noted that "the single most effective antagonist of American business is Ralph Nader who—thanks largely to the media—has become a legend in his own time and an idol to millions of Americans." Powell called for a huge increase in the cash commitment of business, its trade associations, and the wealthy to changing the culture and making the media, universities, and schools much more sympathetic to business and free enterprise. "It is time for American business—which has demonstrated the greatest capacity in all history to produce and influence consumer decisions—to apply their great talents vigorously to the preservation of the system itself." He called for business to dramatically increase spending in the "neglected political arena," through increased lobbying and attention to campaigns such that politicians from both parties are beholden to business interests. And he called for business to direct its attention to the judicial system as much as possible, because "the judiciary may be the most important instrument for social, economic and political change."[135]

What is striking about Powell's memo is that it avoids discussion of specific policies—such as income taxation, trade agreements, the Vietnam war, civil rights—altogether. His entire message is that it is imperative for business to seize the political infrastructure and change the weltanschauung. Soon thereafter much of what Powell called for was in place. Groups and campaigns were established to make news media and higher education more sympathetic to the needs of business by the end of the decade. The great pro-corporate think tanks like the Heritage Foundation, the Cato Institute, and the American Enterprise Institute (AEI) were all created within a few years of Powell's memo. As corporate lobbyist Bryce N. Harlow put it in a speech to business leaders: "We must seek out and liberally support the scholars and the institutions in universities and the AEI kind of private research institutes that are tried-and-true believers in a market-oriented economy and American capitalism. If we fail in that, perhaps all else we attempt will in time be unavailing."[136]

Thanks to journalist and author Timothy Noah, we are now aware of the central role of Harlow—whom Henry Kissinger said "virtually single-handedly created the modern advocacy industry"—in radically transforming corporate political power in Washington, DC, during the 1970s. Harlow worked in the Eisenhower and Nixon administrations, and spent most his career as Procter and Gamble's top Washington lobbyist. He began in the early 1960s, when corporate lobbyists were few and far between. Harlow brought a decided class consciousness to the enterprise. "The Achilles heel of every democracy," he told a group of wealthy businessmen, "has been the drive of the enfranchised to use the mighty weapon of political equality to enforce economic equality. The days of a democracy are numbered . . . when the belly of the system takes charge of the head—when the vagrant on the street corner, resentfully eyeing the passing limousines of the privileged, the talented, and the influential, sets about using his equal vote as he would use a pistol in a bank."[137]

Harlow led the campaign in the early 1970s, after leaving the Nixon administration, to get businesses and trade associations to increase their Washington lobbying efforts dramatically, and to coordinate their activities. "The essence of the problem," he told a group of corporate leaders at the newly formed Heritage Foundation, "is that, unless business can force itself to shape up, and very quickly, in ways that it has been unable to use or has refused to use ever before, it is in for the most disruptive, most disheartening season since the earliest New Deal days of 40 years ago. The important thing to understand from the business point of view is that the old ways of dealing with Congress just won't hack it anymore."[138]

Harlow did have a carrot at the end of his stick: "The hard fact is that, each time American business does unify, does weld together its thunderbolt, it wins hands down in Washington. That very fact gave us the Taft-Hartley Act . . . passed over a veto by a two-thirds vote."[139] Harlow did more than talk. He played a large role in the formation of the Business Roundtable in 1972, a lobbying group with membership restricted to the most powerful corporate CEOs, which is chartered to think in class terms.[140]

Message received, and then some. There was a tenfold increase in corporate federal lobbying by the 1980s—such that it eventually became a $9 billion industry by 2014—and K Street became synonymous with this burgeoning major industry, much like Madison Avenue or Wall Street.[141] Where better to find insider lobbyists than from former members of Congress? In the early 1970s, 3 percent of retiring or exiting members became lobbyists; by 2012 the figure was more like 50 percent, often earning seven-figure incomes after their stint in "public service."[142] Washington, DC, accordingly, went from a sleepy middle-class town of bureaucrats to a booming metropolitan area of high-rolling lobbyists and fat cat government contractors.[143] By 2014, according to Forbes magazine, the greater Washington, DC, metropolitan area housed six of the ten richest counties in the nation.[144] And thanks to a process initiated on the Supreme Court by Justice Lewis Powell in the late 1970s, beginning in 2010 the US Supreme Court overturned a century of legislation and jurisprudence and allowed, in effect, unlimited and unaccountable corporate and individual donations to political campaigns. With this newly shaped and decidedly less-democratic infrastructure, the business domination and control of governance was all but guaranteed.

But that was far from clear in the early 1970s. While the loudest voices of the radical left had disappeared or were speaking in quieter tones, and the student left all but vanished, two related developments threatened to put US business in an even more precarious position.

First, not all young white workers got the memo that they were supposed to be a bunch of Archie Bunker lunkheads, easily manipulated by politicians using jingoistic and dog whistle racist rhetoric. The Vietnam War had been fought largely by poor and working-class Americans, and that experience had a radicalizing effect on more than a few of them.[145] By the early 1970s some of the troops in Vietnam were in semi-open revolt against their commanders, while for many of the rest cynicism abounded, and it was very difficult for the war to be prosecuted. An extraordinary report on the "collapse of the armed forces" by Marine Corps Colonel Robert D. Heinl Jr. was published in a June 1971 edition of the *Armed Forces Journal*. It begins with the following and then goes into detail, particularly about the widespread "fragging"[146] (i.e., murder) of US military officers by the soldiers under their command:

> The morale, discipline and battleworthiness of the U.S. Armed Forces are, with a few salient exceptions, lower and worse than at any time in this century and possibly in the history of the United States.
>
> By every conceivable indicator, our army that now remains in Vietnam is in a state approaching collapse, with individual units avoiding or having refused combat, murdering their officers and non commissioned officers, drug-ridden, and dispirited where not near mutinous.
>
> Elsewhere than Vietnam, the situation is nearly as serious.[147]

Indeed, Army bases were often adjacent to left-wing coffee shops— sometimes affiliated with the FTA[148] movement—and African American, Latino, and a significant number of white GIs were radicalized. It convinced the brass that the draft was no longer viable and led to the institution of a professional army.[149]

When these veterans returned to jobs in American factories they brought an entirely new sensibility to a generation of workers already changing with the times. "With all the shoulder-length hair, beards,

Afros and mod clothing along the line," *Newsweek* observed after a visit to the Lordstown, Ohio, GM plant, "it looks for all the world like an industrial Woodstock."[150] By 1970 the "situation exploded in an upsurge of pent-up rank-and-file militancy," as historian David Noble explained.[151] The early 1970s saw the greatest wave of strike activity, work stoppages, slowdowns, and wildcat strikes since 1946. In 1970 alone 2.4 million workers engaged in large-scale work stoppages of one kind or another. The *Wall Street Journal* characterized the situation as "the worst within memory."[152] There were aggressive attempts led by young workers to take over the steelworkers and mineworkers unions, among others, and throw out the traditional leadership. Management was "dealing with a workforce," *Fortune* informed its readers, "no longer under union discipline."[153]

The concerns of the workers were far more than wages and benefits; after all, real wages for male workers hit their historic peak in 1972. Automation, both in its elimination of jobs and dehumanization of those that remained, was a huge issue for the young workers. As Noble put it, workers were not happy with "management's obsession with and struggle for control over workers."[154] "It is imperative for labor," dissident young longshoremen wrote in a 1971 pamphlet opposing union leadership and management, "to challenge the notion that the employer—in the name of 'progress'—can simply go ahead and slash his workforce or close his factory or, as is being planned in our industry, close an entire port, and to do so without any regard for the people and community involved."[155]

"At the heart of the new mood," the *New York Times* reported, "there is a challenge to management's authority to run its plants, an issue that has resulted in some of the hardest fought battles between industry and labor in the past." The symbol of this new wave was the three-week-long 1972 strike at the Lordstown plant led by "a group of young, hip, and inter-racial autoworkers" whose primary issue was opposing the "fastest—and most psychically deadening—assembly line in the world."[156] There were efforts to link this working-class radicalism to student and antiwar activists and liberals in general. As progressive journalist Jack Newfield put it in 1971, the way to unite these forces was to build around "the root need to redistribute wealth and the commitment to broaden democratic participation."[157]

The crisis in America's workplaces grew so severe that in 1971 Nixon's Secretary of Health, Education, and Welfare, Elliot Richardson, appointed a special task force to study and propose recommendations to address the emergence of "blue-collar blues" and "white collar woes."[158] The subsequent January 1973 report, *Work in America*, began with a quote by Albert Camus—"Without work all life goes rotten. But when work is soulless, life stifles and dies."—and went from there. "Productivity increases and social problems decrease when workers participate in the work decisions affecting their lives, and when their responsibility for their work is buttressed by participation in profits." The "keystone" of the report was a call for "the redesign of jobs," to make them more fulfilling, and there was an important role for unions and workers and government to play in doing this redesign in conjunction with business. "It would give, for the first time, a voice to many workers in an important decision-making process. Citizen participation in the arena where the individual's voice directly affects his immediate environment may do much to reduce political alienation in America."[159]

This extraordinary report, generated by the Nixon administration no less, was in many senses a last hurrah for the era's weltanschauung.

The second development that made the position of US business more uncertain was that in 1974 the United States entered the worst recession since the 1930s; it lasted until 1975 and the official unemployment rate climbed to 9 percent, the highest it had been since the Great Depression. The Watergate scandal as well as the recession gave the Democrats overwhelming control of the Congress after the 1974 elections. The progressive wing of the Democratic party went on the offensive and in the middle of the 1970s advocated strongly for guaranteed full employment, tax reform to make the system *more* progressive, excess-profits taxes on large corporations, Ralph Nader's proposal for a cabinet-level Department of Consumer Protection, same-day voter registration to encourage and increase turnout, labor-law reform to benefit unions, and national health insurance

(Medicare for all), among other things.[160] Polling revealed large corporations were singularly unpopular institutions deep into the 1970s. Business was in a precarious position as it sought policies to reestablish profitability and make it lucrative to invest, especially as it saw austerity—cutbacks in wages and social services for the many and reductions in taxes on business and the wealthy—as the *only* possible course. In 1974 *Business Week* magazine explained the dilemma facing business: "Some people will obviously have to do with less. . . . It will be a bitter pill for many Americans to swallow the idea of doing with less so that big business can have more. Nothing that this nation, or any other nation, has done in modern economic history compares with the selling job that must be done to make people accept this reality."[161]

There was growing elite consensus on the importance of this point. In 1973 the Trilateral Commission was established by business interests to examine the "crisis of democracy" facing the leaders of advanced capitalist nations as they attempted to deal with the problems associated with the ongoing "democratic surge," especially in the United States. This was far from a wingnut operation; it was from the heart of the establishment and was thoroughly bipartisan. Its 1975 report on the United States written by Harvard scholar Samuel P. Huntington stated that "Al Smith once remarked that 'the only cure for the evils of democracy is more democracy.' Our analysis suggests that applying that cure at the present time could well be adding fuel to the flames. Instead, some of the problems in the United States today stem from an excess of democracy."

So the crisis of democracy was . . . too much democracy: "The effective operation of a democratic political system usually requires some measure of apathy and noninvolvement on the part of some individuals and groups."[162] F. A. Hayek, the noted free-market economist, agreed. "Our system of unlimited democracy," he noted despondently, forces "persons at the head of government . . . to do things that they know to be permissive" and wrong, but they must do them to retain their positions.[163]

But how realistic was it to believe such a world-class sales job was possible? The strategy had emerged: an effective sales job by business and its allies on the glories and primacy of "free enterprise" and the evils of big government should be complemented by ongoing efforts to shrink the democratic infrastructure—generating the necessary amount of "apathy and noninvolvement"—such that people would be less likely to interfere with governance. "The effort was undertaken," as political scientist Sheldon Wolin puts it, "to hammer home the astounding principle that a democratically chosen government was the enemy of 'the people.'"[164]

As for the sales campaign, any timidity was cast aside and the operating logic by the late 1970s was that the best defense is a good offense. A tidal wave of material not only promoted the genius of free enterprise, but it also found a new scapegoat to blame for all the nation's increasing economic and social problems: liberals, especially liberal intellectuals. All problems in the nation could be traced to the loony half-baked ideas of liberals and their effete supporters in the media and academia. Now that the economy was broken, the problems there could also be attributed to labor unions and their lazy, pampered, overweight chieftains. Business was a heroic, All-American, job-creating institution that all these deadbeat parasites could never appreciate and wrongly stigmatized. Entrepreneurs and corporate CEOs were the real heroes of society. Milton Friedman, fresh off his 1976 Nobel Prize in economics, argued that liberals, like the kind he was forced to cohabit with at the University of Chicago, were the "intellectual architects of the suicidal course" the country was on.[165] If the Powell Memo was confidential, former Treasury Secretary William E. Simon made the same case in a 1978 bestseller that said what was required was "nothing less than a massive and unprecedented mobilization of the moral, intellectual and financial resources" from those who understood the life-and-death imperative to defend the free enterprise system.[166]

The campaign was a smashing success.[167] The very term *liberal*, which had only a few years earlier been embraced by most Democrats and many Republicans, went from a place of respect for a great political tradition to being filed between drug dealer and pedophile in the popular lexicon. It became unmentionable; the "L" word. And on the congressional front, the entire package of progressive legislation which had seemed likely to pass the day Jimmy Carter was inaugurated in January 1977 went down to ringing defeat within two years as the rejuvenated business lobbies flexed their now gargantuan muscles.[168]

While Reagan defeated Jimmy Carter in the 1980 presidential race to mark the ascension of this "neoliberal" approach to dominance, it has since been forgotten than only a few short years earlier the prospect that someone with Reagan's views might win a national election was seen as preposterous. But to get the full measure of the transition still ongoing, consider the 1980 platform of the Libertarian Party, which featured billionaire David Koch as its vice-presidential candidate. The platform called for, among other things:

- Repeal of all campaign finance laws and unlimited corporate and individual donations
- Abolition of Medicare, Medicaid, the Postal Service, and Social Security
- Abolition of the Environmental Protection Agency, and an end to most consumer regulation
- Privatization of the water system, railroads, public roads, and the highway system
- Abolish all income and capitals-gains taxation
- End all government funding and operation of public schools
- Abolish all social-welfare programs
- Make labor unions "voluntary" for employees, and collective bargaining possible only if employers agree; prohibit the government from enforcing collective bargaining rights
- Repeal of antitrust laws and any government efforts to break up monopolies, as well as abolition of the Federal Trade Commission[169]

This was Milton Friedman's vision of a "free" society with no democratic infrastructure. It is a society where most citizens get nothing of value from the government, and are told they can never get anything of value from the government, so they logically lose their interest in it. As Wolin writes, when politicians proceed "methodically to reduce or eliminate social programs, the result is tantamount to a deliberate strategy of encouraging political apathy among the poor and needy."[170]

Even in 1980 these were all regarded as such batshit crazy ideas that Ronald Reagan wanted nothing to do with them. Yet, their proponents were at last in the on-deck circle. Today some of them have been accomplished at least in part or informally and all of them are legitimate issues for discussion. They have become mainstream political issues, and some of them will be the defining political battles of the coming generation. The weltanschauung has been turned upside down.

This was reflected in political realignments. The Republican Party has moved steadily to the right since the 1970s, purging its entire liberal and moderate wings. Economic and political elites who were associated with the party, and who might still be reasonably liberal on issues such as reproductive rights, made a marriage of convenience with a new entity that came to be known as the "religious right." This uncomfortable but politically potent alliance—a union first conceived by big business as a way to counter the popularity of the New Deal—sought from the start to win votes and elections without dwelling on the self-serving (and unpopular) economic policies of the elites.[171]

The Democratic Party has moved rightward as well. The Democratic Leadership Council was founded by people like Bill Clinton and it successfully remade the party into a far more pro-business party—a champion of deregulation, lower taxes on business and the rich, cutbacks in social services, and secretive trade deals that benefit large corporations and investors but have dubious value for everyone else. The concerns of organized labor and social movements, now reclassified as "special interest groups," were marginalized. The degree to which Democrats moved rightward was obscured by the "polarization" that occurred after congressional white southern Democrats all became Republicans or were defeated by Republicans. With the Democrats losing their southern wing, and the Republicans purging their moderate and liberal wings, there was almost no overlap between the parties, for the first time in history. This has made effective governance by a

two-party system increasingly difficult. Yet the structural constraints
on the process—the lack of a sufficient democratic infrastructure—has
prevented the development of viable third, fourth, and fifth parties that
exist as meaningful alternatives in themselves or in coalitions. Consequently, as the parties have both moved well to the right since the 1970s,
so too has political discourse and the governance of the country.[172]

For four decades the right wing has led the charge to dismantle
or enfeeble the democratic infrastructure. In some of these cases the
Democrats offer resistance, usually tepid. In others, they go with the
flow. And, in too many instances, they join in the deconstruction.

The leaderships of the parties march in lock-step in two areas
where grave damage is being done to the democratic infrastructure.
The first is with regard to militarism. After the defeat in Vietnam
and a rash of scandals involving illegal government surveillance on
American citizens in the 1960s, Senator Frank Church's Senate select committee held unprecedented (and never repeated) hearings in
1975–1976 on the crimes of the federal government, especially by the
unaccountable intelligence community. It consequently passed laws to
reassert congressional control.[173] This mid-1970s moment of honest
reflection about militarism and empire was a nod to the old weltanschauung—it was termed the "Vietnam syndrome"—and quickly forgotten.[174] Both parties now effectively pursue the same policies with
regard to the US military role in the world, and are committed to
a permanent wartime budget, with minimal civilian or congressional
oversight. The United States is in a permanent war against a faceless
enemy that only ends when people in power say it will end, and they
have no incentive to ever end it. When the Soviet Union collapsed
some innocent dreamers imagined the United States would be able
to return to a level of military spending found in other nations, or in
our own pre–Cold War history. America would enjoy a massive "peace
dividend" and could build up its civilian (and democratic) infrastructure. Instead, after what seemed like a thirty-second pause, military
spending remained unchanged and then increased, for no coherent
reason. Continual warfare is now hard-wired into the political economy, a part of the informal constitution.

Second, beginning in the 1980s, for the first time in US history, the federal government began to systematically "privatize" public services and "outsource" to private firms what had traditionally been government activities.[175] States and local governments have followed suit, and both parties participate in the process.[176] The purported reason for privatization and outsourcing was to bring market efficiency to the public sector; it followed from what Tony Judt described as "the intellectual shift that marked the last third of the 20th century . . . the worship of the private sector and the cult of privatization."[177] Research suggests that politics and greed had the most to do with what the government privatized, and that the efficiency claims were rarely realized and often flat wrong. Instead, this became a cash cow for large corporations and wealthy investors and has fanned the flames of corruption.[178] For investors and corporations hard-pressed to locate profitable investments in the sainted "free market," having a chance to grab a fistful of taxpayers' dollars and take over military functions, prisons, public schools, and anything else that wasn't nailed down is a gift from the heavens, especially when the terms are invariably generous, with all-but-guaranteed high rates of return. This also creates powerful lobbies with a decided interest in more militarism, more prisons, and more privatization of schools, so more public money can go into their coffers.[179] The US government, under Republicans and Democrats, seems to be dedicated to fattening the bank accounts of crony capitalists above all else.

But the corruption surrounding privatization and outsourcing is only the beginning of the damage it does to the democratic infrastructure. By removing the government from important functions, it lessens the ability of the citizenry to play a role in the economy and it locks in business domination. Privatization and outsourcing lessens the ability of government to solve social problems and therefore generates cynicism toward it. And, to top it off, evidence suggests privatization has contributed to the rapid escalation of economic inequality.[180] Ironically, the administration of the government by the "free market" crowd proves their exact point: government is corrupt, incompetent, and not to be trusted.[181] The end result is a great demoralization and depoliticization. The weltanschauung has changed, precisely as intended.[182] The cancer of the "excess of democracy" or "unlimited democracy" has been surgically removed and destroyed. Corporations and the wealthy have won, with all the economic benefits outlined in Chapter 2.

For some time now scholars and writers have wrestled with a paradox. In the past, when the United States has had great periods of conservatism where elite interests dominated—such as the original planter/merchant aristocracy, Southern slavery, the Gilded Age, the 1920s—they were followed by major reform periods dedicated to lessening inequality and corruption.[183] By historical standards, the United States is long past due, by a good two decades, for such a reform moment. In our view, the evidence points to the deterioration of the democratic infrastructure as a—perhaps *the*—key factor in delaying or preventing a new era of reform; people have little way to effectively participate in the governing process and they respond (or opt out of responding) accordingly.[184] Until that changes, the paradox will only continue and deepen.

THERE IS NO MYSTERY TO DEMOCRACY

The United States faces a great crisis of unemployment and underemployment, which will be exacerbated by revolutionary developments in technology. It is part of a broader economic malaise, which is made worse by a political system that is mired in corruption and does the bidding of society's very wealthiest inhabitants and largest corporations.

The people who dominate the political economy at present are determined to use their considerable resources and influence to prevent the development and expansion of democratic infrastructure. Indeed, at many turns, they consciously seek the actual deconstruction of that infrastructure. And they will work harder to do so as the social pressures created by technological change, automation, and joblessness are felt more acutely.

Furthermore, the present rulers have spent the past forty years trying to convince everyone that becoming part of an aroused and engaged and organized citizenry is unnecessary and a waste of time. Arguably their greatest victory of the past four decades has been converting the longstanding American optimism that democracy can lick any problem before it into a morose pessimism that there is no alternative, and resistance is futile.

Of course it is frustrating for citizens to be fighting old fights for rights that should have been secured long ago. But the elites know something that should give us all encouragement: the current rulers cannot win a fair fight so they must rig the game. In times of crisis, like the 1970s, their contempt for democracy comes to the surface. In their hands, the United States has become a nation that, as FDR warned it might, is coming to share far too many attributes with fascist societies. Unless there are major structural changes, even those liberties and privileges we enjoy today may be in jeopardy. This is a frightening proposition. But the world the current rulers have made is ill-equipped to address the crisis of unemployment and underemployment, and in no position to advance democratic practices and values. It has to go.

The humane and effective solution to the economic crisis requires that (1) the political system be rejuvenated into a powerful democratic infrastructure that (2) draws people into public policy debates as effective participants. That is the route to the best possible outcomes. Then a frank and effective debate over how best to restructure the economy to serve human interests can occur. In that process the weltanschauung will change, and the crisis will appear as more of an opportunity than as a threat, and human imaginations will be unchained. We can use the technologies to build an egalitarian, humane, sustainable, and democratic society as has never before been seen.

The good news is that nearly all the elements of a democratic infrastructure that we list in Chapter 1 and return to in Chapter 6 have deep roots in American political history. Indeed, what is required to have a credible democracy is well known across the planet.

The other good news is that there is no mystery about what creates democracy and democratic infrastructure. They advance primarily with energy from dynamic popular social movements, as we discuss next, in Chapter 5. Social activism changes everything.

Just as history tells us much about how a democratic infrastructure can and should be constructed, so it tells us much about the formation of those dynamic social movements in times of great economic and social turbulence. In that history, and in the movements that have already taken shape in contemporary America, we see the outlines for the movements to establish the necessary democratic infrastructure for our times.

chapter five

OVERCOMING
THE DEMOCRATIC DISCONNECT

S OMETHING SCARY ABOUT AMERICA, REALLY SCARY, AND REALLY
unsettling, became evident to us as we traveled the United States
on extensive national tours for our two previous books—one of
which examined the collapse of mainstream journalism as a source
of the information that is necessary and sufficient to sustain democracy, and the other of which examined the collapse of democracy
itself under the weight of a campaign-finance system so broken that
it has become the plaything of rogue billionaires and self-interested
CEOs.[1] Everyone understood what we were talking about. We were
examining the fundamentals of the political process as it currently
operates, and condemning that process as a travesty that no longer
serves citizens or communities or the country as a whole. Yet, we
got almost no pushback. Even when we appeared as unapologetic
progressives on conservative or libertarian talk-radio programs, even
when we responded to callers from across the political spectrum,
even when we "debated" those who had positioned themselves as

defenders of traditional values, there was a universal sense that the United States had entered into a period of crisis.

That wasn't the scary part. While the crisis is serious, it would be far worse if people failed to recognize that the country has veered off course.

The scary part was the response of many of the best and brightest people we met to that recognition. As part of these tours, we gave well over a hundred talks on scores of college campuses. The discussions were thoughtful and highly engaged; we were struck by the deep awareness that something had gone askew with America. No one— no student, no professor—jumped up and said, "Hey, you've got it all wrong. The system is working just fine." Back in the late 1990s when we spoke on campuses, we occasionally encountered spirited defenses of the status quo. No more. On our recent tours we found deep recognition of the crisis and a palpable desire to address it: to boldly and genuinely democratize the nation. But we also found a profound and numbing pessimism. Americans live in a time when it often seems that nothing of consequence is ever accomplished by the political system for the benefit of the people—or, at the least, that nothing that is accomplished is as good as was promised, or as permanent as expected. When a putative candidate of the people, Barack Obama, is elected with spellbinding rhetoric and overwhelming, unprecedented support from young voters, the actual results are pretty much business as usual on core economic issues, if not across the board. The message we got from every corner of the country, from every campus and church basement and union hall, was that the experience of politics in recent years has poured gasoline on the flames of cynicism. You can fight the power, we were informed. But you cannot win. Resistance, too many Americans of good sense and good will were telling us, *is* futile.

Scholars and researchers and writers from across the political spectrum point to the certainty that severe economic disruptions, coming in the none-too-distant future, are going to undermine the quality of life for tens of millions of Americans. Few dispute this, at least not with evidence. Most people, too, accept that the democratic infrastructure, as it is currently arranged, is insufficient to foster the necessary response to the challenges that are coming our way. These same people recognize that rebuilding the democratic infrastructure is necessary and long overdue, and would go a long way toward making it possible to reform the economy so we could dramatically improve the human condition. But then the despair sets in. This is impossible, we are told. People will never rise up and make social change. This is as good as it gets. Remarkably, even people who are working hard for change tell us that, in all likelihood, their efforts are for naught. They will struggle on, for reasons of morality and solidarity, they say, but, really, it's hopeless. These good citizens are experiencing the poet Allen Ginsberg's sad, resigned calculus: "America I've given you all and now I'm nothing."[2]

The resulting depoliticization may well be the greatest victory of the counterrevolution launched in the 1970s by the web of corporate-funded think tanks, policy networks, political action committees, and media that has come to dominate the discourse. It has so disillusioned those who know the current system is not working that many of the Americans who should be our most engaged and active citizens see no hope at all. This represents the greatest challenge Americans face today as a people. Yet, it is not a new challenge. Rulers have always found that having their subjects be quiescent of their own volition is the preferable means of maintaining the status quo. But history also tells us that a time comes when the people can stand it no more—when it is not just optimism but necessity that inspires a reaction against conditions that have grown unbearable—when, as Thomas Jefferson wrote in the Declaration of Independence, "evils" are no longer "sufferable."

This will be the case again, and soon. Indeed, there are signs all around us that the roots of a new activism on behalf of economic democracy are growing underneath the corporate media radar. There was no movement for a fifteen-dollar-an-hour minimum wage when we were touring in 2010, and only the barest hints of one when we were touring in 2013. Now, that movement is everywhere. There are parallel movements for a Retail Workers Bill of Rights, for new unions, for a new economy. These movements are not yet so powerful as they will be, and they are not yet so linked together as they will be. But the remarkable response to the presidential candidacy of Bernie

Sanders, which made the linkages in a political context, suggests that the prospect for a transformational moment is real. So, too, does history. Indeed, we can learn from history what it takes for popular forces to not merely engage in electoral campaigns, but to secure a fuller politics and a fairer economy.

We have felt the urgency and seen the activism as we have worked on this book. Something is stirring in the land, because of the economic turbulence that has become so very evident—and because, no doubt, people understand that the turbulence is just the beginning. We still hear plaintive wails of hopelessness. But we also hear talk of organizing, marching, and building something. In fact, one of the most common questions we get at public events these days, sometimes during the formal question-and-answer period, sometimes in furtive conversations that extend late into the evening, has to do with where exhausted citizens who were perfectly willing to expend all that was left of their energy might direct themselves. "What's the most pressing problem?" "What's the most important reform?" "What should I be doing right now?" These people do not want to give up; they know that giving up is not an option. Their numbers are growing. This chapter, and this book, is for them, for you.

AS REAL A REVOLUTION AS THAT OF 1776

We have reviewed the crucial debates concerning democracy at the founding of the nation and in its earliest years. There were also important lessons then about how to make effective social change. "The man who loves his country on its own account, and not merely for its trappings of interest or power, can never be divorced from it, can never refuse to come forward when he finds that she is engaged in dangers which he has the means of warding off," wrote Thomas Jefferson in a 1797 missive that noted threats to liberty coming not from distant kings or tea companies but from elected congressmen and presidents.[3] A few years later, when those threats had become all too evident, and when Jefferson was leading an electoral revolt against the abuses of John Adams's presidency, the author of the Declaration of Independence observed that "it behooves our citizens to be on their guard, to be firm in their principles, and full of confidence in themselves. We are able to preserve our self-government if we will but think so."[4]

Americans still believe this. But they are not, necessarily, "full of confidence in themselves." For that confidence to be renewed, a connection must be made. Not for the first time, but again—as it has been in the past. Jefferson's victory over Adams in 1800 represented the first such American connection. Even at a point when the country fell far short of democracy, when the vast majority of adults could not and did not vote, when editors and members of Congress had been threatened with imprisonment (and in several circumstances were actually jailed) for challenging the authority of an increasingly totalitarian president, a political revolution occurred. Jefferson's defeat of Adams led to much more than the first peaceful transfer of power from a president of one faction to a president of another faction. "The revolution of 1800" was, the new president correctly observed, "as real a revolution in the principles of our government as that of 1776 was in its form; not effected indeed by the sword, as that, but by the rational and peaceable instrument of reform, the suffrage of the people."[5]

A stack of books has been written about the election of 1800, and scholars continue to wrestle with its lessons and consequences. Yet, the explanation of what happened came before the vote from Jefferson himself, in a 1798 letter to John Taylor of Caroline, as the recipient was known. A great advocate of citizen engagement to prevent "a capitalist sect artificially created" from concentrating wealth and power in the new United States, Taylor was agitated by the machinations of Adams and his compatriots, via the Alien and Sedition Acts, to consolidate the authority they had obtained following Adams's narrow 1796 victory over Jefferson.[6] Jefferson counseled that

> a little patience, and we shall see the reign of witches pass over, their spells dissolve, and the people, recovering their true sight, restore their government to its true principles. It is true that in the meantime we are suffering deeply in spirit, and incurring the horrors of a war and long oppressions of enormous public debt. . . .

And if we feel their power just sufficiently to hoop us together, it will be the happiest situation in which we can exist. If the game runs sometimes against us at home we must have patience till luck turns, and then we shall have an opportunity of winning back the principles we have lost, for this is a game where principles are at stake.[7]

An impulsive and often contradictory figure, Jefferson still frustrates biographers. Yet, for all his flaws, he had two remarkable strengths: he was a great popularizer of ideas (second only to Paine) and he was a master of political strategy. Jefferson understood precisely what was required for those who are disempowered to achieve a political revolution. He had experience in this regard, both as the essential author of the Declaration of Independence and as the champion of religious tolerance in colonial Virginia. He understood that there must be "a standard of general feeling" in order to generate both the political will and the political reforms necessary to bend the arc of history. Thus, the key phrase in Jefferson's letter to John Taylor was not the oft-recalled reference to "the reign of witches" but the neglected reference to how "if we feel their power just sufficiently to hoop us together."[8]

What Jefferson was focusing on was the prospect that disparate movements and factions—and there were many in the early days of the American experiment—might be drawn together by a common sense of crisis. And by a common sense of how to respond to that crisis. Though cautious American historians frequently write around this reality, crisis moments in the United States invariably have immediate and clear economic underpinnings. The frequent causes of turbulence are technological, societal, and structural changes to the economy that upset both individual work life and society.

The 1790s saw several financial panics sweep the new United States, as real-estate speculation by foreign and domestic elites created bubbles that burst in much the same way that the speculators of the 1990s and 2000s created boom-and-bust cycles leading up to the financial meltdown of 2008. The speculators often regrouped, but the damage done to the condition of port workers, wage laborers, and shopkeepers lingered—for instance, the Panic of 1797 was still felt in 1800, especially in the port cities along the east coast.[9] This was one of the factors that "hooped together" critics of Adams's presidency and helped Jefferson to win states he had lost in the preceding election, including New York and Maryland. Jefferson's foes in 1800 referred to the Virginian and his supporters as *Jacobins*, borrowing the term first used to describe the most radical of French revolutionaries and then quickly adapted to describe the advocates who, though far from France, shared a taste for upsetting old political *and* economic orders. From afar, the British conservative Edmund Burke warned that Jefferson and his kind were "intoxicated with 'the wild gas' of liberty." Burke was giving Jefferson too much credit, but many of Jefferson's followers were proud to call themselves Jacobins. They joined Democratic-Republican societies that were referred to as "Jacobin Clubs" and that amplified demands not merely for "liberty" but for "equality."[10]

THE URGENT DEMAND OF THE WORKING CLASS

As Jefferson's career was winding down—he left the White House in 1809—the first industrial revolution was transforming England. It was here that technological revolution was fused with a radical transformation of the economy, with explosive effects on the people. The British historian E. P. Thompson provided the deepest insight into the "Pilgrim's Progress" by which disparate individuals and groups of individuals become a class that identifies itself as separate and apart from the political and economic overlords of a nation, with immediate demands for reforms that might alter the nexus of power so that, via democracy, the ruled might become the rulers.[11] Half a century ago, in the introduction to *The Making of the English Working Class*, Thompson reframed and dramatically expanded the discussion of class and class consciousness to establish an understanding of the champions of democracy as a class of citizens seeking to forge a society in which their demands for justice, initially placed through direct-action protests against changes they could not control, might create a circumstance of majority rule:

Like any other relationship, it is a fluency which evades analysis if we attempt to stop it dead at any given moment and anatomize its structure. The finest-meshed sociological net cannot give us a pure specimen of class, any more than it can give us one of deference or of love. The relationship must always be embodied in real people and in a real context. Moreover, we cannot have two distinct classes, each with an independent being, and then bring them into relationship with each other. We cannot have love without lovers, nor deference without squires and laborers. And class happens when some men, as a result of common experiences (inherited or shared), feel and articulate the identity of their interests as between themselves, and as against other men whose interests are different from (and usually opposed to) theirs.[12]

Thompson recognized in the machine-breaking protests of the Luddite rebels against the manifestations of a new industrial age something more than an unthinking rejection of technology and labor-saving devices. He saw the honest expression of a fear—perhaps not fully understood or explained, but fully experienced—that a change imposed by mill owners and "rotten-borough" parliamentarians would render the circumstance of the great mass of workers less humane, less reasonable, less fair. Thompson does not suggest that the initial protests by the Luddites and their fellow insurgents against the oppressive demands of industrialization were all about democracy. Those who protested were often, as author Kirkpatrick Sale has so ably explained, "rebels against the future."[13] But Thompson teaches us that they were also part of something bigger. The historian argues that isolated and seemingly separate protests across the British Isles in the last years of the eighteenth century and the first years of the nineteenth century began to forge a consciousness of the need for democracy—and of how that consciousness eventually led to mass mobilizations on behalf of fundamental and transformative political reform.

With the emergence of an understanding that few significant changes could be achieved by separate economic, social, and political reform movements, but that every change might become possible with a focused and cohesive movement for democracy, the champions of labor rights, religious tolerance, and republicanism turned toward one another. An industrial revolution had thrown everything into question, and in the initial uncertainty the old elites had imposed their will. But the questions were not answered. In fact, they grew more pressing. This, in turn, created a circumstance that provides broad insight into how movements for economic justice produce an agitation for democracy sufficient to permit citizens to repair the breach created by elites.

The first decades of the nineteenth century were a time of epic technological and industrial advances in the United Kingdom, but also of epically irresponsible financial speculation—almost on a scale with what we see today in the United States. That speculation caused cycles of boom and bust that became increasingly devastating for the great majority of workers, farmers, and small shopkeepers. As failed speculators sought to retain their elite status and their comforts by squeezing the poor, it grew increasingly clear that advancing science and industry did not equate to advancing equality. In fact, shifting economic arrangements were creating social chaos. The 1830s saw a banking crisis and then a broader collapse of industrial employment in Britain, such that "grievous reports of distress were being received in 1837 from all the manufacturing districts" of the British Isles. Tens of thousands were unemployed in Manchester, fourteen thousand were out of work in Paisley, while business failures were "alarmingly frequent" in Nottinghamshire and Leicestershire. Riots swept the country as the people rose in opposition to the crude and punishing "Poor Law" of 1834. It consigned impoverished adults and children into workhouses with intentionally deplorable housing and food in exchange for mandatory unpaid labor, of the back-breaking variety—"the operation of which was now for the first time being actively felt."[14] Yet, the response of the economically and politically powerful elites of Great Britain was not to recognize the severity of the crisis and the barbaric consequences for the people. Rather, it was to use the full policing and military force of the central government to put down the protests and to jail and deport those who objected.[15]

It was then that workers and farmers would no longer settle for old inequalities dressed up in an emperor's new clothes of industrial "progress." They began to identify as Chartists, joining their disparate protests, their disparate energies, their disparate fears, and their disparate hopes to the campaign for a "People's Charter" that demanded the democratization of politics and governing:

- All men to have the vote (universal manhood suffrage)
- Voting should take place by secret ballot
- Parliamentary elections every year, not once every five years
- Constituencies should be of equal size
- Members of Parliament should be paid
- The property qualification for becoming a Member of Parliament should be abolished[16]

Today, these changes may appear to be simple and incremental reforms. But at the time they were lodged by the London Working Men's Association, the demands were portrayed as the height of radicalism—anticipating some principles of equal representation that the United States, the supposed exporter of democratic ideals, would not formally embrace for more than a century. Yet, when the People's Charter was first circulated in 1838, the radicals gathered 1.25 million signatures supporting their cause, and then several years later they gained 3 million signatures.[17] The powerful pushed back, often using violence to thwart peaceful protest and direct-action demonstrations, yet even official historians now accept that "the Chartists' legacy was strong" and reforms once imagined as radical were with relative speed accepted as "inevitable."[18] From these reforms came a new politics, and from that new politics came transformations of working life and of society that answered the "clumsy" questions first posed by the Luddites about what would happen to the displaced, the unemployed, the unrepresented masses in a new industrial age.

How did this happen? John Bates, an English Chartist who would eventually immigrate to the United States and continue the democratic struggle by organizing miners into a pioneering American union, offered the best explanation. Recalling the transformative moment when many struggles became one, he explained that in Britain "here were [radical] associations all over the county, but there was a great lack of cohesion. One wanted the ballot, another manhood suffrage and so on. The radicals were without unity of aim and method, and there was but little hope of accomplishing anything. When, however, the People's Charter was drawn up . . . clearly defining the urgent demands of the working class, we felt we had a real bond of union; and so transformed our Radical Association into local Chartist centres."[19] A period of economic and social upheaval spawned a plethora of radical responses that slowly coalesced into a cohesive demand for democracy.

This is an arc of history that must be understood in our times. It provides an indication of the vital role to be played by contemporary campaigners on a host of issues, and of the way in which Americans might confront and tame the digital disruptions that have already occurred and those that are sure to come. Thompson invites us, correctly, essentially, to look for a new set of heroes who are not celebrated in the "official" histories of the past or on the business pages of the *New York Times* or the *Wall Street Journal* today:

I am seeking to rescue the poor stockinger, the Luddite cropper, the "obsolete" hand-loom weaver, the "Utopian artisan," and even the deluded follower of [religious prophetess] Joanna Southcott, from the enormous condescension of posterity. Their crafts and traditions may have been dying. Their hostility to the new industrialism may have been backward-looking. Their communitarian ideals may have been fantasies. Their insurrectionary conspiracies may have been foolhardy. But they lived through these times of acute social disturbance, and we did not. Their aspirations were valid in terms of their own experience; and, if they were casualties of history, they remain, condemned in their own lives, as casualties.

Our only criterion of judgment should not be whether or not a man's actions are justified in the light of subsequent evolution. After all, we are not at the end of social evolution ourselves. In some of the lost causes of the people of the Industrial Revolution we may discover insights into social evils which we have yet to cure. Moreover, this period now compels attention for two particular reasons. First, it was a time in which the plebeian movement placed an exceptionally high valuation upon egalitarian and democratic values. Although we often boast our democratic way of life, the events of these critical years are far too often forgotten or slurred over. Second, the greater part of the world today is still undergoing problems of industrialization, and of the formation of democratic institutions, analogous in many ways to our own experience during the Industrial Revolution. Causes which were lost in England might, in Asia or Africa, yet be won.[20]

Thompson penned those words more than half a century ago, before there was a Google or a Facebook or a Twitter, before there were cellphones or personal computers. Yet, we would update his proposition only in two ways. First, we are certain that Thompson's view of political formation is appropriate not merely to an industrial age but to a digital age. Second, we fear that the timelines Thompson worked on are speeding up, as barriers once thought insurmountable are collapsed in a chaotic age when historian of science James Gleick charts "the acceleration of just about everything."[21]

BREAKING THE YOKE OF SOULLESS INDUSTRIAL DESPOTISM

The advocates of humanity are getting better and better at expressing frustration with expanded inequality and diminished democracy. Yet, they have not succeeded in turning these understandings into a practical politics and governance that can make the change Theodore Roosevelt and his supporters proposed more than a century ago when they spoke of replacing "the tyrannies" of economic and political elites with governance that starts with the premise that "this country belongs to the people who inhabit it. Its resources, its business, its institutions and its laws should be utilized, maintained or altered in whatever manner will best promote the general interest."[22] It was at this moment, in the first decades of the twentieth century, that the

American people created the first great democratic surge in response to the heavy industrialization, widening inequality, and rampant corruption of the Gilded Age.

Roosevelt was not a radical, and he has richly earned his share of criticism. He was a synthesizer of popular ideas that were once considered radical but that were rapidly becoming part of the weltanschauung of a new age. Roosevelt and his allies argued that "it is time to set the public welfare in the first place."[23] But their point of beginning was not with a specific program. Rather, it was with a recognition that the America in which they sought to achieve progressive economic and social change lacked the democratic infrastructure that was needed to reflect the will of the people onto the policies adopted by legislators and executives. In the great framing address of what would come to be a Progressive Era of sweeping reform and social change, Roosevelt explained that

> no sane man who has been familiar with the government of this country for the last twenty years will complain that we have had too much of the rule of the majority. The trouble has been a far different one that, at many times and in many localities, there have held public office in the States and in the nation men who have, in fact, served not the whole people, but some special class or special interest. I am not thinking only of those special interests which by grosser methods, by bribery and crime, have stolen from the people.
>
> I am thinking as much of their respectable allies and figureheads, who have ruled and legislated and decided as if in some way the vested rights of privilege had a first mortgage on the whole United States, while the rights of all the people were merely an unsecured debt. . . .
>
> Now there has sprung up a feeling deep in the hearts of the people—not of the bosses and professional politicians, not of the beneficiaries of special privilege—a pervading belief of thinking men that when the majority of the people do in fact, as well as theory, rule, then the servants of the people will come more quickly to answer and obey, not the commands of the special interests, but those of the whole people.[24]

While casual historians tend to imagine isolated historical events defined by clashes between great men, serious observers of social movements that lead to meaningful change recognize the way in which economic change in general—and patterns of economic instability in particular—bend the arc of history toward moments of initial upheaval and eventual political and social change. This is true in the British experience observed by E. P. Thompson. And this is true in the American experience of Thomas Jefferson and the nation that extended from his Declaration of Independence. America has seen many moments of intensely focused and effective popular engagement in the past, as abolitionists forced the issue of slavery to the center of the nation's agenda, as "vote yourself a farm" campaigners forced the redistribution of public lands to the poor and new immigrants, as populists and trust busters undid the Gilded Age, as New Dealers saw off the "Toryism" of the Wall Street gamblers and unfeeling corporatists whose covetous greed had crashed the global economy, as civil rights campaigners began to give meaning to a two-centuries-old promise that "all men [and women] are created equal."

None of these movements blossomed from thin air. They bloomed with deep and complex root structures, which had grown together over decades. Disparate movements for what had once seemed to be very different causes came, usually in a moment of crisis, to a realization that they were not so different in their fundamental purposes. Thus, an agrarian populist excited by William Jennings Bryan's "Cross of Gold" speech to the 1896 Democratic National Convention might eventually make common cause with an urban do-gooder enthused by Theodore Roosevelt's New Nationalism. Like the Chartists of another land, responding to an earlier stage of an ongoing industrial revolution, Americans came in the early years of the twentieth century to understand the necessity of uniting in pursuit of democratic reforms that were needed to address the corruption, the inequality, and the economic and political violence of a new age of "robber barons." It is no coincidence that the economically and socially unstable period from 1910 to 1920 saw the United States amend its constitution to create an elected rather than an appointed US Senate, to establish an income tax and the infrastructure by which corporations would be taxed and regulated, to extend the franchise to women so that 133 years into the American experiment it might finally be possible to speak of majority rule.[25] The first wave of the modern democratic infrastructure was being constructed.

Nothing was *given* to the American people in this period. These constitutional amendments were demanded by a great movement for reform that crossed lines of gender and race and class and partisanship and immediate self-interest. The political platforms of the 1912 election—in which the Democratic, Republican, Progressive, and Socialist parties competed with a seriousness and an intensity that has not since been matched—did not peddle pabulum. They outlined bold agendas for altering the character of the economy and the direction of society, and they recognized the need for democratic changes that would make it possible to achieve those alterations. The economic critique drew from economist Thorstein Veblen's summary dismissal of then-existing capitalism as irrational and unfair. Of course, the Socialist Party platform of American Railway Union leader Eugene Victor Debs and Milwaukee Mayor Emil Seidel was more radical, but the practical agenda of the Socialists, with its calls for a minimum wage, unemployment insurance, old-age pensions, conservation of natural resources, and an end to child labor, was echoed in the platforms of the other parties. So, too, were calls for an elected Senate, and for women's suffrage. And so, too, in only slightly less ardent language, was the understanding of what was awry. The Socialists argued that "the capitalist system has outgrown its historical function, and has become utterly incapable of meeting the problems now confronting society."[26] They denounced "this outgrown system as incompetent and corrupt and the source of unspeakable misery and suffering to the whole working class." And they explained that

> in spite of the multiplication of labor-saving machines and improved methods in industry which cheapen the cost of production, the share of the producers grows ever less, and the prices of all the necessities of life steadily increase. The boasted prosperity of this nation is for

the owning class alone. To the rest it means only greater hardship
and misery. The high cost of living is felt in every home. Millions of
wage-workers have seen the purchasing power of their wages decrease
until life has become a desperate battle for mere existence.

Multitudes of unemployed walk the streets of our cities or trudge
from State to State awaiting the will of the masters to move the wheels
of industry. The farmers in every state are plundered by the increasing prices exacted for tools and machinery and by extortionate rents,
freight rates and storage charges.

Capitalist concentration is mercilessly crushing the class of small
business men and driving its members into the ranks of property-less
wage-workers. The overwhelming majority of the people of America
are being forced under a yoke of bondage by this soulless industrial
despotism.[27]

Radical? Perhaps. But compare the language of the Socialists with
the program outlined by former President Theodore Roosevelt and
his Progressive Party, which began by announcing that "to destroy
this invisible government, to dissolve the unholy alliance between
corrupt business and corrupt politics is the first task of the statesman-
ship of the day."[28] The Progressives contended that the "test of true
prosperity shall be the benefits conferred thereby on all the citizens,
not confined to individuals or classes, and that the test of corporate
efficiency shall be the ability better to serve the public; that those who
profit by control of business affairs shall justify that profit and that
control by sharing with the public the fruits thereof."[29]

Roosevelt and his compatriots were not socialists. They were simply speaking the language of the moment; it is a clear example of how
the weltanschauung had changed. Indeed, as he prepared his 1912
candidacy, Roosevelt argued that

the absence of effective state, and, especially, national, restraint upon
unfair money getting has tended to create a small class of enormously
wealthy and economically powerful men, whose chief object is to hold
and increase their power. The prime need is to change the conditions

which enable these men to accumulate power which it is not for the general welfare that they should hold or exercise. We grudge no man a fortune which represents his own power and sagacity, when exercised with entire regard to the welfare of his fellows. Again, comrades over there, take the lesson from your own experience. Not only did you not grudge, but you gloried in the promotion of the great generals who gained their promotion by leading the army to victory. So it is with us. We grudge no man a fortune in civil life if it is honorably obtained and well used. It is not even enough that it should have been gained without doing damage to the community. We should permit it to be gained only so long as the gaining represents benefit to the community. This, I know, implies a policy of a far more active governmental interference with social and economic conditions in this country than we have yet had, but I think we have got to face the fact that such an increase in governmental control is now necessary.[30]

Roosevelt was right. Meaningful progress toward the betterment of society could not be achieved without facing the fact that corporations, not citizens, were in charge. The wealthy men who controlled those corporations were absolutely unwilling to act in the public interest, and as such they were employing the great developments of an age of invention and innovation—and the accumulated wealth associated with the mass production of those inventions and the implementation of those innovations—to consolidate their power rather than to improve the condition of the great majority of Americans. Roosevelt recognized that the improvement in the circumstance of that great majority could not be achieved without a democratic revolution. He called it "reform" or "progressivism." His opponents called it "dangerous" or "anarchism." But what Roosevelt proposed in the second decade of the twentieth century was precisely what must be proposed today—an outline for democracy in a new age:

If our political institutions were perfect, they would absolutely prevent the political domination of money in any part of our affairs. We need to make our political representatives more quickly and sensitively responsive to the people whose servants they are. More direct action by the people in their own affairs under proper safeguards is vitally necessary. The direct primary is a step in this direction, if it is associated with a corrupt practices act effective to prevent the advantage of the man willing recklessly and unscrupulously to spend money over his more honest competitor. It is particularly important that all moneys received or expended for campaign purposes should be publicly accounted for, not only after election, but before election as well. Political action must be made simpler, easier, and freer from confusion for every citizen. I believe that the prompt removal of unfaithful or incompetent public servants should be made easy and sure in whatever way experience shall show to be most expedient in any given class of cases.[31]

Specific demands for a democratic revolution were woven into the platforms not merely of Roosevelt's Progressives and Debs's Socialists but of the Republican Party that backed incumbent President William Howard Taft and the Democratic Party that would beat them all with a college professor-turned-politician named Woodrow Wilson. Though the 1912 campaign was one of the hardest fought in American history, a rough consensus on democratic reform was achieved during its course.[32] So it will come as little surprise that, during Wilson's presidency, the Constitution was for the first time since the immediate aftermath of the Civil War amended in relatively rapid succession to end the corrupt practice of appointing senators, to allow for the taxing and regulation of corporations, and to enfranchise women. This was a democratic revolution, and it did much more than clear the way for the immediate changes of the Progressive Era.

These structural changes to American democracy made possible the timid economic and social reforms of the 1910s and 1920s (many of which developed in the states that were recognized then as the nation's "laboratories of democracy"). But they also laid the groundwork for the moment when America would confront the supreme issue outlined by Supreme Court Justice Louis Brandeis in his observation that "we must make our choice. We may have democracy, or we may have wealth concentrated in the hands of a few, but we can't have both."[33] Facing the economic and social breakdown that extended from a Great Depression, Franklin Roosevelt responded with a New Deal that was made possible by the democratization of America. We rarely put democratic reforms in proper perspective, we rarely recognize how different things would be had one change not cleared the way for another. But we need to recognize that FDR's decisive action in 1933 was made possible by reforms initiated in 1913. And we need to recognize how those reforms were achieved.

STUMBLING TOWARD DEMOCRACY

The Progressive Era of democratization did not begin with a speech by Theodore Roosevelt, or even by his worthier antecedent (and frequent scold) Robert M. La Follette. The reforms that eventually became inevitable were not always broadly popular—in fact, they were not always understood as having anything to do with economic injustice. The period after the Civil War in the United States was a time of wild economic instability—of booms and busts that could be a little rough on the rich but absolutely devastating for the farmers, shopkeepers, and day laborers who were struggling to make sense of an economic system that had just been radically reordered by both a war and the arrival of a new age of northern industry, rapid expansion to the west, and fierce financial speculation. The Panic of 1873 rocked the United States so completely that, until 1929, the financial meltdown of the 1870s was referred to as the "Great Depression." When the wave of financial speculation that followed the end of the Civil War crashed, banks collapsed, the New York Stock Exchange closed, and factories began mass layoffs as unemployment soared. Within a matter of months, fifty-five of the nation's railroads had failed; within two years, an estimated eighteen thousand businesses had been shuttered.[34]

The elite response to the meltdown was consolidation, monopoly, and the building of trusts by those like John D. Rockefeller who had the resources and the connections to capitalize on crisis.

The response of the people to the panic was a great agitation about money, which saw farmers associated with the Grange movement and some of their allies form a Greenback Party that argued for easing the gold standard in order to clear the way for the circulation of unbacked paper money, known as greenbacks.[35] This change, the party and its supporters in the labor movement of the day argued, would tip the balance in favor of farmers and workers rather than robber barons and bankers. It was an inspiring prospect, so much so that the *Chicago Weekly Tribune* imagined that the Greenbackers were providing "an opportunity to accomplish something for the country at large—not for the farmers merely, but for all who live by their industry, as distinguished from those who live by politics, speculations and class-legislation."[36] The Greenbackers did indeed have some success at getting candidates elected to state legislatures and the Congress—and considerably more success at introducing ideas such as the eight-hour day, protections for unions, and opposition to monopolies into the political discourse. They decried the "money power" as "the monster of the age" and raged against an "aristocracy of untaxed wealth"—sharing a lexicon with the National Labor Union of the 1870s and the Knights of Labor movement that would rise in the 1880s. Yet, they never gained sufficient traction in a political system that was stacked against the notion of giving economic power to the people. The same went for the People's Party—or Populist Party—that stirred even greater interest around the time of the next great panic, in 1893.[37]

The People's Party built stronger and better alliances between farmers and workers, and had considerably more success at the polls, especially in 1894. But the loose third-party movement never quite succeeded in breaking the stranglehold of the two "old parties," and in 1896 the movement effectively aligned with the Democrats after the surprise nomination of thirty-six-year-old Nebraska populist William Jennings Bryan for the presidency. Bryan was a brilliant public speaker, with immense personal appeal and righteous anger at the bankers and monopolists who had come to rule the Gilded Age. He objected on moral grounds to the impoverishment of farmers and to the violence that was visited upon miners and railway men who sought to organize unions. "The poor man who takes property by force is called a thief, but the creditor who can by legislation make a debtor pay a dollar twice as large as he borrowed is lauded as the friend of a sound currency," growled the Great Commoner. "The man who wants the people to destroy the Government is an anarchist, but the man who wants the Government to destroy the people is a patriot."[38]

Bryan anticipated the New Deal and the modern Democratic Party when he explained to the Democratic delegates of 1896 that "there are two ideas of government. There are those who believe that, if you will only legislate to make the well-to-do prosperous, their prosperity will leak through on those below. The Democratic idea, however, has been that if you legislate to make the masses prosperous, their prosperity will find its way up through every class which rests up on them."[39] Yet, Bryan was in most senses a nostalgic politician who framed his advocacy in deeply religious and romantic terms, pouring his heart and soul into the defense of an agrarian age that was rapidly passing. In effect, he ran against the future, declaring that "you come to us and tell us that the great cities are in favor of the gold standard; we reply that the great cities rest upon our broad and fertile prairies. Burn down your cities and leave our farms, and your cities will spring up again as if by magic; but destroy our farms and the grass will grow in the streets of every city in the country."[40] This was a proper diagnosis, but not a proper appeal.

Against the "money power" assembled by Mark Hanna, the Republican kingmaker who contemporary political grifters such as Karl Rove cite as their hero, Bryan's hapless Democrats were defeated in 1896—and Bryan would lose again in 1900, and again in 1908. The 1896 Democratic platform was thick with talk of gold and silver "standards," but devoid of a vision for how to make a politics that would deliver a new economy.[41] Bryan accepted the political structures that had been assembled to defeat him, and he was, predictably, defeated. The Bryan Democrats, with their emphasis on state's rights, never captured the energy of the burgeoning New Nationalism of the dawning twentieth century. Often more urban, and more adept

at utilizing new tools for communicating and organizing, the rapidly expanding social movements of the period supported women's
suffrage, immigrant rights, labor rights, civil rights, child-labor laws,
and workplace protections so there would be no more industrial di-
sasters like the Triangle Shirtwaist fire that claimed the lives of 146
garment-factory workers (123 of them women and girls as young as
fourteen) in New York City in 1911. They had their own agendas,
but they were beginning to recognize that none of them would be
achieved within the existing calculus of American politics—a calculus
that Bryan had, unwittingly, confirmed could not be upset even with
the most inspired populism.

A critical turning point came with the Panic of 1907, when the speculators busted the economy. The official response will sound familiar to
anyone who was paying attention almost exactly a century later when a
descendent generation of speculators busted the economy. Washington
politicians went to work developing better ways to shore up big banks.
But the conversation among reformers and rebels and radicals began
to turn. Instead of merely answering another crisis with another round
of populist fury at the bankers and their political minions, it began
to dawn on activists and eventually on Americans in general that the
problem wasn't merely a matter of crooked bankers and corrupt politicians. The problem was with a constipated system that offered limited
options for setting things right. Labor activists began to recognize the
vital importance of votes for women—who were so abused in workplaces, and whose children were on the machine floor rather than in
the school room. Suffragettes began to recognize that a monopolized
economy might be as much of a problem as a monopolized politics, and
that the way to address both issues might be by aligning with the trust
busters. And everyone began to recognize that very little was ever going to change if the US Senate was made of men chosen in backroom
deals, men so devoid of shame that the solons had no trouble with
making Nelson Aldrich, the millionaire father of John D. Rockefeller's
son-in-law, the chairman of the National Monetary Commission.[42]

Mass communication played a role in all this. The heart of the system, newspaper journalism, was notoriously corrupt. But a dissident

journalism flowered on the margins and it proved integral to political success. Muckraking writers like Upton Sinclair exposed remorseless bankers and barbarous industrialists.[43] Muckraking magazines like *Cosmopolitan* (yes, that *Cosmopolitan*, but in its earlier incarnation as a crusading journal) published a nine-part series on the "Treason of the Senate," which declared that "treason is a strong word, but not too strong to characterize the situation in which the Senate is the eager, resourceful, and indefatigable agent of interests as hostile to the American people as any invading army could be."[44] Instead of waiting for a "kept press" to tell the truth about machinations of "the money power," progressives such as Robert M. La Follette began to start their own magazines (*La Follette's Weekly*, now the *Progressive*, started in 1909), socialists took local publications such as the *Milwaukee Leader* and the *New York Call* national, and anarchists such as Emma Goldman became editors. The labor press flourished. And the exposés and calls to action grew so loud that the "kept press" in many instances grew a little less kept and a little more conscious that something had to change.

In the period leading up to the 1912 election, connections were constantly made between economic and social ills and the dysfunction of democratic institutions. The "disconnect" of that time between a demand for change and meaningful reform was revealed and reviled. Citizens could organize, advocate, assemble and petition for the redress of grievances; they could raise cries against injustice and against the practical failures of ruling economic elites; and they could decry the economic misdeeds that created a boom-and-bust pattern that seemed always to boom for the wealthy but that frequented busted everyone else. They could combine direct action that yielded isolated victories (particularly for skilled workers involved in industrial disputes) with electoral action that made temporary gains in cities such as Milwaukee and Cleveland, where brutally corrupt Democratic and Republican machines were upended by the transformative administrations of "Sewer Socialists" and other progressive reformers. But the prospect of a whole and meaningful response to the crisis of the age did not become real until the connection between political reform and economic and social progress became a central theme of national politics. The disconnect could no longer be ignored. It had to be addressed.

The political reforms that were demanded and largely achieved in the period from 1910 to 1920—an elected Senate; votes for women; bans on corporate campaign contributions; direct primaries; the option for citizens to petition for initiatives, referendums and recalls; limited protections for labor organizing and collective bargaining; structural shifts that allowed for the development of state banks and municipal utilities; an expanded commitment to public education in general and higher education in particular—did not immediately repair all that ailed America. In some ways, this new democratic infrastructure made things more unstable, more uncertain. But the instability was democratic rather than feudal, and it pointed toward prospects for fundamental change that would be realized as the defeated Democratic vice-presidential nominee of 1920 became the elected Democratic president of 1932.

Franklin Delano Roosevelt frequently celebrated the role that democratic reforms had played in clearing the way for policies that would humanize industry and finance, policies that voice "the deathless cry of good men and good women for the opportunity to live and work in freedom, the right to be secure in their homes and in the fruits of their labor, the power to protect themselves against the ruthless and the cunning. It recognizes that man is indeed his brother's keeper, insists that the laborer is worthy of his hire, demands that justice shall rule the mighty as well as the weak."[45] FDR preached that the essential tool in the pursuit of a humane future was a sense of cohesion around a set of democratic principles and ideals that link all of those who are fighting "against those forces which disregard human cooperation and human rights in seeking that kind of individual profit which is gained at the expense of his fellows."[46] This Roosevelt saw his election not as the start of something but as the next stage in a progression toward democracy.

"It is just as hard to achieve harmonious and cooperative action among human beings as it is to conquer the forces of Nature. Only through the submerging of individual desires into unselfish and practical cooperation can civilization grow," the thirty-second president explained a year after his election, as he celebrated the legacy of Robert M. La Follette and the progressive reformers on a trip to Wisconsin. "In the great national movement that culminated over a year ago, people joined with enthusiasm. They lent hand and voice to the common cause, irrespective of many older political traditions. They saw the dawn of a new day. They were on the march; they were coming back into the possession of their own home land."[47]

It was not merely that the New Deal reforms rested on the shoulders of what had been done in the Progressive Era; they rested on the shoulders of activism across the nineteenth century. As we saw in Chapter 4, the great democratic wave of the 1960s and early 1970s was elevated by the democratic infrastructure created in the New Deal, and much of the activism today that we turn to now finds its most important antecedents in that era. We are not alone, and we are not reinventing the wheel.

A FORMULA FOR DEMOCRATIZING THE FUTURE

Often, when discussing modern society, wise observers will talk about the extent to which human beings feel disconnected. There is now an entire literature devoted to the "bowling alone" phenomenon of collapsing community, just as there are now entire industries devoted to easing and addressing the alienation of modern times.[48] But that's not the "disconnect" that interests us at this point. That's not the crisis. The political crisis facing Americans has to do with a more traditional definition of *disconnect*—the sort that occurs when a fully developed and otherwise functional device does not work because it is not connected to a power supply. The power supply we refer to is the great mass of Americans, many of them already active, many more ready to be engaged. They need a democratic infrastructure that can translate their existing and evolving demands for an economy that translates technological advancement into societal progress.

Think of the economic and social movements that are already active in America, think of the values that Americans already share, think

of our fears and think of our hopes, as sources of immense possibility—a light that might lift the darkness, a phone that might call for
help, a medical device that might keep the heart beating. The ideas
have been developed. The energy to advance them exists. But there
is no connection. They are not plugged into a system that exists with
the purpose of establishing and maintaining what Theodore Roosevelt described as the essential requirement for addressing societal ills
and achieving social progress in a great and prosperous land: "a true
democracy on the scale of a continent, on a scale as vast as that of the
mightiest empires of the Old World."[49]

If we recognize the necessity for democratizing the debate about
dramatic economic and social changes—changes that reveal the extent
to which disenfranchised peoples find themselves with insufficient
tools for shaping their futures—and if we recognize that history provides us formulas for achieving that democratization, then the questions that remain are clear.

Is the current crisis sufficient to inspire a radical response? The answer to our view, indeed the entire point of this book, is to suggest that
we are already in the midst of a transformational crisis that it is rapidly
extending in scope and consequence. Elites in media and politics may
assume, or at the very least pretend to assume, that the great masses of
Americans are sufficiently entertained to remain docile. But this is not
the case. The economic and social changes ushered in by long periods
of deindustrialization, radical workplace change, and stark wage stagnation are creating chaos that benefits 1 percent or so of our population but that leaves the rest of us confused, frightened, and justifiably
angered. The keyword of our moment is *disruptive*.[50]

The economic uncertainty of our times has spawned new movements that reject half-steps and seek to address income inequality and
wage stagnation with immediate initiatives. When President Obama
was being told by Washington insiders, some of whom call themselves
"Democrats," that he was being too bold in proposing to increase
the minimum wage from $7.25 an hour to $9 an hour, fast-food and
retail workers across the country said that simply was not enough.
The argument that full-time workers ought not live in poverty has

been forced into the political debate by low-wage workers, union activists, and proud radicals like Seattle City Council member Kshama Sawant.[51] They aren't settling for incremental change; they are fighting for $15-an-hour wage rates. And they are winning in Seattle and San Francisco and Los Angeles and other communities across the country.[52] The most powerful retailer in the United States, Walmart, has felt the pressure and moved to raise wages for most workers above $10 an hour—significantly more than a supposedly pro-labor president was proposing two years earlier.

This is a movement that has displayed political skills, but it has also embraced old-fashioned direct action. After Seattle's Sawant was arrested at a protest that demanded wage hikes for airline workers, the city councilmember said the airline should be on trial—not her. Asked if it was appropriate for elected officials to be arrested in protests against corporations, Sawant declared, "When workers and faith leaders and community activists are putting their own lives on the line to fight for the rights of workers, it's appropriate for me as an elected public figure to join them in the struggles."[53] She's right. And the struggles in Seattle and other cities are having a dramatic impact. Hundreds of thousands of workers are being lifted above the poverty line not just by organizing to "Fight for 15" but by sophisticated new initiatives—such as a "Retail Workers Bill of Rights," which was enacted in San Francisco after a 2014 campaign spearheaded by the Jobs With Justice movement and its allies. This bill of rights addresses the abusive scheduling and workplace uncertainty that has become endemic in the increasingly app-driven fast-food and retail sectors. It forms a rough outline for a movement not merely to hike wages but to humanize work—and to ensure that workers are not merely whipsawed by that rapid restructuring of traditional industries.[54]

This country has a more militant labor movement than at any time since the early 1970s, possibly even the 1930s. Despite the end of labor reporting by most major media and the replacement of traditional business reporting with "coverage" that is best understood as cheerleading, there are still almost fifteen million union members in the United States today.[55] They are under brutal assault by corporate-funded Republican governors and legislators—and, notably, a number of Democratic mayors—who seek to shut down the steadiest defenders of public services and public education in our politics. Yet, in states such as Missouri and West Virginia, workers have blocked anti-labor right-to-work laws. And in cities such as Los Angeles and New York, and unexpected regions such as the Rio Grande Valley, unions are actually expanding their membership—especially among low-wage workers. Savvy labor leaders such as Rose Ann De Moro of National Nurses United (NNU) recognize that the movement is not as unified or as strategically sophisticated as it needs to be—especially in the face of technological changes that are designed to replace professionals with robots. But, says De Moro, "a movement that has already organized millions of Americans has the potential to be a lot more influential and effective, and right-wing politicians are giving us a lot of reasons to get our act together."[56]

NNU, for example, has been in the forefront of researching so-called digitalized care. While the healthcare industry and new tech companies that have developed to share in the profits are busy developing robots to provide bedside care, the Office of Inspector General, US Department of Health and Human Services, has identified serious and widespread flaws with new systems for healthcare delivery. Not that long ago, the idea of a "robot nurse" would have been the stuff of science fiction but it's a reality now. However, it was not a well-examined reality until NNU launched its own research and education programs to warn that "bedside computers that diagnose and dictate treatment for patients, based on generic population trends not the health status or care needs of that individual patient, increasingly supplant the professional assessment and judgment of experienced nurses and doctors, exposing patients to misdiagnosis, mistreatment, and life-threatening mistakes."[57]

In working on this book, we met with NNU officials and discussed their investment of resources and energy in this project. It's a serious commitment, focused on gathering information, developing statistical databases and, most importantly, identifying for patients and policy-makers the right standards to apply when considering which technologies to utilize and how. "The American health care system already lags behind other industrialized nations in a wide array of essential health barometers from infant mortality to life expectancy. These changing trends in health care threaten to make it worse," explains NNU Co-president Jean Ross, RN. "Behind every statistic is a patient, and their family, who are exposed to unnecessary suffering and risk as a result of the focus on profits rather than what is best for individual patient need."[58] The nurses aren't opposed to technology; they use it all the time. But instead of merely considering the bottom line, they are considering the life-and-death consequences of automation and adding a human component to the equation. And they are expending considerable resources on education campaigns that publicize their conclusions. They fill at least some of the void created by the collapse of serious journalism and the decay of traditional oversight by regulators and legislative and congressional committees. It's not enough, as the nurses were the first to tell us. But this is an important model that ought to be embraced by other unions and activist groups–and that foundations and donors that are serious about getting to the heart of the matter should fund.

Getting workers directly involved with how automation is deployed was considered enlightened thinking in the 1960s, and accepted across much of the political spectrum, at least in principle. It is high time people organize to get us back to that point, and to abandon the suicidal notion that the corporations have an innate right to do whatever they please, social consequences be damned, as long as they are maximizing profits.

This country is seeing the renewal of historic ideals of public and cooperative enterprise. New movements are taking on what Gar Alperovitz, the cofounder of the Democracy Collaborative, refers to as the "huge and agonizing long-term task" of developing and popularizing alternative models for ownership and job creation that involve "nothing less than transforming the underlying institutions that are producing the outcomes we see—in short, one way or another, transforming the system over time, beginning, as always [and as we shall see], in local communities where the pain is greatest."[59] This is big bold stuff, and it has moved way beyond theory. The United States has a vibrant Slow Food movement that has established itself in every state and every major city, along with many small towns. This movement is developing and supporting sustainable models for farming, food production, and eating out—or in. And there is an expanded vision of cooperative enterprise that has begun to renew old ideals of worker ownership and consumer involvement in a country where almost thirty thousand cooperatives have issued almost 350 million memberships.[60] Across the country, there are proposals to democratize finance, with public banking at the state and local levels (along the lines of the century-old and highly successful State Bank of North Dakota), and a coalition of unions and consumer groups is working to renew postal banking as a vehicle to strengthen the US Postal Service and provide access to necessary (and responsible) financial services to low-income and rural communities.[61] "Essentially, a new strategic paradigm—the idea that democratizing ownership can begin locally—is emerging around the nation," argues Alperovitz. "Just beneath the surface of most public reporting, in fact, an explosion of experimentation like this is going on in all parts of the country. It is also beginning to demand—and get—backing from larger institutions, and political backing as well. Such efforts include groups like Prospera, in San Francisco, and Cooperative Home Care Associates, in New York, that bring together women who do home cleaning and home health work, respectively; cab driver co-ops in several cities; food co-ops in most parts of the country; advanced manufacturing co-ops like Isthmus Engineering and Manufacturing in Madison, Wisconsin; and many, many more."[62]

Extending the democratic infrastructure to the economy is the logical next step. It is a topic that requires study and experimentation. And, though you would not know it from media coverage of economic debates, that study and experimentation is burgeoning in communities across the country.

So, too, are movements that refused to be boxed up in neat packages of partisanship. These are the big-picture movements that "get" that the organizing of the future requires a challenge to both major parties and to all of our politics. It's the only way to address essential issues of our time.

This country has a movement to address climate change that recognizes the economic and political challenges outlined by Naomi Klein and Bill McKibben and other visionaries. And it has drawn millions of Americans, especially young Americans, into the streets to demand not merely a transition off fossil fuels but, in the words of Climate Justice Alliance co-director Cindy Wiesner, "an economy good for both people and the planet."[63] An estimated four hundred thousand people joined the September 21, 2014, People's Climate March in New York, and hundreds of thousands more participated in hundreds of marches in communities across the United States—in solidarity with millions more at thousands of rallies across the planet.[64]

This country has a new civil rights movement that has drawn millions of young people—and many of their elders—into the streets and onto social media to declare that "Black Lives Matter." This movement is challenging policing models that have left too many young African American men dead, criminal "justice" models that have substituted mass incarceration for mass employment, and political models that seek to "win" elections by undoing the progress made by the Civil Rights Act and the Voting Rights Act. In states across this country, unprecedented multiracial, multiethnic, multi-religion coalitions that link unions and students and seniors together have surged onto the political scene, declaring as does the Reverend William Barber of North Carolina's Moral Mondays movement that "we need a transformative moral fusion movement that's indigenously led, state-based, deeply moral, deeply constitutional, anti-racist, anti-poverty, pro-justice, pro-labor movement that brings people together, that doesn't wait for somebody to rescue you out of Washington DC, but [that] you mobilize from the bottom up."[65]

This country has a democracy movement that has evolved into the most vibrant crusade for constitutional reform in a century—since the days when progressive reformers sought an elected Senate and votes for women. More than six hundred American communities have formally demanded congressional action to begin the process of undoing the Supreme Court's *Buckley v. Valeo, Citizens United,* and *McCutcheon* decisions. They seek nothing less than a constitutional amendment that will renew the fundamental American premises that money is not speech, that corporations are not people, and that citizens and their elected representatives have a right to shape campaign finance laws to ensure that votes matter more than dollars. Sixteen states have formally requested action to amend the constitution. Millions of Americans have voted in referendums, signed petitions, and appeared before legislatures, city councils, and town boards to demand an electoral politics that is defined by ideas rather than the money power of self-interested billionaires and pay-to-play corporations.[66] Yet, still, when we mention what has happened in speeches to engaged and thoughtful Americans, surprising numbers of them do not know that this movement even exists.

To that end, this country has a media reform movement, steeped in democratic values and a fundamental understanding of civil society's need for robust journalism and unrestrained debate; a movement that in February 2015 beat the most powerful telecommunications corporations on the planet in a fight to preserve a free and open Internet.[67] How? "Four million Americans wrote this agency to make known their ideas, thoughts, and deeply-held opinions about Internet openness," said Federal Communications Commission member Jessica Rosenworcel, who voted with the people and against the conglomerates. "They lit up our phone lines, clogged our e-mail in-boxes, and jammed our online comment system. That might be messy, but whatever our disagreements on network neutrality are, I hope we can agree that's democracy in action and something we can all support."[68]

The number of Americans who are actively involved in the work of addressing the economic and social and political challenges of this moment is astronomical. The critical mass is real. The energy is real. But it is not yet, to borrow an organizing concept from Jefferson, hooped together.

We know this, practically, because so many movements that have drawn so many people to the streets, to the capitals, and to the polls have succeeded by every reasonable measure when it comes to sound-

ing the alarm, making the case, winning the argument, and even winning the election. But they have not succeeded in making big-enough
change—or even in creating the space where the change might be
possible.

There is more to this than the simple challenge of coordination.
Of course this is an issue, but not as much of an issue as might once
have been the case. Climate-change campaigners get that there is an
economic-justice component to their work. Living-wage advocates
understand that there is a racial-justice component to their work. Yes,
there is still a tendency on the part of advocates to imagine that one
issue must go first. We hear powerful and poignant arguments for this
model of prioritization or that. We have made some of them ourselves.
But, if history is any indicator, we know that the defining and uniting
issue will be economic. And we know that the crisis of a jobless future will bring millions of Americans who are not currently engaged
into a fight that extends from the First Amendment–sanctioned direct action of assembling and petitioning for the redress of grievances
through the organizing of new-model labor unions and cooperatives,
to the casting of ballots on behalf of candidates who really are better
than their opponents. But we also know, as was the case two hundred
years ago on the moors of Yorkshire, and one hundred years ago in the
sweatshops of New York, that the political process is weighted against
this activism—indeed, against all activism.

Hence the electoral system is generally the last place social change
leaves its mark. It is a crucial and necessary stage to lock in change,
and election campaigns can be valuable in pushing movements forward, but electoral success is best understood as part of the of the
process. And in these times, where money has corrupted the system
almost beyond belief, the process is frequently frustrating. This is
why the extraordinary enthusiasm generated by US Senator Bernie
Sanders's campaign for the presidency has been so striking. As the
Sanders campaign gained traction in the summer and fall of 2015,
massive crowds and rising poll numbers provided tangible evidence
of the deep reservoir of support for radical social changes that would
reconstruct the economy to suit the needs of the poor and working

class. At a point in American history when frustration was high, and when cynicism about the prospects for change threatened to become debilitating, Sanders was getting people out of their houses and back into a political process that was sorely in need of an infusion of people power. In the senator's hometown of Burlington, Vermont, more than five thousand people showed up to cheer on his announcement of candidacy. Then came ten thousand people in Madison, Wisconsin. Then there were fifteen thousand in Seattle, twenty-seven thousand in Los Angeles, and twenty-eight thousand in Portland. In the first caucus state of Iowa and the first primary state of New Hampshire, the crowds for Sanders were vastly greater than those of any of the other candidates, many of whom had more name recognition, stronger connections to the political establishment in key states, bigger campaign treasuries and massive Super PACs bankrolled by the wealthiest Americans.

What distinguished the Sanders campaign from the start was a focus on the issues that are being raised by the new movements for economic and social change. The newness of the movements created pressures for Sanders; #BlackLivesMatter activists pressed the candidate to speak more forcefully about the need for the reform of policing and for an end to mass incarceration. Instead of resisting the pressure, Sanders embraced it and evolved his campaign and its message. That evolution illustrated how the Sanders run was distinct from standard electoral projects—but not from movements that are in a constant process of updating and extending their activism and their organizing. The explosive growth of the Sanders campaign illustrated the potential for a movement politics that addresses the issues arising from rapid technological and economic change. Indeed, Sanders built his campaign, from the start, around the idea that a "political revolution" would be required to democratize politics and economics. To do this, Sanders spoke, constantly, of the need to rejuvenate the democratic infrastructure with constitutional amendments, sweeping reforms and unprecedented levels of popular engagement. This is the language of a transformative politics—which is, of course, precisely what is needed.

THE POINT AT WHICH EVERYTHING BEGINS TO CHANGE

Transformation is the key. The political process must change—not merely with candidates and parties, but with structural responses that are as bold as was the choice in the 1910s to democratize the selection of senators and to extend the franchise to the majority of citizens. From a new embrace of structural change, in turn, will extend a fresh politics that gives citizens the power to join the debate about how new technologies will be utilized, how new wealth will be shared, and how a new society based on old ideals of liberty and justice for all, equality, and sustainability will take shape.

The way out is a democratic one, but Americans ought not be foolish enough to imagine that the citizenless democracy that currently exists will get us there. This moment's great leap forward will not be made by addressing a single issue. Yet, we ought not neglect or dismiss the single issues around which people have already done so much organizing. We ought not neglect the connections that have already been made. We ought not neglect the concern, the fear, the anger, the passion, the hope, the idealism that have drawn millions of Americans to movements that are so real and so needed—and yet so frustrated. There is a change coming. It is a frightening change. But it need not be overwhelming. Like the Chartists and the Progressives, we arrive at this moment unexpectedly well prepared—if not exactly well organized. Perhaps some of today's radicals are, as their political ancestors were, "without unity of aim and method." Perhaps they have "little hope of accomplishing anything." But the economic turbulence that is already here, and that will grow as technology transforms our circumstance, will clarify much and embolden many. As new movements develop a People's Charter or a progressive platform for our time, "clearly defining the urgent demands of the working class," we will identify the "real bond of union" for our time. What might a People's Charter for these times include? That is the topic for the concluding chapter.

Thomas Jefferson was right: when we overcome the democratic disconnect, when we the people are hooped together, that is the point at which everything begins to change.

chapter six

A DEMOCRATIC AGENDA
FOR A DIGITAL AGE

Change is never the issue. Change is inevitable. The
only real question is whether we will manage change in our
own interest and in the interest of society—or whether we
will simply let it happen to us. Unfortunately, this is the issue that is
most often neglected as we are dazzled and dumbfounded by evolution in real time. The magnitude of the technological, economic,
and social changes that are buffeting us can be so overwhelming, on
so many levels, that it is difficult to grasp what they will mean for
our lives and our futures. It is even more difficult for many of us to
determine whether we will have any say whatsoever regarding the
character and the scope of these changes—let alone when and how
we might intervene on our own behalf. A great fear among environmentalists is that, decades from now, when people fully experience the consequences of decisions that are made today with limited
debate, the sea levels will be rising inexorably, the damage will be

racing out of control, and the range of options for action will be dra-matically narrower and dramatically bleaker. Yet, because the threat is so daunting, because the requirements of a response are so great, it all becomes an abstraction. Even when people read the details of what is coming their way in ten or twenty or thirty years, even when those details are outlined by our best scientists, there is a powerful temptation to wait for a clarifying moment before leaping into ac-tion. The trouble is, environmentalists fear, that when the clarifying moment comes, it will be too late.

We fear that the same could be true when it comes to reports about how the technological revolution under the auspices of con-temporary capitalism is going to create new waves of unemployment and underemployment—with more poverty, wage stagnation, and inequality, and with devastating implications for society and democ-racy. The changes are unfolding now, in our own lives, in our own communities. The apps are being downloaded, the robots are rolling into the hospitals. We're not talking decades. Two years from the moment you read these words, the planet will add more computer power than it did in all previous history. By the late 2030s there will likely be a thousandfold increase in computer power from where we are today.[1] In just a few years Watson, the incredible IBM computer than won at *Jeopardy* in 2011, will compare to other computers like a state-of-the-art 2011 Tour de France bicycle would compare to the race cars at the 2021 Indianapolis 500. That is how fast change is coming.

If the great mass of Americans are going to have any role what-soever in the shaping of this future, if there is to be any chance at all that the twenty-first century will belong to the whole of humanity as opposed to the monopolists of a new Gilded Age, then the defining *economic* issues of the age must become the defining *political* issues of the age. That is not the case now, and there are no guarantees that it will be the case. Americans must recognize that our contemporary political discourse stifles rather than encourages the debates about economic and social responses that might benefit the overwhelming majority of us—in large part because our political infrastructure has been organized to take essential issues off the table.

Putting issues on the table is the most radical and freeing of all political acts, as it opens to everyone the range of possibility that is always available to the elites. This is the essence of democracy. Americans must build out the democratic infrastructure, not only to repair the damage that has been done to it in recent years, but to take it to places that the boldest visionaries of the past could barely imagine. We argue that the extension of democracy to economic planning is imperative. While we mention all the main elements of such an agenda herein, we reject the notion of rank-ordering them because this is an agenda that must integrate with itself.

Our purpose is to illustrate the range of possibility and the free-wheeling—and, yes, disruptive—mindset that must be brought to democratic exploration and innovation. There is a point here that cannot be lost: it is impossible to imagine a decent or desirable society without a strong democratic infrastructure. Only when the democratic infrastructure is in place does it become possible to realize its promise fully. Only then do victories become more permanent, rather than fleeting. Only then do people stop fretting about their powerlessness and start using their power.

It's about time for a new Port Huron Statement, and for a new National Commission on Technology, Automation, and Economic Progress. But, this time, the statements and studies cannot stop with proposals to "humanize" the workplace. What's going on now is much bigger, much broader. The discussion must recognize that the automation of the traditional workplace is already taking place. The focus must move out of the warehouse and office and toward proposals that open up the range of possibility to include new thinking on the organization of global and domestic economies, the balance of jobs and home life, education as it should be, and more. But it can't be an excuse to dust off the tired proposals of the past—including the shopworn proposals of the Left for great sounding but not necessarily transformative initiatives, such as a guaranteed income.[2] Let's start our journey there.

A PHONY SOLUTION

Imagine we were writing a book like this about an ancient civilization, or even some fairly recent society like the Soviet Union in the middle of the twentieth century, that had an economic system that was antithetical in key respects to that of the United States. Assume we provided clear evidence of how the introduction of a technology had radically transformed the society and of how, under the control of the society's unaccountable rulers, the results were disastrous. The conclusion would be obvious: the social structure in the ancient society or in the USSR was a clunker, and for that reason alone technologies that could have advanced civilization by empowering the many instead became tools of repression and scorching societal decay. In such a case study, there would be little debate among contemporary scholars about the nature of the crisis or about what would have been best for those societies: the people should have created a superior economic system that worked for the whole of society and its future, not just the needs of the rulers who were locked into their destructive and short-sighted paradigm.

Existing US capitalism is similarly a dubious fit for the present technological revolution, and it is a bad fit for democracy. This evidence is drawn from scholars and experts who acknowledge that a tension exists between capitalism as currently practiced and what passes for democracy in America. They understand that this puts considerable strain upon the democratic values and institutions of the country. Yet, for the most part, the notion that capitalism itself must be subject to no-holds-barred political debate is unspeakable, even unthinkable. A similar intellectual paralysis among the wise men of an ancient civilization or Soviet scholars would be derided by these same observers as a sign of the society's corruption and the bankruptcy of its intellectual class. Yet there is little self-awareness in the United States today among those who ponder the jobs crisis and the incompatibility automation has with our current political economy.

Indeed, most writers assume capitalism as it has come to be known is the basis for democracy and freedom, and that whatever happens in the future, the necessity of preserving current capitalism (or some sped-up version of it) all but trumps other concerns. Nothing should be done to alter the power of the digital giants or the unquestioned dominance and legitimacy of the profit motive when it comes to defining the future. Even the truest believers in capitalism, if they are honest with themselves, have to recognize that this is a political gambit, a means for taking the biggest issues off the table. When we cannot have a wide-ranging debate about economics, then concentrated economic power translates into general cultural power. This is the nature of the present weltanschauung. We live in a time when it is illegitimate to say that the emperor is wearing no clothes.

This barrier to a no-holds-barred discourse about how best to organize a civil, humane, and deeply democratic future, with liberty and justice for all, warps the debate about the future. It takes not just issues, but ideas, off the table. And it leaves us with too narrow a range of options—even for scholars who have taught us much and care deeply about this country, its peoples, and its future. If changing the economy is off the table, how can the great economic problems outlined in their research, and in all of our books, be addressed? If we may generalize, the one solution that has currency, and that is promoted by scholars who have done so much to identify the concerns outlined in this book (Erik Brynjolfsson, Andrew McAfee, and Martin Ford, among them) is the notion of a basic income or guaranteed annual income for all people in the nation.[3]

The idea is that everyone gets a sufficient income, usually between ten and twenty thousand dollars annually, so that no one starves to death or goes homeless in an era where jobs become far more scarce. The sales pitch to the affluent sector of the population that will pay higher taxes to bankroll the program is twofold: (1) these tens of millions of unemployed people will certainly spend all of this money on goods and services, so it will end up back in your pockets and make the economy much stronger, and (2) unless the wealthy buy off the majority of the population, there will be extraordinary social turbulence that could make the 1930s look like a day at the beach. It says quite a bit about the constricted range of debate today that Brynjolfsson and McAfee assert that basic-income proposals are radical ideas, at the outer limits of what might be acceptable.[4] Ford goes to considerable pains to explain that this project has the free-market seal of approval from Friedrich Hayek and Milton Friedman.[5] God forbid anyone think of a reform that would not be embraced by capitalism's mightiest advocates.

The idea of basic income was first posited by those on the left in the 1960s as a response to an initial automation scare, and this led to a lively debate. It was regarded skeptically by those who saw it as no solution at all, but merely a way for the wealthy to bribe the bulk of the population so they could keep their system and their privileges.[6] At the heart of many basic-income proposals is a calculus that says that once people get their annual check sent to them by a government, that is the end of any services they get from that government. If they want healthcare or transit, or quality education, they have to go buy it in the marketplace, like they would a hamburger or a pair of shoes. In this scenario, all public services would be privatized. The grand irony of "basic income" thinking along these lines is that it leads to the precise opposite of where John Stuart Mill and John Maynard Keynes wanted to end up. Instead of reducing commercialism and the market in a post-scarcity world, it elevates commercialism and the market so that everything is for sale. Hardly a recipe for human happiness. And economist Tyler Cowen makes the astute point that even if this looks like a terrific deal for society's millionaires, it is almost certain they will resist paying taxes to sustain those they regard as deadbeats and freeloaders.[7] Then there develops a massive popular struggle to win and maintain the basic income. If people are going to organize a gigantic battle, they ought to fight for more than this. They ought to fight for a world where their concerns are central, and not struggle to be extras in a world of, by, and for the rich.

In our view, a more humane approach would be to go in the opposite direction and simply remove certain functions from the market altogether as the society grows wealthier. Enhance democracy, don't cash it out. Make broadband Internet access free and ubiquitous. Make healthcare free and ubiquitous. Make extensive public transportation within cities and between them free and ubiquitous. Make all education free and ubiquitous. The list goes on and on. At some point, down the road, inequality is eliminated and humans enter an entirely new phase of their history. The economic problem will have been solved. Which, of course, is why it will be such a difficult political fight to get there.

Education is where the major battle for the future is going on today. A coalition of right-wing, union-hating, high-tech billionaires and hedge-fund managers looking to get rich as schools get privatized is working aggressively to "reform" and effectively end public education in the United States. Most of the arguments are economic: that American kids, who are primarily educated in public schools, are falling behind children worldwide and making the nation less competitive. This is a largely utilitarian view of education that sees it as developing labor skills and high incomes for students. The one reliable measure is testing, and "reformed" school districts have children prepare for and take tests much of their time in schools. Technology is offered as a way to reduce the reliance on human teachers—and in the form of so-called distance learning to eliminate schools themselves. One can only wonder where this leads when there are far fewer jobs and people are increasingly living off basic-income vouchers. There certainly doesn't seem to be much of a reason for schools to exist, except as holding pens for children until they get old enough to collect their own basic-income vouchers and begin shopping around for health insurance companies that will take them.

What is lost in this calculus are the two reasons the United States implemented public education in the first place: (1) to educate young people so they can be engaged and effective citizens and participate fully in the governance of society, and (2) to provide education for all as a great equalizer that gives poor and working-class children a chance to maximize their potential. School reformers often claim they want to create schools to help poor kids become rich adults, but commonly they send their own children to exclusive private schools, with hardly any testing and, ironically, very little technology. Indeed, research shows that a disproportionate percentage of tech billionaires and CEOs went to alternative Montessori schools as children. And in the Silicon Valley many of their children go to alternative Waldorf Schools that emphasize freedom, flexibility, and the arts. In short, these CEOs and their children are educated in an intimate, non-competitive environment with few tests or grades and an emphasis on personal growth, creativity, and critical thinking.[8] Here's our idea: why not make it the national policy that *every* child in America gets the same caliber of education as the children of the wealthy? That seems to be the civilized and humane target for a post-scarcity society. Why not make this the basic premise of every education debate?

ESTABLISHING THE CONTOURS OF DEMOCRACY

American history as it should be taught is that of a centuries-long struggle, often against overwhelming odds, to make real the promise Lincoln enunciated on the blood-soaked fields of Gettysburg, when he spoke of government of, by, and for the people. This history begins with the painful recognition that American "democracy" started as a backroom deal between wealthy, white landholders, many of whom brutally exploited slaves, indentured servants, subsistence farmers, indigenous people, and women. The drama of the story is revealed in the retelling of how dispossessed and oppressed human beings gained for themselves a place at the table of democracy—of how African Americans, Native Americans, Chicanos, women, immigrants, religious dissenters, freethinkers, radical editors, trade unionists, poor people, young people, and gays and lesbians achieved full and meaningful citizenship. This is the greatest American story. These struggles built our democratic infrastructure and an understanding that only through solidarity, through a commitment to one another that bridged difference *and* indifference, could we all be free and prosperous.

This is the story of how the promise of democracy became the reality of democracy. And it is vital to understanding the work of building a democratic infrastructure that is sufficient to the challenges that are coming our way.

From the beginning of the American experiment, there has been an understanding of the basic requirements of democracy:

- elections for positions of public trust by popular vote of constituents
- the rule of law and the control of corruption
- constraints on militarism and "continual warfare"
- the guarantee of an independent, substantial, and uncensored free press
- a government strong enough to address and eliminate excessive economic inequality

Over time, the drafters of state constitutions, as essential frameworks of democracy and governance, have outlined three additional requirements:

- the right to a free education for all citizens, through grade twelve, which is in all state constitutions
- the right to form free trade unions and to engage in collective bargaining, as it is identified in some state constitutions
- the right to a clean and sustainable environment, as it is identified in some state constitutions

The Populist and Progressive Eras recognized that the character of America was changing as a once predominantly rural and agrarian country was becoming increasingly urban and industrial. New democratic practices and arrangements were developed to counter corruption and inequality. The backroom deal was finally ended as a directly elected US Senate was established. Citizens were given the power to write and veto laws via initiatives and referendums and to remove officials via the recall power. Government was given strength and meaning in relation to economic power, via the establishment of the progressive income tax, the authority to tax corporations, and the banning of corporate contributions to campaigns.

But even this progress was insufficient, as the Great Depression and the rise of fascism confirmed with scorching force and immediacy. In response, Franklin Roosevelt proposed a Second Bill of Rights, also known as an Economic Bill of Rights. To realize the full promise of democracy, the United States would need to guarantee the rights to

- meaningful work and a living wage
- healthcare
- an education
- housing
- adequate food, clothing, and recreation
- old-age pensions and social security
- freedom from the abuses of private monopolies in business

This remains an extraordinary agenda. Realizing just what is written above would constitute nothing less than a political revolution, and an economic revolution. Our economy would need to be radically transformed—to get off the drug of militarism, to end crony-capitalism policymaking, to get real about planning and social investment—in order to provide all the elements of the economic bill of rights.

And the transformation would need to be ongoing.

Today's circumstance requires that a few new protections be added to FDR's list. For instance, the ancient sanction against corruption must be updated to guard against the privatization and outsourcing of public education and public responsibilities. It is imperative to remove profiteering from the provision of public goods: education, municipal services, public safety, and the defense of the land from foreign threats. If recent decades have taught us anything, it is that Dwight Eisenhower was right to warn against the threat posed by a military-industrial complex. And it is becoming increasingly clear that, as taxpayers and citizens, we cannot afford a prison-industrial complex or an education-industrial complex. Democracy cannot be maintained when profiteers obtain lucrative contracts and then use the money to hire lobbyists and fund campaigns so that they can obtain yet more lucrative contracts.[9]

Likewise, having an ecology that can sustain human life is not some premium channel a society can select in addition to the democratic basic package. It is not like having satellite radio added to your new car purchase. It is the very foundation for human existence for all societies and must be regarded as such. Environmental movements have come to understand and advance the idea that their success rises and falls with movements for democracy and social justice worldwide. Today's environmental activists recognize that a new more accountable and community-oriented economy is mandatory for human survival, and that the only way to achieve such an economy is through the dramatic extension of democratic infrastructure. As author and environmental activist Bill McKibben argues, it is imperative to "break the intellectual spell under which we live." This is what we have termed *weltanschauung*, and it is joined to the hip of democratic infrastructure. McKibben explains that "the last few decades have been dominated by the premise that privatizing all economic resources will produce endless riches. Which was kind of true, except that the riches went to only a few people. And in the process they melted the Arctic, as well as dramatically increasing inequality around the world."[10]

As the rough outlines of the damage done on a host of environmental, economic, and social issues come into stark relief, a sense of urgency is increasing exponentially. Also increasing is the sense that we are all in this together, and we have common interest in a democratic infrastructure. Elite solutions for the environment, just like the economy, will tend to serve elite interests. As the saying goes, if you are not at the table when decisions are being made, you are the dish that is being served.

A full democratic infrastructure provides more than the right to vote. Full democratic infrastructure provides economic and social security, a free flow of information, and absolute protection against discrimination and corruption so that every citizen—not just those who are wealthy—has the freedom to engage fully in the politics and governance of the nation. None of this presupposes a particular type of economy, yet all of it presupposes that every American will have the right to participate fully and meaningfully in determining what type of economy best serves her—and best frames the future. When a crisis causes a jolt, as will surely be the case with the technological and social transformations that are now unfolding, citizens must retain the power to put economic options on the table—and to embrace the best of those options. If we want to make it through the changes that are headed our way, and to come out on the other side as a nation that enjoys what the New Economy Coalition describes as a "new economy . . . where capital (wealth and the means of creating it) is a tool of the people, not the other way around," then there must be a democratic infrastructure that is sufficient to foster economic democracy.[11]

DEMOCRATIZE THE CONSTITUTION

A certain portion of the work in the coming decades must address the nation's constitutions. Constitutions underpin and frame our democratic infrastructure. Yet, they do not always make it functional. Nothing thwarts political and economic democracy like a constitution so imprecise that it allows right-wing judicial activists to make buying elections easy and voting hard. Instead of democracy, the Constitution of 1787 gave us an unelected Senate and an Electoral College and other structures intended to control rather than empower the unruly masses. Americans who had fought to end the abuses of old elites objected to the prospect of being abused by new ones. They demanded and by 1791 had won the ten amendments known as the Bill of Rights. Seventeen more amendments have come since then. Seven of those amendments overturned Supreme Court rulings, and almost all of them sought to extend democracy, end corruption, and make the federal government more responsive to new times and new challenges.[12]

These amendments made the United States a different and better nation. But we are not different and better enough. Foreseeing our contemporary circumstance, Thomas Jefferson counseled against viewing the Constitution as "too sacred to be touched," warning that "we might as well require a man to wear still the coat which fitted him when a boy, as civilized society to remain ever under the regimen of their barbarous ancestors." Jefferson also argued that "the real friends of the Constitution in its federal form, if they wish it to be immortal, should be attentive, by amendments, to make it keep pace with the advance of the age in science and experience."[13]

The real friends of the Constitution today champion a "move to amend" that would declare that corporations are not people, that money is not speech, and that votes must matter more than billionaires' dollars. Sixteen states and some six hundred communities have since 2010 demanded that Congress initiate a constitutional response to the judicial activism that has allowed elites to commodify our politics and corporatize our governance.[14] At the same time, activists are taking up a proposal by Congressmen Mark Pocan and Keith Ellison to end the crude assault on voting rights with an amendment that establishes, finally and unequivocally, a right to vote and to have every vote counted.[15] These are good starting points, but they are not sufficient.

The Constitution should be clarified so that it sustains rather than throttles democracy. Do away with the Electoral College. Ban the practice of gerrymandering. Close the loophole that allows governors to appoint cronies to vacant Senate seats. Ask why America maintains a House of Lords–like Senate where, today, the vote of a member elected by 121,000 Wyomingites can cancel out the vote of a member elected by 7.8 million Californians.[16] Consider electing members of the House to four-year terms that parallel those of the president, so that the popular will of 131 million voters in a presidential election can't be stymied by 90 million voters in the next mid-term election.[17] Object to any calculus that prevents a majority–African American District of Columbia and a majority–Hispanic Puerto Rico from becoming states.[18] Reexamine every barrier to popular participation, including those of poverty, ignorance, and incapacity. "When it shall be said in any country in the world, my poor are happy; neither ignorance nor distress is to be found among them; my jails are empty of prisoners, my streets of beggars; the aged are not in want, the taxes are not oppressive; the rational world is my friend, because I am the friend of its happiness: when these things can be said, then may that country boast of its constitution and its government," wrote Thomas Paine.[19] He was right, as was FDR when he proposed an economic bill of rights.

No constitution can repair every breach in society, but a renewed US Constitution can clear the way for the people—the whole people, as opposed to a handful of elites—to forge a more perfect union.[20]

The point, after all, is not the perfection of a document, it is the power of the people to shape their future. Something remarkable happens when transformative power is on offer: apathy ends. The advocates of a democratic agenda for a digital age should offer America a vision of a next politics where, as Robert M. La Follette proposed, "the will of the people shall be the law of the land."[21] Going to the root of the matter on behalf of political and economic democracy can be daunting. Constitutional change always faces the open opposition of those who are satisfied with the status quo and the quiet opposition of those who simply do not believe big changes are possible. Progress has never come easily. But progress has come. And here is the good news: progress often comes rapidly.

At the start of the 1910s children who should have been in school were changing bobbins in mills. Workers who dared to organize unions were mowed down by paramilitary forces. Women who could not vote were dying in sweatshop fires. The government lacked the ability to collect revenues necessary to address the basic needs of a nation experiencing rapid yet shockingly unequal growth. Progress in Washington was stymied by millionaires who bribed legislators to secure US Senate seats. Progressive reformers recognized that the "money power" made a mockery of the promise of popular governance. So they established their "covenant with the American people." They explained the changes that were necessary. And they got them. Not with ease, and not through the generosity of the elites. They got them through organizing, marching, rallying, practicing civil disobedience, taking risks, and voting against the failed men of the past who blocked the way to the future. Above all, they got them when the great mass of Americans grew so frustrated, so angry, so determined, so hopeful, that they would no longer accept a fate dictated by distant and disengaged elites. They got them when Americans decided that the people could do a better job of shaping the future than the millionaires and the monopolists.[22]

In a ten-year period, the Constitution was amended so that women were permitted to vote, the Senate was directly elected by the people, and Congress had the power to implement progressive taxation.[23] At the same time, child labor, workplace safety, and pure-food-and-drug laws were implemented; labor unions were on the march; and the rough outlines of what would become the New Deal were taking shape in states that came to be known as "laboratories of democracy." The great leap forward was made possible by recognition that the United States needed fundamental change and that some of that change required amending the Constitution. It was the same in the 1960s and early 1970s, another age of reform that saw constitutional amendments to extend voting rights to the District of Columbia, abolish poll taxes, clarify presidential succession, and allow eighteen-year-olds to vote.[24]

The champions and builders of a democratic infrastructure for the twenty-first century should, when it comes to constitutional reform, seek and expect nothing less from the next ten years.

DEMOCRATIZE JOURNALISM

While constitutional reform is as necessary now as Jefferson suggested it would be, many of the changes that are required to create a full democratic infrastructure do not require any constitutional amendments. Let's start with the information that people need to be their own governors. To get to democracy, there has to be a democratization of communications that ensures that all Americans are sufficiently informed to fully engage as citizens. The great majority of Americans are not getting this now. Old media has been dying slowly for decades, and there is no evidence to imagine that the media that democracy requires will be delivered by app newsrooms or robot reporters. There are no market solutions, no technical fixes, no new economic models. There is only one way out of this mess, and it is to put the people in charge of demanding the solutions that media conglomerates and "click-chasing" reporters will not demand. People—citizens—will need to be in charge of the funding of the next media system.[25] Once we remove the shackles of our stilted political discourse, problems that seem impervious to reform become areas for experimentation and great hope.

American history, and the contemporary experience of the most democratic countries on the planet, tells us this is possible. And the rough outlines of the movement that will be needed to make the change are already in place. Citizens who recognize the essential connection between information and democracy can build on the strength of a media-reform movement that has, under both President George W. Bush and President Barack Obama, prevented bad things from happening. With roots that go back for decades, the media-reform movement came together in its modern form to thwart Bush-era attempts to effectively eliminate limits on the amount of media that one corporation could own in one community—and, by extension, nationally. More recently, it has blocked efforts to undermine net neutrality, the essential tool for defending free speech and the free flow of communications on the Internet. In an age of rapidly changing media, then, the media-reform movement has already engaged millions of Americans in the fight to prevent some very bad things from happening.[26] Now, it must make some good things happen. Media-reform activism must be part of a broad democratic agenda for a digital age.[27]

The goal—every bit as ambitious as those of the most ardent advocates for economic democracy—should be information democracy. Citizens who possess little or no wealth must have the same information that citizens with great wealth now enjoy. Hedge-fund managers and CEOs do not seek information as entertainment. They are not spectators. They get the best information that can be found and they act on it. Citizens who would be their own governors must adopt the same sensibility. For obvious reasons, journalism that democratizes access to information will not be funded by the elites. Bernie Sanders is precisely right when he says that "it's not in the interest of the corporations who own the networks to actually be educating the American people so that we're debating the real issues."[28] But it is in the interest of the people to support journalism that sustains democracy. So the United States should give the people the tools to subsidize independent, not-for-profit journalism.[29]

How? Begin with supercharged funding of public broadcasting and robust support for community media—along the lines already outlined by the most energetic campaigners on behalf of maximized funding for what should be "an American BBC."[30] Those are givens. But we dare not stop there. A democratic agenda must demand substantial public investments in journalism as a "public good." This is nothing new for America. The United States developed a press system that was the envy of the world in the early nineteenth century through massive postal and printing subsidies for newspapers.[31] These subsidies made the cost of production so low that the United States eventually had more newspapers per capita than any other country in the world. The founders of the American experiment were not familiar with the term *public good*, but they treated the press as just that. And they did so in the only way that made democratic sense, by providing generous postal and printing subsidies to all publications—even those that dissented, even those that, like the abolitionist press, proposed radical change—so that none were puppets of the government.[32]

What's the modern model for establishing a nonprofit, noncommercial, competitive, uncensored, and independent press system that embraces digital technology, that recognizes the potential of new-media platforms, and that, above all, provides a journalism that is sufficient to sustain genuine democracy? How about this: every American adult gets a two-hundred-dollar voucher she can use to donate government money to any nonprofit news media of her choice. She can split her two hundred dollars among different qualifying nonprofit media, indicating her choice on her tax return or a simple form. This program would be purely voluntary, like the tax-form check-offs for funding elections or protecting wildlife. Simple universal standards can be developed for media that qualifies for voucher funding, erring always on the side of expanding rather than constraining the number of qualifying newsrooms. A small existing agency, such as the Postal Regulatory Commission (which has some history in this area), could provide necessary oversight and administration.

Based on a proposal from economist Dean Baker, the Citizen News Voucher program we outline here represents a literal and practical response to the transformation of media in the digital age. Baker says it is "designed to maximize the extent of individual choice while taking full advantage of new technologies."[33] The idea borrows from the libertarian movement, in its recognition that vouchers can be used to give greater control over the expenditure of public tax dollars. It combines a healthy hostility to government control over news content with a faith in the power of individuals to make their own choices, and it recognizes the public-good nature of journalism.

A news voucher program would allow public-media organizations to dramatically increase their funding. Imagine if a public television station in a metropolitan area of one million people that was ill-served by existing media—which is to say any and every metropolitan area—managed to get fifty thousand viewers to donate half of their Citizen News Voucher to help with the development of a newsroom to cover state and local elections and government. With a $5 million budget, that station would have the resources to hire top journalists and to provide a quality alternative to dwindling commercial coverage that is invariably surrounded by a slurry of negative campaign commercials.

Now, imagine if most of those fifty thousand viewers donated the other half of their Citizen News Vouchers, in combination with similar numbers of viewers from twenty more metropolitan areas, to develop an evening radio and cable news program along the lines of Amy Goodman's "Democracy Now." That program would have close to $100 million to hire journalists to cover national and international issues. But let's also imagine that two thousand residents and allies of an impoverished and neglected neighborhood in the core city of that metropolitan area were to direct half of the vouchers to fund a community radio station newsroom covering policing issues.

Let's put it all online, with podcasts and apps and alerts so that every one of these initiatives is available to everyone—as news happens and all the time. A condition for getting the vouchers is that everything produced by the nonprofit medium getting the funds must be put online immediately for free; it enters the public domain where anyone can use it as needed. Suddenly old media and new media are working together to produce journalism that matters, and that does not have to rely on advertising or subscriptions or the vagaries of the market. And the people who need information are paying journalists to go out and gather that information and to deliver it to them.

Too good to be true? No. Democratic necessities are never too good to be true. They are simply hard to get. Net neutrality was supposed to be too good to be true. Plenty of pundits said it would be impossible to beat the world's most powerful telecommunications lobbies in a fight to preserve a free and open Internet. Yet, in an era when corporations so frequently get so very much of what they ask for, media reform, civil rights, and community activists made the fight for net neutrality an issue. They put it *on the table*. They were outspent and out-lobbied. But in February 2015 they won a victory that Free Press president Craig Aaron identified as "the biggest win for the public interest in the FCC's history." Aaron explained that "it's the culmination of a decade of dedicated grassroots organizing and advocacy. Millions of people came to the defense of the open Internet to tell Washington, in no uncertain terms, that the Internet belongs to all of us and not just a few greedy phone and cable companies."[34]

Absolute protections for a free and open Internet were impossible to get. Then we got them. The information we need to utilize and maintain a democratic infrastructure will be ours if we make the struggle for that information part of an agenda that recognizes the necessity of political and economic democracy. And if we hoop ourselves together to advance that agenda, we can get it. Indeed, if we hoop ourselves together at a moment when people will be demanding transformative change, we can get a whole lot more.

DEMOCRACY, NOT MONOPOLY

What is striking today is that there is an emerging genre of superb books outlining the stunning increase in economic inequality in the United States over the past four decades and the disastrous implications for our economy, our democracy, and the social structure. It seems like everyone gets it. When the Occupy movement exploded onto the scene in 2011, even Republicans talked about inequality as a problem, albeit for a split-second.[35] For those old enough to remember the 1960s or early 1970s, today's America feels increasingly like a feudal or Third World country, the kind few thought possible fifty years ago. Dramatically lessening economic inequality is required to have a functional democracy; there is no two ways about it. That is one theme that has been central in every period of democratic surge in the nation's history, and it must be so today, because indications are that unless we the people act rapidly and boldly, the current circumstance is only going to get worse, possibly much worse.

One of the essential explanations for mounting economic inequality in the United States is the increasing monopoly power over the economy. This was well understood in the Progressive Era, the New Deal, and even in the 1960s. Monopolies themselves were recognized as singularly anti-democratic constructs that needed to be weakened. Economic concentration is far more prevalent today than in any of those earlier times. The digital economy is nothing if not a hothouse for monopoly. Yet the issue gets barely any serious discussion; massive monopolistic corporations are treated as if they are part of the unchangeable scenery, like the Rocky Mountain range. It shows just how powerful these firms are that they can buy their way out of critical analysis. But the populists, the Progressives, the New Dealers, Ralph Nader, and the 1960s activists all had it right (as did Jefferson and Lincoln): concentrated economic power is not only a threat to smaller businesses, workers, and community enterprise, it is a direct threat to democratic governance. It must be addressed squarely or any hard-earned popular reforms will be fleeting.

Fortunately, the current crisis is sparking a renaissance in thinking with regard to corporate power and monopoly.[36] What's even more encouraging now is that the talk is turning from identification of the crisis toward consideration of what to do about it. When the telecommunications giant Comcast proposed in 2014 to take over Time Warner Cable, in a $45 billion deal that would further monopolize cable and digital communications, there was a general sense that it was a done deal. After all, Comcast was on good terms with leading Democrats as well as Republicans; it was the poster child for crony capitalism, as its core industries were all based on having government monopoly licenses. Even critics of the takeover "assumed that the merger with Time Warner Cable would happen—we just needed to demand concessions on other fronts," recalls Fordham Law School professor Zephyr Teachout. But the done deal was undone. Media reform, civil rights, and consumer groups stirred an outcry and federal regulators started to raise questions. When word leaked that the US Department of Justice might oppose the deal, Comcast backed off in what former FCC Commissioner Michael Copps hailed as "spectacularly good news for consumers concerned about the spiraling cost of cable and broadband and for millions of citizens who want nothing more to do with gatekeeping and consolidation in the communications ecosystem on which our democracy depends."[37] No doubt about that. But it was something else as well. It was a signal that people power may have more capacity to upend corporate power than even the most optimistic activists had imagined.

Teachout took it as such. "Stopping a merger like this is real political power," she explained in the spring of 2015.[38] "The Comcast defeat reminds us that we haven't always accepted big banks, big chicken, big beef, big Monsanto, big patents, big oil, a market defined by bigness instead of competition." To Teachout's view, "the crash of 2008 was the first sign for many people that this concentration of power was bad for people's lives. Although calls to break up the banks failed, the mainstream demand lives on. Banks are bigger and more concentrated than ever, but the consensus ideology was burst. However, the anti-monopoly sentiment stayed largely caged in its own arena, an idea reserved for banks, not for a way of seeing the economy more broadly."

Teachout explained that

a new populist fighting force representing the broad grassroots demand that we break up big companies. When the Sherman Antitrust

Act was passed, Senator Sherman spoke about it in democratic terms, 'A Charter of Liberty,' he said—and until the 1980s we understood that. Comcast, even without the merger, threatens our liberties. One-hundred-and-ten years ago, a group calling itself the Antitrust League held events around the country, demanding the government break up big companies. A few years later, Teddy Roosevelt used the Sherman Act to break up Standard Oil. And while it took until FDR to put in place a persistent, rational antitrust policy, Roosevelt's choice to battle Standard Oil was a critical turning point in American history—it showed we did not have to bow before big monopolists. The modern antitrust leagues are just now forming.

Teachout's not the only one proposing to break up digital giants like Amazon and even Google.[39] Nor is she alone in speaking of the need for new movements and "a new charter of liberty."[40] That's the ticket. But why stop there?

Breaking up monopolies makes sense in some cases, but in others, indeed in the most oppressive of monopoly circumstances, it is virtually impossible to break up a giant company into five or ten competitive parts. These are the "natural monopolies," the kind that dominate the digital economy with its "network effects." What to do? There is an old argument that could be made new again. Worried in the 1930s about the way in which "the corporation is simply running away with our economic (and political) system," University of Chicago economics professor Henry Calvert Simons suggested that "the state should face the necessity of actually taking over, owning, and managing directly . . . industries in which it is impossible to maintain effectively competitive conditions."[41] Simons was no radical. Economist Milton Friedman referred to Simons as "my teacher and my friend—and, above all, a shaper of my ideas."[42] So why did Simons favor nationalization? His reason was both economic and political. "Few of our gigantic corporations can be defended on the grounds that their present size is necessary to reasonably full exploitation of production economies," he argued. Yet, Simons explained, the most powerful corporations could easily thwart attempts at regulation, even blocking moves to apply antitrust laws.

The practical solution was "direct government ownership and operation in the case of all industries where competition cannot be made to function effectively as an agency of control."[43]

Contemporary political economist Gar Alperovitz recalled this analysis after the Wall Street meltdown of 2008, noting that despite the mess they had made of things, the "too-big-to-fail" banks were bailed out and back to their old bad behaviors in no time. Invoking Simons's work, Alperovitz wrote in 2012 that the logic of his argument remains. "With high-paid lobbyists contesting every proposed regulation, it is increasingly clear that big banks can never be effectively controlled as private businesses. If an enterprise (or five of them) is so large and so concentrated that competition and regulation are impossible, the most market-friendly step is to nationalize its functions."[44] That opens up a host of questions that need to be solved. Most important: How can there be accountable and effective management of public enterprises? The track record in the United States and worldwide reminds us that FDR was right: the more democratic a society is, the broader its democratic infrastructure, the more likely public institutions will be honest, effective, and hugely popular.

DEMOCRATIZE PLANNING

In view of the nature of the economic challenges that Americans are experiencing today, and the economic calamity they will experience in coming years, putting economic issues on the table is about more than gently guiding and assisting the private-sector economy, under the assumption that "what is good for Apple is good for America." To this end, we would link the elements of the democratic infrastructure that have already been described to the development of what the United States has never really had: a national industrial policy that

- focuses on creating and retaining meaningful and well-compensated work in all sectors of the economy
- guards against the development of monopolies that reduce competition and innovation, and that threaten small business

- supports research and development—especially in areas where investment is necessary but not necessarily profitable in the short term
- works with private and public employers and communities to establish a proper balance between work and leisure, providing a regulatory framework that defines full-time work and guarantees that compensation is adequate so that employees can support their families without being expected to work excessive hours
- maintains the planning, funding, and support networks needed to guarantee healthcare, disability, and retirement security for all, as well as the education, training, and transportation services that are required by twenty-first-century workers
- encourages economic development in industrial sectors and geographical areas that may not be immediately profitable, but have great social value; by doing so it can make areas eventually cost efficient
- ensures that workers have a voice in their workplaces and, through their unions, in broader economic planning by corporations and governments
- recognizes the value of public utilities and public services to the whole of the economy and to the whole of society, and encourages public ownership and cooperative development
- guarantees that the benefits of technological advances are shared by all, and that changes in the workplace are made to ease economic and social burdens rather than merely to boost profits
- requires that trade policies benefit workers and the environment in the United States and the countries with which it trades
- maintains a steady commitment to environmental protection and climate justice with an eye toward ensuring that economic decisions are made to promote sustainability rather than exploit the planet

- addresses the unique challenges faced by rural and urban Americans, and by people of color and immigrants who have suffered from historical discrimination and contemporary inequity
- establishes a national land-use policy that supports sustainable agriculture and the development of livable communities rather than sprawl and factory farming
- is constantly evolved in a transparent and inclusive manner, with democratic oversight and governance.

Of course, to mention economic planning in the United States in the past few decades is seen as utterly absurd and extremely dangerous. We are told by people who plan all the time to improve their own lives that planning by society will lead to some totalitarian hack—usually a brain-dead bureaucrat who fantasizes about Khrushchev's Soviet Union—interfering with the untouchable market. Everyone who listens to a politician or a corporate spokesperson knows the words by heart. But the truth is we do have serious economic planning in the United States and it has been effective. Trade deals, intellectual property protections, tax policies, farm subsidies, all sorts of monopoly licenses for broadcasting, cable TV, and cellphone spectrum are forms of economic planning. So are choices made with regard to privatization and outsourcing. And let's not forget bailouts of Wall Street and multinational corporations. The market produces its own inefficiencies, its own failures, and—in an age of crony capitalism—its own pathologies that cost taxpayers and the US economy trillions of dollars.[45] Yet, when the market crashes, there are plans to protect those who did the crashing. That's a form of planning, although not a very good one. And nowhere is economic planning more evident in today's United States than in the Pentagon budget, which has been guiding much of the US economy since the 1940s. A significant piece of the US competitive advantage in computing and electronics extends from research bankrolled by the Pentagon. The Internet, itself, was the result of such funding. Large corporations and most of big business are so interlocked with the government that the distinction between them is almost moot.

So we have plenty of economic planning. The problem is that it is done by and for elites with almost no public awareness or participation. And it has become increasingly corrupt. Those purportedly brain-dead bureaucrats of yesteryear are today more likely to be cynical hustlers looking to pass through "the revolving door" between government and the corporate sector. If they do it just "right," as many former congressmen and regulators have, they can make millions in big-ticket private-sector jobs in the industries they oversaw during their period of "public service."

The minimal baseline level of credible planning that once gave the United States the most advanced physical infrastructure in the world has become so corrupt that decisions about how and when to repair that very infrastructure are made not with an eye toward keeping everyone safe and mobile but with an eye toward perfecting the curb cuts around corporate campuses and developing paying-customer lanes on soon-to-be-privatized highways. Oh, yes, there is a lot of planning on behalf of the very wealthy and the very powerful. What's needed is planning for the rest of us. Economic planning needs to be democratized and popularized and made accountable. And this democratic planning must be done locally, regionally, and nationally. It could be that such planning will keep things just as they are, and regard its function as assisting the largest corporations to get even larger. But if that is the case, it should be the result of the informed consent of the people. There is no indication, however, that corporate America believes it can win a fair fight on those terms.

So is economic planning un-American or necessarily radical? Hardly. Most of what is discussed here builds on the industrial policies and approaches to economic planning long embraced by the governors of the strongest economic powerhouses of Europe, especially Germany. We do not hold up the Germans or the Danes or the Norwegians or the Swedes as perfect planners. And we do not suggest that the United States must borrow precise policies—although they are instructive, and we particularly appreciate the groundbreaking work of Britain's Trades Union Congress to show how easily the German model might be adapted to other countries.[46]

What we do suggest is that Jeremy Wiesen, a professor of entrepreneurship (emeritus) at New York University's Stern School of Business, was absolutely right to argue several years ago in the *Wall Street Journal*: "We shouldn't need to implore the government to have at least as many officials focused on new business creation as are measuring GNP and GDP. The term 'industrial policy' should not be seen as a pejorative. It certainly isn't in China. Nor should it be anathema for the U.S. government to provide capital and other incentives to keep scientific and entrepreneurial talent at home, give aggressive trade assistance, and incubate new businesses—all of which is done in China."[47] We believe with economists and Robert Pollin and Dean Baker that "an effective combination of public investments and industrial policies" is necessary "to meet the fundamental challenges at hand."[48] And we emphatically agree with Pollin and Baker that "a public investment/industrial policy agenda is quite viable in principle and has demonstrated its effectiveness in widely varying circumstances, in the U.S. and elsewhere."[49]

Nothing about public investment and industrial policy—nor any of the broader changes that are necessary to democratize economic decision making—will halt, or even slow, the arrival of the future. Rather, these changes will shape the future along humane and equitable lines, rather than along some billionaire's bottom line. There is moral and practical value in establishing an economy that responds to human values and human needs, and that recognizes, as have Green Parties around the world, that

conventional economic policy uses economic growth, inflation, balance of payments and unemployment as "economic indicators," the normal criteria against which progress is measured. Although it is the most usually quoted indicator, gross national product (GNP) is a poor indicator of true progress and does not adequately measure people's sense of well-being. It measures only the activity in the formal sector, regardless of what that activity is. In consequence, current economic theory fails adequately to reflect the real effects of human activity within a finite ecosystem, and is used to "validate" economic activities which are ecologically unsustainable and/or socially unjust.[50]

If it is fair that all citizens should have a say with regard to the policies that shape their future, then it is practical for society to take steps
to strengthen that contribution. The quality of the contribution that
those citizens will make to the debate increases as they enjoy a measure
of economic and social security—and the stability that both provide.
One of the top excuses for Americans who do not vote is that they
simply do not have the time to gather information, get to the polls,
and cast a ballot. "When pollsters have attempted to ask non-voters
why they haven't voted, two of the common answers have been 'too
busy' or 'schedule conflicts'," notes long-time political writer Eric
Black. "A lame excuse by some, perhaps, but not for all."[51] The day-to-
day burdens placed on low-wage workers who put in long hours, often
at some distance from their homes and the neighborhoods where they
would vote, make it hard to meet even the most basic requirements of
democratic engagement, argues Congressman Steve Israel, who explains that millions of Americans simply cannot "find time to vote."[52]
It is true that making voting easier, as Israel and others propose, could
increase turnout. But it is even more true, to our view, that giving
people more job security, steady hours, more workplace flexibility and,
above all, more time away from work, will dramatically increase their
freedom to participate in democracy. That fuller participation ensures
that elections produce governments and policies that are more reflec-
tive of the popular will and more responsive to popular needs. Economic security begets greater economic security, as it allows working
Americans to shape responses to questions about public investment,
planning, and trade that are in the public interest—as opposed to the
often misguided and invariably self-serving whims of CEOs who can
hire lobbyists and fund politicians to do their bidding.

DEMOCRATIZE THE ECONOMY

Economic democracy is not a threat. Economic democracy is a promise.
Economic democracy does not need to be bureaucratic or slow. It can
be fast, and vibrant and brilliant. Think of democratic decision-making
about how to invest the largesse of a great and prosperous nation as the

ultimate crowd sourcing. Economic and social justice and sustainability in the coming digital age are not impossible dreams. The United States can be a prosperous and equitable, innovative, and inspiring country once more. It might even be "the city upon a hill" that John Winthrop imagined in the seventeenth century, and that John Kennedy and Ronald Reagan preached about in the twentieth—a model for other nations to emulate and embrace.[53] But if the experience of the past four decades, and especially of the most recent period of booms and busts, bubbles and bursts, meltdowns and bailouts, wage stagnation and widening inequality teaches us anything it is that there is no market-driven route to justice and sustainability. No billionaire will deliver prosperity and equity. The only way up is democracy. The people have to shape this change.

When the jarring reality of a jobless economy finally and fully hits, as it will, there is going to be an immediate demand for bold and meaningful economic change to ease immediate pain and long-term uncertainty. At this point, every economic and political charlatan in the land, every spin doctor and every paid-off pundit, will have a proposal. So, too, will many honorable yet misguided politicians who want to help but who have no clues. There will be horrible and dangerous plans. There will be those, as there always are, who promise that all will be well if we cede a little more authority to the elites who have been so in charge for so very long. There will be threats to democracy and these will be particularly horrifying—because moments of great turbulence will demand more democracy, not less. And the best way to prepare is to lock in as much democracy as we can.

Alperovitz, a professor at the University of Maryland, has worked for a number of years to get Americans to "contemplate how to rebuild a more equitable economy." Proposals for public banking and real regulation of corporations that are "simply running away with our economic (and political) system" are simply pieces of a greater program he proposes as part of a "new economy" movement that recognizes that "deepening economic and social pain are producing the kinds of conditions from which various new forms of democratization—of ownership, wealth and institutions—are beginning to emerge. The challenge is to develop a broad strategy that not only ends the downward spiral but also gives rise to something different: steadily changing who actually owns the system, beginning at the bottom and working up."[54]

In recent years, Alperovitz has been a happy warrior on behalf of burgeoning movements for worker ownership nationwide. But, as he explains, "The current goal is not simply worker ownership, but worker ownership linked to a community-building strategy." Alperovitz argues that

the strategy must take up the challenge of rebuilding the basic institutional substructure of the local economy in ways that are efficient, effective, stable, redistributive and ongoing. This will include:

- Expanded use of city, school, hospital, university and other purchasing power to help stabilize jobs in a manner that democratizes ownership and benefits for both low-income communities and small- and midsize businesses;
- Expanded use of public and quasi-public land trusts (both for housing and commercial use) to capture development profits for the community and to prevent gentrification;
- An all-out attack on the absurdly wasteful giveaways corporations extract from local governments;
- Coordination with labor unions and community activists to build and sustain momentum.

This is not some utopian fantasy. The United States Federation of Worker Cooperatives, a decade-old national grassroots coalition, now includes more than one hundred member workplaces across the country as part of "a thriving cooperative movement" that provides consulting and technical assistance to cooperatives. Its slogan is "Farther-Faster-Together" and its express mission is to link worker cooperatives to one another and to broader social justice movements. The movement is growing. And they are focusing on communities that have been hit hard by deindustrialization and dislocation. The potential for these models is real, as is the interest in them. "When people start thinking about how they would organize their own workplaces if they had the opportunity and the tools to do it, they get so excited," says Rebecca Kemble, the president of the federation's board. "It frees them up from so much that beats people down, that depresses them. Suddenly, there are possibilities."[55]

There are a lot of possibilities: in new movements by teachers and parents who seek to end the overemphasis on high-stakes testing and rote learning in favor of programs for educating children to think and to act as citizens, in movements to rethink backward models of training and retraining displaced workers for jobs that will soon disappear, in smart thinking about sharing jobs and dialing back the length of the work week, in fresh proposals for full employment and serious infrastructure investment (which recognizes that the infrastructure of the future will require both concrete and fiber optics), and in a renewed understanding of the power and value of public ownership and utilities that meet human needs.

That's a very good start—precisely the sort of thinking that the United States is going to need to address technological change, automation, and the threat of a jobless economy. At the local level, where Kemble says it is still possible to make change, activists are on the move.[56] She was elected in April 2015 to the Madison, Wisconsin, city council and is already working with Mayor Paul Soglin to invest $5 million over five years in "planning, research, grants, loans, and even forgivable loans" to get worker-owned cooperatives up and running. Based on a similar project in New York City, but significantly larger in scale and ambition, the Madison project will focus on both economic and racial justice. "Building a great local economy is not reserved for white males," says Soglin. "We're hoping this will be part of our economic development strategy in areas where there's food insecurity, where there isn't a concentration of jobs, and where significant numbers of households are below the poverty line." Kemble and the mayor hope to shape a new understanding of twenty-first-century economics. "One of the benefits of a program like this is it gives us another opportunity to show that the economics of aggrandizing wealth in the top one percent is stupid," says Soglin.[57]

To bring projects like the one in Madison to scale, to take them national so to speak, remains the challenge. And it is a challenge where the threat of a jobless economy comes into direct conflict with the politics of citizenless democracy. This is where, no matter how beautiful it may be, the dream gets deferred. "[What] we call traditional politics no longer has much capacity to alter most of the negative trends," explains Alperovitz. "To be clear: I think projects, organizing, demonstrations and related efforts are important. But deep down, most people sense—rightly, in my view—that unless we develop a more powerful long-term strategy, those efforts aren't going to make much of a dent."[58]

IMAGINE DEMOCRACY

Imagine if that changed. Imagine if a justifiably frightened and angered American people were to look up from their gadgets and their unemployment forms. Imagine if they realized that the present is unsatisfactory and that the future looks terrifying. Imagine if these Americans recognized that what is terrifying is not the technology, nor even the fact that everything is going to change. What is terrifying is that they have no say about the scope and character and direction of that change. What is terrifying is that they cannot put proposals for a new economy on the table and make them the law of the land and the frameworks for our future. What is terrifying is that the essential economic issues of the time are not the essential political issues of the time. Imagine if the people recognized that they must have a say or they will have nothing at all. And imagine if they were hooped together, finally and fully, across what were once considered lines of division. Imagine if the people were ready to demand a new Constitution, a new politics, a new economy. Imagine if the people were ready, finally, to demand democracy—and all of the freedom, fairness, and human potential that extends from the moment when the profiteers and the pretenders are pushed aside and we, the people, forge our future.

STATISTICAL APPENDIX

R. Jamil Jonna

CHART 1 PERCENTAGE OF QUARTERS WITH 6 PERCENT
OR GREATER REAL GDP GROWTH, 1930–2015

Chart 1 is an update of work originally presented by Fred Magdoff and John Bellamy Foster (2014, 12), who provide a detailed discussion of its significance in the post–Second World War economy of the United States. The bars represent the number of quarters with at least 6 percent real GDP growth divided by the total number of quarters for a given period. Thus the denominator is 40 for each ten-year period, with the exception of 1947–1959 (51 quarters) and 2010–2015q1 (21 quarters). Data for the period covering the Second World War (1940–1946) is considered to be anomalous by economists and is therefore excluded.

Sources: National Bureau of Economic Research. *Gross National Product in Constant Dollars for United States* [Q0896AUSQ240SNBR]. Retrieved from FRED, Federal Reserve Bank of St. Louis, https://research.stlouisfed.org/fred2/series/Q0896AUSQ240SNBR/; US Bureau of Economic Analysis. *Real Gross Domestic Product* [A191RL1Q225SBEA]. Retrieved from FRED, Federal Reserve Bank of St. Louis, https://research.stlouisfed.org/fred2/series/A191RL1Q225SBEA/ (accessed May 7, 2015).

CHART 2 NET PRIVATE NON-RESIDENTIAL FIXED INVESTMENT
AS A PERCENT OF GDP, 1949–2013

Chart 2 was originally conceived by John Bellamy Foster and Fred Magdoff (2009, 103) and is simply updated here with minor modifications. The line represents a ten-year moving average of changes in the percentage of net private non-residential fixed investment.

Sources: US Bureau of Economic Analysis (BEA), "*Table 1.1.5. Gross Domestic Product*," http://www.bea.gov/iTable/iTableHtml.cfm?reqid=9&step=3&isuri =1&903=5; and "*Table 5.2.5. Gross and Net Domestic Investment by Major Type*," http://www.bea.gov/iTable/iTableHtml.cfm?reqid=9&step=3&isuri=1&903 =139 (accessed February 1, 2015).

CHART 3 CASH AND SHORT-TERM INVESTMENTS
OF THE TOP 1,200 NON-FINANCIAL US FIRMS, 1970–2013

All firms in this sample were ranked by the total revenue (REVT variable). Financial firms were excluded by creating a custom three-digit NAICS code variable and dropping the following sectors: 521, 522, and 523.

Sources: Compustat North America, Fundamentals Annual (Standard and Poor 2015); BEA, "Table 1.1.5. Gross Domestic Product," http://www .bea.gov/iTable/iTableHtml.cfm?reqid=9&step=3&isuri=1&903=5 (accessed February 1, 2015).

CHART 4 OFFICIAL AND HIDDEN UNEMPLOYMENT, 1962–2014

Chart 4 is a modified and updated version of data presented in my dissertation (Jonna 2012, 63–70). Hidden unemployment is defined as the sum of "Discouraged," "Long-Term Unemployed," and "Incarcerated." Prior to 1976 it is not possible to determine the precise number of Discouraged and Long-Term Unemployed persons. To get a rough estimate of this part of hidden unemployment for 1962–1975, data is taken from the "Work Experience of the Population" series collected by the Bureau of Labor Statistics (BLS) (a part of the Annual Social and Economic Supplement to the Current Population Survey). For these years, the number of persons unemployed for at least twenty-seven weeks is taken as a proxy for Discouraged + Long-Term Unemployed in later years. While the two sets of data are clearly not directly comparable, the values, though systematically lower (and thus more conservative), correspond closely to data for the years immediately following 1975.

Sources: *Incarcerated*: 1948–1977: "No. HS-24. Federal and State Prisoners by Jurisdiction and Sex: 1925 to 2001," US Census Bureau; 1978–2013: "Prisoners Under State or Federal Jurisdiction, 1977–2004" (December 6, 2005); E. Ann Carson, "Prisoners in 2013" (September 16, 2014). (The most recent data was used whenever possible.) 2014: Estimated based on the percentage change of the previous two years. *Hidden unemployed for 1962–1975*: BLS, "Work Experience of the Population" (various releases). Additional historical data was obtained from the BLS by request. All other figures were tabulated using CPS microdata retrieved from the Integrated Public Use Microdata Series (IPUMS), CPS (see King et al. 2010).

TABLE A-1 Layers of the Labor Market Distress in the US Economy

(thousands)	1980	1990	2000	2010	2014
Official Labor Force [a]	103,339	123,499	140,454	153,413	155,442
Discouraged [b]	1,062	708	727	1,713	1,761
Long-Term Unemployed [c]	2,159	1,706	4,106	5,087	5,253
Incarcerated [d]	330	774	1,394	1,614	1,575
Hidden Unemployed [e]	3,551	3,188	6,227	8,413	8,588
Recalculated Labor Force [f]	106,890	126,686	146,682	161,826	164,031
Officially Unemployed [g]	6,816	6,830	6,116	15,733	10,767
Working Poor [h]	7,351	9,701	11,281	12,693	13,977
Official Rate of Unemployment [i]	10.5%	10.4%	12.5%	13.8%	14.5%
Rate of Labor Market Distress [j]	16.6%	15.6%	16.1%	22.8%	20.3%

Table A-1 totals the various elements of labor market distress in the US economy for selected years. More important, it contains notes explaining each variable and concept used in both the table and chart.

[a] Civilian non-institutional labor force 16 years and older. The age condition is used on all subsequent calculations. LABFORCE=2; AGE (>= 16).

[b] Not in the labor force but has looked for work sometime in the past year. LABFORCE=1; NWLOOKWK (1 ≥ 52).

[c] Not in the labor force and has *not* looked for work in the past year but wants a job now. LABFORCE=1; WANTJOB (2 ≥ 4).

[d] Prisoners under state or federal jurisdiction (see source notes above).

[e] Discouraged + Long-Term Unemployed + Incarcerated

[f] Official Labor Force + (Discouraged + Long-Term Unemployed + Incarcerated).

[g] Jobless but has looked for work in the past month. EMPSTAT=20, 21 or 22.

[h] Employed workers under the poverty line. EMPSTAT=10; OFFPOV=1.

[i] Officially Unemployed / Official Labor Force.

[j] (Hidden Unemployed + Officially Unemployed + Working Poor) / Recalculated Labor Force.

CHART 5 DURATION OF JOB LOSSES IN SELECTED RECESSIONS

Chart 5 is an updated version of data presented by Fred Magdoff (2011, 27). For each recession, the level of employment is fixed and used as a benchmark to assess how long it takes for employment to reach pre-recession levels. The intent is to show that when employment, rather than economic growth, is used as an indicator of recovery a very different picture emerges.

Sources: BLS, *All Employees: Total nonfarm* [*PAYEMS*], https://research.stlouis-fed.org/fred2/series/PAYEMS/; and *NBER based Recession Indicators for the United States from the Period following the Peak through the Trough* [USR-ECD], https://research.stlouisfed.org/fred2/series/USRECD/. Retrieved from FRED, Federal Reserve Bank of St. Louis, January 2015.

CHART 6 CHANGES IN JOB GROWTH BY MEDIAN WAGE
FOR SELECTED PERIODS, 2000–2014

The calculations in Chart 6 use Current Population Survey (CPS) microdata compiled by IPUMS (see King et al. 2010). The two main variables used were HOURWAGE and OCC. Wages were converted to constant 1999 dollars using the IPUMS variable CPI99, and then to 2013 dollars using inflation factors from Sahr (2015). The wage ranges given in National Employment Law Project (2011) were used as a rough guide.

TABLE A-2 Wage Ranges Used for Median Wage Calculations

Wage Range	Low Cutoff	High Cutoff
Low	$5.00	$13.24
Middle	$13.25	$21.99
High	$22.00	$55.00

Table A-2 presents the wage ranges (in 2013 dollars) used for calculations in Chart 6. The OCC variable used in the above calculations reports occupations according to the scheme of the given year. It is important to note that the Census Bureau made significant changes to the occupational categories in 2011. As a result occupations are not directly comparable with previous years (in terms of the number of workers). For example, the occupation "Registered Nurses" was split into four distinct categories: "Registered nurses," "Nurse anesthetists," "Nurse midwives," and "Nurse practitioners." These new occupations were also augmented due to changes in the classification of other occupations. Despite these changes, the calculations above do not depend on any specific definition of a given occupational category because the occupations were categorized by median wage for each year independently. Moreover, changes to the occupational coding did not have a significant effect on the total number of workers in the largest occupational groupings.

CHART 7 INDEX OF REAL MEDIAN HOUSEHOLD INCOME AND REAL GDP, 1967–2013 (1967 = 100)

For Chart 7, Median Household Income data was in constant 2013 dollars and Gross Domestic Product data was in constant 2009 dollars before indexing. The index year is 1967.

Sources: "Table H-5. Race and Hispanic Origin of Householder—Households by Median and Mean Income: 1967 to 2013," US Census Bureau, Historical Income Tables: Households; US Bureau of Economic Analysis, "Table 1.1.6. Real Gross Domestic Product, Chained Dollars," http://www.bea.gov/iTable/iTableHtml.cfm?reqid=9&step=3&isuri=1&903=6 (accessed February 1, 2015).

CHART 8 MEDIAN WAGE AND SALARY INCOME OF PERSONS 18–24 YEARS OLD, WITHOUT COLLEGE EXPERIENCE, 1964–2014

Chart 8 uses CPS microdata (King et al. 2010) to estimate the wage and salary income of eighteen- to twenty-four-year-olds who have not attended college. The age and "Educational attainment recode" variables (EDUC<80) were used to estimate median wage and salary income in 2013 dollars (inflation factors taken from Sahr 2015).

CHART 9 LABOR FORCE PARTICIPATION RATE, MALES, 1948–2014, AND CHART 10 LABOR FORCE PARTICIPATION RATE, FEMALES, 1990–2014

The participation rates reported in Charts 9 and 10 were computed using the following series from the US Bureau of Labor Statistics: Chart 9, "(Unadj) Labor Force Participation Rate—Men" (LNU01300001); Chart 10, "(Unadj) Labor Force Participation Rate—Women" (LNU01300002).

CHART 11 ESTIMATED NUMBER OF MISSING JOBS SINCE 2000
PEAK IN LABOR FORCE PARTICIPATION, 2001–2015

John Bellamy Foster (with help from Fred Magdoff) devised the method of estimating missing jobs used in Chart 11. Foster explains that "missing jobs" represent the "cumulative number of additional jobs needed to maintain employment at the same percent of the civilian noninstitutional population as in 2000" (Monthly Review Editors 2004, 7). The calculation is carried out in two steps: (1) the potential or estimated employment level is determined by multiplying the 2000 peak rate (2000P)—64.4 percent—by the civilian noninstitutional population (CNP) for each subsequent year, thus taking into account demographic and population changes; (2) the number of missing jobs is then determined by subtracting the actual level of employment (EMP) for each year from the estimated employment level arrived at in the first step. The following formula summarizes the calculation: CNP * 2000P – EMP. The civilian population and employment in 2015 are estimated by averaging January, February and March figures. Annual figures represent the average for the given year.

Sources: "Civilian Noninstitutional Population, 16 years and over" (LNU00000000); "(Unadj) Employment Level, 16 years and over" (LNS12000000); "(Unadj) Labor Force Participation Rate" (LNU01300000); and "(Unadj) Civilian Labor Force Level" (LNU01000000), BLS, http://data.bls.gov.

CHART 12 WORKING POOR, HIDDEN UNEMPLOYED,
AND OFFICIALLY UNEMPLOYED, 1968–2014

See Chart 4 for sources and discussion, and particularly Table A-1 as it includes definitions of the Hidden Unemployed and Working Poor (the latter simply defined as employed persons at or below the official poverty line). Data on the poverty status variable does not start until 1967 in the CPS dataset so there is no data for the number of working poor prior to that year. Like Chart 4, Chart 12 is derived primarily from my dissertation (Jonna 2012, 63–70).

CHART 13 UNION MEMBERSHIP AS A PERCENTAGE OF
TOTAL EMPLOYED WORKERS, 1944–2014

Although union membership data prior to 1974 is not directly comparable to later years due to a change in estimation methods (from financial to survey data), the older method was relatively comprehensive and most likely underreports union membership. This means the figures presented in Chart 13 are conservative given the overall trend. In current BLS estimates (available at the BLS site starting in 1984) there is a distinction between "Total Wage and Salary" and "Private Wage and Salary." These distinctions do not exist for earlier years (1944–1974), which makes it impossible to distinguish public from private sector membership.

    Sources: *Union Members*: 1944–1974: "Union membership: 1880–1999" (see Rosenbloom 2006). Prior to 1974, figures are taken from table column Ba4783 (BLS, "Union members"); for 1974, figures are taken from table column Ba4787 (CPS, "Union members among wage and salary workers"). *Union Members*: 1983–2014: BLS. "Total wage and salary workers, Members of unions" (Series LUU0203161800) and "Private wage and salary workers, Members of unions" (Series LUU0203182000). *Total Workers*: BLS. "(Unadj) Employment Level, 16 years and over" (Series LNS12000000). http://data .bls.gov. Retrieved March 2015.

CHART 14 NUMBER OF WORK STOPPAGES IDLING 1,000 WORKERS, 1947–2014

The faint line in Chart 14 is actual data while the darker line represents a ten-year moving average.

    Source: BLS, "Number of Work Stoppages Idling 1,000 Workers or More" (Series: WSU100), http://data.bls.gov.

CHART 15 AVERAGE CHANGE IN INCOME SHARE FOR SELECTED INCOME GROUPS, 1935–2014

Chart 15 is designed to highlight how significant the differences in income share movements are for the top income earners as opposed to those at the bottom. By averaging annual changes in income share over ten-year periods it is possible to assess simultaneously the trend and relative movements in income share for these groups.

    Source: Piketty and Saez (2007). Series updated by the same authors in "The World Top Incomes Database," http://topincomes.g-mond.parisschoolof economics.eu.

CHART 16 UNEMPLOYED FOR AT LEAST 15 WEEKS AS A PERCENTAGE OF THE LABOR FORCE, 1962–2014

Chart 16 uses CPS microdata compiled by IPUMS (see King et al. 2010). The series is constructed using the interval variable DURUNEM2 (≥ 9), which only includes respondents who have looked for work in the last four weeks. This means that "Discouraged" and "Long-Term Unemployed" workers are excluded. The faint line represents actual data and the darker line the five-year moving average.

CHART 17-ADDENDUM Revenue of Top 100 Non-Financial US Firms (by Revenue) as a Percentage of US GDP, 1950–2013

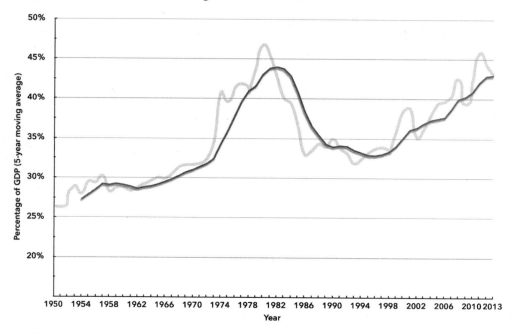

CHART 17 US REVENUE AND US GROSS PROFIT PER EMPLOYEE
OF THE TOP 100 US FIRMS, 1953–2013

In Chart 17 and Chart 17-addendum, firms are ranked by total revenue (REVT variable) for the given fiscal year. If either gross profit (GP variable) or Employment (EMP variable) data were not available for a given year the case was dropped. Actual figures along with case counts and conversion factors for Chart 17 are shown in Table A-3. For Chart 17 the average number of cases for the 1950–2013 period was 97.

Sources: Compustat North America, Fundamentals Annual (Standard & Poor 2015); and US Bureau of Economic Analysis, "*Table 1.1.2. Contributions to Percent Change in Real Gross Domestic Product,*" http://www.bea.gov/iTable /iTableHtml.cfm?reqid=9&step=3&isuri=1&903=2. Accessed February 2015.

It is important to note that the data presented in Chart 17 on average revenue per employee does not distinguish between foreign and domestic workers. The number of foreign workers employed by the largest US multinational corporations has grown considerably. According to data provided by the United Nations Conference on Trade and Development (UNCTAD),

TABLE A-3 Gross Profit and Revenue per Employee with Case
Counts (thousands of 2013 dollars)

Year	Average gross profit per employee	Case Count	Average revenue per employee	Case Count
1953	$44.50	75	$183.93	89
1963	$72.48	98	$250.11	98
1973	$95.59	96	$320.77	96
1983	$110.55	98	$503.76	98
1993	$113.83	99	$469.22	99
2003	$167.84	99	$812.04	99
2013	$224.11	97	$1,504.46	97

about 50 percent of the workforce of the top nonfinancial firms incorporated
in the United States were foreign in 1990 (26 firms); by 2013 it was 60 percent
(23 firms). Moreover, the revenue per worker for foreign workers is typically
about 20 percent higher than for domestic workers (see UNCTAD 2014 and
earlier reports).

CHART 18 NUMBER OF NEW YORK TIMES STORIES
MENTIONING AUTOMATION (THOUGH FEBRUARY 2015)

Research conducted by Grace Hebert, using *New York Times* index.

CHART 19. THEORETICAL GROWTH IN COMPUTING POWER

In computing, "FLOPS" is an acronym for **FL**oating-point **O**perations **P**er
Second, and the preceding "G" stands for giga (or 10^9). Thus a GFLOP is a
billion floating-point operations per second. The measure "GFLOPS per dollar" is used in accordance with the "Law of Accelerating Returns" developed by
Kurzweil (2012: 343–344). The series starts in 1984, when the Cray X-MP/48
supercomputer maxed out at around 0.4 GFLOPS at a cost of approximately
$27 million (2014 dollars), meaning the cost per GFLOP was about $85 million.
From this point, the series simply doubles each period, assuming an exponential
increase in calculations per second per dollar every thirteen months.

SOURCES AND NOTES FOR VOTING FIGURES IN CHAPTER 3

"Total votes" for the majority party is the sum of votes received by that party in the general election of a given year, for either the House or the Senate. For the Senate, the "voting-age population" is the sum of the population eighteen years old and over of the states that had a senatorial race in a given election year. For the House, the "voting-age population" is simply the total population eighteen years old and over in a given election year. Voting-age population figures for 2014 were estimated using the percent change figures (2013 to 2014) reported by the US Census Bureau.

Sources: Voting figures: 1998–2012: "Votes Cast for the U.S. House of Representatives by Party" and "Votes Cast for the U.S. Senate by Party," *Election Results*. Public Records Office: Federal Election Committee; 2014: "*Statistics of the Congressional Election from Official Sources for the Election of November 4, 2014*," Office of the Clerk, US House of Representatives, Karen L. Haas, pp. 53–54, published March 9, 2015, http://clerk.house.gov /member_info/election.aspx. *Population figures*: 1998–2012: "Population Estimates for the U.S. and States by Single Year of Age and Sex"; 2014: "National, State, and Puerto Rico Commonwealth Totals Datasets: Population change and rankings: April 1, 2010 to July 1, 2014," US Census Bureau.

REFERENCES

Foster, John Bellamy, and Fred Magdoff. 2009. *The Great Financial Crisis: Causes and Consequences*. New York: Monthly Review Press.

Jonna, R. Jamil. 2012. "Toward a Political-Economic Sociology of Unemployment: Renewing the Classical Reserve Army Perspective." Edited by John Bellamy Foster. Doctoral Thesis. John Bellamy Foster, Chair. Eugene: Department of Sociology, University of Oregon. doi:10.1080/08854300.2012 .686280.

King, Miriam, Steven Ruggles, J. Trent Alexander, Sarah Flood, Katie Genadek, Matthew B. Schroeder, Brandon Trampe, and Rebecca Vick. 2010. "Integrated Public Use Microdata Series, Current Population Survey: Version 3.0." Minneapolis: University of Minnesota. http://cps.ipums.org/cps.

Kurzweil, Ray. 2012. "On Modis' 'Why the Singularity Cannot Happen.'" In *Singularity Hypotheses*, edited by Amnon H. Eden, James H. Moor, Johnny H. Søraker, and Eric Steinhart, 343–348. Berlin: Springer.

Magdoff, Fred. 2011. "The Jobs Disaster in the United States." *Monthly Review* 63 (2): 24–37. doi:10.14452/MR-063-02-2011-06_2.

Magdoff, Fred, and John Bellamy Foster. 2014. "Stagnation and Financialization: The Nature of the Contradiction." *Monthly Review* 66 (1): 1–24. http:// dx.doi.org/10.14452/MR-066-01-2014-05_1.

Monthly Review Editors. 2004. "The Stagnation of Employment." *Monthly Review* 55 (11): 3–17.

National Employment Law Project. 2011. *The Good Jobs Deficit*. New York, NY. http://www.nelp.org/index.php/content/content_publications/?issue=labor_market_research&type=reports_and_resources.

Piketty, Thomas, and Emmanuel Saez. 2007. "Income and Wage Inequality in the United States 1913–2002." In *Top Incomes over the Twentieth Century*, edited by Anthony B. Atkinson and Thomas Piketty, 141–225. New York: Oxford University Press.

Rosenbloom, Joshua L. 2006. "Union Membership: 1880–1999 (Series Ba4783–4791)." In *Historical Statistics of the United States: Millennial Edition Online*, edited by Susan B. Carter, Scott Sigmund Gartner, Michael R. Haines, Alan L. Olmstead, Richard Sutch, and Gavin Wright. Cambridge, UK: Cambridge University Press. doi:http://dx.doi.org/10.1017/ISBN-97805 11132971.Ba4783–4998.

Sahr, Robert. 2015. "Inflation Conversion Factors for Years 1774 to Estimated 2025, in Dollars of Recent Years." Oregon State University. http://liberalarts.oregonstate.edu/spp/polisci/research/inflation-conversion-factors-convert-dollars-1774-estimated-2024-dollars-recent-year.

Standard and Poor. 2015. "Compustat North America, Fundamentals Annual." Wharton Research Data Services (WRDS). http://wrds-web.wharton.upenn.edu/wrds/ds/comp/index.cfm.

UNCTAD. 2014. *World Investment Report 2014*. New York: United Nations Conference on Trade and Development. http://unctad.org/en/pages/Publication Webflyer.aspx?publicationid=937.

ACKNOWLEDGMENTS

THIS BOOK IS PUBLISHED ON THE TWENTIETH ANNIVERSARY OF A COLLABORATION that began when the two of us began advancing a critique of the consolidation and dumbing down of what has come to be referred to as "old media." Our concern was that a diminishing of journalism would ultimately lead to a diminishing of democracy. As the years passed, this collaboration began to extend from narrow beginnings to a broader consideration of the state of American democratic systems and structures that seemed, to our view, to be under assault at every turn. In a series of books, we examined media and democracy issues, arguing initially for a renewal of journalism as a first step toward a renewal of democracy. After a series of U.S. Supreme Court decisions struck down traditional barriers to the buying of elections by billionaire campaign donors and multinational corporations, we began to link arguments for the renewal of journalism with arguments for a renewal of civic engagement and democratic participation. There was always a measure of nostalgia in our work, a desire to use new technologies and new thinking to renew old structures.

This book is different. It argues, without apology, that the democratic infrastructure and economic understandings of the United States that now exist are not just under stress or broken. They are insufficient to respond to the overwhelming changes that are coming. Political figures such as Bernie Sanders suggest that a "political revolution" is necessary and we would agree with that assessment. But that is not the point of this book, The point of this book is to suggest that the "revolution"—like the American revolution of 1776—will only be a part of a dramatically bigger and bolder rethink of economic and social arrangements. That those arrangements will change is inevitable. What is still at stake is the question of whether the changes will be in the interest of a handful of billionaires or the great mass of Americans—and, indeed, the great mass of human beings around the world. To reach the point where we could write confidently about the changes that are coming and about the responses that are right, we traveled extensively in the United States and internationally. We met with top CEOs of tech companies and with some of the savviest innovators in the world. Our thinking was informed by conversations with scholars and writers who have explored these issues, such as Frank Rieger and others associated with Germany's Chaos Computer Clubs (CCC). Discussions with Nick Bostrom, the director of the Oxford Martin Programme on the Impacts of Future Technology, were incredibly instructive, as were conversations at the forums and events organized by Johannes Winkelhage. Discussions with Noam Chomsky, Naomi Klein, Joel Rogers, Harvey Kaye, and many other thinkers helped us to put the moment in perspective. We were informed, as well, by discussions with labor leaders and activists, including RoseAnn DeMoro, Michael Lighty, Charles Idelson, Jean Ross, RN, and Ken Zinn from National Nurses United, and Joseph Geevarghese of the Change to Win Labor Coalition and the Strategic Organizing Center. We also appreciate the insights provided by Congressmen Keith Ellison and Mark Pocan regarding employment issues, and those we got from the National Employment Law Project, Demos, and state-based research projects such as the Center on Wisconsin Strategies at the University of Wisconsin and Policy Matters Ohio.

Several dear friends gave us many hours of their time to read and comment on several chapters in the book. They include Victor Pickard, John Bellamy Foster, Richard Powers, Dan Schiller, Jeff Cohen, and Matt Rothschild. We received help on specific points in the text from the following friends, journalists, and scholars: Robert Pollin, Timothy Noah, Richard V. Reeves, James Galbraith, James Baughman, David Howell, John Schmitt, Daniel Bowman Simon, Bernie Sanders, Matt Stoller, Inger Stole, Des Freedman, Sigurd Allern, Robert Hackett, Richard Wheeler, Ben Scott, Sundiata Cha-Jua, Fred Magdoff, Robert Reich, and John Murphy. We received invaluable research assistance from Nathan Gerth, Amy Holland, Ali Moll, and Grace Hebert. And, of course, R. Jamil Jonna's talents are on full display in Chapter 2 and in the Statistical Appendix. This book could not exist without the generosity, talent, and wisdom of all these people, though we alone are responsible for any flaws with what lies within.

Our editors at *The Nation*—Katrina vanden Heuvel, Roane Carey, and Richard Kim—were always engaged and encouraging, as were fellow writers such as Naomi Klein, Sarah Jaffe, and William Greider. Ed Schultz and Chris Hayes welcomed our efforts to broaden discussions of employment and workplace rights, as did *Democracy Now*'s Amy Goodman and Juan Gonzalez and radio hosts John "Sly" Sylvester at WEKZ and Joy Cardin on Wisconsin Public Radio. The same goes for Ruth Conniff at *The Progressive*, and of course for Dave Zweifel, Lynn Danielson, and Judie Kleinmaier at the Madison *Capital Times*. Generous research support from the University of Illinois was essential to making the book possible.

This project began with the encouragement of Carl Bromley at Nation Books and, when Carl moved on, it was nurtured by Daniel LoPreto. Alessandra Bastagli, when she took charge at Nation Books, helped us to frame the project and played a pivotal role in making it a success. We appreciate them all, as we do all the folks at Nation Books, PublicAffairs, and the Nation Institute. They made this book possible, as did colleagues and comrades such as Craig Aaron and Joe Torres at Free Press.

Our deepest thanks go to family and friends in Madison, Wisconsin, where we both reside. We cherish Inger Stole, Amy and Lucy McChesney, Mary and Whitman Bottari, and Mary Nichols. We write for them, and for the future.

Robert W. McChesney
John Nichols
Madison, Wisconsin
November 2015

NOTES

INTRODUCTION: WELCOME TO THE FUTURE

1. We have written about these issues in considerable detail in John Nichols and Robert W. McChesney, *Dollarocracy: How the Money and Media Election Complex Is Destroying America* (New York: Nation Books, 2013) and in Robert W. McChesney and John Nichols, *The Death and Life of American Journalism: The Media Revolution that Will Begin the World Again* (New York: Nation Books, 2010). To our view the intersection between the decline of journalism and the rise of saturation campaigning—powered by massive campaign treasuries and outside spending—has redefined the political discourse so that the range of debate is frequently set by campaign donors rather than citizens and independent journalists. Candidates and parties generally, though not always, fit into the framework, rather than trying to challenge it. As a result, political campaigns have become disconnected from issues and ideas that matter—even, it could be argued, from politics.

2. James K. Galbraith, *The End of Normal: The Great Crisis and the Future of Growth* (New York: Simon and Schuster, 2014), pp. 138–145.

3. Jeffrey D. Clements, *Corporations Are Not People: Reclaiming Democracy from Big Money and Global Corporations* (San Francisco: Berrett-Koehler, 2014).

4. Zoe Corbyn, "Robots Are Leaving the Factory Floor and Heading for Your Desk—and Your Job," *Guardian*, February 9, 2015.

5. Frank Swain, "Why I Want a Microchip Implant: With a chip under your skin, you can do everything from unlocking doors to starting motorbikes, says Frank Swain, who has been trying to get his own implant," *BBC*, February 10, 2014, and Rory Cellan-Jones, "Office puts chips under staff's skin," *BBC*, January 29, 2015.

6. Jason Dorrieron, "Burger Robot Poised to Disrupt Fast Food Industry," SingularityHUB, August 10, 2014.

7. Graeme Wood, "The Future of College? A brash tech entrepreneur thinks he can reinvent higher education by stripping it down to its essence, eliminating lectures and tenure along with football games, ivy-covered buildings, and research libraries. What if he's right?" *Atlantic*, September, 2014.

8. Paul Mason, "The End of Capitalism Has Begun," *Guardian*, July, 7, 2015. Mason, one of the leading voices in challenging the madness of austerity, drew the themes for this article from his book *Postcapitalism* (Allen Lane, 2015).

9. Ibid.

10. Nigel Pollitt, "The Non-virtual Elephant in Paul Mason's Postcapitalist Sharing-Economy Room," *Guardian*, July 21, 2015.

11. Michael J. De La Merced, "Eastman Kodak Files for Bankruptcy," *New York Times*, January 19, 2012.

12. Beth Jinks, "Kodak Moments Just a Memory as Company Exits Bankruptcy," *BloombergBusiness*, September 3, 2013, and Matthew Daneman "Kodak Hits 2014 Goals, but Sees a Down '15," *Rochester Democrat and Chronicle*, March 15, 2015.

13. Ian Leslie, "Kodak vs Instagram: This is why it's only going to get harder to make a good living," *New Statesman*, January 28, 2014.

14. Derek Thompson, "A World without Work," *Atlantic*, July–August 2015. For current market values of the largest US corporations, see http://www.iweblists.com/us/commerce/MarketCapitalization.html.

15. Interview with Harvey Kaye, April 20, 2015. Kaye, a scholar of British radical history and the author of groundbreaking books on Thomas Paine and Franklin Roosevelt's "Four Freedoms," is the University of Wisconsin-Green Bay Professor of Democracy and Justice Studies.

16. For an exploration of these themes, see Nichols and McChesney, *Dollarocracy*, pp. 97–128.

17. Rasmussen Reports, "53% Think Neither Political Party Represents the American People," *Guardian*, http://www.theguardian.com/books/2015/jul/17/postcapitalism-end-of-capitalism-begun. According to the Rasmussen analysis, "A new Rasmussen Reports national telephone survey finds that 53% of Likely U.S. Voters think it is fair to say that neither party in Congress is the party of the American people. That's up six points from 47% last October and matches the previous high found in June 2012 during the last national election cycle. Just 28% disagree, while 19% are not sure."

18. Thomas Reese, "Pope Francis: Technology + greed = disaster," *National Catholic Reporter*, August 13, 2015.

19. See Michelle Chen, "New York Fast-Food Workers Win Their Fight for $15: A landmark executive move will serve the state's fast-food workers some long-overdue justice," *Nation*, July 22, 2015.

20. Michael Shavel and Andy Zheng, "The Economics of Automation: Quick Serve Restaurant Industry," Cornerstone Capital Group, March 3, 2015. http://cornerstonecapinc.com/2015/03/the-economics-of-automation-in-the-quick-serve-industry/.

21. Ibid.

22. Kaja Whitehouse and Paul Davidson, "McDonald's Raises Pay for 90,000 Workers," *USA Today*, April 1, 2015.

23. The Real Clear Politics collection of polling data on the direction in which the country is headed—and on a host of other issues related to the mood of Americans with regard to the economy and the country—can be found at http://www.realclearpolitics.com/epolls/other/direction_of_country-902.html. The "wrong direction" sentiment generally outpolls the "right direction" sentiment by about 2–1. Of course, there are many measures that can be taken and we recognize that there are different ways of assessing personal and societal frustration, but we believe the "wrong direction" numbers provide a strong indication of the extent to which Americans are unsatisfied with their collective circumstance.

24. Grace Paley, *Enormous Changes at the Last Minute* (New York: Farrar, Straus and Giroux, 1985).

CHAPTER ONE: INTO THE MAELSTROM

1. Emily Young, "Davos 2014: Google's Schmidt Warning on Jobs," bbc.com, January 23, 2014, http://www.bbc.com/news/business-25872006.

2. The opposition came primarily from people who had not studied the actual technology, as far as we could tell, and dismissed it as ungrounded hyperbole—because massive job displacement had not occurred by 2015 despite decades of technological innovation, why should anyone believe automation would kick in now? For a nice example of this picture in the business press, see Dani Rodrick, "Rise of the Machines," *World Finance*, March 9, 2015.

3. Edward L. Glaeser, "Secular Joblessness," in Coen Teulings and Richard Baldwin, editors, *Secular Stagnation: Facts, Causes and Cures* (London: CEPR Press, 2014), p. 69.

4. The United States now stands as the advanced industrial nation with the highest rate of poverty and the greatest degree of economic inequality, a depressing combination. See Anthony B. Atkinson, *Inequality: What Can Be Done?* (Cambridge, MA: Harvard University Press, 2015), p. 26. For an especially gripping account of how America has become a dramatically less egalitarian and fair society in the past forty years, see Robert D. Putnam, *Our Kids: The American Dream in Crisis* (New York: Simon and Schuster, 2015).

5. Bob Herbert, *Losing Our Way: An Intimate Portrait of a Troubled America* (New York: Doubleday, 2014), pp. 1, 3. There have been many superb books making similar poignant presentations in recent years. See, for example, George Packer, *The Unwinding: An Inner History of the New America* (New York: Farrar, Straus and Giroux, 2013).

6. See Glenn Greenwald, *With Liberty and Justice for Some: How the Law Is Used to Destroy Equality and Protect the Powerful* (New York: Metropolitan Books, 2011).

7. Matt Taibbi, *The Divide: American Injustice in the Age of the Wealth Gap* (New York: Spiegel and Grau, 2014), pp. vxiii, xix.

8. See, for example, the recent work of economists and scholars like Paul Krugman, James Galbraith, Joseph Stiglitz, Dean Baker, Juliet Schor, Jared Bernstein, Robert Pollin, Jeffrey Sachs, and Robert Reich. They have all influenced us a great deal. One recent book that strikes us as eminently sensible, yet entirely outside the boundaries of legitimate debate, is Ralph Nader, *The Seventeen Solutions: Bold Ideas for Our American Future* (New York: Harper, 2012).

9. See, for example, Steven Hill, *Europe's Promise: Why the European Way Is the Best Hope in an Insecure Age* (Berkeley: University of California Press, 2010) and Lane Kenworthy, *Social Democratic America* (New York: Oxford University Press, 2014).

10. See David Broockman and Christopher Skovron, "Politicians Think American Voters Are More Conservative than They Really Are," Scholars Strategy Network, 2013, http://www.scholarsstrategynetwork.org/content/politicians -think-american-voters-are-more-conservative-they-really-are. See also Brendan James, "Study: Lawmakers Assume Voters Are Way More Conservative than They Are," *Huffington Post*, May 21, 2015, http://talkingpointsmemo.com/news /study-lawmakers-liberal-conservative-assume.

11. Kay Lehman Schlozman, Sidney Verba, and Henry E. Brady, *The Unheavenly Chorus: Unequal Political Voice and the Broken Promise of American Democracy* (Princeton: Princeton University Press, 2012); Larry M. Bartels, *Unequal Democracy: The Political Economy of the New Gilded Age* (Princeton: Princeton University Press, 2008).

12. Martin Gilens and Benjamin I. Page, "Testing Theories of American Politics: Elites, Interest Groups, and Average Citizens," *Perspectives on Politics*, 12, no. 3 (September 2014): 564–581.

13. Martin Gilens, *Affluence and Influence: Economic Inequality and Political Power in America* (Princeton: Princeton University Press, 2012), p. 1.

14. Reid Wilson, "Only 36 percent of Americans can name the three branches of government," *Washington Post*, September 18, 2004; "Political Commentary from the LA Times," latimes.com, September 28, 2010; "Two-Thirds of Americans Can't Name ONE Supreme Court Justice," *Huffington Post*, June 3, 2010.

15. Sheldon Wolin, *Democracy Incorporated: Managed Democracy and the Specter of Inverted Totalitarianism* (Princeton: Princeton University Press, 2008), pp. 64, 65.

16. Tony Judt, *Ill Fares the Land* (New York: Penguin, 2010), p. 131.

17. Bob Herbert, *Losing Our Way: An Intimate Portrait of a Troubled America* (New York: Doubleday, 2014), p. 2.

18. John Dewey, *Art as Experience* (Chicago: University of Chicago Press, 1934), ch. 1; we learned of this passage from Thomas Geoghegan, *Only One Thing Can Save Us: Why America Needs a New Kind of Labor Movement* (New York: The New Press, 2014), p. 122.

19. Robert Pollin, *Back to Full Employment* (Cambridge, MA: MIT Press, 2012), pp. 12, 6.

20. See Dean Baker and Jared Bernstein, *Getting Back to Full Employment: A Better Bargain for Working People* (Washington, DC: Center for Economic and Policy Research, 2013).

21. Nicholas Carr, *The Glass Cage: Automation and Us* (New York: W. W. Norton, 2014), p. 16.

22. Herbert, *Losing Our Way*, p. 254.

23. Ben Way, *Jobocalypse: The End of Human Jobs and How Robots Will Replace Them* (Ben Way, 2013), p. 132.

24. Randall Collins, "The End of Middle-Class Work: No More Escapes," in Immanuel Wallerstein, Randall Collins, Michael Mann, Georgi Derluguian, and Craig Calhoun, editors, *Does Capitalism Have a Future?* (New York: Oxford University Press, 2013), p. 51.

25. Derek Thompson, "A World without Work," *Atlantic*, July-August 2015.

26. Judt, *Ill Fares the Land*, p. 177.

27. See Robert W. McChesney, *Digital Disconnect: How Capitalism Is Turning the Internet against Democracy* (New York: The New Press, 2013).

28. For a good discussion of how the Internet is a crucial part of political calculations and machinations by the powerful, see Shawn M. Powers and Michael Jablonski, *The Real Cyber War: The Political Economy of Internet Freedom* (Urbana, IL: University of Illinois Press, 2015). See also Adi Kuntsman and Rebecca L. Stein, *Digital Militarism: Israel's Occupation in the Social Media Age* (Palo Alto: Stanford University Press, 2015).

29. Mike Cooley, "Introduction," in Peter Brodner, *The Shape of Future Technology: The Anthropocentric Alternative* (London: Springer-Verlag, 1990), p. 1.

30. Cited in Peter H. Diamandis and Steven Kotler, *Abundance: The Future Is Better than You Think* (New York: Free Press, 2012), p. 301.

31. Ibid.

32. Kenneth Rogoff, "Is Capitalism Sustainable?" *Project Syndicate*, December 2, 2011.

33. David M. Kotz, *The Rise and Fall of Neoliberal Capitalism* (Cambridge, MA: Harvard University Press, 2015), p. 218.

34. Jeremy Rifkin, *The Zero Marginal Cost Society* (New York: Palgrave Macmillan, 2013), p. 2.

35. David Harvey, *Seventeen Contradictions and the End of Capitalism* (New York: Oxford University Press, 2014), p. 110.

36. *Report of the Commission on Inclusive Prosperity*, co-chaired by Lawrence H. Summers and Ed Balls (Washington, DC: Center for American Progress, January 2015), p. 1.

37. "The Onrushing Wave," *Economist*, January 18, 2014.

38. Brink Lindsey, *Human Capitalism: How Economic Growth Has Made Us Smarter—and More Unequal* (Princeton: Princeton University Press, 2013), p. 72.

39. We have written about these issues in considerable detail in John Nichols and Robert W. McChesney, *Dollarocracy: How the Money and Media Election Complex Is Destroying America* (New York: Nation Books, 2013). See also: Robert E. Mutch, *Buying the Vote: A History of Campaign Finance Reform* (New York: Oxford University Press, 2014); Kenneth P. Vogel, *Big Money: 2.5 Billion Dollars, One Suspicious Vehicle, and a Pimp—on the Trail of the Ultra-Rich Hijacking American Politics* (New York: PublicAffairs, 2014).

40. See Robert W. McChesney and John Nichols, *The Death and Life of American Journalism: The Media Revolution that Will Begin the World Again* (New York: Nation Books, 2010).

41. Aristotle, *Politics*, trans. Benjamin Jowett (Stilwell, KS: Digireads, 2005), p. 60.

42. This is not to say it was not a raging issue across the nation at the time. It was, as Alexander Keyssar documents. It just was not a big debate among the framers of the Constitution in Philadelphia, where the notion of property requirements for white, male-only suffrage was roundly accepted. See Alexander Keyssar, *The Right to Vote: The Contested History of Democracy in the United States* (New York, Basic Books, 2000), p. 15.

43. Milton Friedman, *Capitalism and Freedom* (Chicago: University of Chicago Press, 1962), p. 3.

44. Lewis F. Powell Jr., "Attack on American Free Enterprise System," confidential memorandum for the United States Chamber of Commerce, August 23, 1971. Widely available online.

45. Quotation in P. W. Singer, *Corporate Warriors: The Rise of the Privatized Military Industry* (Ithaca, NY: Cornell University Press, 2008), p. 49.

46. The classic example is the elected socialist government in Chile under Salvador Allende in the early 1970s. For committed democrats, this was the ideal outcome: a free democratic society had determined to change its economy over time following its constitution and the rule of law. It was at all times a democracy and would ever remain so. If the people disapproved of the socialist direction, they had the power to elect a government that would change course. For those who hated communist dictatorship but desired a more egalitarian democracy, this was a development to be embraced.

To those who regard capitalism as sacrosanct, however, Allende's elected government had crossed the line. The United States government surreptitiously organized and bankrolled all sorts of protests meant to disrupt the economy and make life difficult, hence discrediting the government. When those efforts failed, it helped organize a bloody military coup in 1973—with the strong support of the wealthy and upper-middle class in Chile—that installed one of the most barbaric dictatorships of the twentieth century under General Augusto Pinochet. Friedman and some of his fellow economists at the University of Chicago actively supported and advised the Pinochet regime, because it was installing "free market" economics. It was therefore a "free" country. Democracy did not have a right to alter capitalism, and Chile was only allowed to return to democracy when the property system was safe.

In contrast, Friedman and conservatives worldwide applauded the new democracies of Eastern Europe in the 1990s when they rejected Soviet-style communism and embraced markets and a profit-driven economy. That was democracy at its best, and they were its loudest champions. But once those democracies made that decision, they forever lost their right to revisit the matter again. Capitalism was inviolate. You can opt in, but you can never opt out.

47. Robert A. Dahl, *Democracy and Its Critics* (New Haven: Yale University Press, 1989), p. 322.

48. Robert A. Dahl, *How Democratic Is the American Constitution?* (New Haven: Yale University Press, 2002), p. 139.

49. It is because of these factors that private interests tend to find infrastructure projects unprofitable to pursue, unless as a government contract, yet all private interests benefit greatly from their existence. See Brett M. Frischmann, *Infrastructure: The Social Value of Shared Resources* (New York: Oxford University Press, 2012), p. 5.

50. Recent research by Jong-Sung You on East Asian democracies confirms that economic inequality is a crucial factor that increases corruption, and that inequality also makes it much more difficult to implement effective anticorruption measures. Matthew Jenkins, "Inequality and Corruption in Democracies: A Vicious Cycle," *Anti-Corruption Research Network*, February 5, 2014.

51. Elliot Sperber, "Preconditions for an Actually Democratic Society, *CounterPunch*, July 4–6, 2014.

52. Zoltan Tibor Pallinger, "Democratic Infrastructures in the Service of Citizens' Rights: The Swiss Experience," *Working Papers Liechtenstein-Institute*, No. 13, July 2007, p. 11. For a discussion of how the decline of democratic infrastructure has weakened Norwegian democracy, see Tommy Tranvik and Per Selle, "More Centralization, Less Democracy: The Decline of the Democratic Infrastructure in Norway," in Lars Tragardh, editor, *State and Civil Society in Northern Europe: The Swedish Model Reconsidered* (New York: Berghahn Books, 2007), pp. 205–228.

53. Wendell Lewis Willkie, *An American Program* (New York: Simon and Schuster, 1944), pp. 16–18. For Willkie's devotion to free enterprise, see Wendell L. Willkie, *Free Enterprise* (Washington, DC: National Home Library Foundation, 1940).

54. Widespread unionization tends to raise everyone's wages. A 2015 report by the International Monetary Fund demonstrates how those societies with the highest rates of unionization have the lowest rates of economic inequality. See Florence Jaumotte and Carolina Osorio Buitron, "Power from the People," *Finance & Development*, March 2015, pp. 29–31.

55. Naomi Klein, *This Changes Everything: Capitalism vs. the Climate* (New York: Metropolitan Books, 2014), p. 406.

56. Herbert, *Losing Our Way*, p. 255.

57. Ralph Nader, *Unstoppable: The Emerging Left-Right Alliance to Dismantle the Corporate State* (New York: Nation Books, 2014), p. xi.

58. Gar Alperovitz, James Gustave Speth, and Joe Guinan, *The Next System Project: New Political-Economic Opportunities for the 21st Century* (The Next System Project, March 2015), p. 6.

59. Klein, *This Changes Everything*, pp. 461, 459.

60. Chris Hedges, *Wages of Rebellion: The Moral Imperative of Revolt* (New York: Nation Books, 2015).

61. See, for example, Richard Wolff, *Democracy at Work: A Cure for Capitalism* (Chicago: Haymarket Books, 2012).

62. For analysis of the return of fascism, see Samir Amin, "The Return of Fascism in Contemporary Capitalism," *Monthly Review*, September 2014.

63. Dave Renton, *Fascism: Theory and Practice* (London: Pluto Press, 1999), pp. 115, 36.

64. Franklin D. Roosevelt, "Message to Congress on Curbing Monopolies," April 29, 1938. From The American Presidency Project, University of California at Santa Barbara, www.presidency.ucsb.edu.

65. H. W. Brands, *Traitor to His Class: The Privileged Life and Radical Presidency of Franklin Delano Roosevelt* (New York: Anchor Books, 2009), p. 494.

66. Judt, *Ill Fares the Land*, p. 177.

67. Thompson, "A World without Work."

68. "Second Inaugural Address of Franklin D. Roosevelt," January 20, 1937, http://avalon.law.yale.edu/20th_century/froos2.asp.

69. We thank Bob Pollin for educating us on these issues. See Robert Pollin, *Back to Full Employment* (Cambridge, MA: MIT Press, 2012), ch. 2.

70. Michal Kalecki, "Political Aspects of Full Employment," in Michal Kalecki, *Selected Essays on the Dynamics of the Capitalist Economy* (London: Cambridge University Press, 1971), p. 138.

71. Kalecki, "Political Aspects of Full Employment," p. 141.

72. Paul Krugman, *End This Depression Now!* (New York: W. W. Norton, 2012), pp. 94–95.

73. Kalecki, "Political Aspects of Full Employment," p. 141.

74. As Tariq Ali notes, Churchill made these comments in 1927, long before "the abomination of Stalin's purges and the famines resulting from forced industrialization." The Churchill quotes and Ali's discussion of Churchill's stance toward fascism is from Tariq Ali, "Introduction: A Political-Biographical Sketch," in Ralph Miliband, *Class War Conservatism and Other Essays* (London: Verso, 2015), pp. xiii–xiv.

75. This linkage of fascism with democratic socialism rather than with actually existing capitalism is inspired by the classic work of F. A. Hayek, *The Road to Serfdom* (Chicago: University of Chicago Press, 1944), especially ch. 12. Mil-

ton Friedman acknowledged that Nazi and fascist regimes were "fundamentally capitalist," where "private enterprise was the dominant form of economic organization," but he thought fascist regimes allowed more space (and hope) for freedom than communist nations, where the government controlled the economy directly. See Friedman, *Capitalism and Freedom*, p. 10.

76. Robert O. Paxton, *The Anatomy of Fascism* (New York: Alfred A. Knopf, 2004), pp. 207, 10.

77. Hitler quotation from Konrad Heiden, *Der Fuehrer*, translated by Ralph Manheim (Boston: Houghton Mifflin Company, 1944), p. 287.

78. Dave Renton, *Fascism: Theory and Practice* (London: Pluto Press, 1999), pp. 39, 33.

79. Carlo Celli, "Introduction," in Carlo Celli, editor, *Economic Fascism: Primary Sources on Mussolini's Crony Capitalism* (Edinburg, VA: Axios Press, 2013), p. 4.

80. Harold J. Laski, "Foreword," in Robert A. Brady, *The Spirit and Structure of German Fascism* (New York: The Citadel Press, 1971; originally published in 1937), p. xiii.

81. Franklin D. Roosevelt, "Message to Congress on Curbing Monopolies."

82. Henry A. Wallace, "The Danger of American Fascism," *New York Times*, April 9, 1944.

83. Ibid.

84. George Seldes, *Facts and Fascism* (New York: In Fact, Inc., 1947); George Seldes, *Freedom of the Press* (New York: Bobbs-Merrill Company, 1935).

85. Wallace, "The Danger of American Fascism."

86. We take up most of these issues in later chapters. As for the point about the increased degree of economic concentration in the economy today compared to decades past, see John Bellamy Foster and Robert W. McChesney, *The Endless Crisis* (New York: Monthly Review Press, 2012).

87. Many writers have looked at these and other phenomena and raised thoughtful concerns about the drift of the country in such a troubling direction. See, for example, Bertram Gross, *Friendly Fascism: The New Face of Power in America* (Boston: South End Press, 1980); Linda L. Smith, *On the Edge of Fascism: An American Tragedy* (Linda L. Smith, 2013); Eric D. Williams, *The Puzzle of Fascism: Could fascism arise in America or could it already be a Fascist State?* (WhatReallyIsTheMatrix.com, 2007).

88. Robert S. Lynd, "Foreword," in Robert A. Brady, *Business as a System of Power* (New York: Columbia University Press, 1943), p. xvii.

89. Roberto Foa and Yascha Mounk, "Across the Globe, a Growing Disillusionment with Democracy," *New York Times*, September 15, 2015.

90. Taibbi, *The Divide*, p. xx.

91. Considerable research demonstrates that Americans across the political spectrum and people worldwide wish to live in far more egalitarian societies than what actually exist. See Sorapop Kiatpongsan and Michael I. Norton, "How

Much (More) Should CEOs Make? A Universal Desire for More Equal Pay," *Perspectives on Psychological Science*, 9 (2014): 587–593.

92. Klein, *This Changes Everything*, p. 466.

CHAPTER TWO: A JOBLESS ECONOMY?

1. See the Statistical Appendix for information concerning how each of the charts was compiled.

2. Following convention, we leave 1940–1946 out because the war period is highly anomalous for how US capitalism works otherwise.

3. One of us takes this issue up in John Bellamy Foster and Robert W. McChesney, *The Endless Crisis: How Monopoly-Finance Capital Produces Stagnation and Upheaval from the USA to China* (New York: Monthly Review Press, 2012).

4. Tyler Cowen, *Average Is Over: Powering America Past the Age of the Great Stagnation* (New York: Plume, 2013), p. 37.

5. *Report of the Commission on Inclusive Prosperity*, co-chaired by Lawrence H. Summers and Ed Balls (Washington, DC: Center for American Progress, January 2015), p. 30.

6. See Robert Pollin, *Back to Full Employment* (Boston: MIT Press, 2012), p. 41.

7. Hope Yen, "4 in 5 in USA Face Near-Poverty, No Work," Associated Press, September 17, 2013.

8. Cowen, *Average Is Over*, p. 3.

9. Ibid., p. 51.

10. Claire Cain Miller, "As Robots Grow Smarter, American Workers Struggle to Keep Up," *New York Times*, December 15, 2014.

11. The ratio of employment to the civilian non-institutional population (sixteen years and over) stood at 65 percent in 2000, plummeting to 59 percent by early 2015—a considerably greater drop than that of the labor force participation rate.

12. "61 Straight Months of Private Sector Job Growth," Democratic Policy and Communications Center, April 3, 2015, http://www.dpcc.senate.gov/?p=blog&id=172.

13. Jim Clifton, "The Big Lie: 5.6% Unemployment," Gallup.com, February 3, 2015, http://www.gallup.com/opinion/chairman/181469/big-lie-unemployment.aspx.

14. Guy Standing made the concept well known. See Standing, *A Precariat Charter: From Denizens to Citizens* (New York: Bloomsbury, 2014).

15. Victoria Stilwell, "I'm Too Good for My Job. Someone Tell the Fed!" *Bloomberg Businessweek*, November 3, 2014, pp. 18–21.

16. "Generation Jobless," *Economist*, April 27, 2013.

17. John Schmitt, "Inequality as Policy: The United States since 1979," paper published by the Washington, DC–based Center for Economic and Policy Research, October 2009, p. 7.

18. See Stephanie Luce, *Labor Movements: Global Perspectives* (Malden, MA: Polity, 2014).

19. Ruth Milkman and Ed Ott, editors, *New Labor and New York: Precarious Workers and the Future of the Labor Movement* (Ithaca, NY: Cornell University Press, 2014), p. 3.

20. Amanda Becker, "U.S. union membership steady at 11.3 percent in 2013: Labor Department," *Reuters*, January 24, 2014; "Union Members–2014," US Bureau of Labor Statistics, January 23, 2015. Even as the recovery supposedly picked up the pace in the 2010s, union membership declined, or at best remained steady.

21. Ibid.

22. Schmitt, "Inequality as Policy," p. 5.

23. In addition to income, there has been a striking amount of growth over the past several decades in the concentration of wealth—meaning savings and capital—in the smaller number of hands of very rich people. Wealth is the most important measure of economic power in a capitalist economy, because expanding one's wealth is what the system is all about. By 2013 the Credit Suisse *Global Wealth Databook* determined that the United States had the most unequal distribution of wealth among all advanced economies, and was grouped in a cluster that included India, Indonesia, and South Africa. See Credit Suisse Research Institute, *Global Wealth Databook 2013* (Credit Suisse, October 2013), p. 146.

24. Nicholas Kristof, "The Cost of a Decline in Unions," *New York Times*, February 19, 2015.

25. Robert Reich, "Why Wages Won't Rise," *Huffington Post*, January 13, 2015.

26. This is not an accident; those atop the economy understandably desire a healthy dose of unemployment and economic insecurity to keep wages down and workers in line. It also reduces working-class political power. As utilities magnate Samuel Insull famously put it a century ago: "My experience is that the greatest aid to the efficiency of labor is a long line of men waiting at the gate." From Richard Norton Smith, *The Colonel: The Life and Legend of Robert R. McCormick, 1880–1955* (Evanston, IL: Northwestern University Press, 1997), p. 118.

27. Data cited in Nicholas Kristof, "The Cost of a Decline in Unions," *New York Times*, February 20, 2015.

28. Point made by Lawrence Summers in Wonkblog, "Robots Are Hurting Middle-Class Workers and Education Won't Solve the Problem," *Washington Post*, March 3, 2015.

29. Noam Scheiber, "Growth in the 'Gig Economy' Fuels Work Force Anxieties," *New York Times*, July 13, 2015, p. B8. The quote is Scheiber's assessment of the study.

30. Yen, "4 in 5 in USA Face Near-Poverty."

31. Ibid.

32. Lane Kenworthy, *Social Democratic America* (New York: Oxford University Press, 2014), p. 56.

33. This increase in poverty and inequality has the additional effect of making it far more likely that children born into these circumstances will have a much greater likelihood of poverty themselves. See Robert Putnam, *Our Kids: The American Dream in Crisis* (New York: Simon and Schuster, 2015).

34. As James Galbraith has demonstrated, most of the income growth over the fifteen years running up to the Great Recession of 2008 went to a small number of people in a few sectors—most notably military contracting, technology, and finance—who live in a handful of counties that have experienced booms. Virtually everyone else has been left out in the cold. See James K. Galbraith, *Inequality and Instability: A Study of the World Economy before the Great Crisis* (New York: Oxford University Press, 2012).

35. National Employment Law Project, "The Low-Wage Recovery and Growing Inequality," *NELP Data Brief*, August 2012, p. 2.

36. Felix Salmon, "Wall Street's Dead End," *New York Times*, February 13, 2011.

37. Victor Luckerson, "HP's Massive Layoffs Are Doing Wonders for Its Stock Price," *Time*, May 23, 2014.

38. "Coming to an Office near You," *Economist*, January 18, 2014.

39. Reich, "Why Wages Won't Rise."

40. The Nobel laureate economist Joseph Stiglitz notes that "the reason we have a problem is we're so successful in technology. . . . There's no enemy here." Both quotes from Bernard Condon and Paul Wiseman, "Millions of Middle-Class Jobs Killed by Machines in Great Recession's Wake," *Huffington Post*, January 23, 2013.

41. Michael Spence, "Technology and the Employment Challenge," *Project Syndicate*, January 15, 2013.

42. Brad Tuttle, "12 Iconic Stores and Restaurants that Are Rapidly Disappearing," *Time*, July 30, 2014

43. For the source of this data, see addendum to Chart 17 in the Statistical Appendix.

44. Allison Schrager and Peter Coy, "Measuring the State of America's Human Capital," BusinessWeek.com, December 5, 2014.

45. Gary Girod and Eliza Shapiro, "Generation Screwed," *Newsweek*, July 23, 2012, pp. 40–41.

46. Cited in Diane Ravitch, *Reign of Error: The Hoax of the Privatization Movement and the Danger to America's Public Schools* (New York: Alfred A. Knopf, 2013), p. 88.

47. Thompson, "A World without Work."

48. "Generation Jobless."

49. Girod and Shapiro, "Generation Screwed."

50. Even enthusiastic supporters of the market acknowledge that this is "Generation Jobless," though they generally try to find ways the market can

accommodate the tens of millions who are unemployed and underemployed. See Peter Vogel, *Generation Jobless? Turning the Youth Unemployment Crisis into Opportunity* (New York: Palgrave Macmillan, 2015).

51. For pioneering work, see Ursula Huws, *The Making of a Cybertariat: Virtual Work in a Real World* (New York: Monthly Review Press, 2003); for further developments, see Huws, *Labor in the Digital Economy* (New York: Monthly Review Press, 2014).

52. "There's an App for That," *Economist*, January 3, 2015, p. 18.

53. Guy Standing, "On-Demand Taskers: Expanding the Ranks of the 'Precariat,'" *Working-Class Perspectives*, February 16, 2015.

54. Edelman Berland, *Freelancing in America: A National Survey of the New Workforce*, independent study commissioned by Freelancers Union and Elance-oDesk, 2014.

55. Ilana Kowarski, "Freelance Jobs: Half of All New Jobs in Recovery?" *Christian Science Monitor*, June 13, 2011.

56. Noam Scheiber, "Growth in the 'Gig Economy' Fuels Work Force Anxieties," *New York Times*, July 13, 2015, p. B8.

57. Natasha Singer, "Check App. Accept Job. Repeat," *New York Times*, August 17, 2014, sec. B, p. 1.

58. Kowarski, "Freelance Jobs."

59. Kevin Roose, "Does Silicon Valley Have a Contract-Worker Problem?" *New York*, September 18, 2014.

60. *Report of the Commission on Inclusive Prosperity*, pp. 12, 31.

61. Jessica Barrett, "The Death of Lifelong Jobs; Young People Face Uncertainty as the World of Work Changes," *National Post's Financial Post & FP Investing*, November 1, 2014.

62. Simon Baribeau, "Rise of the 'Flex' Economy," *Christian Science Monitor*, June 8, 2014.

63. "There's an App for That," p. 18.

64. Ursula Huws, "iCapitalism and the Cybertariat," *Monthly Review* 66, no. 8 (January 2015): 50.

65. Cowen, *Average Is Over*, pp. 229–230.

66. James K. Galbraith, *The End of Normal: The Great Crisis and the Future of Growth* (New York: Simon and Schuster, 2014), p. 133. For an excellent history of the relationship of capitalism to technology, see David F. Noble, *America by Design: Science, Technology, and the Rise of Corporate Capitalism* (New York: Oxford University Press, 1977).

67. Nicholas Carr, *The Glass Cage: Automation and Us* (New York: W. W. Norton, 2014), p. 31. As the economist Allen Sinai explained to the *New York Times* in 2010, "American business is about maximizing shareholder value. You basically don't want workers. You hire less, and you try to find capital equipment to replace them." See Peter Goodman, "Despite Signs of Recovery, Chronic Joblessness Rises," *New York Times*, February 20, 2010.

68. Sven Beckert, *Empire of Cotton: A Global History* (New York: Alfred A. Knopf, 2014), p. 68.

69. John Maynard Keynes, "Economic Possibilities for Our Grandchildren," in Keynes, *Essays in Persuasion* (New York: W. W. Norton, 1963), pp. 358–373.

70. As the *Economist* notes, "nowadays, the majority of economists confidently wave such worries away" ("The Onrushing Wave," *Economist*, January 18, 2014). The way technology is developed, specifically labor-saving technology, is so closely connected to profit criteria that it is not always easy to determine where the influence of technology ends and the importance of the profit motive begins. They are intertwined, and this can lead to confusion in analysis. At the same time, this explains how critics of what is happening to jobs due to technology are not necessarily critics of technology *per se*, but *per quo*. Their real target is the economic system. Technology is malleable, especially in its early stages of development; once it gets on a specific path, it can be difficult to change its course.

71. Erik Brynjolfsson and Andrew McAfee, *Race against the Machine* (Lexington, MA: Digital Frontier Press, 2011), p. 20.

72. Joseph Schumpeter, *Capitalism, Socialism and Democracy* (London: Routledge, 1943); Paul A. Baran and Paul M. Sweezy, *Monopoly Capital: An Essay on the American Economic and Social Order* (New York: Monthly Review Press, 1966), ch. 8.

73. David F. Noble, *Forces of Production: A Social History of Industrial Automation* (New York: Oxford University Press, 1984), p. 57. See also Noble, "Command Performance: Military Influences on Technological Development and Their Sociological Consequences," in Noble, *Progress without People: In Defense of Luddism* (Chicago: Charles H. Kerr, 1993), pp. 110–124.

74. Noble, *Forces of Production*, p. 67.

75. Norbert Wiener, *The Human Use of Human Beings: Cybernetics and Society* (Boston: Houghton Mifflin, 1950), pp. 187–189.

76. Kurt Vonnegut, *Player Piano* (New York: Charles Scribner's Sons, 1952). See also David Standish, "Interview: Kurt Vonnegut, Jr.," *Playboy*, July 1973.

77. Cited in Carr, *The Glass Cage*, p. 39.

78. Erich Fromm, *The Sane Society* (New York: Rinehart and Co., 1955), p. 289.

79. R. H. MacMillan, *Automation: Friend or Foe?* (Cambridge: Cambridge University Press, 1956), p. 1.

80. Norbert Wiener, *Cybernetics, or Control and Communication in the Animal and the Machine* (1948; reprint, Cambridge, MA: MIT Press, 1962), p. 38.

81. *Automation and Technological Change* (Washington, DC: US Government Printing Office, 1955).

82. Michel Crozier and Georges Friedmann, "Foreword," *International Social Science Bulletin* 10 (1958): 7.

83. Carr, *The Glass Cage*, pp. 159, 37–38.

84. Wiener told Reuther that he had turned down at least one offer from an industrial corporation to advise it on how best to use automation, and he offered

to meet with Reuther to discuss the matter. Norbert Wiener to Walter Reuther, August 13, 1949, in Noble, *Progress without People*, pp. 161–163.

85. "Report of the Director-General, Part I," in *Automation and Other Techno-logical Developments: Labour and Social Implications* (Geneva: International Labour Office, 1957), p. 3.

86. Cited in Frederick Pollock, *Automation: A Study of Its Economic and Social Consequences*, trans. W. O. Henderson and W. H. Chaloner (New York: Frederick A. Praeger, 1957), p. 242.

87. Cited in Noble, *Forces of Production*, p. 253.

88. [Paul M. Sweezy,] *The Scientific-Industrial Revolution* (New York: Model, Roland, and Stone, 1957).

89. To support himself on top of his professional salary and to obtain funds for research, economist Paul Baran occasionally wrote reports for the Wall Street firm of Model, Roland and Stone. He was commissioned to do a report on technology but was pressed for time, so he asked his frequent coauthor Sweezy to do it for him. The resulting report was issued by the firm with no author in-dicated, but Sweezy considered it one of his best pieces of writing. The original copy is in the Sweezy archives at Harvard University. Harry Braverman made use of Sweezy's argument on the scientific-industrial revolution in this pamphlet to construct much of his own argument on the scientific-technological revolution. See Braverman, *Labor and Monopoly Capital* (New York: Monthly Review Press, 1999), p. 115.

90. The German Frankfurt School scholar Frederick Pollock made a detailed study of American automation in the mid-1950s, and was more optimistic than Wiener, but he was struck by the damage that automation would do to smaller businesses and competitive markets. He, too, was alarmed by the likelihood that automation could lead to economic calamity. "The present situation has been summarized in the statement: 'Machines can do practically everything in the economy except buy the goods that are produced.' One might add that—in cer-tain phases of technical progress—there is actually a tendency for new machines to deprive people of their power to consume goods." To Pollock, the solution was economic planning that would "integrate automation with a free and democratic society. Success in such planning would mean that the second industrial revolu-tion could help establish a social system based upon reason." Frederick Pollock, *Automation: A Study of Its Economic and Social Consequences*, trans. W. O. Henderson and W. H. Chaloner (New York: Frederick A. Praeger, 1957), pp. 240, 253.

91. The economist Robert A. Brady completed what was arguably the most comprehensive field examination of automation and the "scientific revolution in industry" in 1961. Like Sweezy, he anticipated a much longer time frame than most contemporary commentators, though he had no doubt about the impor-tance of automation. "In the larger industrial sphere, what appears to be shaping up, with the inevitability of glacial action, is the gradual *de facto* application of one or another of the aspects of automatic machine-operations to the industrial

system at large. . . . The machine takes over, step by step, the entire round of factory operations." Brady, *Organization, Automation, and Society: The Scientific Revolution in Industry* (Berkeley and Los Angeles: University of California Press, 1961), pp. 233, 236.

92. George Terborgh, *The Automation Hysteria* (Washington, DC: Machine and Allied Products Institute, 1965).

93. Todd Gitlin, "The Triple Revolution: Some Questions and Answers," *Monthly Review*, December 1964, p. 524.

94. Robert E. Cubbedge, *Who Needs People? Automation and Your Future* (Washington, DC: Robert B. Luce, 1963), p. 12.

95. Tom Hayden, *The Port Huron Statement: The Visionary Call of the 1960s Revolution* (New York: Thunder Mouth Press, 2005), pp. 79–81. The anarchist Murray Bookchin wrote widely on these themes as well in the 1960s. His work concentrated on "post-scarcity" economies and how technology could be put to humane purposes. See Bookchin, *Post-Scarcity Anarchism* (San Francisco: Ramparts Press, 1971).

96. See Frank Levy and Richard J. Murnane, *The New Division of Labor: How Computers Are Creating the Next Job Market* (Princeton, NJ: Princeton University Press, 2004), p. 1. Text of the memo available at https://www.marxists.org/history/etol/newspape/isr/vol25/no03/adhoc.html. See also The Editors, "The Triple Revolution," *Monthly Review*, November 1964, pp. 417–422.

97. Martin Luther King Jr., "Remaining Awake through a Great Revolution," Presentation at National Cathedral, Washington, DC, March 31, 1968. *Congressional Record*, April 9, 1968, http://mlk-kpp01.stanford.edu/index.php/encyclopedia/documentsentry/doc_remaining_awake_through_a_great_revolution/.

98. Herbert Marcuse, *One-Dimensional Man* (Boston: Beacon Press, 1964), p. 28. Marcuse is quoting the French writer Serge Mallet.

99. George and Louis Crowley, "Beyond Automation," *Monthly Review*, November 1964, p. 423.

100. The Editors, "The Triple Revolution," p. 422.

101. Noble, *Forces of Production*, pp. 249–250.

102. Ibid., pp. 250–251.

103. Herbert A. Simon, *The Shape of Automation for Men and Management* (New York: Harper and Row, 1965), pp. xii-xiii.

104. Cited in Noble, *Forces of Production*, p. 259.

105. Quote in Thompson, "A World without Work."

106. National Commission on Technology, Automation, and Economic Progress, *Technology and the American Economy*, vol. 1 (Washington, DC: US Government Printing Office, 1966), pp. xi, xii.

107. Ibid., pp. 110–112.

108. Ibid.

109. As one labor leader said, "we must, of course, accept the inevitability of automation." Noble concludes that "the unions were on the defensive, and union leaders knew that their own efforts were not enough." This transition is covered well in Noble, *Forces of Production*, pp. 257–261. See also Noble, *Progress without People*, pp. 127–129.

110. Martin Wolf, "Same as It Ever Was: Why the Techno-optimists Are Wrong," *Foreign Affairs*, July/August 2015, p. 19.

111. *Report of the Commission on Inclusive Prosperity*, p. 11.

112. Charles P. Alexander, "The New Economy," *Time*, May 30, 1983.

113. Gene Pylinsky, "The Race to the Automated Factory," *Fortune*, February 21, 1983.

114. Another factor in the decline of automation as a public issue, for reasons we discuss in the next two chapters, is that beginning in the 1970s there was a concerted campaign by big business and its allies to remove anything that might threaten the economic status quo from legitimate political debate. In that environment, the environment Americans still experience today, anything that challenged the right of businesses to use automation to maximize profit or simply to lay off workers as they pleased would be outside the boundaries of legitimate debate. The idea that people were entitled to have a good-paying job if they were willing to work went from being in the heart of the mainstream to the lunatic fringe. With the decline of organized labor, the idea that workers should actively participate in developing technology that gave workers more autonomy, creativity, and satisfaction was similarly tossed into history's dumpster. This is discussed in Seymour Melman, *After Capitalism: From Managerialism to Workplace Democracy* (New York: Alfred A. Knopf, 2001), ch. 7. How could American business remain competitive if the inmates were given the keys to the asylum?

115. Jeremy Rifkin, *The End of Work* (New York: Tarcher Putnam, 1995), pp. xv, xiii.

116. http://www.iweblists.com/us/commerce/MarketCapitalization.html. One of us assesses the emergence and nature of Internet monopoly firms in detail in Robert W. McChesney, *Digital Disconnect: How Capitalism Is Turning the Internet against Democracy* (New York: New Press, 2013).

117. To some, including frustrated workers, this obsession with control made no sense. "The specific form that automation is taking," Barbara Garson observed in a 1988 study of white-collar automation, "seems to be based less on a rational desire for profit than on an irrational prejudice against people." Garson, *The Electronic Sweatshop: How Computers Are Transforming the Office of the Future into the Factory of the Past* (New York: Simon and Schuster, 1988), p. 13.

118. "The New Automation," *Christian Science Monitor*, February 24, 1983, http://www.csmonitor.com/1983/0224/022411.html.

119. Wassily Leontief and Faye Duchin, *The Future Impact of Automation on Workers* (New York: Oxford University Press, 1986), p. 25.

120. Jeremy Rifkin, *The Zero Marginal Cost Society* (New York: Palgrave Macmillan, 2014), p. 123.

121. Ibid., p. 125.

122. As Dan Schiller, perhaps the leading analyst of the role of information and communication technologies in the economy, put it in 2014: "During the final decades of the twentieth century and into the twenty-first, a Herculean reorganization of work tore through corporate production in factories and fields, offices and laboratories. It could never have taken place without ever-more versatile and far-ranging computer-communications. . . . Across an ever-widening front of systems and applications, what was sometimes called "information resource sharing" catalyzed qualitative changes in labor processes, as capital redefined skill requirements across innumerable industries and occupations." It was not just computerization but the connection of these technologies through networks that was key: "Networks participated in this triply: by enabling productivity increases, through shared use of resources and automation of tasks; by enhancing administrative oversight of and intervention into labor processes that had escaped this previously; and by forging linkages between hitherto isolated production processes." Dan Schiller, *Digital Depression: Information Technology and Economic Crisis* (Urbana: University of Illinois Press, 2014), pp. 20–21.

123. Galbraith, *The End of Normal*, p. 141.

124. Wonkblog, "Robots Are Hurting Middle-Class Workers."

125. Erik Brynjolfsson and Andrew McAfee, *The Second Machine Age* (New York: W. W. Norton, 2014), p. 42.

126. Shoshana Zuboff, *In the Age of the Smart Machine: The Future of Work and Power* (New York: Basic Books, 1984), p. 215.

127. Viktor Mayer-Schonberger and Kenneth Cukier, *Big Data: A Revolution That Will Transform How We Live, Work, and Think* (New York: Houghton Mifflin Harcourt, 2013), p. 7.

128. "There's an App for That," p. 18.

129. Brynjolfsson and McAfee, *Race against the Machine*, p. 19.

130. The emergence of quantum computers in the coming years could possibly assure the rate of growth does not slow down appreciably. See "A little bit, better," *Economist*, June 20, 2015, p.p. 77–78.

131. Brynjolfsson and McAfee, *The Second Machine Age*, p. 47.

132. Gill A. Pratt, "Is a Cambrian Explosion Coming for Robotics?" *Journal of Economic Perspectives*, 29, no. 3 (Summer 2015): 51–60.

133. As of 2015, scientists believe they have developed an unbeatable algorithm for playing poker, by incorporating game theory, such that it can successfully navigate whatever opponents might do. See Philip Ball, "Game Theorists Crack Poker," *Nature*, January 8, 2015.

134. Martin Ford, *Rise of the Robots: Technology and the Threat of a Jobless Future* (New York: Basic Books, 2015), p. xiv.

135. Miller, "As Robots Grow Smarter, American Workers Struggle to Keep Up."

136. Mayer-Schonberger and Cukier, *Big Data*.

137. Carr, *The Glass Cage* pp. 11, 17.

138. Vincent Mosco, *To the Cloud: Big Data in a Turbulent* World (Boulder, CO: Paradigm Publishers, 2014), pp. 164–166.

139. Carr, *The Glass Cage*, p. 118.

140. Ford, *Rise of the Robots*, pp. 20–21.

141. "There's an App for That," p. 20.

142. Michael Miller, *The Internet of Things: How Smart TVs, Smart Cars, Smart Homes, and Smart Cities Are Changing the World* (Indianapolis: Que [Pearson Educational], 2015), p. 7.

143. Samuel Greengard, *The Internet of Things* (Cambridge: MIT Press, 2015), pp. xiii–xv. For a more decidedly optimistic vision of the Internet of Things, see David Rose, *Enchanted Objects: Design, Human Desire, and the Internet of Things* (New York: Scribner, 2014).

144. Philip N. Howard, *Pax Technica: How the Internet of Things May Set Us Free or Lock Us Up* (New Haven: Yale University Press, 2015), p. xii.

145. Carr, *The Glass Cage*, p. 195.

146. Alex Webb, "Can Germany Beat the U.S. to the Industrial Internet?" *Bloomberg Businessweek*, September 18, 2015. http://www.bloomberg.com/news /articles/2015-09-18/can-the-mittelstand-fend-off-u-s-software-giants- .

147. Rifkin, *The Zero Marginal Cost Society*, p. 73.

148. W. Brian Arthur, "The Second Economy," *McKinsey Quarterly*, October 2011. We learned of this piece from Carr, *The Glass Cage*, pp. 196–197.

149. Ford, *Rise of the Robots*, p. 6.

150. Ben Way, *Jobocalypse: The End of Humans Jobs and How Robots Will Replace Them* (Charleston, SC: Ben Way, 2013), p. 23.

151. Rifkin, *The Zero Marginal Cost Society*, p. 89.

152. Cited in Diane Ackerman, *The Human Age: The World Shaped by Us* (New York: W. W. Norton, 2014), p. 235.

153. Brynjolfsson and McAfee, *The Second Machine Age*, pp. 37, 90.

154. "The Onrushing Wave."

155. "Coming to an Office near You."

156. Federico Pistono, *Robots Will Steal Your Job, but That's OK: How to Survive the Economic Collapse and Be Happy* (Lexington, KY: Createspace, 2012), p. xvii.

157. "The Onrushing Wave."

158. Zoe Corbyn, "Robots Are Leaving the Factory Floor and Heading for Your Desk—and Your Job," *Guardian*, February 9, 2015.

159. "There's an App for That," pp. 18, 20.

160. Carr, *The Glass Cage*, pp. 110–112.

161. James R. Bright, *Automation and Management* (Cambridge, MA: Division of Research, Graduate School of Business Administration, Harvard University, 1958), pp. 176–195.

162. James R. Bright, "The Relationship of Increasing Automation and Skill Requirements," in National Commission on Technology, Automation, and Economic Progress, *The Employment Impact of Technological Change*, vol. 2: *Technology and the American Economy* (Washington, DC, 1966), p. II-220.

163. Harry Braverman, who made a comprehensive review of all the literature on technology and labor practices for his classic 1974 work *Labor and Monopoly Capital*, correctly termed Bright's pioneering and comprehensive 1950s studies of automation and employment "unique" and especially "important." Braverman, *Labor and Monopoly Capital*, p. 146.

164. Cowen, *Average Is Over*, p. 49.

165. Thompson, "A World without Work."

166. Carr makes the important point that the way jobs are being de-skilled or eliminated by technology is not necessarily a requirement of technology *per se*; it is a requirement of profit-maximizing firms that wish to have total and centralized control over the firm's activities. He points to the extraordinary growth of the video games/computer software games sector, where the technology is built to cultivate the user's interest and challenge her skills. If video games were developed with the same de-skilling logic that is applied to jobs, the industry would be hard-pressed to sell a single unit. It could not exist. Instead, it is user-friendly and wildly popular. One industry report estimates that the industry will have global sales by 2018 approaching $100 billion. Carr, *The Glass Cage*; James Brightman, "Games Software Market to Hit $100 Billion by 2018—FDC," gamesindustry.biz, June 25, 2014, http://www.gamesindustry.biz/articles/2014–06–25-game-software-market-to-hit-usd100-billion-by-2018-dfc. The obvious question is, What prevents a more human-centered logic from being applied elsewhere?

167. "There's an App for That," pp. 18, 20. Early in 2015 the *Guardian* reported that "Uber has launched a research centre focusing on self-driving cars and mapping technology. Is this the end of the cabbie and death of the automobile industry?" Alex Hern, "Are Driverless Cars the Future of Uber?" *Guardian*, February 2, 2015.

168. Corbyn, "Robots Are Leaving the Factory Floor."

169. Robert Reich, "The iEverything and the Redistributional Imperative," Robert Reich blog, March 16, 2015, http://robertreich.org/post/113801138315.

170. "The Onrushing Wave."

171. "As Robots Grow Smarter, American Workers Struggle to Keep Up."

172. Condon and Wiseman, "Millions of Middle-Class Jobs Killed by Machines."

173. Thompson, "A World without Work."

174. Ford, *Rise of the Robots*, pp. 15, 17, 23.

175. Daniela Rus, "The Robots Are Coming: How Technological Break-throughs Will Transform Everyday Life," *Foreign Affairs*, July/August 2015, p. 3.

176. Thompson, "A World without Work."

177. Reich, "The iEverything and the Redistributional Imperative."

178. Carlos Feliciano, "Robot Replacing Nurses: Is It Really That Far-Fetched?" Nurses Together, February 14, 2014.

179. Quotation from Bob Herbert, *Losing Our Way: An Intimate Portrait of a Troubled America* (New York: Doubleday, 2014), p. 207.

180. Peter H. Diamondis and Steven Kotler, *Abundance: The Future Is Better Than You Think* (New York: Free Press, 2012), p. 300.

181. Ford, *Rise of the Robots*, pp. 15, 17, 23.

182. "The Onrushing Wave."

183. James R. Hagerty, "Meet the New Generation of Robots for Manufacturing," *Wall Street Journal*, June 2, 2015. See also "Made to measure," *Economist*, May 30, 2015, pp. 3–4.

184. "The Onrushing Wave."

185. For the former, see John Maynard Keynes, *The General Theory of Employment, Interest, and Money* (1936; reprint, New York: Harbinger, 1964); for the latter see Thomas Piketty, *Capital in the Twenty-First Century*, trans. Arthur Goldhammer (Cambridge, MA: The Belknap Press of Harvard University Press, 2014).

186. Rifkin, *The Zero Marginal Cost Society*, p. 124.

187. Loukas Karabarbounis and Brent Nieman, "The Global Decline of Labor Share," *Quarterly Journal of Economics*, Volume 129, Issue 1 (2014), pp. 61–103.

188. Ford, *Rise of the Robots*, p. 3.

189. Hagerty, "Meet the New Generation of Robots for Manufacturing."

190. Pistono, *Robots Will Steal Your Job*, p. 39.

191. Michael Kan, "Foxconn Expects Robots to Take Over More Factory Work," *PC World*, pcworld.com, February 27, 2015.

192. Consider Sunbird Engineering, a firm owned by Bill Pike that makes mirror frames for heavy trucks at a factory in southern China. Salaries at the plant have risen to a whopping $225 per month, which Sunbird no longer considers competitive. It has already eliminated 15 percent of its workforce through automation, and intends to eliminate much of the rest in the near future. "By automating, we can outlive the labor cost increases inevitable in China," Pike says. "Those who automate in China will win the battle of increased costs." See Condon and Wiseman, "Millions of Middle-Class Jobs Killed by Machines."

193. Keith Bradsher, "Cheaper Robots, Fewer Workers," *New York Times*, April 24, 2015.

194. For a detailed assessment of the massive increase in the global labor pool in the past three decades, especially from China, see Foster and McChesney, *The Endless Crisis.*

195. Thanks to John Bellamy Foster for this specific point. See also Robert Sidelsky, "Labor's Paradise Lost," *Project Syndicate,* June 21, 2012.

196. Rifkin, *The Zero Marginal Cost Society,* p. 125.

197. Galbraith, *The End of Normal,* p. 142.

198. Ibid., p. 144.

199. Ibid., pp. 138–145.

200. Lars Mensel and Max Tholl, "Jeremy Rifkin: In New Economy, 'Social Skills Count More Than Work Skills,'" *The European,* March 2, 2015.

201. Thompson, "A World without Work."

202. Noam Scheiber, "Growth in the 'Gig Economy' Fuels Work Force Anxieties," *New York Times,* July 13, 2015, p. B8.

203. Joe Talton, "Are Robots Better Than Humans? Not If Jobs Are Lost," *Seattle Times,* March 14, 2015.

204. See, for example, Jodi Kantor and David Streitfeld, "Inside Amazon: Wrestling Ideas in a Bruising Workplace," *New York Times,* August 15, 2015, http://www.nytimes.com/2015/08/16/technology/inside-amazon-wrestlingbig -ideas-in-a-bruising-workplace.html?_r=.

205. Sidelsky, "Labor's Paradise Lost."

206. Max Nisen, "Robot Economy Could Cause up to 75 Percent Unemployment," *Business Insider,* January 28, 2013.

207. Sidelsky, "Labor's Paradise Lost."

208. Aaron Smith and Janna Anderson, "AI, Robotics, and the Future of Jobs," www.pewinternet.org, August 6, 2014.

209. Pistono, *Robots Will Steal Your Job,* p. 69.

210. Miller, "As Robots Grow Smarter, American Workers Struggle to Keep Up." Or as Jason Pontin, editor and publisher of the *MIT Technology Review,* put it: "There's no economic law that says the jobs eliminated by new technologies will inevitably be replaced by new jobs in new markets." See Smith and Anderson, "AI, Robotics, and the Future of Jobs."

211. *Report of the Commission on Inclusive Prosperity,* pp. 28–29.

212. Carl Benedikt Frey and Michael A. Osborne, "The Future of Employment: How Susceptible Are Jobs to Computerization?" Oxford Martin School, University of Oxford, September 17, 2013.

213. For Amara's law, see Joel Mokyr, Chris Vickers, and Nicolas L. Ziebarth, "The History of Technological Anxiety and the Future of Economic Growth: Is This Time Different?" *Journal of Economic Perspectives,* 29, no. 3 (Summer 2015): 48. MIT economist David H. Auter, for example, is skeptical that automation is about to take a qualitative leap and argues that "a significant stratum of middle-skill jobs" will continue for decades, but he cautions even that will not necessar-

ily transpire unless the education system produces workers with the necessary skills, which is by no means assured. See David H. Autor, "Why Are There Still So Many Jobs? The History and Future of Workplace Automation," *Journal of Economic Perspectives*, 29, no. 3 (Summer 2015): 3–30.

214. Wonkblog, "Robots Are Hurting Middle-Class Workers."

215. Cited in Carr, *The Glass Cage*, p. 33.

216. Brynjolfsson and McAfee, *The Second Machine Age*, p. 134.

217. "Coming to an Office near You."

218. "There's an App for That," p. 20.

219. "The Onrushing Wave."

220. Greengard, *The Internet of Things*, pp. 151–152.

221. Grave concerns regarding the fate of humanity in this regard have been registered by the likes of Stephen Hawking, Bill Gates, Elon Musk, and Steve Wozniak. See Peter Holley, "Apple Co-founder on Artificial Intelligence: 'The Future Is Scary and Very Bad for People,'" *Washington Post*, March 24, 2015.

222. Carr, *The Glass Cage*, pp. 18, 113.

223. Nick Bilton, "Ava Is Just Sci-Fi (for Now)," *New York Times*, May 21, 2015, p. D2.

224. Future of Life Institute, "Autonomous Weapons: An Open Letter from AI & Robotics Researchers," July 28, 2015, http://futureoflife.org/AI/open _letter_autonomous_weapons.

225. Ford, *The Lights in the Tunnel*, p. 106.

226. Karl Marx and Friedrich Engels, *Manifesto of the Communist Party*, in Harold J. Laski, *The Communist Manifesto of Marx and Engels* (New York: Seabury Press, 1967), p. 135.

227. David Harvey, *Seventeen Contradictions and the End of Capitalism* (New York: Oxford University Press, 2014), pp. 91–111.

228. All taken from bk. IV, ch. VI of John Stuart Mill, *Principles of Political Economy with Some of Their Applications to Social Philosophy*, 6th ed. (London: Longman, Green, 1865).

229. Thorsten Veblen, *The Engineers and the Price System* (New York: B. W. Huebsch, 1921), pp. 8, 9, 68, 121.

230. Keynes, "Economic Possibilities for Our Grandchildren."

231. Ibid., 373.

232. Thompson, "A World without Work."

233. Baran and Sweezy, *Monopoly Capital*, p. 352.

234. Marcuse, *One-Dimensional Man*, p. 37.

235. Paul A. Baran and Paul M. Sweezy, "Some Theoretical Implications," *Monthly Review*, July-August 2012, pp. 26–27. This essay was not published until 2012; it was originally written for inclusion in their book *Monopoly Capital* but was not signed off on by both authors before Baran's untimely death in 1964.

236. Erik Brynjolfsson and Andrew McAfee, "Will Humans Go the Way of Horses? Labor in the Second Machine Age," *Foreign Affairs*, July/August 2015, p. 14.

CHAPTER THREE: CITIZENLESS DEMOCRACY

1. The notion that the people must be in charge is our healthiest obsession as Americans, so much so that 234 years after the Declaration of Independence was written, scholars at the Library of Congress breathlessly announced that, using the newest technologies available for assessing ancient documents, they had discovered that Thomas Jefferson had meticulously smudged his draft of the document to expunge an initial reference to the colonists as *subjects*. He replaced the offending word with *citizens*. "Seldom can we re-create a moment in history in such a dramatic and living way," Library of Congress preservation director Dianne van der Reyden announced in July, 2010. "It's almost like we can see him write 'subjects' and then quickly decide that's not what he wanted to say at all, that he didn't even want a record of it. Really, it sends chills down the spine." See Marc Kaufman, "Jefferson changed 'subjects' to 'citizens' in Declaration of Independence," *Washington Post*, July 3, 2010.

2. Michael Moore and Marcy Kaptur, *Capitalism: A Love Story*, a documentary by Michael Moore, released October 2, 2009.

3. Marcy Kaptur, "Bill Moyers Journal," *PBS*, October 9, 2009.

4. Daniel Wagner and Alison Fitzgerald, "Meet the Banking Caucus, Wall Street's secret weapon in Washington: Lawmakers help industry donors beat back tougher rules," *Center for Public Integrity*, October 31, 2014.

5. Ibid.

6. Robert Scheer, "The Great Deregulator," *TruthDig*, September 10, 2012.

7. "Transcript of Bill Clinton's Speech to the Democratic National Convention," *New York Times*, September 7, 2012.

8. Ron Suskind, *Confidence Men: Wall Street, Washington, and the Education of a President* (New York: Harper, 2011).

9. Andrea Orr, "Too complex to regulate?" Economic Policy Institute Publications, June 8, 2009. Found at: http://www.epi.org/publication/too_complex_to_regulate/.

10. Fabian Kindermann and Dirk Krueger, "High Marginal Tax Rates on the Top 1%? Lessons from a Life Cycle Model with Idiosyncratic Income Risk," NBER Working Paper No. 20601, National Bureau of Economic Research, October 2014.

11. Elizabeth Warren, "Issues: Tax Policy" (from "Leveling the Playing Field" paper), Elizabeth Warren for Senate campaign, http://elizabethwarren.com/issues/leveling-the-playing-field.

12. Chris Isidore, "Buffett says he's still paying lower tax rate than his secretary," *CNNMoney*, March 4, 2013.

13. Rick Ungar, "The Numbers Don't Lie—Why Lowering Taxes for the Rich No Longer Works to Grow the Economy," *Forbes*, September 16, 2012.

14. Katie Sanders, "Bernie Sanders says 99 percent of 'new' income is going to top 1 percent," *Tampa Bay Times* PolitiFact, April 19, 2015.

15. Justin Wolfers, "The Gains from the Economic Recovery Are Still Limited to the Top One Percent," *New York Times*, January 27, 2015.

16. The Editors, "Stacking the Deck: The Phony 'Fix the Debt' Campaign," *Nation*, February 20, 2013.

17. Ibid.

18. Paul N. Van de Water, "Ryan Plan Makes Deep Cuts in Social Security," Center on Budget and Policy Priorities, October 21, 2010. See also, "Rep. Paul Ryan: No Friend of Social Security," Fact Sheet from Social Security Works, http://www.strengthensocialsecurity.org/ryan

19. Kim Dixon, "Obama might back territorial tax, business chief," *Reuters*, January 31, 2013.

20. Jim Provance, "In Ohio, Obama rips Romney tax plan," *Pittsburgh Post-Gazette*, August 2, 2012.

21. Dixon, "Obama might back territorial tax."

22. "Under Obama's Proposed 14% Transition Tax," Citizens for Tax Justice report, February 3, 2015.

23. Robert Goulder, "Bernie Sanders: Swimming against the Tide," *Forbes*, April 27, 2015.

24. Stephen Ohlemacher and Emily Swanson, "AP-GfK Poll: Most back Obama plan to raise investment taxes," February 22, 2015.

25. Aaron Blake, "Elizabeth Warren says the system is rigged for the rich," *Washington Post*, January 9, 2015.

26. Bernie Sanders, "Of the Rich, By the Rich, For the Rich," June 25, 2012, http://www.sanders.senate.gov/newsroom/recent-business/of-the-rich-by-the-rich-for-the-rich.

27. "The Great Recession and the jobs crisis," United Nations Department of Economic and Social Affairs (DESA)–Economic and Social Council (ECOSOC), 2011, http://www.un.org/esa/socdev/rwss/docs/2011/chapter2.pdf.

28. Matthew Bandyk, "Is Unemployment the Worst since the Great Depression?" *US News and World Report*, August 27, 2009.

29. Bob Herbert, "A World of Hurt," *New York Times*, September 15, 2009.

30. "Labor Force Statistics from the Current Population Survey: Unemployment Rate," Bureau of Labor Statistics. Data extracted on: April 28, 2015.

31. John Nichols, "As Unemployment Spikes, Obama's Got a Bigger Problem Than the Debt Ceiling," *Nation*, July 8, 2011. Also: Robert Barone, "Why Jack Welch Has a Point about Unemployment Numbers," *Forbes*, October 16, 2012.

32. Chuck Collins and Felice Yeskel, *Economic Apartheid in America: A Primer on Economic Inequality & Insecurity* (New York: New Press: 2005).

33. Philip Bump, "The Unemployment Rate for Blacks Has Always Been at Least 60 Percent Higher Than for Whites," *Atlantic (The Wire)*, March 7, 2014.

34. "Table A-2. Employment status of the civilian population by race, sex, and age," Bureau of Labor Statistics. Data extracted on: April 28, 2015.

35. Ben Casselman, "How Baltimore's Young Black Men Are Boxed In," fivethirtyeight.com, March 28. 2015.

36. Annie Lowrey, "Do Millennials Stand a Chance in the Real World?" *New York Times*, March 26, 2013.

37. "Labor Force Statistics from the Current Population Survey: Unemployment Rate," Bureau of Labor Statistics. Data extracted on: April 28, 2015.

38. "Mondale's Acceptance Speech, 1984," www.cnn.com, http://www.cnn.com /ALLPOLITICS/1996/conventions/chicago/facts/famous.speeches/mondale .84.shtml.

39. Ibid.

40. Bill Curry, "Neoliberals are killing us: The TED talk, techno-utopian, Thomas Friedman-economy is a lie," *Salon*, April 29, 2015.

41. John Conyers Jr., "H.R. 1000, the "Humphrey-Hawkins Full Employment and Training Act," http://www.johnconyers.com/hr-1000-humphrey-hawkins-full -employment-and-training-act#.VT_nJyFViko

42. William Darity Jr., "Federal Law Requires Job Creation," *New York Times*, December 4, 2013.

43. Conyers, "H.R. 1000"

44. Ibid.

45. Ronald Reagan, "Radio Address to the Nation on the Economic Recovery Program," February 5, 1983.

46. K. O. Jackson, "UAW members rally against plant closure," *Kokomo Tribune*, July 25, 2009.

47. Michael Barone, "Marcy Kaptur," *The Almanac of American Politics* (Chicago: University of Chicago Press, 2014), http://www.nationaljournal.com /almanac/member/254?print=true.

48. Anne O. Krueger, "Willful Ignorance: The Struggle to Convince the Free Trade Skeptics," address to the Graduate Institute of International Studies, Geneva, May 18, 2004. Krueger was then acting managing director of the International Monetary Fund.

49. Paul Gigot, "Opinion Journal: Will Obama Step Up for Free Trade?" March 9, 2015, and Eduardo Porter, "Globalization that Works for Workers at Home," *New York Times*, February 24, 2015.

50. Richard A. McCormack, "President Obama, Wall Street Financiers, Corporate CEOs and Members of Congress Meet Together to Plan Strategy to Sell and Pass Free-Trade Agreements," *Manufacturing and Technology News*, December 17, 2014. For a full text of the president's speech, see "Remarks by the President at Meeting of the Export Council," December 11, 2014.

51. Noam Chomsky, "Manufacturing Consent: Noam Chomsky and the Media," documentary film by Mark Achbar and Peter Wintonick, 1992.

52. "Trade," *AFL-CIO*, January 1, 2015, http://www.aflcio.org/Issues/Trade.

53. Congresswoman Betty Sutton reviewed the figures, did some quick calculations, and went to the floor of the House to deliver a stark message to the Congress and the American people on the eve of the 2012 election campaign, "Many big companies have not created jobs in the U.S. Instead, they've taken many of their jobs to countries with the cheapest labor, the least regulations and few employee rights," Sutton explained. "On that point, every day in the United States, we are losing 15 factories." *Congressional Record–House*, October 25, 2011, HR7063.

54. "Job-Killing Trade Deficits Surge under FTAs: U.S. Trade Deficits Grow More than 425% with FTA Countries, but Decline 11% with Non-FTA Countries," Public Citizen report, February, 2015.

55. Sherrod Brown, "Not Another NAFTA," newsletter, April 6, 2015.

56. Zach Carter, "Elizabeth Warren: Obama Trade Deal Could Undermine Wall Street Reform," *Huffington Post*, December 18, 2014.

57. Daniel J. Ikenson, "Hyperbole Aside, Elizabeth Warren Is Right About the Risk of Investor-State," Cato At Liberty (Cato Institute), February 26, 2015.

58. Michael McAuliff, "Mitch McConnell Pledges Fast Action for Secretive Trade Deals," *Washington Post*, January 7, 2015.

59. Hart Research Associates and Chesapeake Beach Consulting, "Voters' View of Fast-Track Authority for the Trans-Pacific-Partnership Pact," January 27, 2014.

60. "Sen. Mitch McConnell" profile, "Top 20 Industries contributing to Campaign Committee," Center for Responsive Politics, http://www.opensecrets.org/politicians/industries.php?type=I&cid=n00003389&newMem=N&recs=20&cycle=2014.

61. John Nichols, "Obama Talks Tough on Trade," *Nation*, February 13, 2008.

62. Michael Luo, "Memo Gives Canada's Account of Obama Campaign's Meeting on Nafta," *New York Times*, March 4, 2008.

63. Ian Austen, "Trade Pact Controversy in Democratic Race Reaches into Canadian Parliament," *New York Times*, March 7, 2008.

64. Luo, "Memo Gives Canada's Account of Obama Campaign's Meeting on Nafta."

65. Nina Easton, "Obama: NAFTA Not So Bad After All," *Fortune*, June 18, 2008.

66. Ibid.

67. John Nichols, "Obama Goes Soft on Trade," *Nation*, June 19, 2008.

68. Roger Runningen, "Obama Signs Trade Deals with South Korea, Panama, Colombia," *Bloomberg Business*, October 21, 2011.

69. Peter Schroeder, "Warren to Obama: Stop making 'untrue' trade claims," *The Hill*, April 25, 2015.

70. Sarah Green, "How Campaign Finance Reform Could Help Business," *Harvard Business Review*, April, 2012, https://hbr.org/2012/09/how-campaign-finance-reform-co/.

71. We provide long and detailed critiques of contemporary journalism in our last three books: John Nichols and Robert W. McChesney, *Dollarocracy: How the Money and Media Election Complex Is Destroying America* (New York: Nation Books, 2013); Robert W. McChesney and John Nichols, *The Death and Life of American Journalism: The Media Revolution that Will Begin the World Again* (New York: Nation Books, 2010); and John Nichols and Robert W. McChesney, *Tragedy and Farce: How the American Media Sell Wars, Spin Elections, and Destroy Democracy* (New York: The New Press, 2005).

72. John Nichols and Robert W. McChesney, "Dollarocracy: Special Interests Dominate Washington and Undermine Our Democracy," *Nation*, September 11, 2013.

73. Matt Isaacs, Lowell Bergman, and Stephen Engelberg, "His Man in Macau: Inside the Investigation into Sheldon Adelson's Empire," Investigative Reporting Program of the University of California and FRONTLINE, July 16, 2012; Hannah Groch-Begley, "Bribery, Money-Laundering, and Islamophobia: The Sheldon Adelson Story the Media Forgot," Media Matters for America, March 31, 2014.

74. Luisa Kroll, "Billionaire Sheldon Adelson Was Year's Biggest Winner, with Fortune Jumping $15 Billion," *Forbes*, December 23, 2013.

75. Igor Bobic, "Koch Brothers Plan $300 Million Spending Spree in 2014," *Huffington Post*, June 14, 2014.

76. "Sheldon Adelson No. 8 in Forbes' Billionaire Rankings; Bill Gates No. 1," Associated Press, March 3, 2014.

77. Nichols and McChesney, *Dollarocracy*, pp. 35–66.

78. Nicholas Confessore, "Koch Brothers' Budget of $889 Million for 2016 Is on Par with Both Parties' Spending," *New York Times*, January 26, 2015; "Democrats Daunted by Conservative Group's $900 Million for 2016 Campaign," *Reuters*, January 28, 2015.

79. Elizabeth B. Wydra, "Roberts Court: Easier to Donate, Harder to Vote," *Reuters*, April 4, 2014. We have long argued that mass movements to address this reality are essential to restoring and renewing the battered democratic infrastructure of the United States—in fact, we wrote a bluntly titled 2013 book on the subject: *Dollarocracy: How the Money and Media Election Complex Is Destroying America*. But it is important to recognize that undoing the *Citizens United, McCutcheon,* and *Shelby* decisions would only get the United States back to 2010, which was not exactly the high water mark for American democracy.

80. Jillian Berman, "Walmart PAC, Walton Family Political Contributions Favor Conservatives: Report," *Huffington Post*, June 18, 2013.

81. John Nichols, "Voters Say 'Yes' to the Republican Who Said 'No' to Wall Street," *Nation*, May 6, 2014.

82. William Greider, "How the Democratic Party Lost Its Soul: The trouble started when the party abandoned its working-class base," *Nation*, November 11, 2014.

83. Samuel P. Jacobs, "Democrats may join Republicans' push for early convention in 2016," *Reuters*, March 20, 2013.

84. John Nichols, "Martin O'Malley Declares that the Democratic Debate Schedule Is 'Rigged,'" *Nation*, August 30, 2015.

85. Center for Responsive Politics, "Election to Cost Nearly $4 Billion, CRP Projects, Topping Previous Midterms," October 22, 2014, http://www .opensecrets.org/news/2014/10/election-to-cost-nearly-4-billion-crp-projects -topping-previous-midterms/. Spending on state, local, and judicial elections, as well as referendum votes, will likely push the final figure well over $5 billion. With a full accounting of dark-money spending and related projects, it could perhaps go as high as $6 billion.

86. A *Huffington Post* headline on an article by the Reverend Al Sharpton published as the campaign was getting going declared: "The 2014 Midterms Just Might Be More Important than the 2016 Presidential Election." *Huffington Post*, July 28, 2014.

87. John McCormick, "Biden: This Election More Important than 2008 or 2012," *BloombergPolitics*, October 27, 2014.

88. The Editorial Board, "The Worst Voter Turnout in 72 Years," *New York Times*, November 11, 2014.

89. Lindsey Cook, "Midterm Turnout Down in 2014: New data for the midterm elections show turnout dropped in most states," *U.S. News and World Report*, November 5, 2014.

90. Bernie Sanders, "Make Election Day a National Holiday," November 7, 2015, http://www.sanders.senate.gov/democracyday

91. United States Elections Project, "2014 November General Election Turnout Rates," December 30, 2014: http://www.electproject.org/2014g.

92. Ibid.

93. Lindsey Cook, "Midterm Turnout Down in 2014: New data for the midterm elections show turnout dropped in most states."

94. The Center for Media and Democracy, "Interesting ALEC Quotes." A transcription of the quote and a video of Weyrich's 1980 speech can be found at http://www.sourcewatch.org/index.php?title=Interesting_ALEC_Quotes.

95. See the discussion in the Statistical Appendix for sources and notes.

96. International Institute for Democracy and Electoral Assistance (International IDEA), "Voter Turnout," http://www.idea.int/vt/.

97. Howard Steven Friedman, "American Voter Turnout Lower than Other Wealthy Countries," *Huffington Post*, July 10, 2012.

98. International Institute for Democracy and Electoral Assistance (International IDEA), "Voter turnout data for Germany," http://www.idea.int/vt /countryview.cfm?CountryCode=DE.

99. International Institute for Democracy and Electoral Assistance (International IDEA), "Voter Turnout," http://www.idea.int/vt/.

100. Rafael López Pintor and Maria Gratschew, "Voter Turnout since 1945: A Global Report" and "Voter Turnout in Western Europe since 1945: A Regional Report," International Institute for Democracy and Electoral Assistance (International IDEA), http://www.idea.int/publications/voter_turnout_weurope /index.cfm.

101. United States Elections Project, "Voter Turnout," http://www.elect project.org/home/voter-turnout.

CHAPTER FOUR: DEMOCRATIC INFRASTRUCTURE

1. Robert A. Dahl, *How Democratic Is the American Constitution?* (New Haven: Yale University Press, 2002), p. 139.

2. For a good discussion of this, see Cass Sunstein, *Designing Democracy: What Constitutions Do* (New York: Oxford University Press, 2001).

3. Staughton Lynd, *Doing History from the Bottom Up* (Chicago: Haymarket Books, 2014), p. xii.

4. Ben Railton, "The Paragraph on Slavery that Never Made It into the Declaration of Independence," *Huffington Post*, July 3, 2015, http://talkingpoints memo.com/cafe/slavery-declaration-of-independence-juy-4.

5. Gerald Horne, *The Counter-Revolution of 1776: Slave Resistance and the Origins of the United States of America* (New York: New York University Press, 2014).

6. Sean Wilentz, "Constitutionally, Slavery Is No National Institution," *New York Times*, September 16, 2015. See also, Lawrence Goldstone, "Slavery Is Indeed a National Institution," NewRepublic.com, September 17, 2015, http://www.newrepublic.com/article/122843/constitutionally-slavery-indeed -national-institution.

7. Thomas Paine, "African Slavery in America," *Pennsylvania Journal and the Weekly Advertiser*, March 8, 1775, http://www.constitution.org/tp/afri.htm. For two recent enlightening books on this subject, see Horne, *The Counter-Revolution of 1776*, and Roxanne Dunbar-Ortiz, *An Indigenous Peoples' History of the United States* (Boston: Beacon Press, 2014).

8. Woodrow Wilson, *Division and Reunion, 1829–1889* (New York: Longmans, Green, and Company, 1893), pp. 12–13.

9. Bruce Hartford, "The Historical Context of Voting Rights," *Civil Rights Movement Veterans Network*, crmvnet.org, March 21, 2015.

10. The Twenty-Fourth Amendment to the US Constitution, which abolished the poll tax, was approved by Congress August 27, 1962. It was formally ratified January 23, 1964.

11. Alexander Keyssar, *The Right to Vote: The Contested History of Democracy in the United States* (New York, Basic Books), p. 11.

12. Cited in John Nichols, *The "S" Word: A Short History of an American Tradition . . . Socialism* (New York: Verso, 2011), p. 49.

13. Gore Vidal, "Homage to Daniel Shays," *New York Review of Books*, August 10, 1972.

14. William Hogeland, *Founding Finance: How Debt, Speculation, Foreclosures, Protests, and Crackdowns Made Us a Nation* (Austin: University of Texas Press, 2012), p. 57.

15. Ibid., pp. 43, 70–71.

16. Ibid., pp. 1, 229, 2.

17. Walter Dean Burnham, "The Constitution, Capitalism, and the Need for Rationalized Regulation," in Robert A. Goldwin and William A. Schambra, editors, *How Capitalistic Is the Constitution?* (Washington, DC: American Enterprise Institute, 1982), p. 77.

18. Sven Beckert terms this preindustrial capitalist era as *war capitalism*. Far from some idyllic and benign world of small farmers and happy townsfolk, it was "based not on free labor but on slavery." It was "based as often as not on violence and bodily coercion." Far from a "laissez faire" state, war capitalism was based on "massive expropriations" by the state. See Sven Beckert, *Empire of Cotton: A Global History* (New York: Alfred A. Knopf, 2014), p. xvi.

19. There is some debate about the exact first time the word *capitalism* is used and some have placed it in the middle of the nineteenth century. But Williams has got it right from what we can see, and we rely upon his explanation. See Raymond Williams, *Keywords: A Vocabulary of Culture and Society* (New York: Oxford University Press, 1976), p. 51.

20. Benjamin Franklin to Robert Morris, December 25, 1783. In *The Founders' Constitution*, Volume 1 (Chicago: University of Chicago Press, 1987), Ch. 16, Document 12, http://press-pubs.uchicago.edu/founders/documents/v1ch16s12 .html.

21. Quoted in Beckert, *Empire of Cotton*, p. 81.

22. David H. Gans and Douglas T. Kendall, "A Capitalist Joker: The Strange Origins, Disturbing Past, and Uncertain Future of Corporate Personhood in American Law," *John Marshall Law Review*, 44 (2011): 643–699.

23. By 1825, for example, Jefferson was alarmed by the Federalists then in power, "who having nothing in them of the feelings or principles of '76 now look to a single and splendid government of an Aristocracy, founded on banking institutions and monied in corporations under the guise and cloak of their favored branches of manufactures commerce and navigation, riding and ruling over the plundered ploughman and beggared yeomanry." From Thomas Jefferson

to William Branch Giles, December 26, 1825, Founders Online, National Archives, http://founders.archives.gov/documents/Jefferson/98–01–02–5771.

24. Thomas Jefferson to George Logan, November 12, 1816, Papers of Thomas Jefferson *Retirement Series*, Vol. 10, p. 522, http://tjrs.monticello.org /letter/1392; http://hdl.loc.gov/loc.mss/mtj.mtjbib022651.

25. Cass Sunstein, *The Second Bill of Rights: FDR's Unfinished Revolution and Why We Need It More than Ever* (New York: Basic Books, 2004), p. 115.

26. Emily Zackin, *Looking for Rights in All the Wrong Places: Why State Constitutions Contain America's Positive Rights* (Princeton, NJ: Princeton University Press, 2013), p. 12.

27. Even Alexander Hamilton, the "pro-capitalist" framer who advocated a strong manufacturing sector, was hardly a proponent of laissez faire; he thought the federal government had to take an active hand in establishing a manufacturing sector, and had no qualms with its doing so. See Robert Heilbroner and Aaron Singer, *The Economic Transformation of America*, 4th Edition (Boston: Wadsworth, 1999), pp. 85–87.

28. Matthew J. Hegreness, "An Organic Law Theory of the Fourteenth Amendment: The Northwest Ordinance as the Source of Rights, Privileges, and Immunities," *Yale Law Journal*, 120, no. 7 (May 2011): 1823, 1841.

29. John Adams to John Jebb, September 10, 1785, http://rotunda.upress .virginia.edu/founders/FOEA-03–01–02–0254. In John Adams, *The Works of John Adams, Second President of the United States: With a Life of the Author, Notes and Illustrations*, Volume 9 (Little, Brown, 1854), p. 540. In his essay on John Adams's defense of constitutions, Neal Pollack wrote: "The idea of equal access to education, to the great intellectual advancements of the Enlightenment, to reasoned inquiry, is at the core of all Adams' writing, and indeed was the intellectual core of this country's founding. Without it, the specter of tyranny begins to cast its shadow." Neal Pollack, "Introduction," in John Adams, *A Defence of the Constitutions of Government of the United States of America* (New York: Akashic Books, 2004), pp. 20–21.

30. Thom Hartmann, *The Crash of 2016* (New York: Twelve, 2014), p. 64.

31. Sunstein, *Second Bill of Rights*, p.116.

32. Cited in Michael J. Thompson, *The Politics of Inequality* (New York: Columbia University Press, 2011), p. 57.

33. Dahl, *How Democratic Is the American Constitution?*, pp. 34–37.

34. Ibid., p. 37.

35. Quoted in Thomas Geoghegan, *Only One Thing Can Save Us: Why America Needs a New Kind of Labor Movement* (New York: New Press, 2014), p. 34.

36. Zephyr Teachout, *Corruption in America: From Benjamin Franklin's Snuff Box to Citizens United* (Cambridge, MA: Harvard University Press, 2014), pp. 14, 20, 5.

37. Publius (Alexander Hamilton), "The Danger of a Standing Army: 'An Intention to Mislead the People," *The Federalist* XXIV, December 19, 1787. In

The Debate on the Constitution, Part One (New York: Library of America, 1993), p. 576.

38. Madison Debates, "In Convention," August 17, 1787, Avalon Project, Yale Law School, http://avalon.law.yale.edu/18th_century/debates_817.asp.

39. Akhil Reed Amar, *The Bill of Rights: Creation and Reconstruction* (New Haven: Yale University Press, 1998), p.59.

40. Cited in Robert Scheer, *They Know Everything about You* (New York: Nation Books, 2015), p. 194.

41. Cited in John Nichols, *The Genius of Impeachment: The Founders' Cure for Royalism* (New York: The New Press, 2006), p. 121.

42. Cited in John Nichols, editor, *Against the Beast: A Documentary History of American Opposition to Empires* (New York: Nation Books, 2005), p. 14.

43. George Washington, "Farewell Address," 1796, http://en.wikisource.org/wiki/Washington%27s_Farewell_Address.

44. Walter Dean Burnham, "The Constitution, Capitalism, and the Need for Rationalized Regulation," in Goldwin and Schambra, *How Capitalistic Is the Constitution?*, p. 81.

45. This episode and tradition are covered in Andrew J. Bacevich, *Breach of Trust: How Americans Failed Their Soldiers and Their Country* (New York: Metropolitan Books, 2013), ch. 9.

46. The Editors, "War Profiteering," *Nation*, May 12, 2003, http://www.thenation.com/article/war-profiteering#.

47. Sunstein, *Second Bill of Rights*, p. 239.

48. For two classic statements, one from the 1960s and the other from 2010, imploring the United States to reject its new imperialism and return to its pre-1940s ways, see Eugene J. McCarthy, *The Limits of Power: America's Role in the World* (New York: Holt, Rinehart, and Winston, 1967), and Chalmers Johnson, *Dismantling the Empire: America's Last Best Hope* (New York: Metropolitan Books, 2010).

49. See Andrew P. Napolitano, *Suicide Pact: The Radical Expansion of Presidential Powers and the Lethal Threat to American Liberty* (Nashville: Nelson Books, 2014). See also William F. Grover and Joseph G. Peschek, *The Unsustainable Presidency: Clinton, Bush, Obama, and Beyond* (New York: Palgrave Macmillan, 2014).

50. *Papers of Thomas Jefferson*, vol. 11: 48–49, http://press-pubs.uchicago.edu/founders/print_documents/amendI_speechs8.html.

51. Nichols and McChesney, *Tragedy and Farce*.

52. It was a radical notion, too radical it would turn out for Washington, who was ill at ease with Paine's challenges to organized religion, consolidated wealth, and authority in general. All of this history is covered in detail in McChesney and Nichols, *The Death and Life of American Journalism*.

53. Covered in detail in McChesney and Nichols, *The Death and Life of American Journalism*.

54. Alexis de Tocqueville, *Democracy in America* (New York: Penguin, 2003), pp. 215, 604.

55. *Whitney v. California*, 274 US 357 (1927), cited in Gene Kimmelman, "Deregulation of Media: Dangerous to Democracy," text of speech given at University of Washington Law School, Seattle, WA, 6 March 2003.

56. The AP argued the First Amendment prevented the government from enforcing antitrust laws against its monopoly. Consider us "absolutists" with regard to Hugo Black's magnificent majority opinion in that case, which ruled against AP:

> It would be strange indeed however if the grave concern for freedom of the press which prompted adoption of the First Amendment should be read as a command that the government was without power to protect that freedom. The First Amendment, far from providing an argument against application of the Sherman Act, here provides powerful reasons to the contrary. *That Amendment rests on the assumption that the widest possible dissemination of information from diverse and antagonistic sources is essential to the welfare of the public, that a free press is a condition of a free society.* Surely a command that the government itself shall not impede the free flow of ideas does not afford non-governmental combinations a refuge if they impose restraints upon that constitutionally guaranteed freedom. Freedom to publish means freedom for all and not for some. Freedom to publish is guaranteed by the Constitution, but freedom to combine to keep others from publishing is not. Freedom of the press from governmental interference under the First Amendment does not sanction repression of that freedom by private interests" (our emphasis). *Associated Press v. United States*, 326 US 1 (1945), http://caselaw.lp.findlaw.com/scripts/getcase.pl?court=US&vol=326&invol=1.

57. Potter Stewart, "Or of the Press," *Yale Law Report*, 21, no. 2 (Winter 1974–1975): 9–11.

58. Cited in Donald R. Simon, "Big Media: Its Effect on the Marketplace of Ideas and How to Slow the Urge to Merge," *John Marshall Journal of Computer and Information Law* 20, no. 2 (Winter 2002): 273.

59. These points are developed in detail in Robert W. McChesney, *Digital Disconnect: How Capitalism Is Turning the Internet against Democracy* (New York: The New Press, 2013). The proposal we favor was inspired by the work of Milton Friedman, such that we sometimes term it the Milton Friedman News Voucher plan. See Robert W. McChesney, *Blowing the Roof Off the Twenty-First Century: Media, Politics, and the Struggle for Post-Capitalist Democracy* (New York: Monthly Review Press, 2014), pp. 230–236.

60. The three Reconstruction amendments are of great importance, as they change the fundamental relationship of the national government to the states and its citizens. They are outside the main concerns of this chapter, however.

See Eric Foner, "The Second American Revolution," in Bertell Ollman and Jonathan Birnbaum, editors, *The United States Constitution* (New York: New York University Press, 1990), ch. 20.

61. Daniel Lazare, *The Frozen Republic: How the Constitution is Paralyzing Democracy* (New York: Harcourt Brace and Company, 1996), p. 9.

62. Paul Zummo, "Thomas Jefferson's America: Democracy, Progress, and the Quest for Perfection," Ph.D. Dissertation, Catholic University, 2009, p. 116.

63. John Kincaid, "State Constitutions in the Federal System," in *State Constitutions in a Federal System*, Annals of the American Academy of Political and Social Science, 496 (March 1988): 14.

64. Alexander Keyssar, *The Right to Vote: The Contested History of Democracy in the United States* (New York, Basic Books), pp. 15–21.

65. John F. Dinan, *The American State Constitutional Tradition* (Lawrence, KS: University Press of Kansas, 2006), p. 1.

66. Zackin, *Looking for Rights in All the Wrong Places.*

67. Ibid., p. 105.

68. For chapter-length discussion of each of these areas, see Zackin, *Looking for Rights in All the Wrong Places.*

69. Katherine Twomey, "The Right to Education in Juvenile Detention under State Constitutions," *Virginia Law Review*, 94, no. 3 (May 2008): 788.

70. Christopher Lasch, *The Revolt of the Elites* (New York: W. W. Norton, 1995), p. 147.

71. Cited in the remarks of Carolyn B. Maloney, *Congressional Record*, August 2, 2001.

72. Diane Ravitch, *Reign of Error: The Hoax of the Privatization Movement and the Danger to America's Public Schools* (New York: Alfred A. Knopf, 2013), p. vii.

73. Ibid., p. 237.

74. In W. F. Doughty, "School Administration Problems in the South," *The American School Board Journal*, 44, no. 2 (February 1912): 19.

75. Because census data at the time does not permit an easy calculation of the over-twenty-one population, we use the overall population for the vote assessment in 1804.

76. See Robert O. Paxton, *The Anatomy of Fascism* (New York: Alfred A. Knopf, 2004), for a discussion of this.

77. Franklin D. Roosevelt, "Message to Congress on Curbing Monopolies," April 29, 1938. From The American Presidency Project, University of California at Santa Barbara, www.presidency.ucsb.edu.

78. For two superb studies, see Harvey J. Kaye, *The Fight for the Four Freedoms: What Made FDR and the Greatest Generation Truly Great* (New York: Simon and Schuster, 2014), and Sunstein, *Second Bill of Rights.*

79. Wendell L. Willkie, *Free Enterprise* (Washington, DC: National Home Library Foundation, 1940), p. 27.

80. Franklin D. Roosevelt, "Annual Message to Congress on the State of the Union," January 6, 1941, http://www.presidency.ucsb.edu/ws/print.php?pid=16092.

81. Kaye, *The Fight for the Four Freedoms*, p. 87.

82. "The more avidly conservatives, reactionaries, and corporate capitalists tried to deny, appropriate, or alter the Four Freedoms," Harvey Kaye writes, "the more passionately did union, consumer, and civil rights activists promote them." This and the other quotes in the paragraph from Kaye, *Fight for the Four Freedoms*, pp. 142, 111, 120, 116–117.

83. Franklin D. Roosevelt, "State of the Union Message to Congress," January 11, 1944, http://www.presidency.ucsb.edu/ws/print.php?pid=16518.

84. "Franklin Roosevelt's Address Announcing the Second New Deal," New York, NY, October 31, 1936, http://docs.fdrlibrary.marist.edu/od2ndst.html.

85. Roosevelt, "State of the Union," January 11, 1944.

86. Willkie, *Free Enterprise*.

87. Kaye, *Fight for the Four Freedoms*, p. 116.

88. Wendell Lewis Willkie, *An American Program* (New York: Simon and Schuster, 1944), p. 11.

89. Ibid., pp. 17–18.

90. Ibid., p. 29.

91. Sunstein, *Second Bill of Rights*, p. 16.

92. David M. Kennedy, *Freedom From Fear: The American People in Depression and War, 1929–1945* (New York: Oxford University Press, 1999), pp. 786–787.

93. Henry A. Wallace, "The Danger of American Fascism," *New York Times*, April 9, 1944.

94. Wright Patman, "Foreword," in Legislative Reference Service of the Library of Congress, *Fascism in Action: A Documented Study and Analysis of Fascism in Europe* (Washington, DC: United States Government Printing Office, 1947), pp. v-vii.

95. Ibid., p. 204.

96. Victor Pickard, *America's Battle for Media Democracy* (New York: Cambridge University Press, 2014).

97. Patman, "Foreword," *Fascism in Action*, p. vii.

98. Pickard, *America's Battle for Media Democracy*, pp. 121, 205.

99. John C. Culver and John Hyde, *American Dreamer: A Life of Henry A. Wallace* (New York: Norton Paperback: 2001).

100. The story is told in Seymour Morris Jr., *Supreme Commander: Mac-Arthur's Triumph in Japan* (New York: Harper Collins, 2014).

101. *The Constitution of Japan* (Tokyo: Ministry of Justice, 1946), pp. 1, 3.

102. We write about the postwar press policies in occupied Japan and Germany at length in McChesney and Nichols, *The Death and Life of American Journalism*, pp. 241–254.

103. According to the *Economist's* 2014 Democracy Index, Germany is the second most democratic of the fifty nations with populations over 25 million,

while Japan ranks fifth, http://en.wikipedia.org/wiki/Democracy_Index. They also ranked first and fifth in the world in 2014, respectively, for press freedom for the fifty nations with over 25 million population, according to the annual report of Freedom House, https://freedomhouse.org/report/freedom-press-2014/press-freedom-rankings#.VQnFbOFpFJB.

104. Sunstein, *Second Bill of Rights*, pp. 2–3.

105. Ibid., p. 102.

106. Judith Blau, "Our 18th Century Bill of Rights Needs Revising," *Truthout*, June 27, 2015, http://www.truth-out.org/opinion/item/31510-our-18th-century-bill-of-rights-needs-revising#.

107. Dahl, *How Democratic Is the American Constitution?*, p. 3.

108. In the past decade the new constitutions of Iraq and Afghanistan, written and approved after the United States invaded and overthrew the previous governments, similarly invoked aspects of the Second Bill of Rights and/or the Universal Declaration of Human Rights.

109. Jefferson Cowie, *Stayin' Alive: The 1970s and the Last Days of the Working Class* (New York: The New Press, 2010), p. 12.

110. Bob Herbert, *Losing Our Way: An Intimate Portrait of a Troubled America* (New York: Doubleday, 2014), p. 4.

111. Lyndon Baines Johnson, "The Great Society," May 22, 1964, http://www.lbjlib.utexas.edu/johnson/lbjforkids/gsociety_read.shtm.

112. Dwight D. Eisenhower to Edgar Newton Eisenhower, November 8, 1954. Widely available online. See http://www.snopes.com/politics/quotes/ikesocial.asp.

113. "Democratic Party Platform of 1972," July 10, 1972. Readily available online. See http://www.presidency.ucsb.edu/ws/?pid=29605.

114. See Paul LeBlanc and Michael D. Yates, *A Freedom Budget for All Americans* (New York: Monthly Review Press, 2013).

115. Richard Nixon, "Annual Message to the Congress on the State of the Union," January 22, 1970, http://www.presidency.ucsb.edu/ws/?pid=2921.

116. The same point holds true for Clinton and Obama. In different times, like the late 1960s or early 1970s, they may have been more progressive presidents.

117. John Bellamy Foster and Robert W. McChesney, "A New New Deal under Obama?" *Monthly Review*, 60, no. 9 (February 2009): 1–11.

118. See, for example, Julian E. Zelizer, "LBJ's Voting Rights Speech Shows the Power of Grassroots Activism," *Atlantic*, March 12, 2015.

119. See Edward P. Morgan, *What Really Happened in the 1960s? How Mass Media Culture Failed American Democracy* (Lawrence, KS: University Press of Kansas, 2010).

120. For a fascinating examination of the intersection of rock music and radical politics in the 1960s, see Peter Doggett, *There's a Riot Going On: Revolutionaries, Rock Stars, and the Rise and Fall of the '60s* (New York: Canongate, 2007).

121. Charles A. Reich, *The Greening of America* (New York: Random House, 1970).

122. Ibid., pp. 1–2.

123. See Thomas Frank, *The Conquest of Cool* (Chicago: University of Chicago Press, 1997).

124. Murray Bookchin, *Post-Scarcity Anarchism* (San Francisco: Ramparts Press, 1971), pp. 50, 53, 54. Bookchin continued his work along these lines until his death in 2006. See Murray Bookchin, *The Next Revolution: Popular Assemblies and the Promise of Direct Democracy* (New York: Verso, 2015).

125. Mark Stencel, "The Reforms," *Washington Post*, June 13, 1997.

126. See *A Public Trust: The Landmark Report of the Carnegie Commission on the Future of Public Broadcasting* (New York: Bantam Books, 1979), ch. 2; *Public Television: A Program for Action: The Report of the Carnegie Commission on Educational Television* (New York: Harper and Row, 1967).

127. Ravitch, *Reign of Error*, pp. 279–280.

128. See Sunstein, *Second Bill of Rights*, pp. 5, 107–108, 153–159.

129. Robert Lekachman, "Capitalism or Democracy," in Goldwin and Schambra, editors, *How Capitalistic Is the Constitution?*, p. 131.

130. See Molly Niesen, "From Gray Panther to National Nanny: The Kidvid Crusade and the Eclipse of the U.S. Federal Trade Commission, 1977–1980," *Communication, Culture & Critique* (2015), pp. 1–18; for the debate over prisons in the early 1970s, see Michelle Alexander, *The New Jim Crow: Mass Incarceration in the Age of Colorblindness* (New York: New Press, 2010).

131. David Vogel, *Fluctuating Fortunes: The Political Power of Business in America* (New York: Basic Books, 1989), p. 59.

132. Ralph Nader, "Introduction," in Morton Mintz and Jerry S. Cohen, *America, Inc.: Who Owns and Operates the United States* (New York: Dell, 1971), p. 18.

133. "Analyzing Youth," *Richmond Times Dispatch*, July 7, 1971.

134. We discuss Powell, his memo, and his subsequent career on the Supreme Court in some detail in Nichols and McChesney, *Dollarocracy*, ch. 3.

135. Lewis F. Powell, Jr. "Attack on American Free Enterprise System," confidential memorandum for the United States Chamber of Commerce, August 23, 1971. Widely available online.

136. "Remarks by Bryce N. Harlow at the Business Government Relations Council Annual Meeting," September 16, 1977. In Bryce N. Harlow Collection, 1960–1978, Box 3, Folder 19, The Carl Albert Center, University of Oklahoma.

137. Timothy Noah, *The Great Divergence: America's Growing Inequality Crisis and What We Can Do about It* (New York: Bloomsbury Press, 2012), pp. 118, 117.

138. "Remarks by Bryce N. Harlow at Conference on Government and Business," January 23, 1975. In Bryce N. Harlow Collection, 1960–1978, Box 2, Folder 162, The Carl Albert Center, University of Oklahoma.

139. "Remarks by Bryce N. Harlow to Labor Policy Association," February 26, 1972. In Bryce N. Harlow Collection, 1960–1978, Box 2, Folder 25, The Carl Albert Center, University of Oklahoma.

140. Jacob S. Hacker and Paul Pierson, *Winner-Take-All Politics* (New York: Simon and Schuster, 2010), p. 120.

141. Ibid.

142. Lawrence Lessig, *Republic Lost: How Money Corrupts Congress—and a Plan to Stop It* (New York: Twelve, 2011), pp. 99, 123.

143. See Lee Fang, "The Shadow Lobbying Complex," *The Investigative Fund*, February 20, 2015.

144. "America's wealthiest counties: Six of top 10 richest counties in D.C. area," wtop.com, April, 2014, http://wtop.com/news/2014/04/americas -wealthiest-counties-six-of-top-10-richest-counties-in-dc-area/.

145. Christian G. Appy, *Working-Class War: American Combat Soldiers and Vietnam* (Chapel Hill, NC: University of North Carolina Press, 1993).

146. One of us (Bob) was teaching a class at the University of Illinois when the subject of fragging in Vietnam came up while discussing *Breach of Trust: How Americans Failed Their Soldiers and Their Country* (New York: Metropolitan Books, 2013) by military scholar Andrew Bacevich. Many of the students understandably found it difficult to believe. Then a student raised his hand and mentioned that his father had gone to West Point, graduating in 1970, and went on to a career in the military. The student said his father had three roommates at West Point, and that two of them had been fragged in Vietnam within a year of their graduation.

147. Robert D. Heinl Jr., "The Collapse of the Armed Forces," *Armed Forces Journal*, June 7, 1971, https://msuweb.montclair.edu/~furrg/Vietnam/heinl .html. We thank Michael D. Yates for alerting us to this report. See Michael D. Yates, "Honor the Vietnamese—Not Those Who Killed Them," *Monthly Review*, 67, no. 1 (May 2015): 1–16.

148. Free the Army, or Fuck the Army in some iterations. See, for example, Barry Levine, "Fuck the Army," *Harvard Crimson*, August 1, 1972, http://www .thecrimson.com/article/1972/8/1/fuck-the-army-pbob-hope-and/.

149. This issue is covered in Bacevich, *Breach of Trust*. See also Derek Seidman, "Paper Soldiers: The *Ally* and the GI Underground Press during the Vietnam War," in James L. Baughman, Jennifer Ratner-Rosenhagen and James P. Danky, editors, *Protest on the Page: Essays on Print and the Culture of Dissent Since 1865* (Madison: University of Wisconsin Press, 2015), pp. 183–202.

150. Quoted in Cowie, *Stayin' Alive*, p. 12.

151. David F. Noble, *Progress without People: In Defense of Luddism* (Chicago: Charles H. Kerr, 1993), p. 20.

152. Ibid., p. 21.

153. Ibid.

154. Ibid., p. 64.

155. Ibid., p. 21.

156. Cowie, *Stayin' Alive*, pp. 2, 7–8.

157. Jack Newfield, "A Populist Manifesto: The Making of a New Majority," *New York* magazine, July 19, 1971, p. 40.

158. Noble, *Progress without People*, pp. 24–25.

159. *Work in America: Report of a Special Task Force to the Secretary of Health, Education, and Welfare* (Cambridge, MA: MIT Press, 1973), pp. xx, xvii, xviii.

160. Harold Meyerson, "The Ghost of Democratic Agenda," *American Prospect*, February 13, 2009; Hacker and Pierson, *Winner-Take-All Politics*, p. 99.

161. Editorial, *Business Week*, October 12, 1974.

162. Michael Crozier, Samuel P. Huntington, and Joji Watanuki, *The Crisis of Democracy* (New York: New York University Press, 1975), pp. 113, 114.

163. F. A. Hayek, "Foreword," in William E. Simon, *A Time for Truth* (New York: Berkley Books, 1978), pp. xvii–xviii.

164. Sheldon S. Wolin, *Democracy Incorporated: Managed Democracy and the Specter of Inverted Totalitarianism* (Princeton: Princeton University Press, 2008), p. 156.

165. Milton Friedman, "Preface," in William E. Simon, *A Time for Truth* (New York: Berkley Books, 1978), p. xiv.

166. Simon, *A Time for Truth*, p. 246.

167. For as chronicle of the defeat for labor and public interest values, see Erik Loomis, *Out of Sight: The Long and Disturbing Story of Corporations Outsourcing Catastrophe* (New York: New Press, 2015).

168. Hacker and Pierson, *Winner-Take-All Politics*, p. 120.

169. http://issuepedia.org/US/Libertarian_Party/platform/1980. Note that the Libertarians in 1980 and thereafter tended to oppose the militarization of American life in no uncertain terms; this aspect of their belief system was never mainstreamed, because, unlike their other proposals, there are no strong corporate interests that benefit by demilitarization and many that would be gravely damaged.

170. Wolin, *Democracy Incorporated*, p. 156.

171. For exceptional research and analysis of this topic, see Kevin M. Kruse, *One Nation under God: How Corporate America Invented Christian America* (New York: Basic Books, 2015).

172. For a superb discussion of the parties, see Hacker and Pierson, *Winner-Take-All Politics*, Part III.

173. See Robert Scheer, *They Know Everything about You* (New York: Nation Books, 2015), ch. 7; Glenn Greenwald, *With Liberty and Justice for Some: How the Law Is Used to Destroy Equality and Protect the Powerful* (New York: Metropolitan Books, 2011), ch. 2.

174. By 2015 research showed to no one's surprise at all that the enacted reforms were entirely worthless. See Elizabeth Goitein and Faiza Patel, *What Went*

Wrong with the FISA Court? (New York: Brennan Center for Justice at New York University School of Law, 2015).

175. See Jacques V. Dinavo, *Privatization in Developing Countries* (Westport, CT: Praeger, 1995), ch. 1.

176. For a discussion of Democratic Mayor Rahm Emanuel's embrace of privatization in Chicago, see Rick Perlstein, "How to Sell Off a City," *In These Times*, January 21, 2015.

177. Tony Judt, *Ill Fares the Land* (New York: Penguin, 2010), p. 107.

178. See Daphne T. Greenwood, "The Decision to Contract Out: Understanding the Full Economic and Social Impacts," paper published by the Colorado Center for Policy Studies, University of Colorado, Colorado Springs, March 2014.

179. See P. W. Singer, *Corporate Warriors: The Rise of the Privatized Military Industry* (Ithaca, NY: Cornell University Press, 2008); Jeremy Scahill, *Blackwater: The Rise of the World's Most Powerful Mercenary Army* (New York: Nation Books, 2007).

180. Richard Wilkinson and Kate Pickett, *The Spirit Level: Why Greater Equality Makes Societies Stronger* (New York: Bloomsbury Books, 2009), pp. 250–251.

181. This point was made most brilliantly in Thomas Frank, *The Wrecking Crew: How Conservatives Rule* (New York: Metropolitan Books, 2008).

182. British Prime Minister Margaret Thatcher championed this turn away from community-mindedness and toward selfishness, once saying that her "free market" economic policies were simply a method; "the object is to change the heart and soul" (Ronald Butt, "Mrs. Thatcher: The First Two Years," *Sunday Times*, May 3, 1981). Mission accomplished, there and here. "As recently as the 1970s, the idea that the point of life was to get rich and that government existed to facilitate this would have been ridiculed: not only by capitalism's traditional critics, but also by many of its staunchest defenders," Judt observed. He noted that a survey of English schoolboys in 1949 found that the more intelligent the boy the more likely he would choose an interesting career at a reasonable wage over a job that would merely pay well. "Today's school children and college students can imagine little else but the search for a lucrative job" (Judt, *Ill Fares the Land*, p. 39). The same appears true on this side of the pond. UCLA's annual "Freshman Survey," which has been conducted for decades, found that whereas in 1974, 44 percent of college freshmen regarded "being very well-off financially" as "very important" or "essential," that figure has steadily risen to where it stood at 82 percent by 2014 (Dan Berrett and Eric Hoover, "College Freshmen Seek Financial Security Amid Emotional Insecurity," *Chronicle of Higher Education*, February 5, 2015).

While ignorance of politics and social life may be rational, it is by no means bliss. There is little evidence that depoliticized and demoralized people—simply looking out for number one—are especially happy or content. "In an age when young people are encouraged to maximize self-interest and self-advancement,"

Judt notes, "the grounds for altruism or even good behavior become obscured" (Judt, *Ill Fares the Land*, p. 130). Studies in the United States show a sharp decline in empathy among young people over the past thirty-five years (Jamil Zaki, "What, Me Care? Young Are Less Empathetic," *Scientific American*, December 23, 2010). Nicholas Carr chronicles the mounting evidence—from the huge increase in the use of anti-depression prescription drugs to the increase in the rate of suicide—that suggests these are deeply troubled times for the American psyche (Nicholas Carr, *The Glass Cage: Automation and Us*, New York: W. W. Norton, 2014, p. 220). This is a complex issue, of course, and cannot be attributed to depoliticization or the changing weltanschauung exclusively, but it clearly plays a role. In 1970, Americans, especially young Americans, were an optimistic people. Far less so today.

183. See Steve Fraser, *The Age of Acquiescence: The Life and Death of American Resistance to Organized Wealth and Power* (New York: Little, Brown and Company, 2015). For a detailed look at the 1970s, see Judith Stein, *Pivotal Decade: How the United States Traded Factories for Finance* (New Haven: Yale University Press, 2010).

184. Our argument complements in some respects that of Robert Putnam and the decline of social capital. See Robert D. Putnam, *Bowling Alone: The Collapse and Revival of American Community* (New York: Simon and Schuster, 2000).

CHAPTER FIVE: OVERCOMING THE DEMOCRATIC DISCONNECT

1. The books discussed here are John Nichols and Robert W. McChesney, *Dollarocracy: How the Money and Media Election Complex Is Destroying America* (New York: Nation Books, 2013), and in Robert W. McChesney and John Nichols, *The Death and Life of American Journalism: The Media Revolution That Will Begin the World Again* (New York: Nation Books, 2010).

2. Allen Ginsberg, "America," *Howl and Other Poems* (San Francisco: City Lights Publishers; Reissue edition, 2001).

3. Thomas Jefferson to Elbridge Gerry, 1797, *The Writings of Thomas Jefferson: Memorial Edition* (Washington: Lipscomb and Bergh, editors, 1903–04), 9:407.

4. *The Jeffersonian Cyclopedia* (New York: Funk and Wagnalls, 1900), p. 684.

5. Susan Dunn, *Jefferson's Second Revolution: The Election of 1800 and the Triumph of Republicanism* (Boston: Houghton Mifflin Harcourt, 2004), p. 274.

6. John Taylor (edited by F. Thornton Miller), *Tyranny Unmasked* (Indianapolis: Liberty Fund, 1992).

7. Scott Horton, "Jefferson on the Reign of Witches," *Harper's Magazine*, July 4, 2007.

8. Ibid.

9. Bruce H. Mann, *Republic of Debtors: Bankruptcy in the Age of American Independence*. (Cambridge, MA: Harvard University Press, 2002), pp. 173–205.

10. Willard Sterne Randall, *Jefferson: A Life* (New York: Henry Holt and Co., 1993), pp. 493–547. See also, Michael Kennedy, "The French Jacobin Club in Charleston, South Carolina, 1792–1795," *South Carolina Historical Magazine* 91, no. 1 (Jan. 1990): 4–22.

11. E. P. Thompson, an independent historian who became one of the most influential writers of his time, developed an approach to studying the formation of political movements that paid close attention to both economic and social trends. His writings placed a great emphasis on cultural shifts and the many factors that go into the formation of a clearly defined and understood working class.

12. E. P. Thompson, *The Making of the English Working Class* (London: Victor Gollancz, 1963), from the Preface.

13. Kirkpatrick Sale, *Rebels against the Future: The Luddites and Their War on the Industrial Revolution; Lessons for the Computer Age* (Cambridge, MA: Perseus Publishing, 1996). Sale's book was highly influential in reintroducing the Luddites, especially to Americans. Author Bill McKibben credits Sale with rescuing the Luddites "from the old caricature of head-in-the-sand machine breakers, and restores them to their rightful place: as prophets of what industrialism would mean for most men, women and communities." McKibben's assessment is featured as a blurb on the paperback edition of Sale's *Rebels against the Future: The Luddites and Their War on the Industrial Revolution: Lessons for the Computer Age.*

14. Arthur Redford, *Labour Migration in England, 1800–1850* (Manchester: Manchester University Press, 1964) p. 103.

15. Paul Carter, "The Battle of Bradford 1837: Riots against the New Poor Law," *The Bradford Antiquary* (Journal of the Bradford Historical and Antiquarian Society), volume 10 (2006), pp. 5–15.

16. "The People's Charter," British Library online resources, http://www.bl.uk/learning/histcitizen/21cc/struggle/chartists1/historicalsources/source4/peoplescharter.html.

17. The Chartist Movement," U.K. Parliament: Living Heritage, http://www.parliament.uk/about/living-heritage/transformingsociety/electionsvoting/chartists/overview/chartistmovement/.

18. Ibid.

19. Dorothy Thompson, *The Chartists: Popular Politics in the Industrial Revolution* (London: Pantheon Books, 1984), p. 60.

20. Thompson, *The Making of the English Working Class*, Preface.

21. James Gleick, *Faster: The Acceleration of Just About Everything* (New York: Vintage, 2000).

22. Platform of the Progressive Party, adopted August 7, 1912, http://www.pbs.org/wgbh/americanexperience/features/primary-resources/tr-progressive/.

23. Ibid.

24. Patricia O'Toole, *When Trumpets Call: Theodore Roosevelt after the White House* (New York: Simon and Schuster, 2006), p. 156. O'Toole brilliantly puts

Roosevelt's "New Nationalism" speech in context. For a transcript of the speech, which the former president delivered August 31, 1910, in Osawatomie, Kansas, see http://www.theodore-roosevelt.com/images/research/speeches/trnationalismspeech.pdfl.

25. Nichols and McChesney, *Dollarocracy*, pp. 256–284. See also: Michael McGerr, *A Fierce Discontent: The Rise and Fall of the Progressive Movement in America* (New York: Oxford University Press, 2005), and Ray Ginger, *The Bending Cross: A Biography of Eugene V. Debs* (Chicago: Haymarket Books, 2006).

26. "The Socialist Party Platform of 1912," adopted in Indianapolis, Indiana, May, 12, 1912, http://sageamericanhistory.net/progressive/docs/SocialistPlat1912.htm.

27. Ibid.

28. Platform of the Progressive Party, http://www.pbs.org/wgbh/american experience/features/primary-resources/tr-progressive/.

29. Ibid.

30. Theodore Roosevelt, "The New Nationalism," http://www.theodore -roosevelt.com/images/research/speeches/trnationalismspeech.pdfl.

31. Ibid. See also, James Chace, *1912: Wilson, Roosevelt, Taft, and Debs—The Election that Changed the Country*. (New York: Simon and Schuster, 2004), and George E. Mowry, *Theodore Roosevelt and the Progressive Movement* (Madison: University of Wisconsin Press, 1946).

32. See Chace, *1912*.

33. Irving Dilliard, editor, *Mr. Justice Brandeis, Great American* (St. Louis: Modern View Press, 1941), p. 42.

34. Nicolas Barreyre, "The Politics of Economic Crises: The Panic of 1873, the End of Reconstruction, and the Realignment of American Politics." *Journal of the Gilded Age and Progressive Era*, 10, no. 4 (2011): 403–423. See also, Eric Foner, *A Short History of Reconstruction 1863–1877* (New York: Harper and Row, 1990), and Charles Kindleberger, *Manias, Panics and Crashes: A History of Financial Crises* (New York: John Wiley and Sons, 2005), p. 137.

35. Darcy G. Richardson, *Others: Third Party Politics from the Nation's Founding to Greenback-Labor Party*, Volume 1 (New York: iUniverse, 2004).

36. Ibid, p. 451.

37. Lawrence Goodwyn, *The Populist Moment: A Short History of the Agrarian Revolt in America* (New York: Oxford University Press, 1978).

38. William Jennings Bryan, "First Speech against Unconditional Repeal," February 9, 1893. See: William Jennings Bryan, *Speeches of William Jennings Bryan* (New York: Funk and Wagnall's, 1909) pp. 78–146.

39. Ibid, pp. 238–250. Bryan referred to the address as "In the Chicago Convention," but today it is widely recalled as the "Cross of Gold" speech.

40. Ibid.

41. "Democratic Party Platform of 1896," adopted July 7, 1896. American Presidency Project, http://www.presidency.ucsb.edu/ws/?pid=29586.

42. David Graham Phillips, "The Treason of the Senate," *Cosmopolitan*, February, 1906.

43. See Kevin Mattson, *Upton Sinclair and the Other American Century* (Hoboken, NJ: John Wiley and Sons, 2006), and Greg Mitchell, *The Campaign of the Century: Upton Sinclair and the EPIC Campaign in California* (New York: Atlantic Monthly Press, 1991).

44. David Graham Phillips (edited with an introduction by George E. Mowry and Judson A. Grenier), *The Treason of the Senate* (Chicago: Quadrangle Books, 1964).

45. Franklin D. Roosevelt, "At Green Bay, Wisconsin," *Public Papers of the Presidents of the United States: F. D. Roosevelt, 1934*, Volume 3. See also: Franklin D. Roosevelt, "Address Delivered at Green Bay, Wisconsin," August 9, 1934, American Presidency Project, http://www.presidency.ucsb.edu/ws/?pid=14738.

46. Ibid.

47. Ibid.

48. Robert Putnam, *Bowling Alone: The Collapse and Revival of American Community* (New York: Touchstone Books by Simon and Schuster, 2001).

49. Theodore Roosevelt, "The Right of the People to Rule," address delivered March 20, 1912, at Carnegie Hall, New York, http://www.americanrhetoric.com/speeches/teddyrooseveltrightpeoplerule.htm.

50. Leslie Shaffer, "Why We Can't Measure Disruptive Technology," *CNBC.com*, March 19, 2015, http://www.cnbc.com/id/102521238. Ashish Dhawan, "A Tale of Two Disruptive Technologies," *FirstPost*, March 23, 2015, http://www.firstpost.com/business/tale-two-disruptive-innovations-2168409.html.

51. John Nichols, "A Socialist Wins in Seattle: Kshama Sawant's City Council victory reflects broad trends: polls show voters are increasingly immune to red-baiting," *Nation*, November 26, 2013.

52. Chris McGreal, "Seattle minimum wage: $15 figure represents 'historic victory' for workers: Move will benefit around 100,000 working people in city and is expected to give momentum to campaigns across the US," *Guardian*, June 3, 2014.

53. Hana Kim, "Seattle's Kshama Sawant arraigned on disorderly conduct charge stemming from wage protest," Q13 FOX News, February 19, 2015.

54. John Nichols, "It Is Time for a Retail Workers' Bill of Rights," *Nation*, December 1, 2014.

55. "Union Membership," United States Department of Labor: Bureau of Labor Statistics, January 23, 2015.

56. Interviews by John Nichols with Rose Ann DeMoro, May, 2014.

57. "Nurses Launch New Campaign to Alert Public to Dangers of Medical Technology and More," National Nurses United Press Release, May 13, 2014, http://www.nationalnursesunited.org/press/entry/nurses-launch-new-campaign-to-alert-public-to-dangers-of-medical-technology/.

58. Interviews with Rose Ann DeMoro, Jean Ross, and Michael Lighty of National Nurses United and the California Nurses Association and the

Minnesota Nurses Association were tremendously instructive and helped us to frame our understanding of the practical impact of robotics and automation in healthcare and other sectors.

59. Gar Alperovitz, "Inequality's Dead End—And the Possibility of a New, Long-Term Direction," *Nonprofit Quarterly*, March 10, 2015.

60. "Overview: Cooperatives," www.community-wealth.org, http://community -wealth.org/strategies/panel/coops/index.html.

61. John Nichols, "Why We Need a Bank at the Post Office: Senator Elizabeth Warren points out that reviving this old institution would provide basic services to millions of underserved Americans," *Nation*, March 3, 2014.

62. Alperovitz, "Inequality's Dead End."

63. Nadia Prupis and Sarah Lazare, "Front-Lines Communities Rising Up: Dispatches from People's Climate March," www.commondreams .org, September 23, 2014, http://www.commondreams.org/news/2014/09/23 /front-lines-communities-rising-dispatches-peoples-climate.

64. "Largest Global Call for Climate Action in History: Nearly 400,000 march in NY, events in over 150 countries," www.peoplesclimate.org, September 21, 2014.

65. "Transcript of the Rev. Dr. William Barber at NN14," www.dailykos .com, http://www.dailykos.com/story/2014/07/24/1316230/-I-m-glad-I-didn-t -miss-it.

66. John Nichols, "America's Most Dynamic (Yet Under-Covered) Movement: Overturning 'Citizens United,'" *Nation*, July 5, 2013.

67. Craig Aaron, "How We Won Net Neutrality," *Huffington Post*, February 26, 2015. http://www.huffingtonpost.com/craig-aaron/how-we-won-net-neutrality _b_6759132.html.

68. Jessica Rosenworcel, "Statement of Commissioner Jessica Rosenworcel," www.fcc.gov, February 26, 2015. See also Rebecca R. Ruiz and Steve Lohrfeb, "F.C.C. Approves Net Neutrality Rules, Classifying Broadband Internet Service as a Utility," *New York Times*, February 26, 2015.

CHAPTER SIX: A DEMOCRATIC AGENDA FOR A DIGITAL AGE

1. Erik Brynjolfsson and Andrew McAfee, *The Second Machine Age* (New York: W. W. Norton, 2014), p. 251.

2. Veronique de Rugy, "Time for a Guaranteed Income? The pros and cons of a welfare idea championed by liberals and libertarians alike," *Reason*, March 2014.

3. There is also considerable activism—especially outside the United States— around using the Internet and social media to provide "a platform for democracy." We think this work has great value as part of a broader movement. For a quarter century now, there have been advocates for "Democracy 2.0" theories that seek, as Argentina's Net Party activists propose, "to weave a bridge between

the click and the vote" (Matthew Carpenter-Arevalo, "How the Net Party aims to create a new UI for democracy in Argentina," *The Next Web [TNW Blog]*, May 11, 2013). We understand the appeal of the arguments made by the Net Party and the various European Pirate Parties, as well as some of the more tech-savvy young campaigners who have remade traditional liberal parties in Europe. They are absolutely right to argue that "democracy has stagnated" and they are absolutely right to imagine that one way to engage and excite citizens is with experiments in direct democracy. We are as intrigued as they are by "a hybrid model of representative and direct democracy in which candidates representing (a political party) are elected to the country's governing bodies but their vote on any given issue is determined by the collective intelligence of the party's members." After all, people had their doubts about shopping on the web and that came together rather nicely for Amazon. Why not shop for policies, candidates, and parties?

There is no question that digital democracy has a future. There was every reason to cheer on Iceland's attempt—as part of a much broader and frequently quite radical period of transformation following the country's wrenching 2008 financial crisis—to cheer on the decision by drafters of a new national constitution "to use social media to open up the process to the rest of the citizenry and gather feedback on 12 successive drafts." As political theorist Hélène Landemore explained, "Anyone interested in the process was able to comment on the text using social media like Facebook and Twitter, or using regular email and mail. In total, the crowdsourcing moment generated about 3,600 comments for a total of 360 suggestions. While the crowd did not ultimately 'write' the constitution, it contributed valuable input. Among them was the Facebook proposal to entrench a constitutional right to the Internet, which resulted in Article 14 of the final proposal." It was unfortunate that, despite broad popular support for the "crowdsourced constitution," as expressed in a 2012 referendum, Iceland's parliament blocked its implementation. We share Landemore's view that "although it didn't result in any actual constitutional change, the Icelandic experiment has definitely challenged the view that a constitutional process must be exclusionary and secretive, creating a precedent for a more democratic design. Let us hope it will inspire more experiments of the kind in the near future" (Hélène Landemore, "We, All of the People: Five lessons from Iceland's failed experiment in creating a crowdsourced constitution," *Salon*, July 31, 2014). We highly recommend Landemore's deeper investigation of the Icelandic experience in her article, "Inclusive Constitution-Making: The Icelandic Experiment," *Journal of Political Philosophy*, February 25, 2014.

4. Erik Brynjolfsson and Andrew McAfee, *The Second Machine Age* (New York: W. W. Norton, 2014), pp. 232–239.

5. Martin Ford, *Rise of the Robots: Technology and the Threat of a Jobless Future* (New York: Basic Books, 2015), pp. 257–279.

6. The Editors, "The Triple Revolution," *Monthly Review*, November 1964, pp. 417–422.

7. Tyler Cowen, *Average Is Over: Powering America Past the Age of the Great Stagnation* (New York: Plume, 2013), p. 233.

8. Diane Ravitch, *Reign of Error: The Hoax of the Privatization Movement and the Danger to America's Public Schools* (New York: Alfred A. Knopf, 2013), p. 174; Brynjolfsson and McAfee, *Second Machine Age*, pp. 196–197.

9. Dwight Eisenhower, "The Farewell Address," Eisenhower Archives, January 17, 1961, http://www.eisenhower.archives.gov/research/online_documents /farewell_address.html.

10. Bill McKibben, "The Commons Offers a New Story for the Future," in Jay Walljasper, *All that We Share: A Field Guide to the Commons* (New York: New Press, 2010).

11. "What Is the New Economy?" New Economy Coalition, http://new economy.net/about/what-is-the-new-economy.

12. John Bonifaz: "Restore Democracy to the People with 28th Amendment," *Capital Times*, December 4, 2011.

13. Thomas Jefferson to Robert Selden Garnett, February 14, 1824. National Archives: Founders Online, http://founders.archives.gov/documents/Jefferson /98–01–02–4052.

14. John Nichols, "America's Most Dynamic (Yet Under-Covered) Movement: Overturning 'Citizens United,'" *Nation*, July 5, 2013. Also, "Democracy for All Amendment Resources," Public Citizen: Democracy is for People, http:// www.democracyisforpeople.org/page.cfm?id=2.

15. "Pocan and Ellison to Introduce Right to Vote Constitutional Amendment," www.pocan.house.gov, January 22, 2015, http://pocan.house.gov/media -center/press-releases/pocan-and-ellison-to-introduce-right-to-vote-constitutional -amendment.

16. Ezra Klein, "If You're from California, You Should Hate the Senate," *Washington Post*, March 11, 2013.

17. William A. Galston, "Four-Year House Terms Would End the Gridlock: Eisenhower and LBJ knew members need more time to learn to govern," *Wall Street Journal*, February 25, 2014.

18. "DC Vote's Mission, Vision and Purpose," DC Vote. Link: http://www .dcvote.org/dc-votes-mission-work

19. Thomas Paine, *The Rights of Man*, 1790, "Part 2.7 Chapter V. Ways and means of improving the condition of Europe, interspersed with miscellaneous observations." From Eric Foner, editor, *Thomas Paine—Collected Writings: Common Sense; The Crisis; Rights of Man; The Age of Reason; Agrarian Justice* (New York: Library of America: 1995).

20. A useful and instructive literature has emerged in recent years by scholars making strong cases for how the Constitution should be amended to make the US political system more functional and democratic. See, for example, Larry J. Sabato, *A More Perfect Union* (New York: Walker and Company, 2007).

21. Robert M. La Follette, *The Political Philosophy of Robert M. La Follette* (Madison: Robert M. La Follette Publishing Company, 1920), pp. 13–27.

22. John Nichols and Robert W. McChesney, *Dollarocracy: How the Money and Media Election Complex Is Destroying America* (New York: Nation Books, 2014), pp. 255–284.

23. John R. Vile, *A Companion to the United States Constitution and Its Amendments* (Santa Barbara: ABC-Clio LLC, 2010).

24. Nichols and McChesney, *Dollarocracy*, pp. 259–261.

25. The arguments in this section were formulated for our book, Robert W. McChesney and John Nichols, *The Death and Life of American Journalism: The Media Revolution that Will Begin the World Again* (New York: Nation Books, 2010) but have been substantially updated to reflect the developments of recent years, which have only made the need for intervention more urgent.

26. John Nichols, "The Activists Who Won Net Neutrality Must Defend It in 2016," *Nation*, February 26, 2015.

27. John Nichols and Robert W. McChesney, "Free the Media! It's time to get back to our roots—the grassroots—to fight for reform of an increasingly monopolistic and manipulative media," *Nation*, November 6, 2013.

28. Karin Kamp, "What the Mainstream Media Won't Let Bernie Sanders Talk About," *Moyers and Company*, October 30, 2014.

29. Note the emphasis on not-for-profit journalism. There is little future for democracy-sustaining for-profit journalism. Subscriptions have never paid for journalism, and they never will. For a time, advertising sustained a reasonable measure of journalism. But in a new age of "smart" and targeted digital advertising, corporations no longer bother to place ads on sites that citizens might go to for news. Instead, corporations purchase target audiences directly and place ads through Internet ad networks that locate the desired target wherever they are online. Advertisers no longer need to support journalism or content creation at all. This explains why Rupert Murdoch, the greatest corporate media visionary of our times, abandoned his iPad/smartphone news venture, the *Daily*, in 2012; and this explains why editors of the *Guardian*, who maintain one of the most heavily trafficked and respected news websites in the world, tell us they have no idea how they could support their journalism if they were forced to rely upon Internet revenues. (See John Nichols and Robert W. McChesney, "How to Save Journalism: The patriotic case for government action," *Nation*, January 7, 2010, and Robert W. McChesney, "Rejuvenating American Journalism: What the FTC will hear today from Robert McChesney," *Columbia Journalism Review*, March 10, 2010.) As Matthew Hindman's book, *The Myth of Digital Democracy* (Princeton: Princeton University Press, 2008), so convincingly demonstrated, the Internet is not some "Wild West" incubator, where a new and more democratic journalism is being hatched. Internet traffic mostly gravitates to sites that aggregate and reproduce existing journalism, and the

web is dominated by a handful of players, not unlike old media. Indeed, many of the same players who ran old media into the ground are now in charge of running new media into the ground (Nichols and McChesney, "How to Save Journalism"). Journalism has to be recognized now as a classic "public good"— something that society needs and that people want but that market forces are now incapable of generating in sufficient quality or quantity. The institution should be understood in the same way that we understand universal public education, national security, public health, and transportation infrastructure. Necessities that are not maintained and sustained by the market remain necessities, and a civil society makes policies and appropriations to meet them.

30. See "Public Media," Free Press, http://www.freepress.net/public-media.

31. From the days of Washington, Jefferson, and Madison through those of Andrew Jackson to the mid-nineteenth century, enormous printing and postal subsidies were the order of the day. The need for them was rarely questioned, which is perhaps one reason they have been so easily overlooked. They were developed with the intention of expanding the quantity, quality, and range of journalism—and they were astronomical by today's standards. If, for example, the United States had devoted the same percentage of its GDP to journalism subsidies in 2009 as it did in the 1840s, we calculate that the allocation would have been $30 billion. In contrast, the federal subsidy in recent years for all of public broadcasting, not just journalism, was around $400 million.

32. The argument for restoring the democracy-sustaining subsidies of old— as opposed to the corporation-sustaining ones of recent decades—need not rest on models from two centuries ago. When the United States occupied Germany and Japan after World War II, Generals Eisenhower and MacArthur instituted lavish subsidies to spawn a vibrant, independent press in both nations. The generals recognized that a docile press had been the handmaiden of fascism and that a stable democracy requires diverse and competitive news media. They encouraged news media that questioned and dissented, and even at times criticized US occupation forces. They did not gamble that the "free market" would magically produce the desired outcome.

33. "Citizens' News Vouchers: $200 for Everyone?" The Benton Foundation, April 6, 2010.

34. Nichols, "Activists Who Won Net Neutrality."

35. "Mitch Daniels Response to State of the Union: Text & Video," *Huffington Post*, January 24, 2012, http://www.huffingtonpost.com/2012/01/24/mitch -daniels-response-_n_1228467.html.

36. Financial writer Barry Lynn has for a number of years been writing and speaking about a "new age of monopoly," and "an economy controlled by the few." Barry Lynn, *Cornered: The New Monopoly Capitalism and the Economics of Destruction* (Hoboken, NJ: Wiley, 2010). Author William Petrocelli describes "the relentless drive towards consolidation in almost every business and the almost inevitable transfer of power to a few financial giants." William Petrocelli,

"Monopolies on the Loose!" *Washington Post*, April 12, 2010. *Washington Post* writer David Ignatius decries "financial giantism." David Ignatius, "The Right Roosevelt?" *Washington Post*, March 5, 2009.

37. Michael Copps, "Common Cause Hails Reported Collapse of Comcast/ Time Warner Cable Merger," www.commoncause.org, April 23, 2015.

38. Zephyr Teachout, "Quashing the Comcast Merger Is Just the Beginning: A new antitrust movement is on the march," *Nation*, May 18, 2015.

39. Samuel Gibbs, "Does Europe have the power to break up Google? Regulatory matters have become a political issue as members of the European parliament clash with the European commission," *Guardian*, November 26, 2014. Franklin Foer, "Amazon Must Be Stopped: It's too big. It's cannibalizing the economy. It's time for a radical plan," *New Republic*, October 9, 2014.

40. Teachout, "Quashing the Comcast Merger," with comments from a draft by Teachout of a broader article on monopoly reviewed by the authors.

41. Cited in Gar Alperovitz, "Wall Street Is Too Big to Regulate," *New York Times*, July 22, 2012.

42. Milton Friedman, "The Monetary Theory and Policy of Henry Simons," *Journal of Law and Economics* 10 (October 1967): 1–13.

43. H. C. Simons, *The Chicago Tradition in Economics 1892–1945* (London, Routledge, 2002), edited by Ross B. Emmett, p. 18. See also Gar Alperovitz, "Nationalize Banks that Overwhelm Regulation," *New York Times*, January 13, 2014, and Alperovitz, "Wall Street Is Too Big to Regulate."

44. Alperovitz, "Wall Street Is Too Big to Regulate."

45. "The true cost of the bank bailout," Need to Know on PBS, *PBS*, September 3, 2010. "We all know about TARP, the Troubled Asset Relief Program, which spent $700 billion in taxpayers' money to bail out banks after the financial crisis. That money was scrutinized by Congress and the media," reported PBS. "But it turns out that that $700 billion is just a small part of a much larger pool of money that has gone into propping up our nation's financial system. And most of that taxpayer money hasn't had much public scrutiny at all. According to a team at Bloomberg News, at one point last year the U.S. had lent, spent or guaranteed as much as $12.8 trillion to rescue the economy."

46. Trades Union Congress, "German Lessons: Developing Industrial Policy in the UK," January 2012, published by TUC, Congress House Great Russell Street London WC1B 3LS.

47. Jeremy Wiesen, "The U.S. Needs Its Own Industrial Policy: China's government incubates business with capital and other incentives. So should America's," *Wall Street Journal*, September 13, 2010.

48. Robert Pollin and Dean Baker, "Public Investment, Industrial Policy and U.S. Economic Renewal," *Working Paper Series: Number 211* (produced for the Political Economy Research Center/ Center for Economic and Policy Research), December 2009.

49. Pollin and Baker, "Public Investment, Industrial Policy."

50. The Green Party, "Economy: Indicators," Green Party of England and Wales, March 2015. See also Heather Stewart, "Beyond GDP: Greens spark debate on a better measure of progress," *Observer*, January 31, 2015.

51. Eric Black, "Why Is Turnout So low in U.S. Elections? We make it more difficult to vote than other democracies," *MinnPost*, October 1, 2014.

52. Steve Israel, "Weekend Voting Act," http://israel.house.gov/issues /weekend-voting-act.

53. It is worthy of note that, while today Americans often look to other countries for examples of innovation and efficiency, as recently as the 1960s European intellectuals were writing books such as Jean-Jacques Servan-Schreiber's *Le Défi Américain* (*The American Challenge*), a 1967 bestseller that argued European nations had to overcome their stodgy approaches to innovation and their aversion to transnational cooperation.

54. Gar Alperovitz, "How to Democratize the US Economy: A long-term plan to renovate the American dream begins at the local level and scales up," *Nation*, October 8, 2013.

55. Conversation with Rebecca Kemble, May 1, 2015.

56. Rebecca Kemble, "Northside Rising," April 5, 2015, http://www.kemble4 district18.com/.

57. Jay Cassano, "Madison, Wisconsin, Is Investing $5 Million in Worker Cooperatives: The best part: the businesses will stay local, because co-ops don't up and move to cities offering more attractive incentives," *Fast Company: Co.Exist*, February 2, 2015.

58. Alperovitz, "How to Democratize the US Economy."

INDEX

Aaron, Craig, 263
activism, 31–33, 184–188, 208,
   234–243, 337n3; and big-picture
   movements, 238–239; and climate
   change movement, 239; and
   cohesion, need for, 240–241; and
   democracy movement, 239–240;
   and democratic disconnect, 243;
   and economic reform, 211–212; and
   economy, democratizing the, 238;
   and election campaigns, value of,
   241–242; and finance, proposals to
   democratize, with public banking,
   238; and labor movement, 235–237;
   and media reform movement, 240,
   260; and minimum wage, 211,
   234–235, 335n52; and new civil
   rights movement, 239, 242; and
   ownership, democratizing, 238;
   and political process, need for
   change in, 242–243; and political
   reform, 211–212; and public and
   cooperative enterprise movement,
   237–238, 274–276; and sustainable
   farming and food production,
   238; and transformative moment,
   212, 234; and US Postal Service,
   strengthening of, 238, 336n61. See
   also specific movements
Adams, John, 160, 212–213, 215,
   322n29

Adams, John Quincy, 162
Adelson, Sheldon, 140–141
AEI. See American Enterprise
   Institute
Afghanistan, 327n108
African-American slaves, 153–154, 162
Aldrich, Nelson, 230
Alien and Sedition Acts, 213
Allende, Salvador, 296n46
Alperovitz, Gar, 237, 238, 267,
   273–274, 276
Amar, Akhil Reed, 163
Amara, Roy, 105
Amash, Justin, 142
Amazon, 92, 103–104, 266
America, Inc. (Nader), 193
American Enterprise Institute (AEI),
   195
American Federation of Labor-
   Congress of Industrial
   Organizations, 133
An American Program (Willkie),
   178–179
Anderson, John, 187
Apple, 92
"Are Human Beings Necessary?"
   (Russell), 76
Argentina, 337n3
Arthur, W. Brian, 94
Articles of Confederation, 162
artificial intelligence, 92, 106–107

Associated Press v. United States, 168, 324n56

AT&T, 7

automation, 32, 247; acceleration of, 3; and artificial intelligence, 92; and big data (digitized information), 92–93, 95; and capitalism, 73–74, 77–78, 79; in China, 311n192; and cloud computing, 92–93; and computing power, exponential rise in, 88–93, 91 (chart 19), 95, 285–286; and control system, 95; and core paradoxes of the profit system, 107–113; and corporations and minimum wage, 10–11; decline in stories mentioning, 84, 85 (chart 18), 285; and disintermediation, 68–69; and economic crisis, 305n90; and fast-food restaurants, 4; and free time, 112; and growth and employment, divergence of, 68–69; and guaranteed basic income, 80–81, 83, 249–250; hysteria, of the 1960s, 79, 88; and Internet of Things (billions of human-made devices connected by universal computing infrastructure), 93–94; and job displacement, 13–15, 20–21, 293n2; and jobs, future of, 95–107, 310n163; and Moore's Law, 88–90; optimistic vision of, 87; as outside boundaries of legitimate debate, 307n114; as public issue, decline of, 84, 86, 307n114; qualitative leap in, 312–313n213; and robotics, 90, 92, 94, 98–99; and robotics and computers, and perceptual parts of the brain, 90, 92; and shift to profits, 78; short history of, 73–88; and smart machines, 95; solution to challenges of, 19; and 3D printing, 94–95; time frame, 87, 305–306n91; and unions, 77, 81–82, 84

Automation and Management (Bright), 96

"Automation and Technological Change," subcommittee of the Joint Committee on the Economic Report of the US Congress hearings on, 76

automobile industry, 102–103

automobiles, self-driving, 97, 98, 310n167

bailouts. *See* government bailouts

Baker, Dean, 262, 271

Balls, Ed, 72, 105

Bank of New York, 158

bankers, 5, 15, 133, 138, 139, 228–229, 230–231. *See also* bank(s)

bank(s), 124–125, 158, 217, 238, 322n23; bailout, and financial crisis of 2008, 117, 118–120, 267, 341–342n45; legislation to regulate, attempts to undermine, 119. *See also* bankers

Baran, Paul, 74, 112, 305n89

Barber, Rev. William, 239

Barbour, Haley, 145

basic income. *See* guaranteed basic income

Bates, John, 218–219

Beckert, Sven, 73, 321n18

Bell, Daniel, 82

Bellman, Richard, 79

Biden Joe, 145

big business, and crisis of democracy, 193–202

big data (digitized information), 92–93, 95

big-picture movements, 238–239

Bill of Rights, 160, 162, 169, 182, 256–257. *See also* US Constitution

billionaires and corporations: and campaign contributions, 23–24, 140–141, 145, 196; education of, 251–252; tax breaks for, 120–125. *See also* corporations

Black, Eric, 272

Black, Hugo, 324n56

Black Lives Matter, 239, 242

Black Panther Party, 190–191
Blau, Judith, 182–183
"Blue Book" campaign, 180
Bookchin, Murray, 190
Brady, Robert A., 41, 305–306n91
Brandeis, Louis, 116, 168, 226–227
Braverman, Harry, 305n89, 310n163
Bright, James R., 96, 310n163
Broockman, David, 16
Brooke, Edward, 187
Brown, Sherrod, 134
Bryan, William Jennings, 222,
    228–230
Brynjolfsson, Erik, 74, 88, 89, 90, 95,
    106, 114, 249–250
Buchanan, Brooke, 142
Buckley, Ray, 143
Buckley v. Valeo, 240
Buffett, Warren, 121
Burke, Edmund, 215
Burnham, Walter Dean, 164
Bush, George H. W., 121
Bush, George W., 260
Business Roundtable of 1972, 196

campaign contributions: from
    billionaires and corporations,
    23–24, 140–141, 145, 196. *See also*
    election(s)
Camus, Albert, 199
Canada, 137–138
capitalism, 21–27; and automation,
    73–74, 77–78, 79; and climate
    change and inequality, 32; and
    computer technology, and job
    elimination, 102–106; and
    democracy, 26–28; and democracy,
    in Chile, 296–297n46; vs.
    democratic socialism, and fascism,
    38, 298–299n75; and depressed
    environment, investors, and
    government intervention, 35–36;
    as dubious fit for democracy,
    248–249; as dubious fit for
    technological revolution, 248–249;
    and economic debate, 22–23, 24–25;

end of, 5; and freedom, 25–26; and
    government policies and subsidies,
    24; and politics, and economics,
    interchangeability of, 24–25;
    and production vs. production
    capacity, 108–113; and property and
    democracy, 25–26; and relationship
    of democracy to economy, 25;
    and relationship of economy to
    governance, 25; and relationship to
    democracy, 24; and social labour,
    22; and technology, potential vs.
    reality, 21–22; and unemployment,
    35–36, 43–67; and US Constitution,
    157–159, 158n; and wealth and
    property, endless increase of,
    157–159; in a world where work is
    unnecessary, 22; as wrong economic
    system for emerging material world,
    113–114
Capitalism: A Love Story (film), 117
capitalism, first use of term, 158,
    321n19
Carr, Nicholas, 20, 73, 77, 92, 93–94,
    96, 304n70, 332n182
Carter, Jimmy, 118, 128, 202
Carter, Zach, 134–135
Cato Institute, 195
CEOs, 4, 10–11, 122–123, 132–133,
    138, 196, 201, 209, 272; education
    of, 251–252; wages of, vs. workers,
    63
change, demand for, and meaningful
    reform, disconnect between,
    231–232
Chartists/People's Charter, 218–219,
    222, 243
Chile, 296–297n46
China, 100–102, 134, 136–137, 271,
    311n192
Chomsky, Noam, 132
Chrysler, government bailout of,
    130–131
Church, Frank, 204
Churchill, Winston, 38, 298n74
Cisco, 94

citizen engagement, 8; and election of 1800, 212–215; need for, and democracy, 115–117. *See also* citizenless democracy

citizenless democracy, 16–17, 17–19, 24, 116, 243; and demoralization and disconnect, 19; and economic crimes, 117; and the media, 139–140; and trade policy, 139; and the wealthy elite, 151–152. *See also* citizen engagement; democracy

Citizens for Tax Justice, 124

Citizens United v. Federal Election Commission, 142, 240, 318n79

civil rights movement (new), 239

Civil War, 164, 227

Clifton, Jim, 57, 60

climate change, 17, 32, 245–246

climate change movement, 239

Clinton, Bill, 119–120, 133, 134, 203, 327n116

Clinton, Hillary, 137, 144

Clinton administration, 188

cloud computing, 92–93

Cohen, Jeff, 23

colleges, replacement for, 4, 251

Collins, Chuck, 126

Collins, Randall, 20

Colombia, 138

Comcast, 264–266

Common Sense (Paine), 156

communication technology, 74, 308n122

communism, 180–181, 182n

Communist Manifesto (Marx and Engels), 108–109

community-mindedness, vs. selfishness, and economic policy, 331–332n182

computer power: exponential rise in, and automation, 88–93, 91 (chart 19), 95, 285–286; thousandfold increase in, 246

computer technology, 86–87, 102–106

computerization: and core paradoxes of the profit system, 107–113; existential questions about, 106–107

computers, 74–75; near-workerless factories run by, 87, 308n122; and perceptual parts of the brain, 90, 92; and ratio of jobs eliminated to jobs created, 103

Condon, Bernard, 68

Confidence Men (Suskind), 120

conservatism, overestimates of, 16

conservatives, and anti-democratic elements of today, 157

constitutional conventions, 152–153, 153n

constitutional traditions, 152–153

constitutions, 337n3; and anti-democratic elements, 152–162. *See also* state constitutions; US Constitution

control system, and automation, 95

Conyers, John, Jr., 129–130

Cooley, Mike, 21

Coolidge, Calvin, 149

cooperative enterprise movement, 237–238, 274–276

Cooperative Home Care Associates, 238

Copps, Michael, 265

Cornerstone Capital Group, 10

corporate think tanks, 195–196

corporations: and colleges, replacement for, 4; and job creation, 3; and minimum wage and automation, 10–11; as people, 3; and political setbacks, 193; and raising wages while eliminating jobs, 11; tax breaks for, 120–125; and trade policy, 133–135; and US Constitution, 159, 322n23. *See also* billionaires and corporations

Cosmopolitan, 231

counterculture of the 1960s, 188–191, 211

counterrevolution of the 1970s, 211

Cowen, Tyler, 54, 72, 96, 250

creative destruction, 14, 16–17, 68–72

crowdsourced constitution, 337n3

Cubbedge, Robert E., 79

Curry, Bill, 127
cybernation, 79–81, 112, 190

Dahl, Robert A., 27, 28, 152, 153, 161–162, 183
Darity, William, Jr., 128
DARPA. *See* Defense Advanced Research Projects Agency
Davis, John W., 149
De Moro, Rose Ann, 236
de-skilling, and job elimination, 96–97, 96n, 310n166
debate, need for no-holds-barred, 249
Debs, Eugene Victor, 223, 226
Declaration of Independence, 153–154, 314n1
Defense Advanced Research Projects Agency (DARPA), 90
democracy, 206–208, 252–256; basic requirements of, 253–254; and capitalism, 26–28; and capitalism, in Chile, 296–297n46; and capitalism, in Eastern Europe, 297n46; capitalism as dubious fit for, 248–249; and citizen engagement, need for, 115–117; citizens' demand for, 276; and corporate-government collusion, 41; crisis of, and big business, 193–202; digital democracy, 337n3; direct democracy, 337n3; disillusionment with, 41–42; effective popular participation in, 27; and fascism, 39–42, 173–174; Internet and social media as platform for, 337n3; vs. monopoly, 263–267, 341n36; political and economic, 11, 12; and property ownership and capitalism, 25–26; proven enemies of, 29; relationship of capitalism to, 24; and socialism, 296–297n46; unlimited, 200, 206; and unrestrained capitalism and limited government, 31. *See also* citizenless democracy
democracy as pejorative term, 157
Democracy Collaborative, 237

democracy movement, 239–240
democratic disconnect, 19, 231–232, 243; definition of, 233–234; and democratic infrastructure, 233–234
democratic infrastructure, 28–34, 151–152, 172–183, 247; and anti-democratic elements, and constitutions, 152–162; battle for, 31; and civil liberties, 29; and constitutions, 152–172; decay of, 117; and democratic disconnect, 233–234; and economic crisis, 31; and economic structure, 29–30; and fascism, 40–41, 179–181; and free press, constitution on, 165–169; history of development of, 150; and jobs crisis, 31, 32; and militarism, constitution on, 162–165; need to protect, 42; need to rebuild, 210–211; and progressive Era, 221; role of, 255–256; and social change/activism, 31–33; and state constitutions, 170–171; and unions, 30; and voting rights, 28–29; and weltanschauung, 30–34
democratic infrastructure (1900 to 1970), crucial policies enacted during, 172–173
democratic infrastructure (1930s and 1940s), 173–183; and fascism, 179–181; and "Four Freedoms," 174–176, 178, 180, 181–182, 326n82; and post-World War II, 181–182; and radio broadcasting, 180–181; and Second Bill of Rights (Economic Bill of Rights), 174, 176–178, 180, 181–183, 187, 192, 254, 257, 327n108; and Universal Declaration of Human Rights, 182–183, 327n108
democratic infrastructure (1960s to early 1970s), 183–193; and corporations, and political setbacks, 193; and counterculture, 188–191; and Democratic Party, 1972 platform of, 185–187; and democratic surge, 183–193;

and economic growth, 183; and
Johnson's Great Society, 183–184;
and Nixon administration,
187–188; and post-scarcity
generation, 183–184, 189–190;
and social movements, 184–188;
and social reforms, 192; and
Vietnam War, 191, 191n; wealth
and privilege during, 192–193; and
weltanschauung, 185, 190–191
democratic infrastructure (1970s),
193–202; and automation, and
union dissidents, 198; and big
business, and crisis of democracy,
193–202; and big business sales
campaign strategy, 194–195, 196,
200–202; and big business scapegoat
strategy, 201–202; and Business
Roundtable of 1972, 196; and
corporate campaign contributions,
196; and democracy, unlimited,
200, 206; and judicial system, and
big business, 194; and Lewis Power
Memorandum of August 1971,
194–195; and lobbyists, 195–196;
and management's authority,
challenge to, 198–199; and pro-
corporate think tanks, 195–196; and
recession of 1974, 199; and Vietnam
War, radicalizing effect of, 197–199;
and Watergate scandal, 199; and
weltanschauung, 195, 199
democratic infrastructure (1980s to
present), 202–206; deconstruction
of, by the economic elite, 206–207;
and Democratic Party, and
shift to the right, 203–204; and
demoralization and depoliticization,
206, 332n182; deterioration of, as
key factor in preventing reform,
206; and election 1980 Libertarian
Party platform, 202–203; and
illegal government surveillance,
204; and militarism, 204; and
privatization and outsourcing,
205–206; and Republican Party,
and religious right, 203–204; and

weltanschauung, 203, 204, 206,
332n182
democratic infrastructure (future):
attempts to deconstruct, 206–208;
and public policy debates, 207;
rejuvenation of, 207; and social
activism, 208; and weltanschauung,
207
democratic reforms, and Industrial
Revolution (Great Britain),
215–220, 222
democratic socialism, vs. capitalism,
and fascism, 38, 298–299n75
democratic surge, of the 1960s and
early 1970s, 183–193
democratization: demands for, during
Industrial Revolution, 218–219; of
economic planning, 247, 267–272;
of the economy, 238, 272–276; in
the future, 233–243; of journalism,
259–263; and Progressive Era,
220–233; of the US Constitution,
256–259
depression, and anti-depression drugs,
332n182
Dewey, John, 18, 171
Diamondis, Peter H., 98
digital communication, 74–75
digital democracy, 337n3
digital revolution, 15, 21, 86–87, 106,
116, 118; and efficiency, 3; political
and economic realities of, 4–5
Digital technological revolution, 72
direct democracy, 337n3
disconnect. *See* democratic disconnect
disruptive technologies, 234
distance-learning certificate programs,
4, 251
Dobbs, Lou, 125
Dow Chemical, 135
Duchin, Faye, 87
Durr, Clifford, 180, 181
Dyson, George, 106

Eastern Europe, 297n46
Economic Bill of Rights. *See* Second
Bill of Rights

economic crimes, and citizenless
    democracy, 117
economic crisis, 31; and automation,
    305n90; and democratic
    infrastructure, deconstruction of,
    206–208; and economic system,
    reform of, 113–114, 116–117;
    solutions to, 107–108, 113–114,
    116–117. *See also* financial crisis of
    2008
economic democracy, 272–276
economic elite: and creative
    destruction, 16–17; and democratic
    infrastructure, deconstruction of,
    206–207; and financial crisis of
    2008, 118, 119–120; and politics,
    impact on, vs. average Americans,
    17–18. *See also* wealthy elite
economic growth: and cash and
    short-term investments of top non-
    financial US firms, 1970–2013, 44
    (chart 3), 278; and employment,
    divergence of, and automation,
    68–69; and GDP, net private
    non-residential fixed investment
    as a percentage of, 46 (chart 2),
    277–278; and GDP and household
    income, split between, 1967–2013,
    50, 52 (chart 7), 281; and GDP
    growth, percentage of quarters
    with 6 percent or greater real,
    1930–2015, 44 (chart 1), 277; and
    income inequality, 65n, 302n33; and
    income shares, 1935–2014, 63, 65,
    66 (chart 15), 283; post–World War
    II, 183; rate of, and unemployment,
    43, 44 (chart 1), 45, 46 (chart 2), 47
    (chart 3); and US Constitution, 158
economic inequality, 15–16, 263–264,
    293n4; and unions, 30, 297n54;
    and US Constitution, 161. *See also*
    income inequality; living wage
economic insecurity, as aid to labor
    efficiency, 301n26
economic planning, 270;
    democratization of, 247, 267–272
economic policy, and community-

mindedness vs. selfishness,
    331–332n182
economic reform, 211–212, 255–256;
    prevention of, 206
economic structure, and democratic
    infrastructure, 29–30
economic system: capitalist, as wrong
    system for emerging material
    world, 113–114; and production vs.
    production capacity, 108–113
economics, politics, and capitalism,
    interchangeability of, 24–25
economy: democratization of, 238,
    272–276; layers of labor market
    distress in, 279 (table A–1); and
    monopolies, and fascism, 173–174;
    new American Dream, 127
education, 192; and battle for the
    future, 251–252; of billionaires
    and CEOs, 251–252; and state
    constitutions, 171; and US
    Constitution, 160–161, 322n29
education-industrial complex, 254
egalitarian society, desire for, 42,
    299n91
Eisenhower, Dwight, 41, 120, 185,
    254, 340n32
election(s), 241–242; 1800, 212–215;
    1894, 228; 1896, 228–229, 229;
    1900, 229; 1908, 229; 1912, 223,
    224–226, 231; 1924, 149; 1932,
    232–233; 1936, 149; 1968, 192;
    1972, 185–187, 191; 1980, 202–203;
    2010, 146–147; 2012, 148; 2014,
    144–145, 145–147, 319n85; 2016,
    9–10, 241–242; and electoral
    process, viability of, 144. *See also*
    campaign contributions; political
    campaigns; voter turnout
Eli Lilly, 135
Ellison, Keith, 257
employment: and AT&T and
    Google, 7; and growth, divergence
    of, and automation, 68–69; and
    Kodak and Instagram, 6–7; ratio
    of, to civilian non-institutional
    population, 300n11. *See also* full

employment; hidden employment; underemployment; unemployment

energy technology, 74

Engels, Frederick, 108–109

entitlement reform, 122–123

environmental issues, 17, 133–135. *See also* climate change

environmental movements, 255

Europe, economic planning in, 270

European Pirate Parties, 337n3

Exxon Mobil, 135

Facebook, 7, 220, 337n3. *See also* social media

factories: loss of and trade policy, 134, 317n53; near-workerless, run by computer programs and robotics, 87, 308n122

faith, as basis for optimism about job creation, 104

farming and food production, sustainable, 238

fascism, 34–42; characteristics of, 180; definition of, 35n; and democracy, 39–42, 173–174; and democratic infrastructure, 40–41, 179–181; and democratic socialism vs. capitalism, 38, 298–299n75; and economic problems, and monopolies, 173–174; and FDR, 173–174, 178, 207; and full employment, 37–38; overshadowed by "communist" threat, 180–181; post-World War II, 182; and removal of capitalism objections to full employment, 37–38; requirements to minimize threat of, 180; in 1930s, 34–35; and unemployment, 35–36, 128

fast-food restaurants, and automation, 4

fast-food workers, and corporations, minimum wage, and automation, 10–11

"Fast Track" trade Promotion Authority, 135–137

federal government, functions of, and US Constitution, 160, 322n27

Feingold, Russ, 140

"Fight for 15," 235

finance, proposals to democratize, with public banking, 238

financial crisis of 2008, 214; and economic elite, 118, 119–120; and gains of recovery to top 1 percent, 122, 122n; and government bank bailout, 117, 118–120, 267, 341–342n45; and legislation to regulate banks, attempts to undermine, 119; and recession, 119 (*see also* Great Recession). *See also* economic crisis

financial panics, 214–215. *See also* specific panics

food production and farming, sustainable, 238

Ford, Gerald, 124

Ford, Martin, 3, 92, 93, 94, 97–98, 99, 107, 249, 250

Four Freedoms, 174–176, 178, 180, 181–182, 326n82

Foxconn, 100–102

fragging, in Vietnam, 197, 329n146

Francis, Pope, 10

Franklin, Benjamin, 159

free press, and US Constitution, 165–169

free time, 112

Free Trade Agreements (FTAs), 131–139

freedom, and capitalism, 25–26

freelance sector, 71–72

Friedman, Howard Steven, 148

Friedman, Milton, 25, 26, 193n, 201, 202–203, 250, 266, 296–297n46, 298–299n75

Fromm, Erich, 76

FTA movement, 198, 329n148

FTAs. *See* Free Trade Agreements

full employment, 19–20; and fascism, 37–38; policies during Great Depression, 128, 130; policies during Great Recession, 129–130, 130–131; policies in the 1980s, 129, 130; policies in the 1970s, 128–129;

proposals to create, 15–16. *See also* employment
Full Employment and Balanced Growth Act of 1978, 128
Fuller, Walter D., 175
Future of Life Institute, 106–107
"Future of the Internet" survey, 104

Galbraith, James, 3, 73, 88, 102, 103, 302n34
game theory, 308n133
General Electric (GE), 76, 87, 94
general purpose technology (GPT), 74, 88, 102
generation jobless, 302–303n50
George, King, 153–154
Germany, 100, 148, 181–182, 182n, 327n103, 340n32
GI Bill, 179
Gilens, Martin, 17
Gingrich, Newt, 133
Ginsberg, Allen, 211
Glaeser, Edward L., 14
Gleick, James, 220
Goldman, Emma, 231
Goldwater, Barry, 187
Goodman, Amy, 262
Google, 7, 13, 92, 266
Goolsbee, Austin, 137
Gou, Terry, 101
government, role of, 26–28
government bailouts, 15, 117, 118–120, 130–131, 267, 341–342n45
government surveillance, 204
GPT. *See* general purpose technology, 74, 88
Great Britain, Industrial Revolution in, 215–220, 222
Great Depression, 102, 111, 125, 127, 227; and election of 1936, 149; full employment policies during, 128, 130
Great Recession, 45, 50, 69, 88; full employment policies during, 129–130, 130–131; and unemployment, 125–131. *See also* financial crisis of 2008
Great Society, 183–184

Greece, 34
Greenback Party, 228
Greengard, Samuel, 93, 106
The Greening of America (Reich), 189
Greenstone, Michael, 63
Greider, William, 143
gross profit, and revenue per employee, with case counts, 1953–2013, 285 (table A–3)
guaranteed basic income, 80–81, 83, 249–250. *See also* income inequality; living wage; minimum wage

Hamilton, Alexander, 158, 163–164, 322n27
Hanna, Mark, 229
Harlow, Bryce N., 195–196
Harris, Townsend, 171
Harvey, David, 22, 109
Hawkins, Augustus, 128
Hayden, Tom, 79–80
Hayek, F. A., 200, 250
healthcare industry, 236–237
Hedges, Chris, 34
Heilbroner, Robert, 86
Heinl, Robert D., Jr., 197
Herbert, Bob, 15, 18, 20, 32, 125, 183
Heritage Foundation, 195–196
hidden employment: 1962–2014, 45, 48 (chart 4), 50, 278; 1968–2014, 59 (chart 12), 60–61, 282. *See also* employment
Hitler, Adolf, 38
Hogeland, William, 156–157
Horne, Gerald, 154
Howard, Philip, 93
Huberman, Leo, 81
human responsibility, vs. technological development, 10
Humphrey, Hubert, 128
Humphrey-Hawkins Full-Employment Act, 128
Humphrey-Hawkins Full-Employment and Training Act, 129
Hunt, H. L., 185
Huntington, Samuel P., 200
Huws, Ursula, 72

IBM, 92, 94, 95
Iceland, 337n3
Ikenson, Daniel, 135
income inequality, 2, 122, 234–235.
    See also economic inequality;
    inequality; living wage
India, 99, 100, 101
Industrial Revolution, 2, 15, 95, 96n,
    118
Industrial Revolution (Great Britain),
    215–220; and banking crisis
    of 1830s, 217; and Chartists/
    People's Charter, 218–219, 222,
    243; and cohesive demand for
    democracy, 219; and demands for
    democratization of politics and
    governing, 218–219; and financial
    speculation, 217; and Poor Law of
    1834, 217; and protests, 217–218;
    and transformative moment, 219
inequality, 32, 302n33; proposals to
    reduce, 15–16. *See also* economic
    inequality; guaranteed basic
    income; income inequality; living
    wage; poverty; social inequality
information democracy, 260–261
information technology, 5, 308n122
infrastructure projects, 28, 297n49
Instagram, 6–7
Insull, Samuel, 301n26
Internet, 86–87, 169; as platform for
    democracy, 337n3; and ratio of
    jobs eliminated to jobs created,
    103
Internet of Things (billions of
    human-made devices connected by
    universal computing infrastructure),
    93–94
Investor-State Dispute Settlement
    mechanisms, 134
Iraq, 327n108
ISDS mechanisms. *See* Investor-State
    Dispute Settlement mechanisms
Israel, Steve, 272
Isthmus Engineering and
    Manufacturing, 238
Italy, 38, 39

Jacobstein, Neil, 21
Japan, 99, 100, 181–182, 327n103,
    340n32
Jefferson, Thomas, 25, 153–154, 159,
    163, 170, 171, 211, 222, 240, 264,
    314n1; and democratic disconnect,
    243; and economic inequality, 161;
    and election of 1800, 212–215; and
    free press, 165–167, 169; and US
    Constitution, 256–257, 259
job creation, 104–105, 125, 312n210;
    and corporations, 3; faith as basis
    for optimism about, 104; and future
    possibilities, 103, 104
job displacement, 13–15, 20–21,
    293n2
job elimination, 102–106; and "at
    risk" jobs, 97–102, 103–104,
    105; and de-skilling, 96–97, 96n,
    310n166; and middle-class service
    jobs, 105, 312–313n213. *See also*
    unemployment
job growth, changes in, by median
    wage, 2000–2014, 50, 51 (chart 6),
    280
jobless economy, 9
jobs: and college graduates and high
    school graduates, competition for
    low-paying, 69, 71; and current
    working conditions, 104; future of,
    and automation, 95–107, 310n163;
    loss of good-paying, 2; outsourcing,
    86
Jobs With Justice movement, 235
Johnson, Lyndon Baines, 80, 96,
    183–184
Jones, Walter, Jr., 142
journalism, 140, 167–169; collapse
    of, 23–24; corruption in, 230–231;
    democratization of, 259–263;
    dissident, 230–231; and political
    campaigns, 291n1; subsidized
    independent, not-for-profit, 261,
    339–340n29, 340n31, 340n32. *See
    also* media
judicial system, and big business,
    194

Judt, Tony, 18, 20–21, 35, 205, 331–332n182

Kalecki, Michal, 36–38
Kaptur, Marcy, 117–118, 118–119
Karabarbounis, Loukas, 100
Kasparov, Garry, 92
Katzman, John, 98
Kaye, Harvey, 8, 292n15, 326n82
Kemble, Rebecca, 275
Kennedy, Anthony, 168
Kennedy, John F., 82, 273
Keynes, John Maynard, 36, 111–112, 113, 116, 130, 250; and technological unemployment, 73–74
Keyssar, Alexander, 156
King, Martin Luther, Jr., 80, 187, 191, 191n
Kissinger, Henry, 195
Klein, Naomi, 21, 32, 33–34, 42, 239
Knights of Labor movement, 228
Koch, Charles, 141
Koch, David, 141, 202
Kodak, 6–7
Kotler, Steven, 98
Kotz, David M., 22
Krueger, Anne O., 131
Krugman, Paul, 37, 105–106
Kurzweil, Ray, 89

La Follette, Robert M., 149, 227, 231, 233, 258
labor efficiency: and technology, 73, 303n67; and unemployment and economic insecurity as aids to, 301n26
labor market distress, layers of, in US economy, 279 (table A-1)
labor movement, 235–237
labor unions. See unions
Landemore, Hélène, 337n3
Landon, Alf, 149
Laski, Harold J., 39
Lazare, Daniel, 169–170
Leontief, Wassily, 87
Leslie, Ian, 7

Lewis Powell Memorandum of August 1971, 26, 194–195, 201
liberal as pejorative term, 201–202
libertarians: and militarization, 330n169; and party platform, election 1980, 202–203; and US Constitution, 160
life-expectancy, 15
Limbaugh, Rush, 142
Lincoln, Abraham, 158n, 177, 264
Lindsey, Brink, 23
living wage, demand for, 11. See also economic inequality; guaranteed basic income; income inequality; minimum wage
lobbyists, 195–196
Logan, George, 159
Looney, Adam, 63
Luddites, 8, 73, 84, 216, 218, 219, 333n13
Lynd, Robert S., 41
Lynd, Staughton, 153

MacArthur, Douglas, 182, 340n32
MacMillan, R. H., 76
Madison, James, 25, 161, 162, 163, 166–167, 169, 170
Magdoff, Fred, 45
The Making of the English Working Class (Thompson), 215
management, challenge to authority of, 198–199
Mann, Horace, 171
manufacturing co-ops, 238
Marcuse, Herbert, 81, 112
Marx, Karl, 36, 108–109
Mason, George, 162–163
Mason, Paul, 5–6, 8
McAfee, Andrew, 74, 88, 89, 90, 95, 106, 114, 249–250
McCloskey, Pete, 187
McConnell, Mitch, 135–136
McCutcheon v. Federal Election Commission, 142, 240, 318n79
McDonald's, 99; and raising wages while eliminating jobs, 11
McGovern, George, 185, 187, 191

McKibben, Bill, 239, 255, 333n13
Meany, George, 81–82
media: and campaign contributions from billionaires and corporations, 23–24, 140–141; and citizenless democracy, 139–140; and government policies and subsidies, 167–169, 342n52; and political campaigns, 140; and voter turnout, 140. *See also* journalism
media reform movement, 240, 260
median wage: and job growth, changes in, 2000–2014, 50, 51 (chart 6), 280; wage ranges used for calculations of, 280–281 (table A-2)
mercantile classes, interests of, 155–156
Mexico, 100, 137, 164
microchip implants, 1, 4
Microsoft, 92
militarization, 330n169
military-industrial complex, 254
military industry, 75
military/militarism, 17, 204; and professional army, 197; and US Constitution, 162–165
Mill, John Stuart, 109–110, 250
Miller, Michael, 93
minimum wage, 211, 234–235, 335n52; vs. corporations and automation, 10–11. *See also* living wage
Mondale, Walter, 127
monopoly: vs. democracy, 263–267, 341n36; and economic problems, and fascism, 173–174
Monopoly Capital (Baran and Sweezy), 112
Moore, Gordon, 88
Moore, Michael, 117, 119
Moore's Law, 88–90
Moral Mondays movement, 239
Mosco, Vincent, 93
muckraking magazines, 231
Musk, Elon, 106
Myrdal, Gunnar, 80

Nader, Ralph, 188, 191, 193, 194, 199–200, 264
NAFTA. *See* North American Free Trade Agreement
National Commission on Technology, Automation, and Economic Progress, 82–83, 96, 247
National Labor Union, 228
National Monetary Commission, 230
National Nurses United (NNU), 236–237
Native Americans, 153, 166
Nazi Germany: and fascism, 35, 37–38, 38–39; and full employment, 37–38
Net Party, 337n3
New Deal, 36, 130, 181, 203, 227, 233
Newfield, Jack, 198–199
newspapers: and corruption, 230–231; government subsidized, 167–169, 261, 340n31, 340n32, 342n52
Nieman, Brent, 100
Nixon, Richard, 124
Nixon administration, 187–188
NNU. *See* National Nurses United
Noah, Timothy, 195
Noble, David F., 75, 198
North American Free Trade Agreement (NAFTA), 130–131, 133, 134, 135, 136–138
Northwest Ordinance, 160
Notes on the State of Virginia (Jefferson), 159
Nye, Gerald, 164

Obama, Barack, 129, 145, 188, 210, 234, 260, 328n116; and the new American Dream economy, 127; and "territorial tax" scheme, 123–124; and trade policy, 132, 135–139
Occupy movement, 264
O'Malley, Martin, 144
One-Dimensional Man (Marcuse), 81
optimism, and realism, reconciliation of, 5–6, 8

Orr, Andrea, 120
outsourcing, 205–206, 254
ownership, democratizing, 238

Page, Benjamin I., 17
Paine, Thomas, 154, 156, 167, 214, 257, 324n52
Paley, Grace, 12
Pallinger, Zoltan Tibor, 29
Panama, 138
panic of 1790s, 214–215
Panic of 1797, 215
Panic of 1873, 227
Panic of 1893, 228
Panic of 1907, 230
Paris uprising of 1968, 190
Patman, Wright, 180, 181
Pauling, Linus, 80
Pax Technica (Howard), 93
Paxton, Robert O., 35n, 38
peer-production, 5, 6
People's Climate March, 239
People's Party/Populist Party, 228
Percy, Charles, 187
Peterson, Pete, 123
Picard, Rosalind, 98
Pike, Bill, 311n192
Pinochet, Augusto, 296n46
Pistono, Federico, 95, 104
Player Piano (Vonnegut), 76
Pocan, Mark, 257
political campaigns: and campaign contributions from billionaires and corporations, 23–24, 140–141, 145, 196; and campaign fund-raising and expenditures, 141; and debates, 143–144; and journalism, 291n1; and the media, 140; and political parties, 142–144; and US Supreme Court decisions (Citizens United, McCutcheon, and Shelby), 142, 240, 318n79; and voter turnout, 140. See also elections
political debates, 143–144
political movements, formation of, 215–216, 333n11
political parties: distrust of, 292n17; and future plan, lack of, 9–10; and political campaigns, 142–144
political reform, 211–212, 242–243; and citizen engagement, and election of 1800, 212–215; desire to address, 210; hopelessness, despair, and cynicism regarding, 210–211; of Progressive Era, 231–233; recognition of need for, 209–210
politics: cynicism about, 139; and economics, and capitalism, interchangeability of, 24–25; impact on, by the economic elite vs. average Americans, 17–18
Pollack, Neal, 322n29
Pollin, Robert, 19–20, 271
Pollitt, Nigel, 6, 8
Pollock, Frederick, 305n95
population, restraint on, 109
Port Huron Statement, 79–80, 247
post-scarcity generation, 183–184, 189–190
poverty, 15, 63, 65, 65n, 293n4, 302n33, 302n33. See also inequality
Powell, Lewis, 26, 194–195, 196, 201
Pratt, Gill A., 90
PricewaterhouseCoopers, 94
Priebus, Reince, 143
prison-industrial complex, 254
private interests, and infrastructure projects, 28, 297n49
privatization, 205–206, 254
profit motive, 304n70
profit system, 3, 26–28; core paradoxes of, and computerization and automation, 107–113
profiteering, 254
Progressive Era, 32; and constitutional amendment, 222–223, 226; and democratic infrastructure, lack of, 221; of democratization, 220–233; and political platforms of 1912 election, 223, 224–226; reforms during, 231–233; and Roosevelt, Theodore, 220–221, 222, 224–226

Progressive Party/Progressives, 181, 224, 243. *See also* Progressive Era
property ownership, 25–26, 157–159, 296n42
Prospera, 238
public and cooperative enterprise movement, 237–238, 274–276
public broadcasting, 192

quantum computers, 308n130

racism, 181
radio broadcasting, 180–181
Randolph, A. Philip, 181, 187
Randolph, Edmund, 157
Ravitch, Diane, 171
Reagan, Ronald, 26, 129, 130, 168, 202, 203, 273
realism, and optimism, reconciliation of, 5–6, 8
recession of 1974, 199
reconstruction amendments, 169, 325n60
Red Scare, 181
Rees, Sir Martin, 106
Reich, Charles, 189
Reich, Robert, 97, 98
religious right, 203–204
Renton, Dave, 35
Retail Workers Bill of Rights, 11, 211, 235
Reuther, Walter, 77, 82, 304n70
revenues: and gross profit per employee, with case counts, 1953–2013, 285 (table A–3); and gross profit per employee of top US firms, 1953–2013, 69, 69n, 70 (chart 17), 284; as percentage of GDP of top non-financial US firms, 1950–2013, 284 (chart 17–A)
Richardson, Elliot, 199
Rifkin, Jeremy, 22, 86, 94, 100, 103
Roberts, John, 142
robotics, 94, 98–99; in China, 100–102; existential questions about, 106–107; and healthcare

industry, 236; near-workerless factories run by, 87, 308n122; and perceptual parts of the brain, 90, 92
Rockefeller, John D., 227, 230
Rockwell, Norman, 176
Rogoff, Kenneth, 22
Romney, Mitt, 123
Roosevelt, Eleanor, 182
Roosevelt, Franklin D., 35, 39–40, 41, 164; and constitutional amendments, 177; and election of 1932, 232–233; and election of 1936, 149; and fascism, 173–174, 178, 207; and Four Freedoms, 174–176, 178, 180, 181–182, 326n82; and GI Bill, 179; and New Deal, 36, 130, 181, 203, 227, 233; and Second Bill of Rights (Economic Bill of Rights), 174, 176–178, 180, 181–183, 187, 192, 254, 257, 327n108; and World War II, 174–175
Roosevelt, Theodore, 171, 220–221, 222, 224–226, 227, 234, 266
Rosenworcel, Jessica, 240
Ross, Jean, 237
Rove, Karl, 229
Rus, Daniela, 98
Russell, Bertrand, 76
Ryan, Paul, 119, 123

Saez, Emmanuel, 122
Sale, Kirkpatrick, 216
Salk, Jonas, 188
Salmon, Felix, 65
Sanders, Bernie, 2, 9–10, 124, 125, 138, 142, 211–212, 260; and election campaign, 241; and voter turnout, 146, 149–150
The Sane Society (Fromm), 76
Sawant, Kshama, 235, 335n51
Schakowsky, Jan, 124
Scheer, Robert, 119
Schiller, Dan, 308n122
Schmidt, Eric, 13–14, 42
Schmitt, John, 61, 63

Schumpeter, Joseph, 74
Second Bill of Rights (Economic Bill of Rights), 174, 176–178, 180, 181–183, 187, 192, 254, 257, 327n108
secular joblessness, 14
Seidel, Emil, 223
Seldes, George, 40
selfishness, vs. community-mindedness, and economic policy, 331–332n182
The Shape of Automation (Stein), 82
shaping progress, 8
shareholders, vs. workers, 303n67
sharing economy, 5, 6
Shay's Rebellion, 156
Shelby County v. Holder, 142, 318n79
Sherman Antitrust Act, 265–266
Sidelsky, Robert, 104
Simon, Herbert, 82
Simon, William E., 201
Simons, Henry Calvert, 266–267
Sinai, Allen, 303n67
Sinclair, Upton, 231
Sirota, David, 138
Skovron, Christopher, 16
slavery, 153–154, 162
Slow Food movement, 238
smart machines, 95
Smith, Adam, 96n
Smith, Al, 200
social activism. *See* activism
"Social Consequences of Automation" (*International Social Science Bulletin*), 76
social democracy, 36
social inequality, 15–16. *See also* inequality
social media, 7, 220; as platform for democracy, 337n3
social mobility, 65
social movements, 184–188. *See also* activism
social problems, and privatization and outsourcing, 205
social reforms, of the 1960s and early

1970s, 192
socialism, and democracy, 27, 296–297n46
Soglin, Paul, 275
Solow, Robert, 82
Somerset v. Stewart, 154
South Korea, 100, 138
Soviet Union, collapse of, 204
spectacular deprivation paradox, 110–111
spectacular productivity paradox, 110–111
Spence, Michael, 68
Sperber, Elliot, 29
Standard Oil, 266
state constitutional conventions, 152–153, 153n
state constitutions, 152–153, 153n, 159–160; and democratic infrastructure, 170–171; drafting and redrafting of, 170–171; and education, 171; and positive rights and social welfare, 159–160. *See also* US Constitution
stationary state, 110
Stewart, Potter, 168
Stiglitz, Joseph, 302n40
Students for a Democratic Society (SDS), 79–80
suicide, 332n182
Summers, Lawrence H., 23, 72, 88, 105
Sunbird Engineering, 311n192
Sunstein, Cass, 160, 192
Suskind, Ron, 120, 182
sustainable farming and food production, 238
Sutton, Betty, 317n53
Sweden, 148
Sweezy, Paul M., 74, 77–79, 81, 112, 305n89

Taft, William Howard, 226
Taft-Hartley Act, 196
Taibbi, Matt, 15, 41–42
TARP. *See* Troubled Asset Relief Program

tax policy: vs. entitlement reform,
122–123; and financial crisis and
gains of recovery to top 1 percent,
122, 122n; and "fix the debt"
firms, 123; and progressive income
taxation, 121; and support for taxing
billionaires and banks at higher
rates, 124–125; and tax breaks
for corporations and billionaires,
120–125; and "territorial tax"
scheme, 123–124
Taylor, John, 213–214
Teachout, Zephyr, 162, 265–266
technological development, vs. human
responsibility, 10
technological revolution, 1–2, 4–5,
22, 107, 116, 151, 246; capitalism as
dubious fit for, 248–249
technological unemployment, 73–74
technologies, disruptive, 234
technology: and capitalism,
potential vs. reality, 21–22; and
change, magnitude of, how to
address, 245–247; and creative
destruction, 68–72; and general
purpose technology, 74, 88; and
healthcare industry, 236–237; and
impact comparable to Cambrian
Explosion, 90; job-killing, 68;
and labor efficiency, 73, 303n67;
and labor substitutive innovation,
88; oppressive prospects of,
11–12; and profit motive,
304n70; and unemployment and
underemployment, 206, 207
telecommunications, 264–266
"territorial tax" scheme, 123–124
Thatcher, Margaret, 331n182
Thompson, Derek, 20, 36, 69, 96, 97,
103, 111–112
Thompson, E. P., 215–216, 219–220,
333n11
3D printing, 94–95
thrift paradox, 108
Tocqueville, Alexis de, 167
TPP. See Trans-Pacific Partnership
trade policy: and citizenless

democracy, 139; and corporate
interests vs. workers and the
environment, 133–135; and factory
losses, 134, 317n53; and "Fast
Track" authority, 135–137; and free-
trade agreements, 131–139; and
ISDS mechanisms, 134; and trade
deficit, 134
Trans-Atlantic Trade and Investment
Partnership (TTIP), 138
Trans-Pacific Partnership (TPP),
135–136, 138
transformative moment/crisis, 212,
219, 234
transportation technology, 74
Triangle Shirtwaist fire (NYC), 230
Trilateral Commission of 1973, 200
triple revolution, 80–81
Troubled Asset Relief Program
(TARP), 341–342n45
Truman, Harry, 181
TTIP. See Trans-Atlantic Trade and
Investment Partnership
Turner Broadcasting System v. FCC, 168
Twitter, 220, 337n3. See also social
media
Twomey, Katherine, 171

Uber, 97, 310n167
underemployment, 19–20, 20–21,
36, 60, 206, 207, 246. See also
employment; hidden employment;
unemployment
unemployment, 246; as aid to labor
efficiency, 301n26; and capitalism,
35–36, 43–67; and economic
growth, rate of, 43, 44 (chart 1),
45, 46 (chart 2), 47 (chart 3); and
fascism, 35–36, 128; and Great
Recession, 125–131; and job losses,
duration of, in selected recessions,
49 (chart 5), 50, 280; and labor
force participation rate, decline
in, 54, 55 (chart 9), 56 (chart 10),
57, 58 (chart 11), 60, 281, 282; and
labor force participation rate, for
females, 54, 55 (chart 9), 281; and

labor force participation rate, for males, 54, 56 (chart 10), 281; long-term, as percentage of labor force, 1962–2014, 65, 67 (chart 16), 283; official and hidden, 1962–2014, 45, 48 (chart 4), 50, 278; official and hidden, 1968–2014, 59 (chart 12), 60–61, 282; political solutions to, 107, 114; predictions, 20–21, 105; in 1930s and 1940s, 173; in 1930s and 1940s, government solution to, 35–37; and technology, 206, 207; and union membership, as percentage of total employment workers, 1944–2014, 61, 62 (chart 13), 282–283, 301n20; and union strikes and works stoppages, 1947–2014, 61, 63, 64 (chart 14), 283; and wages, decline in, for persons 18–24, 53 (chart 8), 54, 281. *See also* employment; job elimination

unemployment rate: for blacks, 126–127; during Great Depression, 126–127; and the new normal, 127; official and unofficial, 126, 127

Unger, Rick, 121

union membership, as percentage of total employment workers, 1944–2014, 61, 62 (chart 13), 282–283, 301n20

union(s), 30, 131, 182, 297n54; and automation, 77, 81–82, 84, 198; dissidents, and automation, 198; and strikes and works stoppages, 1947–2014, 61, 63, 64 (chart 14), 283; and trade policy, 133. *See also specific unions*

United Auto Workers, 131

United States Federation of Worker Cooperatives, 276

Universal Declaration of Human Rights, 182–183, 327n108

Uruguay, 148

US Constitution: and African-American slaves, 153–154, 162; and anti-democratic elements, 152–162; and capitalism, 157–159, 158n; and conservatives and anti-democratic elements of today, 157; and corporations, 159; and *democracy* as pejorative term, 157; democratization of, 256–259; and economic growth, 158; and economic inequality, 161; and education, 160–161, 322n29; and federal government, functions of, 160, 322n27; and free-market libertarians, 160; and free press, 165–169; intent of original, 154–155; and militarism, 162–165; and Native Americans, 153; and newspapers, government subsidized, 167–169, 342n52; and political economy of the time, 157; and popular uprisings, 156; and Progressive Era constitutional amendment, 222–223, 226; and reconstruction amendments, 169, 325n60; revisions and updates to, 169–170; and suffrage, 161, 172; and US Constitutional Convention, first meeting of, 156–157; and US Postal Service, 167–168; and wealthy and mercantile classes, interests of, 155–156. *See also* Bill of Rights; state constitutions

US Constitutional Convention, first meeting of, 156–157

US Department of Justice, 265

US Postal Service, 167–168, 238, 336n61

US Supreme Court, 142, 168, 240, 318n79. *See also specific cases*

Van der Reyden, Dianne, 314n1

Veblen, Thorstein, 110–111, 113, 223

Vietnam War, 191, 191n, 204; and fragging, 197, 329n146; and FTA movement, 198, 329n148; radicalizing effect of, 197–199

vision, evolution of, 90

Vogel, David, 193

Vonnegut, Kurt, 76

voter turnout, 117, 144–150, 272; 1924 election, 149; 1936 election, 149; 2012 election, 148; 2010 midterm election, 146–147; 2014 midterm election, 145–147, 148; since 1970s, marked decline in, 149; in US vs. other countries, 148. *See also* elections

voting-age population, 147–148, 286

voting rights, 28–29, 192; and property ownership, 25, 296n42; and US Constitution, 161, 172

wage stagnation, 234. *See also* minimum wage

wages: of CEOs vs. workers, 63. *See also* living wage

Wallace, Henry A., 39–40, 41, 179, 181, 185–187

Walmart, 141, 142, 235; and raising wages while eliminating jobs, 11

Walton family, 141

war capitalism, 321n18

Warner Cable, 264–265

Warren, Elizabeth, 2, 121, 125, 138, 142, 336n61

Washington, George, 164, 167, 324n52

Watergate scandal, 199

Watson, Thomas, 82

Watson (IBM computer), 92, 95, 246

Way, Ben, 20, 94

wealth, 109–110; concentration of, 301n23; endless increase of, and capitalism, 157–159; and privilege, in the 1960s and early 1970s, 192–193. *See also* wealthy elite

The Wealth of Nations (Smith), 96n

wealthy elite: and citizenless democracy, 151–152; and US Constitution, 155–156. *See also* economic elite; wealth

Webster, Noah, 161

Weicker, Lowell, 187

weltanschauung, 30–34, 178, 181, 207, 255; 1960s and early 1970s, 185, 190–191; 1970s, 195, 199; 1980s to present, 203, 204, 206, 332n182

White, William Allen, 175

Whitney v. California, 168

Who Needs People? Automation and Your Future (Cubbedge), 79

Wiener, Norbert, 75, 76, 77

Wiesen, Jeremy, 271

Wiesner, Cindy, 239

Willkie, Wendell, 30, 174, 178–179, 181

Wilson, Woodrow, 154–155, 226

Winthrop, John, 273

Wiseman, Paul, 68

Wolf, Martin, 84

Wolfers, Justin, 122, 122n

Wolin, Sheldon, 18, 201, 203

work, importance of, 111–112

Work Fusion, 97

Work in America report, 199

workers: and the environment vs. corporate interests and trade policy, 133–134, 134–135; vs. shareholders, 303n67; wages of, vs. CEOs, 63

World War I, 164

World War II, 40, 164, 174–175; government subsidized journalism during, 340n32; post-, 181–182

"wrong direction" sentiment, 293n23

Wydra, Elizabeth B., 142

Yeskel, Felice, 126

Zackin, Emily, 160, 170

Zuckerberg, Mark, 7

Brent Nicasio

ROBERT W. MCCHESNEY is the Gutgsell Endowed Professor in the Department of Communication at the University of Illinois at Urbana-Champaign and the author or editor of twenty-three books. His work has been translated into thirty languages. He is the cofounder of Free Press, a national media-reform organization. In 2008 the *Utne Reader* listed McChesney among their "fifty visionaries who are changing the world." He lives in Madison, Wisconsin.

Robin Holland

JOHN NICHOLS, a pioneering political blogger, has written the *Nation*'s Online Beat since 1999, is their Washington, DC, correspondent, and is a contributing writer for the *Progressive* and *In These Times*. He is also the associate editor of the *Capital Times*, the daily newspaper in Madison, Wisconsin, and a cofounder of Free Press. His articles have appeared in the *New York Times*, *Chicago Tribune,* and dozens of other newspapers, and he frequently appears on MSNBC, NPR, BBC, and other broadcast media outlets as a commentator on politics and media issues. Nichols lives in Madison, Wisconsin, and Washington, DC.

The Nation Institute

NATION
BOOKS

Founded in 2000, **Nation Books** has become a leading voice in American independent publishing. The inspiration for the imprint came from the *Nation* magazine, the oldest independent and continuously published weekly magazine of politics and culture in the United States.

The imprint's mission is to produce authoritative books that break new ground and shed light on current social and political issues. We publish established authors who are leaders in their area of expertise, and endeavor to cultivate a new generation of emerging and talented writers. With each of our books we aim to positively affect cultural and political discourse.

Nation Books is a project of The Nation Institute, a nonprofit media center dedicated to strengthening the independent press and advancing social justice and civil rights. The Nation Institute is home to a dynamic range of programs: the award-winning Investigative Fund, which supports ground-breaking investigative journalism; the widely read and syndicated website TomDispatch; the Victor S. Navasky Internship Program in conjunction with the *Nation* magazine; and Journalism Fellowships that support up to 25 high-profile reporters every year.

For more information on Nation Books, The Nation Institute, and the *Nation* magazine, please visit:

www.nationbooks.org

www.nationinstitute.org

www.thenation.com

www.facebook.com/nationbooks.ny

Twitter: @nationbooks